An Illuminating Study of Mao Tse-tung's
Role in China and World Communism

MAO
and the Perpetual Revolution

By Franz Michael

I. E. Cadenhead, Jr.
Editor

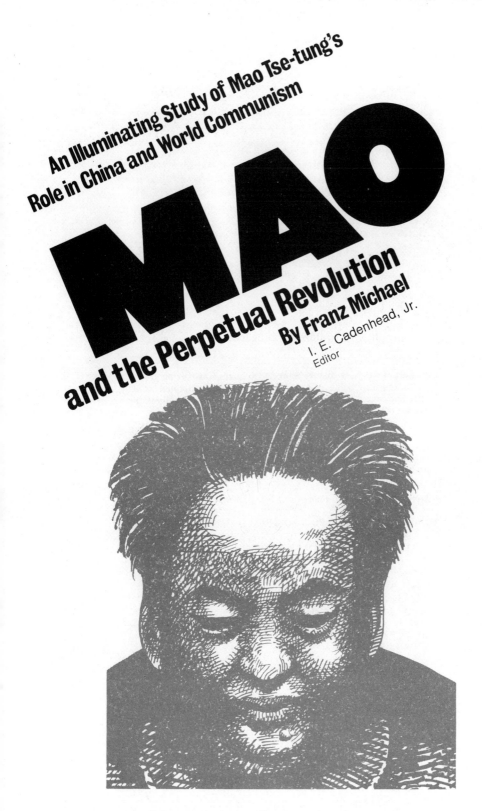

BARRON'S / WOODBURY, NEW YORK

To Dolores

All inquiries should be addressed to:
Barron's Educational Series, Inc.
113 Crossways Park Drive
Woodbury, New York 11797

Library of Congress Catalog Card No. 77-24400

International Standard Book No. 0-8120-5132-7

Library of Congress Cataloging in Publication Data
Michael, Franz H.
  Mao and the perpetual revolution.

  Includes index.
  1. Mao, Tse-tung, 1893-1976. 2. Heads of state—
China—Biography. 3. China—Politics and government
—1949-   I. Title.
DS778.M3M516   951.05'092'4[B]   77-24400
ISBN 0-8120-5132-7

PRINTED IN THE UNITED STATES OF AMERICA

Contents

EDITOR'S FOREWORD

No figure in modern times other than Chairman Mao has held a position of leadership over so much of the world's population. The continuing importance of the nation he did so much to create is clear to anyone, and the importance of Mao's wife in the affairs of China is only now becoming known to most non-specialists.

This timely book by Professor Michael describes the lengthy career of Mao, including the turbulent times, his conflict with Chiang Kai-shek, and his contributions to the development of a Chinese ideology important to the entire world.

Drawing upon extensive research and an obvious knowledge of his subject, the author has presented an understandable discussion of the complexities of Chinese history while, at the same time, providing the reader with insight into the human side of the Chinese leaders.

Though it is too early as yet to have a true "Verdict of History" on Mao, the chapter with this title is especially significant in placing Mao and his writings into historical perspective, providing direction for further study, and pointing up some of the debate that has already gone on over proper interpretations of the Chairman's role. The appendix contains documents illustrative of Mao's work and provides, in a convenient form, the basis for preliminary discussion of Mao's thought by the relatively uninitiated.

Professor Michael, a political scientist with the Institute for Sino-Soviet Studies at George Washington University, has written here not only a worthy addition to the Shapers of History Series but a new and important interpretation of the career and times of Mao Tse-tung. Its importance can only grow as further studies of the subject are produced.

I.E. Cadenhead, Jr.

AUTHOR'S PREFACE

Mao Tse-tung, the Chinese Communist leader, was clearly one of the great revolutionaries of our time. Revolutions are a means to overthrow a given social order and to replace it with the new order, as envisaged by the revolutionaries. The revolutionary process, however, is not a goal in itself. The question is, what social order do the revolutionaries intend to bring about?

The Western social order, as we know it today, has been brought about through three major revolutionary transformations of the medieval world. First, there was the prolonged English revolution, broadening participation in government, based on the key document of the Magna Carta limiting royal authority which eventually led to representative government of the Western democratic tradition. The French Revolution of 1789, with the noble goal of *Liberté, Egalité, Fraternité,* commenced as an attack against the aristocracy and led to the institutionalization of the rule of that bourgeoisie that had risen in the towns and cities of Europe by the end of the Middle Ages. The American Revolution of 1776 had its deepest roots in the English and Western tradition. While initially a struggle against colonial rule, it declared the broadest form of freedom for the individual and his or her right to life, liberty and the pursuit of happiness.

By the twentieth century, the pendulum of revolution had begun to swing backward. The revolutionary goal was by now concerned not with individual freedom, but with the distribution of material goods. The utopian goal of Karl Marx and the Marxist-Leninists became the self-regulating collective, a projected, idealized social order based on the principle "from each according to his ability and to each according to his need." Under the new doctrine of class struggle, the freedom of the Western tradition was attacked as bourgeois chimera; and with the condemnation of freedom of the individual, came the attack against the principle of intellectual freedom that had been fought for since the Age of Reason in the eighteenth century. The very basis of the Western concept of free scholarship, "the objective search for truth," was denied as bourgeois prejudice. Truth became whatever served the purpose of the proletarian revolution.

It was within this Marxist-Leninist tradition that Chairman Mao placed his stamp on Chinese history. Strong-willed and domineering, Mao might well have asserted himself in any historical period. He was born, however, at the end of the nineteenth century and played his part in the framework of the ideas and concepts of the twentieth century. Fusing what he had learned from Marx and Lenin with his own utopian dreams derived from a simplified version of Darwinism, Mao came to regard eternal struggle as the basis of all existence. When challenged by the leading comrades of his party, Mao did not hesitate to attack the party structure itself and to found a leader cult, elevating himself to the position of leader of the masses and final arbiter of all policy making. Mao's own political life was a constant struggle to the very end, confirming his belief in struggle as the essence of existence.

The title of this book, *Mao and the Perpetual Revolution,* was chosen to characterize this aspect of the life of Chairman Mao, who started within the Marxist-Leninist system and later struck out on his own course, on an extraordinary venture in ever-recurring revolution, whose utopian goal was almost by definition forever unreachable.

This book, though not an exhaustive account, is meant as a comprehensive assessment of the Chinese leader. It is intended to introduce the general reader to the story of the man and his part in the Communist world and in the shaping of events in China for over half a century. There are many works on Chinese communism and on the life of Mao Tse-tung, his personality, actions, thought, the ramifications of his political role and even on his poetry or his psyche. The author has profited from them. If the analysis provided here should stimulate debate with specialists on controversial issues and interpretations—all the better.

Over a period of many years of reading and discussions with colleagues and specialists in the field in the United States, Europe and East Asia, the author has enjoyed the give and take of countless debates and has learned from many studies of his colleagues—too many to list here. To single out but the best known—the works of Stuart Schram and Benjamin Schwarz have been very helpful, as has been the well-informed and stimulating recent biography on Mao by Edward Rice. These and others are listed in the selected bibliography. What the author has perhaps stressed more than is usually the case in these works is the Soviet connection under which Mao came to power. Providing crucial doctrinal and material support for over two decades until the Communist victory in China, the link continued during the first years of the People's Republic of China. Without reference to this part of Mao's story, the poignancy of Mao's assertion of independence and his challenge to Moscow would be largely lost.

Much had to be omitted, but the flavor of Mao's style as expressed in certain speeches and key documents and in an example of his poetry is provided in the appendix.

The picture that emerges is that of a unique revolutionary who lived and died in the midst of struggle; who, through his singular authoritative personality and willpower, inspired masses of fanatical followers, destroyed millions of people for the sake of his revolutionary goals, kept China in turmoil and left a heritage of perpetual revolution without a known successor of equal stature and single-minded revolutionary zeal.

Washington, D.C.   Franz Michael

CHRONOLOGY

1893   *December 26* — Mao Tse-tung is born of a peasant family in Hsiangtan, Hunan.

1911   Mao enters Middle School in Ch'angsha in Hunan.

            October 10 — National Revolution breaks out in Wuchang.
                        — Mao joins a revolutionary army in October.

1912   Mao leaves the army and returns to Hunan Middle School.

1918   Mao graduates and in September goes to Peking and works as an assistant in the Peking University Library. Meets Ch'en Tu-hsiu, Li Ta-chao and other leftists who form a society for the study of Marxism.

1919   *March* — Mao returns to Hunan via Shanghai. Becomes politically active and edits the *Hsiang-Chiang Review.*

            May 4 — Student movement begins in Peking and quickly spreads to students in Shanghai and elsewhere.

            December — Mao returns to Peking and is politically active among Hunanese there.

1920   *April* — Mao visits Shanghai again, has talks with Ch'en Tu-hsiu and becomes a confirmed Marxist.

            July — Mao returns to Ch'angsha to become director of a primary school attached to the Teacher's Training School.
                   — Marries Yang K'ai-hui.

1921   *July* — Founding of the Chinese Communist party in Shanghai. Mao is one of twelve or thirteen in attendance.

            October — Mao establishes Chinese Communist branch in Hunan. Becomes first secretary.

            December — Mao organizes Hunan branch of the Socialist Youth Corps and party cell at Anyüan Mines.

1922   *July* — Mao misses the Second Chinese Communist Party Congress held in Shanghai.

1923   *January 26* — Sun-Joffe Agreement is announced.

April — Mao leaves Hunan under threat of arrest. Works at Chinese Communist party center in Shanghai.

June — Third Congress of the Chinese Communist party held in Canton. Mao attends and is elected to the Central Committee. Congress agrees to cooperate with Kuomintang.

July — Mao returns to Shanghai to arrange cooperation between the Chinese Communist party and the Kuomintang.

December — Mao leaves for Canton to attend First Kuomintang Congress.

1924   *January* — Mao elected alternate member of the Central Executive Committee of the Kuomintang.

November — Mao falls ill and returns to Hunan.

1925   *January* — Fourth Chinese Communist Party Congress meets in Canton. Mao loses post in Central Committee.

March — Dr. Sun Yat-sen dies in Peking.

July — Mao leaves Hunan for Canton.

August — Mao becomes director of the Kuomintang Training Institute for the peasant movement. Later becomes also secretary and deputy head of the propaganda department of the Kuomintang.

December — Mao returns to Shanghai where he works with Kuomintang leaders.

1926   *January* — Mao reelected alternate member of the Kuomintang Central Committee at the Kuomintang Second Congress in Canton.

1925-26   Mao divides his time between Canton-Hunan-Shanghai working within both the Chinese Communist party and the Kuomintang, and is active in the peasant movement.

1926   Mao heads the Chinese Communist party peasant department in Shanghai.

December — Mao is sent to Hunan by the Party to investigate the peasant unrest in the province.

1927   *March* — Mao's report on the peasant movement in China is published.

April — Suppression of Communist organization in Shanghai. Formation of Nanking Government.

May — Fifth Communist Party Congress at Wuhan. Mao alternate member of Politburo.

August 1 — Nanchang uprising.

August 7 — Emergency meeting of the Chinese Communist Central Committee at Kiukiang called by the Comintern representative, Lominadze.
   — Ch'en Tu-hsiu deposed.
   — Planning of Autumn Harvest uprising in four provinces. Mao sent to Hunan to participate in uprising there.

September 19 — Autumn Harvest uprising in Hunan fails. Mao escapes, leads remnants of force to Chingkangshan.

November — Party Politburo meeting in Shanghai. Mao censored and dismissed from position as alternate member of the Politburo and as a member of the party Provincial Committee in Hunan.

1928 *April* — Chu Teh and Mao Tse-tung join forces at Ching-kangshan.

June — Sixth Congress of the Chinese Communist party in Moscow.

December 28 — Chu-Mao forces move into Southern Kiangsi and Western Fukien and establish Kiangsi Soviet with capital at Juichin.

1929 *December* — Kut'ien Conference. Mao formulates basic principles of guerilla warfare.

1930 *April* — Mao is ordered to Shanghai for consultation by party leadership but refuses to go.

June — Chinese Communist strategy under Li Li-san promotes attackes on cities in contravention to Moscow's policy.

August-September — Chu-Mao forces attack Nanch'ang and fail.

September-November — Li Li-san purged and sent to Moscow. The 28 Bolsheviks (Chinese leaders trained in Moscow) assume party leadership.

December — Fut'ien incident. Mao arrests and executes a large number of Li Li-san adherents in the whole area.

1930-34   Five "annihilation" campaigns by National Government against Kiangsi Soviet.

1931   *September 18* — Mukden incident, Japanese invasion of Manchuria.

           November 1 — First All-China Soviet Congress opens at Juichin.

           December — Mao elected chairman of National Soviet Government.
           — Chou En-lai arrives in Juichin; beginning decline of Mao's authority.

1933   *January* — Communist party Politburo leaders arrive in Juichin.

           October — Chiang Kai-shek begins *block house* strategy to strangle Juichin Soviet in Fifth Annihilation Campaign.

           Fall — Communist military agent, Otto Braun, arrives in Juichin.

1934   *January* — Second All-China Soviet Congress held at Juichin.

           October — Communists break through Kiangsi blockade. Long March begins.

1935   *January* — Tsunyi Conference. Mao elected chairman of Revolutionary Military Council.

           June — Mao and Chang Kuo-t'ao forces meet at Maokung in Szechwan.

           August 5 — Maoerhkai Conference between Mao and Chang. Mao secretly marches with his troops to Shensi. Arrives in October at Wayaopao, end of Long March.

           December — New United Front policy adopted at Politburo meeting.

1936   *November* — Anti-Comintern Pact signed between Nazi Germany and Japan.

           December — Kidnapping of Chiang Kai-shek at Sian resulting in the end of the civil war.

1937   *January* — Mao moves his headquarters to Yenan in Shensi.
           — Trial of Chang Kuo-t'ao.

           July 7 — Marco Polo Bridge incident. The undeclared war between China and Japan begins.

August — Politburo meeting at Lochuan in North Shensi to discuss cooperation with the Kuomintang.

September — Eight Route Army is organized and North Shensi Soviet is renamed Shensi-Kansu-Ninghsia border region.

October — Communist victory against Japanese at battle of P'inghsingkuan.
— Wang Ming returns from Moscow.

During 1937 Chiang Ch'ing becomes Mao's companion and eventually becomes his third wife.

1937-39   Communist border governments established.

1938   *January* — New Fourth Army formed in lower Yangtze Region.

1940   *January* — Mao publishes his essay called "On the New Democracy.

August-December — One Hundred Regiment Campaign launched by Eighth Route Army against the Japanese.

1941   *January* — New Fourth Army incident.

1941-42   Cheng-feng movement, Mao's purge of the opposition.

1944   *November* — Ambassador Hurley flies to Yenan to promote negotiations between the Communists and the National Government.

1945   *February* — Yalta Agreement.

April-June — Seventh Chinese Communist Party Congress begins. Mao's speech on coalition government. Mao elected chairman of Central Committee.

August 14 — Sino-Soviet Treaty of Friendship and Alliance.

August 18 — Japan surrenders.

August 28 — Mao flies to Chungking with Hurley to negotiate with Chiang Kai-shek.

October — Mao and Chiang Kai-shek sign the October 10 Agreement.

December 22 — General Marshall arrives as President Truman's special envoy to China.

1946   *January-February* — Political Consultative Conference convenes.

              July — Fighting between the Nationalists and Communists begins.

              November — Chou En-lai leaves for Yenan ending the negotiations between Nationalists and Communists.

1947   *May-June* — Battle of Ssup'ingchieh. Decisive Nationalist victory. American pressure on Chiang Kai-shek to cease attack and shift to a defensive war in order to resume negotiations.

              December — Mao declares that the revolutionary war has changed from defensive to offensive war.

1948   *Spring* — Communist offensive in Manchuria.

              November — Manchurian campaign ends with complete Communist victory.

1948-49   *November-January* — Battle of Hsüchow, Communist victory.

1949   *May* — Communist troops cross Yangtze River. Rapidly occupy all mainland China.

              September — People's Political Consultative Conference called by Mao in Peking. Approves the Organic Law and Common Program.

              October 1 — The establishment of the People's Republic of China.

              December — Mao leaves for an eight-week visit to Moscow to negotiate Sino-Soviet Treaty of Friendship and Alliance.

1950   *June* — Outbreak of the Korean War.

              October — Mao sends "volunteers" to Korea.

1950-53   *June* — Period of political drives and terror.

1953   Initiation of First Five-Year Plan and beginning of collectivization.

1954   *September* — First National People's Congress held. Proclaims a constitution for the People's Republic and elects Mao Tse-tung chairman of the People's Republic of China.

1955   *July* — Speeding up of collectivization by Mao.

1956   *February* — Twentieth Party Congress of Soviet party. Khrushchev's secret "de-Stalinization" speech.

1956-58   Eighth Chinese Communist Party Congress. New party statutes eliminates Mao's Thought from preamble.

1957   *February* — Mao's speech "On the Correct Handling of Contradictions Among the People" inaugurates "Let a Hundred Flowers Bloom" campaign.

     June — Beginning of "Anti-Rightist" campaign.

     November — Mao visits Moscow to participate in the First Communist Intraparty Conference in Moscow. Delivers a speech stating "the East Wind prevails over the West Wind."

1958   *May* — Mao launches the Great Leap Forward, introduces a policy of the commune system and the Three Red Flags.

     December 10 — Central Committee meeting decides on a retreat from the Great Leap Forward. Mao resigns as chairman of the People's Republic of China.

1959   *July* — Lushan meeting of the Central Committee. Defense Minister P'eng Teh-huai attacks Mao's Great Leap Forward policy. P'eng is purged and succeeded by Lin Piao.

     October 1 — Ten Year Anniversary of the People's Republic of China. Khrushchev among many visiting Communist dignitaries.

1959-65   Build-up of the Cult of Mao and of the Thought of Mao, initiated by Lin Piao who issues *The Little Red Book* of Chairman Mao's sayings.

1960   Second Intraparty Conference in Moscow. Chinese delegation without Mao. Sino-Soviet polemics begin.

1961   *January-December* — Sino-Soviet polemics worsen.

1962-63   Peking denounces Soviet "Modern Revisionism." Sino-Soviet conflict becomes public.

1962-64   Socialist Education movement as a tug-of-war between Mao and the party leadership under Liu Shao-ch'i.

1964   *October* — Khrushchev falls. China explodes its first atomic bomb.

1965   Struggle between Mao and the Chinese Communist party under Liu enters the universities.

1966   *July 16* — Mao's swim in the Yangtze River.

1966-69   Mao launches the Great Proletarian Cultural Revolution to attack the party and purge its leaders.

1966   *June 2* — Mao's directive suspends school admissions, promises proletarization of education, formation of student activists groups, later called Red Guards.

            August — Mao calls Eleventh Plenary Session of the Central Committee in Peking.

            August 8 — Sixteen article resolution on the Great Proletarian Cultural Revolution.

            October-November — Nine mass meetings of eleven million students at T'ien-an-men Square in Peking.

1967   *January 6* — Mao's directive to the Red Guards to seize power.

            January 21 — Mao directive to the People's Liberation Army to "support the left."

            January 28 — Mao's directive to the People's Liberation Army circumscribing People's Liberation Army action.

            February 5 — Establishment of the People's Commune in Shanghai to be changed two weeks later to a Revolutionary Committee.

            July — Wuhan incident.

1968   *July 28* — Mao blames five Red Guard leaders for their failure in the Cultural Revolution.

            September — Revolutionary Committees chiefly under People's Liberation Army control are established in all twenty-nine provinces and municipalities in China: China is "all red."

1969   *Spring* — Sino-Soviet border incidents.

            April-May — Ninth Congress of the Chinese Communist party. Lin Piao is named Mao's successor. New party statutes.

            September — Soviet Premier Aleksei Kosygin meets with Chou En-lai at airport in Peking. Sino-Soviet talks on border disputes begin.

December — Sino-Soviet talks stalemated. Propaganda war resumes.

1970   *April* — Chou En-lai visits Pyongyang.
     — Chou En-lai chairs conference in South China dealing with Chinese support of the Indochina War of Liberation. China claims to be "reliable rear area."

December — Politburo meeting in North China critical of Lin Piao.

1971   *July* — Dr. Kissinger visits Peking.

September 11-12 — Purge of Lin Piao.

1972   *February* — President Nixon visits the People's Republic of China; Shanghai Communique.

1973   *April* — Rehabilitation of Teng Hsiao-p'ing.

August 7 — Beginning of anti-Confucius drive.

August 24-28 — Tenth Chinese Communist Party Congress.

September 29 — Joint editorial of *People's Daily, Liberation Daily* and *Red Flag;* militia's task is redefined.

1975   *January* — National People's Congress.

December 27 — China releases Soviet helicopter and crew, captured eight months earlier.

1976   *January 8* — Chou En-lai dies.

April 5 — Massive anti-Mao demonstrations in Peking and other cities. Purge of Teng Hsiao-p'ing.

Hua Kuo-feng becomes prime minister and deputy chairman of the Central Committee of the Party.

September 9 — Mao Tse-tung dies.

Birthplace of Mao Tse-tung, Hunan Province.   *Wide World Photos.*

CHAPTER

I

Communism in China: The Man, The Strategy, and The Organization

Fʀᴏᴍ ᴛʜᴇ ᴛɪᴍᴇ of the founding of the Communist party in China in 1921 to the tumult of the Great Proletarian Cultural Revolution and its aftermath, Chinese communism has taken a special course away from established Marxist-Leninist lines into new directions of political and social experimentation. The man responsible for this course was Mao Tse-tung. Although Mao was only a minor figure at the beginning of the Chinese Communist party organization in the early 1920s and was not the creator of Chinese Communist strategy, he placed his stamp so markedly on the development of Chinese communism that it appears proper to speak of this phase of development in China, the period from the founding of the Chinese Communist party in 1921 to the third decade of the Chinese People's Republic in the late 1970s, as the era of Mao Tse-tung. As in all important periods of human history, it was the intertwining of the special historical setting and the outstanding ability of a leading personality which determined the course of events. Chinese communism made Mao a world figure and Mao turned Chinese communism into an instrument to build his political power and transform China according to his revolutionary image.

I

THE MAN: Mao Tse-tung, The Making of a Leader

A great deal has been written about the family background and origin of Mao Tse-tung in an attempt to explain his personality and character. Though it may be futile to try to understand the mysteries of personality in terms of the genes or of social environment, it may still be of importance to point to the factors that affected the formation of the individual. Mao Tse-tung was born on December 26, 1893, in a village in the Chinese province of Hunan, south of the Yangtze, the largest river and communications system of central China, and south of the great lake area of Tung-t'ing Hu, from which the province of Hunan—"South of the Lake" —takes its name. Hunan, like other provinces south of the Yangtze, is made up of the basin of the Hsiang River that flows into the Tung-t'ing lake and is surrounded by mountainous areas and other valleys, all with a drainage toward the lake and the Yangtze River. Mao's birthplace in Shaoshan village in Hsiang-t'an district is located in the east of the province. As in other southern provinces separated by mountains from neighboring areas, a distinctive dialect developed in Hunan, and the Hunanese are regarded as having a stubborn and strong-willed character. Natives of the province have taken pride in the substantial list of native sons who stood out in Chinese history as men of character and accomplishment.

Though of peasant origin, a fact that has been stressed often, Mao did not come from a family without means. Mao's father, through his own hard work and business activities, raised his status to what the Communists and Mao himself later called "middle peasant" and eventually to that of a rich peasant. He became a trader and grain merchant.[1] Therefore the family was able to provide their son with the kind of education which the child of a poor peasant family could not easily obtain. Mao's father possessed at least a basic literacy, enough to enable him to keep records of his business activities. Mao's mother was, as were most village women, illiterate with a strong leaning toward Buddhism, which made some impression on her son.

Mao himself, as his pictures of that period show, was a slender youth. His face was rather round and was marked by a pronounced mole, later often retouched in official pictures. In later years, Mao gained considerable weight. His appearance has been described by one Western observer as rather feminine.[2] He had a high-pitched voice and spoke in a strong Hunanese dialect, characteristics which handicapped him as a public speaker.

Much has been made of the clash of personalities between father and son in the Mao family. The father used the traditional authority in the

Chinese family system and has been described as extraordinarily domineering. Mao's rebellion against his father's commands at one time led him to threaten suicide by jumping into the village pond, a threat that forced his father to relent. Mao thus appears to have been able to assert his will in this clash of personalities, an incident reported by Mao himself which may be one indication of the extraordinary willpower exerted by him in his early conflicts and one of the main personal traits that characterized Mao's later victories in the many conflicts of the hard school of Communist politics.

His father saw to it that at the age of eight his son received the traditional education of the upper class of Chinese society. This Confucian education had in the past been the basis of the rise to power through the examination system which qualified the Confucian elite to hold office and to assume the role of leadership in society. During Mao's childhood, however, this system had already lost its traditional importance; and indeed the Chinese examination system on which the Confucian order rested was abolished in 1905, to be replaced by Western education introduced first through missionary schools. Mao thus received the rudiments of a classical education which gave him a limited familiarity with the classical texts, memorized by the students during the first few years of schooling.

When Mao was 13, his father took him out of school, apparently feeling that further education was unnecessary. Young Mao labored on the land and aided his father with the simple bookkeeping needed for his business ventures. Mao soon opposed his father on the subject of further education and, characteristically asserting himself, was able by the age of 16 to enter a Western higher primary school in a neighboring district. Mao thus became a product of this age of transition between the classical Confucian education and the modern Western-oriented schooling. In his traditional education Mao retained not only an acquaintance with the classics, but also a love for famous Chinese novels and histories, such as *Romance of the Three Kingdoms, Water Margin, Journey to the West, Rebellion Against the T'ang Dynasty.* and other stories of rebellions.[3] This historical tradition and its literature stressed the heroic role of rulers, military leaders and statesmen, a major aspect of the Chinese interpretation of their own history in romantic and heroic terms. In spite of the rebellion against the past that was carried on by the younger generation of Chinese growing up during this time of transition, this glorification of military heroism remained one of the traits of the Chinese tradition that was carried over into modern times, adding its contribution to the emerging nationalism of the end of the nineteenth and beginning of the twentieth centuries. For Mao it remained a factor even in the late years of his Communist leadership.

From his own account, we know that Mao read many books about these Chinese heroes, as well as great men in Western history. His ideas of the latter were derived from a popular book called *Great Heroes of the World*. From Mao's personal account, we know that he was keenly interested in Napoleon and George Washington, the latter for his perservance during long years of bitter warfare. One of Mao's Chinese heroes was the Emperor Ch'in Shih Huang-ti, who founded the unified empire in the third century B.C. In the traditional Chinese interpretation, the first Emperor was damned because of his suppression of the Confucian opposition. In 213 B.C. this Emperor had given the order to burn all the books that presented the political view of his opponents and to have buried over 400 Confucian scholars alive. To interpret these acts as heroic feats signified Mao's willingness towards a ruthless break with the traditions and moral concepts of the Confucian world—an attitude which again found expression towards the end of Mao's career in the Maoist attack against Confucius. In his youth, Mao also began to read about the reform movement of the time, personified by the great political philosopher K'ang Yu-wei and his student and follower Liang Ch'i-ch'ao, both of whom impressed Mao greatly.[4] As other young students of his time, Mao just got a glimpse of the world outside China, of the greatness of Chinese past history, especially its martial aspects, and of the new problems of the transition of the period.

In 1911, the year of the Chinese Revolution, Mao at the age of 18 went to the provincial capital Changsha, where he entered Middle School. It was here that Mao learned of the outbreak of the Revolution in Wuhan on October 10. As were his fellow students, Mao was tremendously excited about the great events of the times which soon affected the city of Changsha itself. Mao's participation in the Revolution was of somewhat minor nature; he and a number of fellow students cut off their queues, the symbol of submission to the alien Manchu dynasty, the Ch'ing, which had ruled China for over 250 years, and then went to work cutting off queues from fellow students not courageous enough to act by themselves.[5] Mao then joined the army of a local military leader for about half a year; but then, presumably disenchanted by this short experience of a private soldier's life, he left again to resume his student existence.[6] After some experiences at other schools, and a time of study by himself in which he read rather indiscriminately translations of Western works of Darwin, Mill, Montesquieu and Spencer, Mao entered in 1913 a provincial normal school at Changsha from which he graduated in 1918.

During his student days at the Changsha Normal School, Mao came in contact through some of his teachers with the new intellectual life of his time. Among those who influenced Mao most was one of his teachers, Yang Ch'ang-chi, through whom Mao became acquainted with the journal *The New Youth (Hsin Ch'ing-nien)* edited by Ch'en Tu-hsiu, dean of the Faculty of Letters at Peking University. The journal advocated a total break with China's traditional past and promoted the idea of Chinese complete westernization. Influenced by Western readings, Ch'en Tu-hsiu expounded the concept that democracy and science, the idols of Western nineteenth century belief in progress, were the symbols under which China should break with the past and enter a modern phase of development along Western lines. In propagating these thoughts, Ch'en Tu-hsiu even personified "Mr. Democracy" and "Mr. Science" as the figures which were to save China from her outmoded stagnation and bring her into the modern world. It was thus Ch'en Tu-hsiu, later to become the chief founder of the Chinese Communist party and first secretary-general of the Central Committee, who led a revolutionary intellectual attack against the Chinese cultural tradition, which made a deep impression on the youth of the time.

Ch'en Tu-hsiu had also accepted the essays of another young Chinese scholar, Hu Shih, who, as a student of John Dewey, brought the American pragmatist's thinking onto the Chinese scene and was responsible for inviting Dewey himself to give a lecture course in China. Hu Shih had promoted the concept of what he called a "literary renaissance," an attempt to broaden Chinese literacy through abolishing the classical style of Chinese writing, the monopoly of a scholarly elite, and to replace it by *pai hua,* the actual spoken language used by the people. *The New Youth* journal used and popularized this form of writing which led to a vast growth of Chinese literature, especially after the May Fourth movement in 1919.

Mao's teacher, Yang Ch'ang-chi, propagated this journal and his ideas to Mao and other students, although in his own view he was not willing to abandon China's national culture through complete westernization, but rather thought that it could be transformed under the impact of the new thinking. Mao's own interest at the time, in line with his belief in the heroic and warlike aspects of Chinese history, was aimed at physical training of the Chinese people to strengthen their military spirit and overcome their weakness in the face of military threats. Through his teacher, Mao placed an article under the title of "A Study of Physical Culture," into *The New Youth* in April 1917, which, in essence, represented his view that "the principal aim of physical education is military heroism."[7]

After his graduation in 1918, Mao went to Peking University and became an assistant librarian. Under the influence of Li Ta-chao, director of the Peking University Library and professor of history, Mao became acquainted with Marxism and joined a Marxist study group which had been established by professor Li at the university.

As has sometimes been pointed out, Li Ta-chao, though a doctrinaire Marxist, never quite overcame his penchant for Chinese nationalism which gave his Marxist interpretation a somewhat different slant from that of Ch'en Tu-hsiu and other Chinese Communist leaders. It may be possible to overestimate this influence, but it has been held that Li's ideas may have influenced young Mao and strengthened his admiration for China's heroic tradition. Under this influence of professors Ch'en and Li, Mao formed his impressions of Western thought and learned about Marxism. The Marxist study group in which Mao participated approached Marxism as a topic of discussion rather than an instrument of political or academic discipline.

When Mao left Peking in February or March, 1919, to return to Hunan, his thinking was therefore in his own words still rather "confused" though more and more radical. On the way home, Mao stopped in Shanghai to bid farewell to some fellow students departing for further study abroad. These student journeys were supported by a group of young scholars in their overseas studies—a project in which Mao had participated. Mao appears never to have wanted to study abroad himself since, according to his own account, he did not feel sure enough about France or any foreign country; however, according to other accounts, he was not good at foreign languages. After his return Hunan, Mao took part in political activities that resulted from the May Fourth movement.[8]

The May Fourth movement of 1919 was a political demonstration by Chinese students and young intellectuals that was triggered by the news of the Treaty of Versailles and its disregard for the Chinese Nationalist demands of restoring the territorial rights China had lost to Japan during World War I. The Japanese military and political expansion in China during the period of World War I, when China was weak and the Western powers were preoccupied with fighting in Europe, had created a deep resentment among China's educated youth. Japan's success at the treaty table served as a catalyst in releasing these pent-up feelings and resulted in large student protests in Peking, Shanghai, and other cities.[9] The student demonstrations of this time have remained a vivid memory in the minds of Chinese intellectuals who later became the leaders of Modern China. The new thought that was forming under the impact of Western ideas and the bitterness of China's humiliation under the unequal treaties imposed by the Western powers since the middle of the nineteenth century found an open forum of expression in these street demonstrations.[10] In Peking, the demonstrations found their outlet in physical attacks on the officials who were held responsible for China's defeat at the Peace Conference, but the movement soon led to a much larger expression of the new Chinese nationalist feelings. An outburst of writings in pamphlets, journals and essays provided a new literature for the young China of the time. A drive to boycott Japanese goods, participated in by Chinese merchants, was directed against Japan's economic predominance in China.

Mao took part in the activities of the May Fourth movement in his province of Hunan, forming groups for "promoting national goods" and linking the efforts of students, merchants and workers for the common national purpose. As editor of one of the new local journals prospering during the May Fourth period, the *Hsiang-Chiang Review,* Mao wrote an article, "The Great Union of the Popular Masses."[11] It has been said that this article and the thinking of Mao at that time may have already expressed that trend towards "populism" which remained characteristic of Mao throughout his later career.[12] Indeed, the widely applied use of the term "masses," so characteristic of Mao, may be seen to date back to this early time.[13]

In his editing of the *Hsiang-Chiang Review,* Mao made use of the new *pai hua* form of writing that the literary renaissance had introduced. The articles which appeared in the *Review,* many of them from Mao's own pen, dealt with the popular radical themes of the time. When the journal was suppressed by the authorities, Mao, in line with general practice, switched to another local student paper, *Hsin Hunan,* which was in turn forbidden by the authorities. Mao then began to write for a local regular newspaper, the *Ta Kung pao* of Changsha. He wrote on topics popular among the students—the free choice of marriage partners, and the evil of control of young people by their parents. This activity, together with his reorganization of the students' association, brought Mao to the attention of the provincial authorities and placed him in danger of arrest. He therefore left Hunan and, with a group of student representatives, returned to Peking in December, 1919.

This was the time when leading Marxist publications, such as *The Communist Manifesto,* and Kautsky's *Karl Marx ökonomische Lehren* were translated and read in Peking where they made an impression on Mao. From Peking, Mao went to Shanghai where he discussed his new impressions with his mentor Ch'en Tu-hsiu, who had himself now accepted Marxist beliefs and whose views helped to strengthen Mao's acceptance of Marxist concepts as an answer in his search for the formulation of his radical ideas. From Shanghai, where Mao made a living by working in a laundry, Mao was soon called to Hunan by a former teacher, I P'ei-chi, who had returned to Changsha when the Nationalist military and political leaders gained control of the province. I P'ei-chi had become director of the Normal School and invited Mao in the summer of 1920 to take the position of director of a primary school attached to the Normal School. For the first time Mao had gained a respectable appointment and an income which enabled him to marry Yang K'ai-hui, daughter of Yang Ch'ang-chi, his former teacher who had introduced Mao to modern Western thought at the Normal School in Changsha.[14] By this time, Mao had become, as stated by himself in retrospect, a convinced Marxist, though his Marxist education was clearly rudimentary. What Mao had obtained in his earlier years as a student and political activist, was the martial view of Chinese history and the populist approach to politics, both trends which characterized his career throughout his later life.

THE STRATEGY: The National Liberation Movement

The historical setting in which Mao rose to international eminence was determined not only by the general framework of a Communist system but also by a special Communist strategy originated by Lenin for the nonindustrial world, applied first to China. This was the strategy of *wars of national liberation.*

According to Marxist doctrine, Communism was to be brought about in the age of capitalism by a revolution of the politically most advanced class of the time, the working class: in Communist terminology, the *proletariat.* The revolution was to occur in the industrial countries of the capitalist world, through urban uprising by the proletariat, started by general strikes and ending in a forcible seizure of power in the industrial centers of the world. The Bolshevik Revolution in Russia was regarded as such a proletarian uprising leading to a socialist state and society. Lenin, the leader of this revolution, had created the Communist party, a small disciplined group of revolutionaries which was to be the *vanguard* of the proletariat, acting as its guardian and tutor.

In the view of the leaders of the Bolshevik Revolution, success could only be secured if the seizure of power in the Soviet Union did not remain an isolated world event but spread to other countries, thus broadening the revolutionary base. This indeed was the great hope of the leaders in Moscow in 1917 who expected that their own seizure of power in Russia would be followed by a Communist takeover in Germany, Hungary and throughout Europe. In the excited statements of the time, it was to be only a matter of weeks or months until the Soviet Union in Russia would merge with a larger European Communist-Soviet Union. The revolutionary uprising in Munich and Bela Kun's short-lived regime in Hungary seemed to be the beginning of this trend towards a world Soviet Union predicated in the name of the Union of Soviet Socialist Republics and unrestrained by any geographical location. To promote this revolutionary cause in Europe, Lenin founded in 1919 the Third Communist International, the Comintern.[15]

When this hoped-for European revolution perished with the Communist collapses in Hungary and Munich, followed by the later defeat of the German Communists, Lenin turned toward the East. He was well aware of the revolutionary potential in the colorful and quasi-colonial world of eastern Asia, because of the positive reaction of the minority people of Russian Asia towards the Bolshevik Revolution. To use this potential for a Communist purpose required, however, a fundamentally different strategy from that of a proletarian revolution. The countries of Asia were not yet industrialized and provided no proletarian class. For such countries to play their part in a world Communist revolution, their actions had to be planned and explained in terms that permitted promising revolutionary action within the framework of Communist beliefs. For this purpose, Lenin developed the strategy of *national liberation movements* and *wars of national liberation* for the colonial world of Asia.[16] This strategy (which may be termed Communist strategy No. 2 in contrast to strategy No. 1: the proletarian revolution) had a long history of theoretical debate among socialist leaders before the Bolshevik Revolution.[17]

Two measures by Lenin, one theoretical and one practical, provided the basis for this new strategy in Asia. Theoretically, Lenin's theory of imperialism justified Communist support of nationalist aspirations in the colonial world of what today are called the *developing countries*. According to Lenin's theory of imperialism, the exploitation of the colonial countries through the *monopoly capitalism* of the industrial world had replaced the exploitation of the working class by the *capitalists* in their own countries. The struggles for national independence occurring in many colonial countries in the early 1900s were, in this interpretation, determined by economic factors with which the Communists could make common cause. The slogan for this cooperation between the Communists and the national movements in each country was a *united front.*

Lenin's creation of the Communist party as the proclaimed vanguard of the proletariat made it possible to organize such parties in countries that were not at all or not fully industrialized and had therefore no substantial working class or proletariat. In such countries the Communist parties would represent the world proletarian movement and work for the world revolution. This movement was to be organized by the Comintern which now turned its major work towards Asian countries, especially China. Its first task was to organize a local Communist party as the instrument through which to gain and maintain influence over the united front of a common policy of national liberation movements. In these countries with little or no working class the Communists claimed to exploit the revolutionary potential of the other social classes which in the Communist view were ready for revolutionary action: the peasants and the bourgeoisie.

The peasant societies of Asia were in Communist terminology *feudal*. If China did not know serfdom, the attachment of the peasant to the land, a hereditary upper nobility of lords and a lower nobility of knights, feudal contracts or any feudal concepts which could provide a parallel to the period of feudalism in the West, Chinese society had, so the Communist doctrine asserted, the characteristics of economic feudalism found in the relationships of landlord and tenants.[18] Within this conceptual framework the Communists aimed at exploiting peasant dissatisfaction and unrest. This was the *agrarian revolution* which communism would foster.

The second element which the strategy of the national liberation movements was to make use of, was the *bourgeoisie* in terms of Marxist doctrine. The capitalists of the colonial countries were themselves exploited by the monopoly capitalism of the imperialist powers. The *nationalist capitalists* of the colonial world were therefore fighting for their own survival. They could be the allies of the Communists in the battle against monopoly capitalism. A united front could therefore be formed with the national bourgeoisie and the *petit bourgeoisie* of the colonial countries. In the Communist view, Sun Yat-sen was indeed the representative of the Chinese bourgeoisie. This bourgeoisie was in doctrinal terms *progressive*.

China became the main theater of operation for this strategy of national wars of liberation. These were the decisive years between 1920 and 1923, when Chinese communism was organized under Comintern leadership and a united front was formed with the Chinese Nationalist movement.

Moscow's policy in China was actually three-pronged. First of all, a Chinese Communist party had to be created to become the chief instrument of the Communist Revolution. The establishment of such a Communist party in 1921 was to provide the necessary tool for Communist infiltration and eventual control of the Nationalist movement. Like all Communist parties established by the Comintern, the Chinese Communist party was to be organized after the model of the Soviet party. The principle of so-called democratic centralism of these Communist parties demanded that all party members had to be absolutely obedient to the orders given by the party leaders in the Central Committee and Polit-buro—where the real power rested. This total party discipline gave the leadership, in practice always in the hands of one man—a Lenin, a Stalin, a Mao Tse-tung—absolute power over the party members. Through the Comintern the Soviet leaders in turn controlled and directed the leaders and policies of the Communist parties worldwide.

The second task was to form a united front with the Nationalist move-ment in China. The Nationalist movement was led by Sun Yat-sen, the father of the Chinese Nationalist Revolution. After the overthrow of the imperial government in 1911, Sun's Nationalist party, the Kuomintang, tried unsuccessfully to establish a viable government. While China was divided among many autonomous warlords who fought among each other for territory and supremacy, Sun precariously maintained a political foothold in the South at Canton through the tolerance of a local warlord, Ch'en Chiung-ming, a military friend and collaborator of Sun. Deserted by this warlord, his local backing withdrawn, Sun was looking for other support and money to carry on his revolution, and was therefore willing to receive Soviet assistance through funds, equipment and political and military advisers. Along with this Soviet support Sun, presumably in the belief that he would remain in full control of his own party, accepted the cooperation of the Chinese Communists, who not only became members of the Nationalist party but obtained high positions in that party while maintaining their Communist allegiance.

The cooperation between Sun Yat-sen and Moscow was formalized by the Sun-Joffe Agreement of January 26, 1923 (Joffe was Moscow's Com-intern representative) in which the Soviets promised their support to Sun Yat-sen's Nationalist party.[19] The agreement was concluded after pro-longed contact and talks between Sun and Comintern representatives, which included discussions on the military aspects of Soviet support.[20]

The third Soviet approach was in the area of state relations. From 1916 to 1927, the formal government of China was located in Peking under the alternating control of several major and some lesser warlords of the North. In 1924 Moscow concluded a treaty with this government abrogating the "unequal treaties of the Czarist time." The treaty of 1924 served as a propaganda weapon for Soviet policy and neutralized potential international opposition from major Western powers to Soviet influence in China. The three Soviet moves thus established the Soviet position in China which would enable her to intiate and support a Chinese Communist strategy of wars of national liberation.

The Revolutionary Army

In contrast to the *proletarian revolution* which was to be based on the strategy of general strikes and political action in the cities, led by the Communist party, *national liberation movements* were to make use of a very different strategy: the application of military force through prolonged warfare. National liberation movements became, in practice, *wars of national liberation.* The instrument of this strategy was the *revolutionary army,* a politically indoctrinated military force, led by officers who combined political motivation and planning with professional military ability. This was to be an army altogether different from those of the warlords, an army recruited nationwide from idealistic, nationalistic students, who saw in military service their chance to translate into action their hopes for building a strong nation, free from the chaos and corruption of warlord exploitation and the humiliations of the unequal treaties imposed by Western powers.

When Sun Yat-sen received a promise of Soviet support for his revolution under the Sun-Joffe Agreement of 1923, a crucial part of this support referred to the promise of funds, equipment and advisers for establishing a Nationalist revolutionary army. After his bitter experience with unreliable provincial warlord forces, Sun readily agreed.[21] With Soviet help he established a military academy near Canton, the Whampoa Academy, which was to train cadets for the officer corps of the new Nationalist army. The Whampoa Academy became the cradle of a new Nationalist army. Two years later, characterizing this army and its role, Stalin emphasized the Communist view of the differences between this type of army and armies of the past. In Stalin's words:

> *Formerly, in the 18th and 19th centuries revolutions usually began with an uprising of the people, for the most part unarmed or poorly armed, who came into collision with the army of the old regime, which they tried to demoralize or at least to win in part to their own side. This was the typical form of the revolutionary outbreaks in Russia in 1905. In China, things have taken a different course. In China, the troops of the old government are confronted not by an unarmed people, but by an armed people in the shape of its revolutionary army. In China the armed revolution is fighting the armed counter-revolution. That is one of the special features and one of the advantages of the Chinese revolution. And therein lies the special significance of the revolutionary army in China.[22]*

This statement by Stalin was later taken up by Mao Tse-tung who restated it in these words, "In China the main form of struggle is war and the form of organization is the army."[23] It is this statement from which Mao eventually derived his oft-quoted slogan that "Political power grows out of the barrel of a gun."

However, the idea of creating a new revolutionary army in China developed by stages. Since the Chinese Revolution had been made possible with the backing of regional warlord armies that supported Sun Yat-sen's revolution of 1911, the use of these armies seemed at first the logical way to provide the necessary military backing for the new Nationalist revolution, supported by Moscow. Members of the small Communist party were all academics and intellectuals, lacking any military experience or background. The warlord armies which Sun Yat-sen had relied on in Canton had also at first been relied upon by Chinese Communist leaders and Moscow in their search for military support. Li Ta-chao, the co-founder of the Chinese Communist party, approached the northern warlord, Wu P'ei-fu, in Peking in an attempt to gain his support but failed. The most promising of the military leaders of the warlord period from the Communist point of view appeared to be Feng Yu-hsiang, a warlord, at that time based in the Northwest, who went to Moscow on the invitation of Stalin and was promised and given Soviet aid. But such temporary cooperation with warlords proved impractical because of the character of warlord regimes, and when the Sun-Joffe Agreement provided for massive Soviet support of the Nationalist movement through the United Front, it became practical to establish a Chinese Nationalist army with Soviet support. The revolutionary army of that time was, according to the Communist concept, a Chinese Nationalist rather than a Communist army. It was this army to which Stalin referred in 1926. As the United Front enabled the Communists to work in the Nationalist party, so the Whampoa Academy was to make it possible for the Communists to penetrate the new military organization.

The United Front was militarily as well as politically an ideal framework for Communist infiltration and eventual takeover from within. Only when this attempt failed and the Chinese Communists were expelled from the Kuomintang in 1927 were they forced to establish their own military organization, the Chinese Red Army which became the main force of the Communist Revolution in China, the People's Liberation Army (PLA) of today.

THE ORGANIZATION: *Mao and the Chinese Communist Party*

The Chinese Communist party was a creation of the Comintern, the agency established by Lenin in 1919 to extend the Communist organization on a worldwide basis. The Bolshevik Revolution of 1917 in Russia had a strong impact on China. The successful power seizure in Russia was regarded by many intellectual leaders in China as an outstanding example of a revolution that had succeeded. The attraction of the Soviet example was all the greater since the new Soviet government promised to abandon all privileges of the "unequal treaties" and deal with China on the basis of equality.[24] Within China, the Chinese Revolution of 1911 had been a disappointment. The years of the First World War had brought nothing but chaos and civil war. Power had fallen into the hands of military men. After the death of Yuan Shih-kai, China's first president and military strongman of the North, no outstanding leader had been able to hold the country together even in military terms. China was then divided among the warlords who fought each other for control of more land, which would bring more taxes with which to pay larger armies, so as to increase their respective bases and their power. In Canton, Sun Yat-sen was surviving on warlord tolerance; and in the constant large-scale military operations carried on by these *tufu,* military governors, there was no revolutionary purpose left in a period of decline and despair.

In this ideological void, there was no clear concept of any system of political and social values which could replace those of the past. The condemnation of the old traditions, voiced by the intellectuals, found its most ardent expression in the May Fourth movement of 1919, which rejected the Confucian past and opened the door for new Western ideas. Marxism was only one of many Western systems of thought which were now propagated in China. Yet there was little understanding of Marxism even among the group of intellectuals in Peking who had been interested in it, the circle of Ch'en Tu-hsiu and Li Ta-chao. This was the group to which Mao had become attached, although at the time he had only become acquainted with the rudiments of Marxist ideas.[25]

Like other young members of this Marxist-oriented group, Mao Tse-tung went all out in his newly gained Marxist views which to him meant a division of all people the world over into capitalists and proletarians. In Changhsa, Mao had begun to distribute Marxist material to students and when he received material from Peking in October, 1920, on a Socialist Youth Corps which had been established in the capital, Mao organized a branch of this youth organization in January, 1921. To do his part in the struggle between capitalists and the proletariat, Mao also tried his hand for a short time at labor organization. In his enthusiastic efforts, Mao personified the new, somewhat unsophisticated Marxian views held by some Chinese intellectuals at the time. What their efforts lacked was organization, discipline and funds, which were soon provided by Moscow through the Comintern.

The Chinese Communist party was founded in July, 1921, in a meeting in Shanghai, called and directed by the Comintern agent, Gregory Voitinsky. A small group of these Chinese Marxist-inclined intellectuals, thirteen in number, met with Voitinsky and a second Comintern agent, a Dutchman, H. Sneevliet, known under the *nom de guerre* of Maring, to discuss and accept the rudiments of a party organization. As a representative of the political action group in Hunan province, Mao participated as a lesser figure in this meeting. From the records of the Congress, it is apparent that the Chinese participants were more inclined to express their newly-gained radical notions than come to terms with a seasoned strategical appraisal of the situation. The two most senior Chinese Marxists, Li Ta-chao and Ch'en Tu-hsiu, were unable to attend; Li had remained in Peking and Ch'en had been called to Canton by Sun Yat-sen.

The record of this first founding meeting of the Chinese Communist party stressed the goal of the overthrow of the capitalist class and the establishment of a dictatorship of the proletariat without providing for any extensive political program of directives on the strategy to be followed.[26] The Comintern representatives from the outset had the somewhat difficult task of restraining the radical, unschooled enthusiasm of the participants. They appeared, however, to have obtained the important agreement that regular monthly reports on party affairs should be sent to the Comintern. The minutes of the meeting indicate that the Chinese group ignored the strategy of the United Front. The reason may be that neither Voitinsky nor Maring were present at the final session and therefore could not guide the writing of the resolutions. This absence may explain the shortcomings, in terms of Moscow policy, of the declaration arrived at, especially a sentence that strongly opposed cooperation with other parties.[27] The meeting was held at a girl's school in the French Concession in Shanghai, but when the French police, alerted by an informant, approached, the participants hurriedly dispersed to meet again on a boat on the South Lake near Chiahsing in Chekiang province to continue their deliberations without the Comintern representatives.

At this point it apparently was more important for Moscow to establish the organization itself; the proper directives and the right program could always be introduced later. When Ch'en Tu-hsiu, who became the first chairman of the Party's Central Committee, took over, he received such directives from Moscow and followed them properly.[28] The radical statements of the First Congress were therefore of no lasting importance.

Whether Mao Tse-tung played any part in the discussion is unknown. His official biographies credit Mao with taking a view opposed to the radical resolutions, presumably to prove his conformity with Moscow's plan of a broad-based united front, but this assertion cannot be documented.[29] In any case, as a member of the newly organized Chinese Communist party, Mao was now under party discipline and was to carry on the party's work. After his return to Changsha, Mao formally set up the Hunan branch of the Chinese Communist party and became its secretary. Earlier he had used his position in the school system to good advantage to disseminate Marxist teachings and Marxist literature. When Mao's activities in organizing strikes in Hunan province, particularly at the Anyüan coal mines and the Canton-Hankow Railroad, led to the suppression of labor unions and orders for the arrests of their leaders, Mao fled to Canton in April, 1923. In Canton, Mao was to participate in the united front work that represented the broader base of Lenin's strategy.[30]

The Soviet plan for cooperation between the Chinese Nationalists and Communists was outlined to the Chinese in January, 1922, at the First Congress of the Toilers of the East, held in Moscow and Petrograd, and attended by both Communist and Kuomintang Chinese. In the summer of 1922, Sun Yat-sen discussed the form of cooperation between his party, the Kuomintang, and the Communists with Comintern agents in Shanghai and they agreed that Chinese Communists would be permitted to join the Kuomintang on an individual basis. In July, the same plan was taken up by the Comintern representatives at the Second Congress of the Chinese Communist party held in Shanghai which adopted a resolution forming an alliance with the Kuomintang. Mao Tse-tung did not participate in this Congress because, according to him, he could not find the secret meeting place, although he was actually in Shanghai. However, in August, 1922, another meeting was called in Hangchow where the Comintern agent, Maring, transmitted a directive to the effect that some of the Chinese Communist party members should join the Kuomintang as individuals and without vitiating their Communist "party membership," as had already been agreed to by Sun Yat-sen.[31]

On the basis of this agreement, Mao Tse-tung like other Communist leaders joined the reorganized Nationalist party in Canton. Mao became an alternate member of the Kuomintang Central Committee, which included three Communist full members and five other Communist alternates. Mao Tse-tung's first assignment in the Kuomintang was in the important field of propaganda.[32] Next, in 1925, as director of the Institute for the Peasant Movement, he was given the vital function of preparing cadres for instigating and directing the *agrarian revolution*.[33] Among the students of the institute were several dozen young Communists and many came from Hunan, Mao's province.[34] Some of the Hunanese students at the institute did not finish their studies but returned to Hunan by the end of 1925 as special commissioners of the peasant movement which was under the auspices of the Hunan Provincial Committee of the Kuomintang. Most of them were assigned to work in the areas along the railroads. They set up several township peasant associations, whose members were drawn from the ranks of poor peasants and some educated elements such as primary school teachers.[35]

This peasant organization had to be handled with restraint in order not to alienate the Kuomintang members who came from urban bourgeois or landlord families and who would have strongly opposed any violence that threatened their families in the rural areas. Indeed, the agrarian revolution, as far as it went, was to be organized under Nationalist auspices and it was in an agency of the Kuomintang that Mao Tse-tung got the assignment of training agrarian functionaries.

The rudiments of the organization of agrarian discontent were taught to the Chinese Communists in Canton in lectures by the Soviet adviser, Borodin, in which Mao participated. This Soviet policy as derived from Lenin and continued by Stalin has been little understood. The myth that Moscow, at least under Stalin, was concerned only with proletarian uprisings in the cities and that only the Chinese Communist leaders, that is, Mao Tse-tung, discovered the peasant and invented the peasant strategy is factually untenable. From the very beginning the importance of the peasant as a revolutionary class factor had been recognized by Lenin, and the program in Canton duly laid the foundation for this policy in the United Front. However, as long as cooperation with the Kuomintang existed, the peasant organizations and uprisings had to be restricted in order not to effect unfavorably the attitude of the Nationalist leaders, especially the military officers, many of whom came from the families who had a vested interest in land holdings.

FUTURE ANTAGONISTS: Chiang Kai-shek and Mao Tse-tung and the Crumbling of the United Front

The most important assistance given to Sun Yat-sen by the Comintern was the funds, advisers and equipment for the establishment of the military academy, the famous Whampoa Academy, for the training of officers for the new Nationalist army. To set up and direct the Academy, Sun Yat-sen chose a young officer who had been a member of his party and had been consulted by him in the difficult Canton years.

Chiang Kai-shek, who was born in 1887 in the small town of Ch'i-k'ou in the district of Fenghua in Chekiang province, of modest family background, had been a cadet at the Paotingfu Academy of Hopeh province from where he had been sent to Japan for further training. There he had joined Sun's party, the Tung Meng Hui. As a young officer in Shanghai, Chiang participated in the revolution of 1911. At a most critical time in Sun's career, during his conflict with Ch'en Chiung-ming, in Canton, Chiang Kai-shek had come to Sun's assistance and had thus become Sun Yat-sen's trusted military adviser. In 1923, assuming his position as president of the new Academy, Chiang was sent to Moscow with a Chinese delegation which included a number of Chinese Communists.[36] In gathering background for the new military academy, Chiang Kai-shek interviewed Soviet political and military leaders, and visited various military establishments, and was told about the concept of a *revolutionary army*.[37] Under this concept, the new Chinese Nationalist army was not only to be professional, but also a political force. It was not only to be trained in military skills, it was to be politically indoctrinated as a revolutionary vehicle—in fact, the main force of the revolution.

To carry out this indoctrination the Whampoa Academy followed the example of the Soviet Red Army, adding Communist party representatives to its staff. There was a difference, however, between the party representatives of the new Chinese revolutionary Nationalist army and the commissar system in the Soviet Red Army. In the Soviet case, Trotsky had introduced the commissars to supervise the commanders of the troops, most of whom had been former Tsarist officers who could not be trusted politically. In China, the commissars were not to supervise the commanders but to indoctrinate the whole army as a revolutionary force. The fact that this task of indoctrination of the Nationalist army was in the hands of Communists, such as Chou En-lai, seemed to provide a further guarantee that the army would eventually be taken over by Communist leadership.

The Whampoa Academy became the cradle of the new type of Chinese military leadership. At a time of strong Nationalist spirit, so many young people applied for admission that the Academy could select an outstanding group of students. This student body was welded together by an *ésprit de corps* and formed a totally different type of force from that of the warlord armies—in fact, so superior in human quality and training that it was soon able to defeat much larger warlord units and secure Kuomintang control over the area of Canton. This was in preparation for the main campaign by the new Nationalist army which was to march north from Canton to Nanking and Peking, defeat the armies of the warlords who had divided China among themselves for the last decade and unify the country for the first time under a Chinese Nationalist Government. Some warlords had already joined the Nationalists, giving strength to the Nationalist cause.

From the beginning, however, the cadets of the academy were divided in their political loyalties, and a struggle for power was carried on between the Soviet advisers and Chiang Kai-shek. The conflict was further aggravated by the fact that the substantial number of Chinese Communist party members who had been accepted as cadets soon organized within the academy their own society, the Association of Young Soldiers. The Kuomintang cadets thereupon formed the Sun Yat-sen Society, and Chiang Kai-shek had his hands full in his endeavor to maintain peace between the two groups.[38]

During the first two years of the Academy's existence, Chiang Kai-shek as president succeeded in maintaining unity and cooperation. He stressed the spirit of personal sacrifice and loyalty and established a system according to which soldiers and officers were mutually responsible to each other in battle. It was this spirit which transformed the cadet army into a formidable force. Later, however, when the Nationalist and Communist officers found themselves on opposite sides in a military confrontation, this common background accentuated the bitterness with which they fought for their conflicting convictions.

The conflict between the two groups at the Whampoa Academy came to a head in the so-called *Chungshan* incident on March 20, 1926. The incident was explained as a Communist attempt to remove Chiang Kai-shek, who stood in the way of their control of the academy. It began with the unauthorized movement of a gunboat—the *Chungshan,* which was commanded by a Communist officer—and was believed to have been an attempt to kidnap Chiang Kai-shek and remove him from the academy, possibly to send him to Moscow.[39] In quick reaction to the move and to defeat the presumed conspiracy, Chiang Kai-shek used a loyal unit to disarm his opponents, place the Soviet advisers under arrest and reassert his control over the academy. In the following negotiations with the chief Soviet adviser, Michael Borodin, who had been absent during the coup, a compromise was reached. Some of the Soviet advisers involved in the coup were returned to Soviet Russia; the Chinese Communists were to continue cooperation in the Kuomintang, but Chiang Kai-shek ordered the Communist cadres who served as party representatives expelled from the Nationalist army; it was agreed that the Nationalist forces should immediately start their military campaign against the warlord armies by marching north from Canton.

The timing of this campaign had previously been an argument between Chiang Kai-shek and the Soviet advisers. Chiang, who realized the impossibility of escaping Soviet control in Canton, where all equipment and funds for the academy and its armies were provided by Moscow, had long pressed for the beginning of the northern campaign, which would enable the Nationalist forces to obtain access to military weapons and funds other than from the Soviet Union and thus escape the Soviet vise. The Soviets had delayed action in order to strengthen their hold over the Nationalist party and army and obtain control in Canton before the northern campaign took place. They also intended to direct the march towards Wuhan in central China where they hoped to maintain their control of funds and war materiel, in view of the fact that the warlord of the northwest, Feng Yü-hsiang, had been receiving Soviet support and was believed to be dependent on Moscow. Chiang Kai-shek on his side wanted to march towards Nanking and Shanghai to attain access to the arsenal in Shanghai and to Chinese and Western funds available there. Following the *Chungshan* incident, negotiations led to a compromise according to which the Nationalist forces divided into right and left wings, moving to Nanking-Shanghai and Wuhan, respectively. It was this agreement and the success of Chiang Kai-shek in curbing the Communist influence which laid the foundation of Chiang's eventual victory in freeing the Nationalist party from Soviet and Communist control and in establishing in 1927 the National Government in Nanking under his own leadership.

Mao Tse-tung was not present in Canton during much of this time and played no active part in the Communist-Nationalist conflict. He had left first for Shanghai and then for his home province of Hunan for reasons which have never been fully explained. Before he left Canton, Mao had participated in the meetings of the Central Committee of the Kuomintang where he had proposed measures of administrative decentralization which, if applied, might have benefitted the Kuomintang administration.[40] It was a proposal for the establishment of regional party bureaus in about a dozen places where there were favorable conditions for political development. Mao's proposal was in essence a program that aimed at development of the Kuomintang.

In Shanghai, Mao worked closely with such Kuomintang leaders as Hu Han-min and Wang Ching-wei. In fact, he worked so actively within the Kuomintang that he came under attack by his Communist colleagues for his excessive efforts to cooperate with the Kuomintang.[41] Then Mao left Shanghai claiming illness and returned to Hunan, but from there, he fled again under threat of arrest by local authorities and returned to Canton, there to continue his work with the Kuomintang as *de facto* head of the propaganda department, editor of the political department's weekly, and director of the Kuomintang Peasant Movement Training Institute. The graduates of this institute, especially the Communist party members, were now sent to the rural areas of the northern provinces to prepare the ground for the advance of the Nationalist armies on their northern campaign. Mao again went to Shanghai at the end of 1926 to become head of the Chinese Communist party's peasant department but soon returned once more to Hunan.

During this time, then, Mao Tse-tung continued to work in the Moscow framework of close cooperation with the Kuomintang. In fact, he has been described as the Chinese Communist party member who was closest to the Kuomintang leadership. This period of Mao's activities is clearly underplayed in the later records of the Chinese Communist history written under Mao's control. What is important to the historian is the fact of Mao's close adherence to the Moscow line at this early stage of Chinese Communist politics, and indeed, throughout his rise to power. Though Mao was in charge of the training of rural agitators, he was not particularly stressing any rural policy, and what he learned about the importance of organizing peasants for the agrarian revolution was closely derived from Moscow's political directives and training by Borodin.

In this period of Kuomintang-Communist cooperation, Mao thus played an important part in working with the Kuomintang and was given an opportunity to be active in peasant policy which, as directed from Moscow, was carried out within the framework of the Kuomintang organization. He divided his time between Canton, Shanghai and Hunan, getting acquainted with rural and urban situations and serving in several capacities. When the Fourth Communist Party Congress met, in January, 1925, he was absent and as a result was not reelected to the Central Committee.

Mao's new role began after the split between the Kuomintang and the Soviet advisers and Chinese Communists, which led to the period of civil war and a new Communist strategy of rural-based insurrection.

Young Mao addresses a conference in Kiangsi Province, 1933. *Wide World Photos.*

CHAPTER

II

Mao and the Agrarian Revolution

T HE *Chungshan* incident in Canton may be considered a turning point in Sino-Soviet relations, the beginning of the end of Chinese Nationalist dependence on Moscow. The outcome of the incident was, however, a compromise reached between Chiang Kai-shek and Borodin which permitted the Chinese Communists, including Mao Tse-tung, to remain within the Kuomintang; and Chinese Communist officers retained command of units within the Nationalist army during the northern campaign.

In Moscow, Stalin was asserting his authority over his rivals among the Soviet leaders. The question of which policy to follow in China became one of the issues in this power struggle. Stalin intended to continue the United Front with the Kuomintang as long as possible. In his words, he wanted to "squeeze out the lemon and then throw it away." He had misjudged Chiang Kai-shek.

The realization that the Chinese Communist position in the Kuomintang and in the Nationalist army was endangered led, however, to preparations for an alternative policy, should the cooperation of the United Front with the Nationalists collapse.

THE NEW COURSE: From United Front to Agrarian Revolution

From 1926 on, messages from Stalin directed towards the Chinese Communists warned them to be ready for the eventual necessity of reyling on their own military strength.[1] In the same vein the Executive Committee of the Comintern stressed several times the need to turn to "agrarian revolution," leading finally in February, 1928, to a resolution "on the Chinese Question" in which it emphasized the need to organize "in the sovietized peasant areas Red Army detachments which can subsequently be united into a single National Chinese Red Army."[2]

Among the Kuomintang leaders, opinions were divided on the question of cooperation with the Soviets and the Chinese Communists; at issue was the marching route of the northern campaign. The Kuomintang Central Committee, influenced by Borodin, was willing to march toward Wuhan and continue the Soviet connection. Chiang Kai-shek was determined to march toward Shanghai to shake off Soviet control. A fragile compromise was reached by dividing the campaign: the right wing under Chiang Kai-shek moved towards Nanking and from there to Shanghai where Chiang wanted to gain access to non-Communist financial sources and military equipment; the left wing of the campaign under the Kuomintang Central Committee marched to Wuchang, accompanied by Borodin, who hoped to maintain his influence over the Kuomintang and link up with the northwestern warlord Feng Yü-hsiang. Chiang Kai-shek tried first to bring some of the Kuomintang's political leaders to his headquarters while the Kuomintang Central Committee ordered Chiang to come to Wuchang. When Chiang refused, the Central Committee deprived him of his position as commander-in-chief. The conflict was now in the open. In Shanghai, Chiang succeeded in gaining the support of the business community and the non-Communist labor leaders. After securing control of the city, he broke the Communist stronghold in the Shanghai industrial sector by arresting and executing a large group of Communist leaders and supporters. Chiang Kai-shek had thus broken with the Communists as well as with the left wing of the Kuomintang.

The split between Moscow and the Chinese Communists and the leftist leadership of the Kuomintang in Wuchang occurred shortly thereafter. It was triggered, in the end, by the Comintern agent, M. N. Roy, who showed Stalin's telegram to the Kuomintang leader, Wang Ching-wei.[3] Once the Kuomintang leaders at Wuchang had proof of Moscow's demand that they accept the new Soviet policies of violent land revolution and an independent Chinese Communist army, they too broke with Moscow and the Chinese Communists. The Chinese Communists were expelled from Wuchang and the Soviet advisers sent home.

This final break with the Communists made it possible to reunite the Nationalist leadership. Within the year, the National Government, which was to rule the mainland for the next twenty-two years, was established in Nanking under Chiang Kai-shek. The period of the National Government, from 1927 to its defeat on the mainland in 1949, was one of continuous turbulence, civil war and the disastrous war with Japan which was to culminate in World War II. Yet the first decade before the war with Japan was also a period of great successes in building a modern nation state. In the rapidly expanding area it controlled, the National Government introduced major measures of modernization: a system of Western laws, modern economic development in banking, trade, industry, and communications, as well as a modern educational system. The economy grew, the living standard improved, and the government began to eliminate some of the territorial privileges and rights of the foreign powers.

It was against this government that a new Communist strategy was to be applied; Communist military bases in suitable areas had to be established from which to launch revolutionary warfare. The National Government's neglect of a policy of agrarian reform facilitated this new Communist approach. The urban proletarian base of communism in Shanghai had been decimated by Chiang Kai-shek's surprise attack against the Communist infrastructure in April, 1927. Although the Communist Central Committee was reassembled at Shanghai, the labor base of Chinese communism had been gravely weakened, making it all the more important to develop rural-based military forces as a source of Communist power.

The new Communist rural-based army was to be derived from two sources. The professional core was to consist of those units which could be extracted from the Nationalist army since they were commanded or controlled by Communist officers, while the new revolutionary forces of the Communist army were to be recruited from the rural population through the peasant associations. To carry out this program of the twofold genesis of the Chinese Communist army, two types of actions were taken. One was the Nanchang uprising of August 1, 1927, and the other the Autumn Harvest uprising in August and September of that year. Both these ventures failed but they can still be regarded as the beginnings of the establishment of a Chinese Red Army. Indeed, August 1, the date of the Nanchang uprising, became Red Army Day in Communist China and is celebrated as such in the People's Republic today.

The Nanchang uprising was an action designed to separate from the Nationalist army those units which were commanded or infiltrated by the Communists and to establish with them an independent Communist organization through the temporary capture of the city of Nanchang.[4] The plan was to gather these Communist-controlled troops for a withdrawal to the south to link up with rural areas which appeared promising as a base for agrarian revolution and prolonged warfare.[5] The Communist hope was that as many Nationalist troops as possible could be enticed to join the uprising and defect to the Communist side. The plan of the Nanchang uprising had been approved by Moscow and by its Comintern representative in China, Lominadze; and the Soviet military adviser, Galen, attempted to persuade one of the leading Nationalist commanders, Chang Fa-k'uei, to join the rebellion, but failed.[6]

Some 10,000 soldiers under Communist military officers occupied Nanchang on August 1 and set up a Revolutionary Council; they left the city four days later in search of a rural base. At the end of September they took the city of Swatow in Kwangtung but could not hold it and retreated towards the Canton area. During the difficult march and the constant skirmishes with Nationalist forces, the Communist army evaporated through battle losses and desertions until the main force disintegrated. Only the leaders escaped and fled to Shanghai to fight another day. The only remnant of this Nanchang uprising that survived was a small rear guard force of two battalions under the command of Chu Teh that was left in northern Kwangtung.[7] It retreated into southern Hunan, there to establish a base at Ichang in early 1928. This unit first raised the Communist flag and named itself the Fourth Red Army; it became the professional core of the new Communist army.[8]

The more important part of the Communist military program called for rural uprisings in several Chinese provinces where conditions seemed favorable to recruit from the peasantry a new rural military force. To discuss this plan, a special emergency meeting of the Central Party leadership, which became known as the August 7 Emergency Conference, was called by the Comintern representative, Lominadze, in Kiukiang. It was attended by twelve members and three alternate members of the Central Committee of the Party plus some representatives of the Communist Youth League and of local party units. The original plan was to organize a rural uprising in four provinces: Hunan, Hupeh, Kiangsi and Kwangtung.[9] Actually, no action was taken in Kiangsi and Kwangtung and the Hupeh uprising was soon abandoned; only one of the uprisings got under way, the one in Hunan, and it was here that Mao Tse-tung was assigned to play a leading role.

The choice of Mao as organizer of the Hunan uprising was a logical one. Hunan was Mao's home province, and, in anticipation of future activity, Mao had been sent by the Party Central to Hunan in the fall of 1926 to study the situation of peasant unrest in the province. At that time the peasant insurrections in Hunan had created a problem for the Communists because of the difficulties they had caused in the relationship with the Kuomintang before the breakup of the United Front. Peasant outbreaks in Hunan had been marked by violence and some of the landlords had been killed. Kuomintang officers who came from Hunan had seen their families and property threatened by the outbreaks; the military cooperation was therefore in danger. To allay the fears of the Kuomintang leaders in Wuhan with whom they were then still allied, the Communists condemned the "excesses" of the peasant outbreaks. To explain their disapproval, the Communist leaders argued that these "excesses" had been caused by the poorest section of the peasants — loafers, gamblers, and paupers, a sort of "Lumpen peasants," — not a class-conscious group, but rather a substandard stratum comparable to the "Lumpen proletariat," as Marx had described the lowest level of the working class that could not be used for the proletarian revolution.[10] Now, in preparation for the shift to the agrarian revolution, the Party was to reassess the situation and Mao was best suited to give a report on the situation in his home province.

Mao's "Report on the Investigation of the Agrarian Movement in Hunan," published in March, 1927, was an enthusiastic description of the revolutionary character of the peasant movement, emphasizing the great potential for agrarian uprisings in Hunan. Mao described the actions taken by the peasants in most euphemistic terms. The peasants had successfully attacked and swept away the privileges and prerogatives of the landlords and had taken over authority in the villages. In Mao's Marxist terminology, "the partriarchal, feudal local bullies and bad gentry together with the illegitimate landlords, were not only the foundation of the dictatorial regime of the past several thousand years [but also] the tools of the imperialist warlords and corrupt officials." The poor peasants who had taken the lead in the movement had abandoned, according to Mao, their former bad habits of gambling and loafing and had become "reformed, able and hardworking people." They deserved support, rather than repression, because: "This leadership by the poor peasants is very essential."[11] Mao was clearly carried away by his enthusiasm. He predicted: "Within a short time, hundreds of millions of peasants will rise in central, south and north China, with the fury of a hurricane; no power, however strong, can restrain them." They would, so Mao proclaimed, "break all the shackles" that bound them, and "all imperialists, warlords, corrupt officials, and bad gentry will meet their doom at the hands of the peasants." In a rhetorical question, Mao asked whether the Party was to "fight them from the opposite camp" or rather "get in front of them and lead them."[12] Mao used these overenthusiastic terms, which proved to be a misjudgment of the actual situation, to promote what he knew to be the coming party line. When Mao spoke of "the rising up of the democratic forces in the countryside, who overthrow the feudal forces in the villages, which is the true goal of the National Revolution," his terminology was in line with the strategy of national liberation movements. Mao called the expected uprising not a "socialist," but rather a "national" and "democratic" revolution, adding that this was the goal for which Sun Yat-sen had labored 40 years. Without offending the united front concept, Mao obviously pleased his sponsors in Shanghai. His report was accepted by the Party Central and was also printed in Moscow in the international journal, *Imprecor,* as the worthwhile product of a Chinese comrade.[13]

Yet, despite these expressed opinions, Mao still followed the tortuous line of the peasant policy of the Chinese Communist party, which during the spring and summer of 1927, continued to disapprove of the "excesses of the peasant movement," because of the fact that they would endanger the already precarious cooperation with the Kuomintang. Through his report, however, Mao had established himself as the person best acquainted with the local conditions in Hunan; he was therefore ordered in August, 1927, to assume the responsibility for the peasant uprising there.

The Autumn Harvest uprising in Hunan was the first attempt of the Chinese Communist leaders to translate the theoretical principle of land revolution into practice. The plans for these uprisings are, therefore, still of great interest today. They were, in essence, drawn up under Lominadze's supervision by the Emergency Central Committee that had been called in Kiukiang on Lominadze's request.

For the new policy, a new leadership of the Party was needed. It was the August 7 Emergency Conference which finally removed Ch'en Tu-hsiu from the party leadership. The conference then reconstituted the party leadership by establishing a provisional Central Politburo to act for the Central Committee at the present time. The new policy decreed by the Eighth Comintern Central Committee plenum of May, 1927, was thus to be carried out under the leadership of a group newly selected by Moscow. Mao Tse-tung was not a member of this special group of leaders which was headed by Ch'ü Ch'iu-pai. The choice of Ch'ü was based on the fact that he was known for his strong emphasis on land revolution and the new policy; however, he never gained the commanding authority that his predecessor, Ch'en Tu-hsiu, had held.

The program accepted at the August 7 conference clearly stressed agrarian revolution. The urban program was moderate; the workers were to fight for economic rather than political concessions and for reforms, such as higher wages, unemployment assistance, and an eight-hour working day.[14] The agrarian program, however, was the mainstay of the new policy. The Autumn Harvest uprising was to be carried out by "hundreds of thousands of peasants" rising "from below."

The autumn harvest period was selected because this was the time when the landlords collected the payment of rents and loans from the peasants and the tax was due. This was the time when the peasants could be aroused in defense of their share of the crops. The resolution of the conference authorized the peasant associations to arm the peasants and to confiscate the land of large and middle landlords. Whether the small landlords were to be affected was left uncertain and depended on local action. It was understood that local conditions differed, and the four provinces of Kiangsi, Kwangtung, Hupeh and Hunan were chosen in the belief that they harbored explosive conditions for unrest which could be exploited. After the Nanchang uprising of August 1, it became clear, however, that no suitable organization or preparation for peasant uprising existed in the province of Kiangsi. In Kwangtung province some preparations were made but with the defeat at Swatow of the main Communist force from Nanchang, nothing was undertaken. Actual plans were prepared only for Hupeh and Hunan. The Hupeh insurrection, though well planned by the Party Central, failed in all its moves at the beginning and so it was only in Hunan where the Autumn Harvest uprising led to some actual revolutionary actions. It was this province which was the basis for Mao Tse-tung's local leadership and eventual emergence as the key figure in the new strategy.

Though Mao and others had been active in the organization of peasant associations, none of them had any practical experience with the kind of military action based on peasant uprisings that were not contemplated. As has been pointed out by one of the leaders of the time, it was difficult for the Communists to translate slogans into action and to understand how to make peasant revolution.[15] Mao himself admitted later that he had no previous experience in the practical organization of such uprisings, and this may explain his early failures and his disregard for the directives given him by the Party Central.[16]

While in his report Mao expressed all the right slogans about the importance of land revolution and peasant uprising, the actual plan he drew up for the Hunan Autumn Harvest rebellion was the opposite of Moscow's concept. According to correspondence between the Party Central and the Hunan branch, a letter in Mao's own writing, though not signed, outlined the plan for the insurrection which centered on Changsha, the capital of the province, which he wanted to capture first.[17] To take the city, Mao asked for the use of two regiments of regular Nationalist troops which would, according to Mao, be willing to cooperate and take the city, a plan which was later criticized as "military adventurism." In the letter, Mao also proposed to establish Chinese soviets in the areas of the Autumn Harvest uprisings under the flag of the Communist party. He further submitted a program of confiscation of the property of small and middle as well as big landlords.[18] The Party Central, in clearer perception of the Comintern intention, criticized this proposal on all counts, pointing out that in the proposed plan there was no indication of adequate preparation of mobilizing the "peasant masses." Without such mobilization, any attempt to capture any major city would require regular military forces and this was not in line with the program of land revolution. The Party Central gave, therefore, detailed instructions for preparation of insurrection in the rural districts, not only in the area around Changsha, but also in a number of other Hunanese areas, in southern, as well as central Hunan. The Party Central also criticized Mao's proposal to establish Chinese soviets and his plan to confiscate all land, including that of small landlords and peasant owners. While such expropriation should not be opposed if it actually happened, it should not be consciously promoted.

In his answering letter to the Hunan provincial committee, Mao defended his proposal, explaining that in his view the capture of Changsha was merely the starting point of the insurrection and the two regiments of troops were to be used only as an auxiliary force. He also believed that other districts would fall once Changsha had fallen. In essence, therefore, Mao did not answer and possibly did not understand the crucial difference between his own plan and the Comintern program transmitted to him by the Party Central. On the issues of Chinese soviets, Mao remained silent. To his letter of August 30, the Party Central answered on September 5, repeating its previous criticism and stressing the importance of the "peasant masses" rather than the use of regular military forces. The letter claimed that if the peasants were organized as the principal force of insurrection, the towns would later automatically fall.[19]

Mao did not change his plan even after having been admonished by the Central leadership not to focus on Changsha. Little preparation was undertaken in the rural areas of western Hunan as had been demanded or in eastern Hunan, which became the theater of actual insurrection. The main action of the Hunan uprising directed by Mao was undertaken by a Wuhan garrison force that had originally been attached to the Second Front Army of the Kuomintang commanded by Chang Fa-k'uei, whose regimental commander and deputy commander were both Communists. They had earlier attempted unsuccessfully to link up with the insurrection in Nanchang. This force was supplemented by other units including rural self-defense corps of miners and peasants, and was eventually divided into four regiments. The political training of this mixed force was, according to Mao himself, extremely limited.[20] This force of four regiments initiated the Autumn Harvest uprising at the beginning of September, 1927. The regiments, formed in Kiangsi, marched from there by three different routes toward Changsha. En route, the Second Regiment deserted and the First Regiment had to be reorganized. According to the record, the military aspect of the insurrection, though at first leading to some advances and successes, collapsed in a few days, and, when no uprising occurred in Changsha, the remaining forces retreated. The ease with which this military action was countered by the Nationalists is an indication of the weakness in the preparation and the inadequacy of intelligence and security.

Mao's movements during this critical time have never been fully explained. According to his own account, Mao was captured by a Kuomintang militia unit when moving from one of his regiments to another. He was to be executed but narrowly escaped.[21] Realizing that the uprising had been defeated, Mao then ordered the remaining forces of his First Regiment to retreat to the Hunan-Kiangsi border where the Third Regiment of his force had already arrived. He then decided to retreat with the remainder of his troops to Chingkangshan, a mountain range located on the Kiangsi-Hunan border. At that time he had only about 1,000 men left.[22]

The whole Autumn Harvest uprising ended thus in failure. In the inevitable post mortem, the party leadership sought the cause for this failure, not without justification, in the lack of proper peasant organization. In a November politburo session, the Party condemned the provincial organizers and party leaders responsible for the failures.[23] The Hunan leadership was found guilty of having completely violated the main line of party policy for organizing peasants and having instead, despite the express warning sent to them by the Party Central, used military "opportunism" and "putschism." As a result, Mao Tse-tung, together with the leading members of the Hunan provincial committee, was dismissed from the provincial committee, and as an alternate member of the Politburo.

There is certainly some truth in the Party Central's accusation of Mao and the provincial leadership, that they had ignored and mishandled the party directive. But beyond that, there may well have been a problem of what in Communist parlance were the "objective conditions" for the uprising as planned. Though there was clearly a great deal of peasant organization, discontent, and unrest, the problem for the Communists may well have been the unwillingness of the large majority of the peasantry to follow Communist doctrine and leadership any more than the proletariat was willing to follow the Party in the industrial countries. It was not the organized peasantry, but rurally based military organization that provided the means by which the Communists survived and eventually obtained another opportunity for the seizure of power made possible by the Japanese attack at Marco Polo Bridge in 1937 and the long-drawn-out and disastrous suffering of China during World War II.

But first, a decade of civil war lay ahead.

The Kiangsi Soviet

When Mao retreated with his small remaining force from the Hunan insurrection to Chingkangshan, he was, according to his own account, in charge of a ragged and undisciplined group. Two elements were necessary for the establishment of a viable Communist military force. One was a core of professionally trained and experienced troops and the other, political indoctrination. The first was available from the regular forces that survived the Nanchang uprising. This was Chu Teh's unit which had split off the main force and, though embattled, had survived. The second, political indoctrination, Mao could provide as leading political party figure on the spot.

On the mountain crest of Chingkangshan, Mao was joined by bandit forces who in addition to augmenting Mao's troops provided intelligence information about the area. Chu Teh had established his base at Ichang under the Communist flag. Both Mao and Chu Teh, however, were forced by Nationalist troops to abandon their positions. The party headquarters in Shanghai then ordered Chu Teh to join forces with Mao in order to strengthen their situation. In May, 1928, their combined troops, which became known as the Chu-Mao force, returned to Chingkangshan. Again pressed by surrounding Nationalist troops, they were forced to abandon the mountain and escaped on December 28 into the border area of Kiangsi and western Fukien province, where they eventually established their base at Juichin in southern Kiangsi. This so-called Central Army group in control of what became the Kiangsi Soviet was soon to be the main center of the new rural strategy.

The period of the Kiangsi Soviet and its aftermath was crucial for Mao's rise to power in the Chinese Communist movement. Mao's demotion and removal from the provisional Politburo of the Central Committee affected his standing in the Party. The retreat from Chingkangshan of the Chu-Mao force further weakened Mao's reputation. According to some reports of that time, Mao was also not too popular with the troops and there were conflicts between Chu Teh and Mao. There was also disagreement on military tactics. Chu's plans for guerilla raids in the nearby area were attacked by Mao as "bandit" tactics.[24] The Party

Central in Shanghai, informed of these conflicts, sided with Chu Teh and attempted several times to remove Mao from the Kiangsi Soviet by inviting him to Shanghai, but Mao refused to go. When Chu Teh, in following his policy, had carried out a raid into central Fukien province and was defeated by government troops, Mao exploited the setback of his rival. He called a congress of the party organization of the soviet region to meet in December, 1929, at Kut'ien. Making good use of Chu's defeat, Mao attacked Chu's "purely military viewpoint," strengthening his own position.

By this time Mao Tse-tung had fully grasped and developed the program of agrarian revolution. In theory Chinese Communists were to fight against Western imperialism in China, regarded as the main enemy oppressing and exploiting the Chinese people. This oppression was carried out, or so Mao claimed, in cooperation with and through the warlords, the more immediate target of the Chinese Revolution. A closer enemy still, in terms of the agrarian revolution, were the landlords who became the local butt of Communist propaganda. In linking the targets of Communist policy, the slogan was therefore: Destroy the landlord class, the warlords and imperialism. In practical terms the goal of agrarian revolution was the destruction of the landlords, and the distribution of their land among the poor and landless peasants. This proclaimed policy remained silent on the long-range Communist goal of land collectivization. It was clearly a tactical measure, an appeal to the peasants' desire to own their own land, designed to gain peasant support for the Communist cause.

In the resolution of the Kut'ien Conference, Mao declared that it was the task of the Red Army to lead in this agrarian revolution. The Red Army was not only a fighting force, but also a political force whose mission it was to agitate, organize and arm the common people, in Communist parlance, "the masses."[25] Organizing the masses meant the establishment of a political structure of Communist party and government institutions. The Communist party organization in Kiangsi Soviet generated by the Red Army became thus an army-party organization in which the military and political administrations were inseparably fused.

To establish such a military-political organization in the countryside, it was essential to gain the full cooperation of the majority of the population, the peasants. Armies in China had more often than not mistreated the villagers and had become feared and despised. To overcome this fear and gain the confidence of the people was a primary condition for the program of agrarian revolution. Strict rules had therefore to be enforced for the behavior of the soldiers towards the people. Such rules were first adopted and formulated at a conference at Chingkangshan when Chu

Teh and Mao Tse-tung joined forces. They were reformulated several times and became known as the *Three Main Disciplines* and *Eight Rules.* Of the various versions that came into existence, the best known has been rendered as:

The Three Main Disciplines:
1. Obedience to orders;
2. Take not a needle or thread from the people;
3. Turn in all confiscated goods.

The Eight Rules:
1. Replace all doors and return all straw on which you sleep before leaving;
2. Speak courteously to the people and help them whenever possible;
3. Return all borrowed articles;
4. Pay for everything damaged;
5. Be honest in business transactions;
6. Be sanitary—dig latrines a safe distance from the houses and fill them up with earth before leaving;
7. Never molest women;
8. Do not mistreat prisoners. [26]

Most of the rules contained in this Chinese Communist version had been used earlier in Chinese history to enlist popular support for military forces. Similar rules were also drawn up by the Nationalist army, and even some armies of the warlords, though the problem was that they could be enforced only in well-disciplined units.

The Communist version contained, however, some special rules that were related to Communist guerilla warfare. The order not to take anything from the people referred to the soldiers' attitude towards the poor peasant population. The property of landlords and wealthy peasants was fair prey, but it was to be confiscated rather than looted and the confiscated goods had to be turned in by the soldiers under threat of severe punishment. This confiscated property became a main source of supply and income for the Communist soviet.

Similarly, the rule about the treatment of prisoners was a major part of Communist strategy. It had been applied by Chinese government armies during earlier rebellions when occasionally prisoners were permitted to leave for home and even provided with travel funds as a matter of propaganda. Under Mao this system became broadly applied. Captured soldiers and low-ranking officers were given the choice of enlisting in the Communist army or leaving for home with travel expenses provided. Most of them joined up and provided additional strength to the Communist armies. Those who left very effectively spread the news of the humane attitude of the Communist armies among the common soldiers and the population in government areas.

The Red Army's control over the population was realized through quasi-military organizations, the Red Guards and the Young Pioneers. Most of the population of the area was incorporated into these local forces. All adults from sixteen to forty years of age were Red Guards.[27] Nominally this service was voluntary but in practice everyone enlisted except elements such as landlord families who were counted as enemies of the regime.

The Red Guards formed quasi-military units under the command of special military departments in each district. They were organized into squads, companies, battalions, regiments and divisions, established within the geographical units; in fact, they were an armed militia. They also served as a recruiting ground and supplementary force for the Red Army, equipped with rifles and spears. Like the Red Army they were under military discipline and indoctrinated by political commissars. Red Guard model companies joined in the actual regular warfare, and in time of major battles, other units of the Red Guard were thrown into combat as supplementary regiments.

Aside from their quasi-military role, the Red Guards had the most important function of maintaining political control in the rear, liquidating landlords and their families and guarding against political opposition. Through the organization of the Red Guards, the population of the Kiangsi Soviet was militarized and indoctrinated into faithful adherence to the Communist revolutionary program. In addition to the Red Guards, children of school age and adolescents were members of the Young Pioneers organized in military units like the Red Guards. The Young Pioneers were an additional reserve force which was used for the training of the young generation. They served as informants as well as an auxiliary force for service under the Red Army. Through these militarized political organizations, Mao had created a system of political and military control that could serve to enlist the population of the soviet area in the Communist revolutionary program.

Mao's opportunity to expand his political control further came at the time of a leadership crisis in Shanghai. The head of the Party at that time was Li Li-san, who had made his Communist career in labor organization and urban work and was by inclination and experience leaning towards an urban strategy. When the Comintern's policy line changed, Li Li-san

misunderstood or disregarded Moscow's directives and attempted to
order attacks on urban centers thus placing himself in opposition to the
Moscow line.[28]

Because of this "deviation," a special session of the Central Committee
was called in September, 1930, to criticize Li Li-san and remove him from
leadership. The man entrusted by the Comintern for this task was Li
Li-san's predecessor, Ch'ü Ch'iu-pai, who was then in Moscow but who
was sent back to China to carry out the purge. In the absence of any
Comintern representative, Ch'ü Ch'iu-pai arranged a compromise and
reconciliation with Li Li-san. The Comintern, totally dissatisfied with the
outcome of the Central Committee meeting, now turned against Ch'ü
Ch'iu-pai. On November 22, an enlarged meeting of the Chinese Politburo was called at which both Li Li-san and Ch'ü Ch'iu-pai lost their
positions of party leadership. Li Li-san was recalled to Moscow for
reeducation. In turn, the so-called Internationalists, or Bolsheviks, Chinese students who had been trained in Moscow and were loyal to the
Comintern line, assumed control of the Chinese party.

The fall of Li Li-san and the temporary weakening of the Party Central
leadership in Shanghai because of the purges gave Mao Tse-tung the
opportunity to broaden his authority in the Kiangsi Soviet region. In an
attempt to strengthen his power, Li Li-san had placed some of his own
followers in positions of commissars to local Communist groups in Kiangsi province, a counterweight to the Chu-Mao force. In the so-called
Fut'ien incident in December, 1930, Mao, with the help of Chu Teh,
arrested these Li Li-san supporters and summarily executed them. According to some accounts, the blood purge affected as many as 2,000 to
3,000 Communist functionaries whom Mao at the time accused of belonging to the so-called A-B group, an alleged "Anti-Bolshevik" unit.[29] Only
much later would Mao justify this massacre as his fight against the "Li
Li-san line."[30] With this action, Mao had temporarily strengthened his
leadership in Kiangsi. But the new Shanghai Central group, the so-called
Internationalists, were soon concerned with establishing their control
over the rural bases.

By this time, the Kiangsi Soviet had been reorganized and strengthened. Under the leadership of Mao Tse-tung, the first National Soviet
Congress was called in November, 1931, at the new soviet capital, Juichin,
to select a central soviet government in China. Mao claimed that this
government represented not only the Juichin base but also other Communist rural soviet areas, several of which had been established in central
and south China by this time. The most important of these O-yü-wan, was
located north of the Yangtze River at the border of Hupeh, Honan and
Anhwei provinces. It was headed by Chang Kuo-t'ao, a leading member

of the Politburo and chief rival of Mao in his rise to party leadership. Since he was present at Juichin, Mao made himself chairman of the newly established Chinese Soviet Republic while Chang Kuo-t'ao, in absentia, was elected as deputy chairman with little actual authority. To direct military affairs in the Kiangsi Soviet, a Revolutionary Military Council was established under the chairmanship of Chu Teh; but its direction was also for all practical purposes in the hands of Mao Tse-tung, who therefore assumed both military and political power.[31] The congress at Juichin in November, 1931, was the high point of Mao's power at the time.

During all this time, the Communist rural bases were engaged in constant civil war with the National Government in which their survival was at stake. Chiang Kai-shek's plan was first to destroy the internal Communist threat before he could attempt the inevitable final stand against Japanese aggression. Chiang's effort was handicapped by a series of other conflicts with warlord armies and ambitious rebellious leaders but most of all by the Japanese themselves. During the years 1931 to 1933 the Japanese conquered Manchuria and set up the puppet state of Manchukuo; in 1935 they threatened north China, trying to separate the provinces north of the Yellow River from the National Government, and finally in 1937 they started the China incident, an all-out war against China's independent survival. The war with Japan forced Chiang Kai-shek to end the civil war and accept another United Front with the Communists in the face of the common danger.

Punctuated by these interruptions Chiang Kai-shek organized in the years 1930 to 1934 five *bandit suppression campaigns* against the Kiangsi Soviet which eventually forced the Communists to abandon their Kiangsi base and break through the Nationalist encirclement in search of a new suitable and defensable rural area. The first three Nationalist campaigns fell under the period of Mao's political and military leadership. Their defeat laid the foundation for Mao's reputation as the creator of a successful guerilla strategy.

The development of guerilla warfare was part and parcel of this new strategy of agrarian revolution. The Comintern resolution on the Chinese Question in February, 1928, advocated guerilla warfare and the Sixth Congress of the Chinese Communist party held in Moscow in the summer of 1928 prescribed guerilla warfare in its "Resolution on the Peasant Question."[32] From the very beginning then it was the task of the Communist leaders to devise rules and methods for this type of warfare. These were the methods that came to be applied in the Kiangsi period. They were sloganized into the following sentences as reported by Mao in April, 1929, to the Central Committee in Shanghai.[33]

> *Disperse the forces among the masses to arouse them, and concentrate the forces to deal with the enemy.*
>
> *The enemy advances, we retreat; the enemy halts, we harass; the enemy tires, we attack; the enemy retreats, we pursue.*
>
> *In an independent regime with stabilized territory, we adopt the policy of advancing in series of waves. When pursued by a powerful enemy, we adopt the policy of circling around in a whirling motion.*
>
> *Arouse the largest numbers of the masses in the shortest possible time and by the best possible methods.*
>
> *These tactics are just like casting a net; we should be able to cast the net wide or draw it in at any moment. We cast it wide to win over the masses and draw it in to deal with the enemy. Such are the tactics we have applied in the past three years.*

The best known of these slogans are the short sentences of the second paragraph, which have usually been ascribed to Mao. Actually, Mao never claimed personal authorship of any of the rules of guerilla warfare which, in his words, "grew out of many years of collective military and political experience."[34]

The tactics of guerilla warfare and the regulations that secured the popular support on which the Red Army and its intelligence depended enabled the Kiangsi Soviet to withstand the first Nationalist attacks. The first Nationalist anti-Communist campaigns in December, 1930, and May, 1931, were carried out mainly by provincial troops against whom Mao successfully applied this type of elastic warfare, first attacking the enemy's roads of supply and then destroying the attacking units in a piecemeal fashion through a strategy of rapid maneuver that avoided major confrontations but concentrated in each engagement a superior force against a smaller enemy unit.

The failure of these first two Nationalist campaigns led to a third campaign in July and September, 1931, this time directed by Chiang Kai-shek himself and carried out by elite Nationalist divisions. In this third campaign, the Communist strategy of harassment and flanking attacks did not substantially retard the National advance into the soviet area. The fall of the Communist capital of Juichin appeared imminent when, at the last moment, the Japanese attack in Manchuria, on September 18, 1931, forced the National Government to abandon the campaign temporarily in order to face the Japanese aggressor. This deflection appears to have saved the soviet area and provided a respite that was used for reorganization and entrenchment of the Communist forces.

The survival of the Kiangsi Soviet and other Communist rural areas contrasted sharply with the fate of the Communist party in the major cities, especially in Shanghai, during that year of 1931. The Communist infrastructure in the urban centers had been largely destroyed in a relentless drive mounted by the National Government's police. In April, 1931, the Nationalist police captured Ku Shun-chang, an underground organizer serving in the Communist secret police, then headed by Chou En-lai. To save his life, Ku gave the Nationalists full information about the Communist secret organization, not only in Shanghai but in other cities of China and Hong Kong. The effect of this information could be measured by such an important catch as that of the Vietnamese Comintern agent Ho Chi Minh, who had been working with Borodin and who was arrested by the British in Hong Kong. The Chinese Communist frustration over Ku Shun-chang's defection could be recognized by the cruel action of Chou En-lai, who ordered Ku Shun-chang's whole family and friends executed—a total of 48 persons.[35] But the damage had been done. Under the circumstances, the Communist position in the cities became very precarious. Under Comintern directive, the Party decided to move its headquarters to the central soviet area in Kiangsi. This was done by stages. Chou En-lai, who was the first to move, arrived in Juichin in December, 1931. When he arrived in Kiangsi, Chou En-lai became vice chairman of the Revolutionary Military Committee—the chairman was Chu-Teh—and concurrently political commissar of the First Front Army under the First Army Corps. Chou's arrival marked therefore the beginning of the decline of Mao's control over the Army. Mao's power evaporated further when the leaders of the Central Committee, Po Ku (Ch'in Pang-hsien) and Lo Fu (Chang Wen-t'ien), were transferred from Shanghai to Kiangsi in the summer of 1933. To provide them with the professional advice they needed for directing the military affairs of Kiangsi and other soviet areas, these Chinese Central Committee leaders were given the assistance of a Comintern army adviser Otto Braun, alias Li Teh, who was sent from Shanghai to Kiangsi in the fall of 1933. Otto Braun's role in directing Communist military strategy was important as long as the Internationlist group was in charge. Later when Mao reasserted his power, Braun's influence lessened, though he remained with the Communist leadership through the Long March and in Yenan until 1937, as an important witness of intra-party struggle and Communist strategy for that period.[36]

In his memoirs published in 1969, Otto Braun has described his impressions of the Kiangsi Soviet as observed upon his arrival. "The Kiangsi Soviet was situated in a wide fertile plain with harvested fields, clean houses and industrious people." Because the bombing by Nationalist planes had largely destroyed the capital town, Juichin, the government was located in a "restricted zone," at some distance from Juichin. The people there "moved about freely," and, despite the blockade by the Nationalist armies, the economic situation was "not bad." The observer was particularly impressed by the tireless work of men, women and children, who then "harvested the second crop of the year, carried rice and pickled vegetables to the collecting points, even delivered pigs and chickens, plaited bast and straw sandals for the Red Army soldiers, and sewed uniforms from imported cotton." This popular support was based on "the extraordinary correct relationships toward the population maintained by the Red soldiers." The population in turn provided military support through partisan detachments, Red Guards, young guards, and other peasant self-defense organizations, though all of these participated only in limited and local battle activities. Comparing them with the soviet workers during the First Five-Year Plan, this Comintern eyewitness admired the "unsurpassed heroism" of Chinese peasants who "could not read nor write," but "worked with the same dedication for their soviet and fought for it at the front." As a result, agricultural production was sufficient for the population and at least in part for the Red Army, which gained its additional needs not only of weapons and ammunition, but also food and textiles through incursions into Kuomintang territory. A lively commerce was carried on with south Fukien and north Kwangtung, including the export of tungsten, tobacco and other agrarian products in exchange for the import of salt, textiles and other needed goods.

The impression given in Braun's account is that of a viable military and political organization backed by peasant support, which obtained additional economic and military supplies through raids and trade from neighboring territory. Basically, this Communist success had to be credited to Mao Tse-tung.

In praising this system of "war communism" under the slogan "everything for the front," the pro-Moscow observer expressed in retrospect his criticism of the "grave mistakes" committed by Mao Tse-tung during this early phase of the Kiangsi Soviet.[37] This criticism of Mao echoes the political conflict of the time in which the Chinese leaders from Shanghai, the so-called Internationalists, shouldered Mao out of his leadership in the Kiangsi Soviet. The reason that Mao survived politically at all was that Moscow still regarded his early role in rural party work as important enough to protect him against the Internationalists intention of removing him completely from power. After all, it was his success in the Chu-Mao Kiangsi base that provided a refuge for the Party and the hope for continuing the revolution.

In 1933 Chiang Kai-shek started the fourth campaign against the Chinese soviet areas. By that time the reorganized Communist leadership attempted a coordinated action of the Kiangsi Soviet with the other soviets north and south of the Yangtze in Honan and Szechwan, defended by the Second and Fourth corps of the Red Army. The strategy, as actually formulated by the Central Committee then still in Shanghai, was to have the Red Army forces of the Second and Fourth corps surround Wuhan, create peasant unrest and interfere with Nationalist military movements in the area, while the Central Red Army in Kiangsi would complete its preparations in anticipation of the new National offensive. The Nationalists succeeded, however, in forcing the Second and Fourth corps out of the Soviet areas, and then turned in full force against the Kiangsi Soviet. The sheer numerical superiority of the Nationalist armies and a newly adopted Nationalist strategy of mobility made it impossible to hold the Communist soviet north of the Yangtze River and raised serious questions as to whether the Kiangsi Soviet would be able to survive. Which defensive strategy to follow became a matter of serious argument among the leaders in Juichin. A so-called offensive-defense was adopted, designed on the advice of Otto Braun to throw the attacking forces off balance. This policy succeeded in inflicting some serious setbacks on the Nationalist offensive in Kiangsi. Mao Tse-tung at the time opposed the offensive-defense strategy and demanded a retreat within the Kiangsi Soviet and the use of guerilla warfare there. When he was defeated in the Conference, Mao became ill and retired from any further political and military activity. Mao therefore had little to do with the military policy during the last phase of the Kiangsi Soviet.

Actually what ended the fourth campaign of the Nationalists was not Communist military action but rather a renewed Japanese military threat against north China, which forced Chiang to break off the offensive in order to again face the Japanese. Having conquered all of Manchuria and established their puppet state of Manchukuo, the Japanese temporarily halted their advance, however, and concluded in 1933 a truce with the National Government. The truce ended the fighting between the Nationalist forces and Japanese and enabled Chiang Kai-shek to resume his anti-Communist offensive in the fifth and final campaign.

The year 1933 brought other global events that affected the Chinese scene. Hitler's seizure of power in Germany had begun to raise the specter of a possible two-front war for the Soviet Union in case of cooperation between Nazi Germany and expansionist Japan. With Soviet blessings, therefore, the Chinese Communists initiated a policy of adding to their anti-Kuomintang propaganda a call for national unity and joint Chinese military action against the Japanese agression in China.

This Communist clamor for resistance against the Japanese coincided with the rebellion of a Nationalist army in Fukien against Chiang Kai-shek. The mutinous soldiers had gained a reputation for their heroic stand against the Japanese during their attack on Shanghai the year before. They were therefore receptive to any propaganda that stressed the importance of anti-Japanese resistance over the continuation of civil war. The Communists exploited both the Manchurian incident and the anti-Japanese feelings that it had provoked throughout China through a propaganda offensive for a united front designed to broaden their support within China.

When the Fukien rebellion occurred, the possibility immediately arose of cooperation between the Fukien rebels and the soviet area in Kiangsi. For the Chinese Communists, an alliance with the Fukien rebels would not only impair the Nationalist attacks against the Kiangsi Soviet but also possibly secure an outlet to the sea, permitting access to Soviet supplies. The Comintern therefore sent a telegram in favor of Chinese Communist cooperation with the Fukien rebels.

The Chinese Communists were ready to support the Fukien uprising in military, if not in political, terms. A tentative agreement was reached providing for a move by Chinese Communist troops into Fukien province, a move which would have meant a threat against the flank of the Nationalist troops advancing towards the provincial capital. This promised Communist military move was delayed, however, by the opposition of Mao Tse-tung for reasons which have never been fully explained.[38] In the meantime, the Nationalist troops rapidly advanced and the Fukien rebellion collapsed within less than two weeks. The setback was later blamed on Mao's obstructionism and resulted in a further decline of Mao's position. Chou En-lai took over the position of political commissar for the entire Red Army.[39]

The fifth campaign of the National Government, which soon followed, resulted in a Nationalist victory. The Nationalist success was not only the result of a far superior military force consisting of elite divisions but also of a new strategy that successfully countered the Communist flexible guerilla warfare. This was the *blockhouse* strategy designed by Chiang Kai-shek and his advisers on the basis of their experience in previous campaigns. The essence of the strategy was the establishment in depth of a network of strongpoints and blockhouses that prevented any Communist contact with the outside and resulted in a noose that was being tightened step by step to compress the Communist base and eliminate the flexibility of Communist military moves. It deprived the Communists not only of supplies but also threatened to bottle them up and force them into a final showdown within a limited area when the Nationalist superiority in numbers and equipment would clearly determine the outcome.

There was a heated argument among the Communist leaders as to how to face the threat. The decision taken was the modification of several different views and was basically the concept of an offensive-defense suggested by the Comintern representative Otto Braun, meaning hit-run attacks against advancing Nationalist troops, a strategy that did not prove too successful in view of the Nationalist refusal to be deflected from the gradual advance. Mao Tse-tung later claimed that his idea of withdrawal into the rear areas of the Juichin soviet would have provided a better answer to the threat, but in view of the massive superiority of the Nationalist forces, it is doubtful whether any successful defense would have been possible.

It was therefore agreed that the Kiangsi Soviet be abandoned and an attempt made to break through the blockade and find another suitable location to continue the Communist rural strategy.

In October, 1934, the Communist troops established their columns for the breakthrough. Marching at night while within the soviet area and through the border area between the provinces of Hunan and Kwang-tung-Kwangsi, they sought to avoid major battles within the blockhouse region. The breakthrough was successful and was carried out with limited losses to the combat units.[40] In the middle of December, the combat columns reached operative space behind the blockaded fortress area. The pursuing Nationalist elite divisions arrived too late to prevent the Communists from reaching a crucial river crossing. Having shaken off the pursuit, the Communists reached the county seat of Tsunyi where they rested and held a two-day session of the Central Committee at the beginning of January. In this session Mao asserted his leadership.

The Tsunyi Conference and the Long March

The Tsunyi Conference in January, 1935, was slated as an enlarged session of the Central Committee of the Party. In reality it was a well-prepared meeting of Mao's supporters among the Party's military commanders.[41] Of the thirty-five to forty participants at the conference, at least two-thirds, probably three-fourths, were not members of the Central Committee of the Communist Party, let alone the Politburo. Some were cadres of the Kiangsi government, but most of them were commanders and commissars of the Red Army who, under the impact of the critical military situation, were willing to listen to Mao's plans for a change in strategy. Mao gave them the right to vote at the conference.

At the meeting Mao gave the main report on the results of the Fifth Nationalist campaign, in his words a major defeat for the Communists. He sharply attacked the leading Chinese comrades as well as the Comintern advisor, Li Teh (Otto Braun). Mao's criticism did not refer to any major political line but dealt with the tactics of the campaign itself. The offensive-defense plan of Li Teh was held responsible for the necessity to abandon the Kiangsi Soviet, and the leadership of the Internationalists was accused of bringing about the dangers of the present situation. Chu Teh and several other leading officers did not participate actively in the discussion, so that there was no open opposition to Mao. Most important for Mao was the willingess of the highest ranking political leader present, Chou En-lai, to vote with Mao. Chou, who later proved to be the most flexible of the Communist leaders, appears to have recognized the shift of power in time to join the winning side. Mao assumed the chairmanship of the Revolutionary Military Council, replacing Chou En-lai, who yielded apparently by choice. This position gave Mao again control of the military organization, the true source of power. Immediately after having asserted his leading position, Mao sent a representative to Moscow to report on the elections. While not gaining complete control of the Army and the political structure, Mao had thus secured the position of dominance; later, in Yenan, Mao was to expand this dominance into complete control of the Communist organization.[42]

Henceforth Mao led what was to become known in history and legend as the *Long March*. Mao led the army first into Szechwan province in the hope of linking up there with the forces of the Second and Fourth army corps under Ho Lung and Chang Kuo-t'ao, which had marched into Szechwan after being driven from their respective bases by Nationalists troops. At the border of Kueichow and Szechwan provinces, Mao's force was met by superior Nationalist units which stopped Mao's advance and forced him to return to Tsunyi. There Mao's leadership was reassured by a military success. In an ambush Mao's troops gained a surprise victory over the Nationalists, which secured for them a breathing spell.

From that time on, however, the Long March became a costly, exhaustive and desparate affair for both troops and leaders. From Tsunyi through Kueichow into Yunnan province and from there northward, battle losses, death from illness and starvation reduced the size of the force drastically. Several precarious escapes from total destruction dramatized the march, which occasionally took on the character of a desperate flight. At the Chinshakiang, the upper course of the Yangtze River, the crossing was barred by a well-entrenched defensive force. Pressed from all sides, Mao's unit escaped only through a ruse which made the crossing possible. A Communist unit, dressed in Nationalist uniforms, was mistaken by the defenders as reinforcements and was supplied by them with boats which enabled the Communists to cross without interference and to disarm the hapless Nationalist defenders.

After this success, Mao called a war council, and it was decided to continue northward into Szechwan. During the march through the highlands of southwest Szechwan there occurred the heroic crossing of the Tatu River, a tributary of the Yangtze. The terrain of this route was forbidding, leading over steep mountain trails and through deep gorges that exposed the troops in very precarious positions to constant harassment and attacks by the inhabitants of the region. These were non-Chinese minority people who had been previously attacked by Communist forces who had killed many of the mountain people and looted their property, and they now took their revenge. The inhabitants successfully withheld any supplies from the Communists so that several thousand troops perished by starvation. Indeed the strategy of this part of the campaign is, in retrospect, a matter that could be seriously questioned. But the core of the troops and the leaders got through and survived.

In mid-June of 1935 at Maokung in Szechwan, Mao's force finally met the units of the Fourth Communist Corps under the leadership of Chang Kuo-t'ao. This force, after being driven out of its Hupen-Honan-Anhwei border area, had been more successful than Mao's troops. It had maintained strength and effectiveness and had established itself in Szechwan province. At the time of the meeting, the number of troops under Mao had been reduced to some 10,000 men, while Chang Kuo-t'ao's unit consisted of over 45,000 men, who were in much better condition than those of Mao. From the point of view of actual power, Chang Kuo-t'ao appeared, therefore, to have a decided advantage over Mao Tse-tung. No wonder that Chang Kuo-t'ao refused to recognize the elections held at the Tsunyi Conference at which he and his supporters had not participated. A compromise agreement, according to which Chang and several of his supporters were co-opted to the Central Committee, did not satisfy Chang and did not provide a permanent solution. While there was no open hostility between the two groups and their leaders, the leadership remained divided. In fact, both Mao and Chang maintained their own independent units, even their own political organizations, so that there were now two Communist central committees and two independent military forces stationed side by side, linked only by contacts and discussions of their respective leaders. No actual integration was therefore possible; and while discussions were held about future strategy and troop movements, there was no agreement either on military plans or march routes. Chang Kuo-t'ao suggested a move into western Szechwan and from there into Sinkiang province for the purpose of establishing contact with the Soviet Union and obtaining Soviet support. Mao had previously held similar ideas but would not agree with Chang Kuo-t'ao's plan now. He therefore suggested a move towards the northwest into

Shensi province to join up with Communist local units in that area and open contact with the Soviet Union via Mongolia. No agreement was reached. Under constant Nationalist pressure, the forces moved northward, each on its own, but held another emergency conference at Maoerhkai in northern Szechwan on August 5. The disagreement about strategy and political integration continued. Each side based its position in this confrontation on the backing of its own military force. Mao Tse-tung maintained his original proposal of a march north into Shensi province. Chang Kuo-t'ao maintained that the march north through the steppeland would be disastrous and declared that his proposal of setting up a base in western Szechwan and from there establishing contact with the Soviet Union through Turkestan was much more promising. The deadlock continued.

In this situation, Mao acted alone. Without notifying his rival or the other commanders, Mao secretly left one night with his whole force and Central Committee to march northward to Shensi. He was to suffer additional losses during his march through hunger, disease and battle, and only a remnant of the combat force, according to various accounts consisting of between 2,000 and 7,000 men, reached northern Shensi by October, 1935, and there linked up with a local Communist force. While the majority of the soldiers were lost, the commanding officers survived and provided the core from which the Communist forces could be expanded again by new recruitment and reorganization.

Deserted by Mao Tse-tung during the night, Chang Kuo-t'ao moved his troops into western Szechwan and formally established his own Central Committee of the Party so that the Communist party and leadership was actually divided into two opposed factions. This split in the Communist leadership continued until a new directive from Moscow led to a temporary reunification of Chang Kuo-t'ao's group with that of Mao Tse-tung.

For Mao and his followers the Long March was more than an escape from destruction and a battle for power. The epic of the march itself, the proof of the endurance in overcoming endless and extreme natural and military adversities and dangers gave the survivors an emotional bond of shared glory that greatly strengthened their cohesion throughout the civil war and in the building of a Communist state. The hundreds of skirmishes and dozens of battles, the heroic fight for the suspension bridge at the crossing of the Tatu River, the precarious paths along precipitous mountain ridges and gorges, the last horses perishing—the deaths in the "great grassland—when a sheep was worth the price of a human life," the sufferings through illness and exhaustion in the crossing of high altitude swamps, rapid mountain rivers and icy glaciers, when typhus and amoebic dysentary took their heavy toll, taken in all provided an incredible story of determined survival that helped to strengthen the image of Chinese Communism and of Mao at home and abroad.

Route of the Long March.　　*Union Research Institute, Hong Kong.*

Mao Tse-tung with his wife Chiang Ch'ing in Yenan, circa 1945.   *Wide World Photos.*

CHAPTER

III

Yenan

IN THE FALL of 1935, a year after the breakthrough of the blockade in Kiangsi, the remnants of the First Army Corp under Mao reached the small district town of Wayaopao in Shensi province. Mao's decimated army, consisting of only a few thousand men, joined forces with the unit of the local soviet which had been established in Shensi by two Communist leaders, the Political Commissar Kao Kang and the Commander Liu Chih-tan. The Liu-Kao unit, officially designated as the Fifteenth Army Corps, consisted of some 20,000 men.[1] Mao Tse-tung, as the leading figure in the Party's Central Committee, incorporated this local force into his own under the command of Lin Piao, the most trusted of Mao's commanders.[2] Wayaopao became for a short time the headquarters of the new soviet base under Mao's control.

The establishment under difficult circumstances of the new headquarters of the Chinese Communists in Shensi province would normally have indicated a further weakening of the Communist position. In driving the Communists toward the northwest, the National Government pursued three objectives: removing the Communists from Kiangsi was to free the rear of the Nationalist forces for the approaching confrontation with

Japan; driving the Communists into a barren area would deprive them of adequate resources for a new base; opening an opportunity for the Communists to retreat from Chinese soil into Soviet-controlled territory would obviate the need for a final military showdown.

The province of Shensi in northwest China, not far from Soviet-controlled Outer Mongolia, is a dry, barren area, characterized by its soil, called *loess*. Loess is windblown sand that has been carried for thousands of years by seasonal winds from the deserts of Central Asia into North-west China, where it has over centuries been deposited to a depth of some hundreds of feet. It is highly porous and has a spongelike quality, retaining water which on the surface evaporates in the dry air and leaves a hardened surface. This soil which has been cut deeply by river gorges forms a terrace-like landscape. In many areas caves have been dug into the vertical slopes for housing, which is cool in summer and warm in winter. This dramatic landscape became the new center for the Communists who also lived in caves, first in Paoan and later in Yenan, and organized cultivation of the land to increase the meager food supply available.

The Second United Front

By this time, however, the international scene had changed. In spite of its poverty, Shensi province proved to be of extreme importance, strategically located as it was in the geographical center between the National Government in Central China, the Japanese in Manchuria and north China, and the Soviet Union, the major parties in a coming confrontation.

As a result of the rapid strengthening of the ties between Nazi Germany and Japan in the mid-thirties, the Soviet Union, in fear of the danger of a two-front war, initiated a policy of a new global united front which was transmitted to the Communists in China. The change of the Soviet position from an independent policy to cooperation with all potential allies against this Nazi-Japanese danger occurred while the Chinese Communists were on the Long March. After Berlin and Tokyo concluded the Anti-Comintern Pact in November, 1936, this policy was pursued with new urgency. Internationally, the Soviet Union joined the League of Nations, and in describing the Western countries changed the nomenclature from "imperialist powers" to "Western democracies" with whom it was possible to cooperate in the fight against fascism and nazism. In Asia, the heightened danger of a Japanese attack led to the new Soviet United Front policy vis-a-vis the National Government of Chiang Kai-shek, adopted at a Comintern Congress in July-August, 1935. On August 1,

Wang Ming, the Chinese representative at the Comintern, issued a manifesto to proclaim this new United Front.[3]

During their stay in Kiangsi the Chinese Communists had begun to use the Japanese attack as an opportunity for propagating a *national resistance* against Japanese imperialism. The question of cooperation with non-Communist groups in China had first become acute during the Fukien rebellion but had gotten nowhere.

During the Long March the Communist leadership was unaware of the shift in Comintern policy. Chang Kuo-t'ao, who campaigned in Szechuan with his own units, had independently promoted the idea of united National Chinese resistance against Japan in place of a continued fight against the National Government.

Finally in December, 1935, at Wayaopao, Mao learned of the new policy through a Chinese emissary from Moscow, and at a politburo meeting on December 25, the new Soviet policy was discussed and officially accepted. However, there was already a difference of attitude towards the new line on the part of the Chinese Communist leaders. The issue was whether this new United Front with the Nationalists should include cooperation with the National Government of Chiang Kai-shek or whether the United Front should be directed against both Japan and Chiang Kai-shek, who was pictured as a traitor to the cause of national resistance. Here, as later, Mao Tse-tung represented the second view, attempting to maintain his independence from National Government control.[4]

The resolution agreed upon at the meeting supported Mao's view. While the Communists aimed at gaining broader popular support through a modification of their social and economic measures, the main thrust of the Comintern line was ignored. This coincided with the attitude of Chiang Kai-shek, who had disregarded all proposals for abandoning the anti-Communist campaign in favor of joint resistance against Japan.[5]

Mao continued the campaign against the forces of the National Government, and in the spring of 1936 he led a foray into Shensi and Suiyuan provinces to reestablish contact with the Soviet Union through Outer Mongolia and thus strengthen the Communist position. The campaign was successful in local skirmishes with provincial troops, but it did not reach Outer Mongolia. During the absence of the main force, local provincial troops made a surprise attack against the Communist headquarters at the town of Wayaopao. Headquarters had to be hurriedly abandoned by the small garrison force headed by Chou En-lai, who had remained behind. The capital was now moved to Paoan, a small town in a mountainous area with few buildings but numerous caves which served as housing for the poor farming population. Here Mao returned with his forces to celebrate a proclaimed victory in the campaign towards the West. Here he reasserted his full control over the Communist party and armies.

In the fall of 1936 the armies of Chang Kuo-t'ao and Ho Lung, who had joined forces in Szechuan, arrived together at Mao's headquarters in Shensi province. Before his arrival sometime in June, 1936, Chang Kuo-t'ao had received a wire from Mao informing him of the shift in Comintern policy toward a united front with the National Government. The telegram contained the suggestion that the two independent central committees, that of Chang Kuo-t'ao and that at the Shensi headquarters under Mao, should be dissolved and, after both forces were combined, a new central leadership would be elected.[6] Chang accepted the proposal and dissolved his Central Committee; but when in October, 1936, his troops met with units of Mao's First Army, he found out that Mao's Central Committee had not been dissolved and that he had obviously been outmanuevered by Mao. Embittered, Chang Kuo-t'ao led his troops into a new campaign into the Kansu Corridor in the hope of establishing his own link with the Soviet Union through Chinese Turkestan. However, Chang's troops were defeated by pro-Nationalist troops under Governor Ma Pu-fang, and when Chang returned to Shensi in December, 1936, with the decimated remainder of his original force, he had lost his military power. Early in 1937, Mao brought Chang to trial for his mistakes.[7] The comparatively mild verdict which only ordered Chang to study and rectify his errors can in part be explained by the considerable support which Chang Kuo-t'ao may still have enjoyed among other Communist leaders, but more likely by the Comintern exhortation to avoid personal conflicts and maintain unity for the sake of the new United Front policy. After the practical elimination of his chief opponent, Mao Tse-tung could shift more openly to the new United Front policy.

One result of the new policy was an agreement between the Communist leadership and the Chinese administrator of the Peking area, General Sung Che-yüan.[8] On the Communist side, the negotiations were led by Liu Shao-ch'i, Mao's man, who at that time worked underground in Peking as the head of the Northern Bureau of the Chinese Communist party. The agreement provided for the release by Sung Che-yüan of a number of Chinese Communists who had been imprisoned by Sung and who were now permitted to leave after a formal pledge that they had renounced communism and would not continue their political activities.[9] This co-operation with Sung Che-yüan could, however, still be interpreted as a move towards a United Front without cooperation with Chiang Kai-shek.

The issue whether the new United Front was to include Chiang Kai-shek was brought to a decisive test in December, 1936, by the kidnapping of President Chiang Kai-shek at Sian. At that time, Chiang Kai-shek had ignored all Communist appeals for ending his anti-Communist campaign and joining a united front against the Japanese aggressor. Chiang had planned a sixth campaign to drive the Communists from Shensi and had ordered the troops stationed at Sian to attack the Communists and to carry out his campaign. These troops were Manchurian Chinese units under the command of the young Marshall Chang Hsüeh-liang, who had been driven out of Manchuria by the Japanese attack during the Manchurian incident. Chiang's troops were particularly vulnerable to the Communist propaganda appeal of stopping the civil war and turning against the Japanese who had occupied their homeland. Chang Hsüeh-liang made proposals to Chiang Kai-shek to stop the civil war, establish a united front and enter into an alliance with the Soviet Union against Japan. These proposals were rejected by Chiang Kai-shek. Unbeknownst to Chiang Kai-shek, Chang Hsüeh-liang had, however, come under the influence of the Chinese Communists who concluded with him an agreement for cooperation in an anti-Japanese front without Chiang Kai-shek —the policy of Mao Tse-tung at the time.[10]

When Chang Hsüeh-liang procrastinated, Chiang Kai-shek went in person to Sian in December, 1936, to cajole the recalcitrant troops and their leader into carrying out their assignment of attacking the Communist armies. With disregard for personal danger, Chiang Kai-shek had brought with him only a small bodyguard. When he failed to obtain compliance from his disobedient commander, Chiang Kai-shek threatened to relieve Chang Hsüeh-liang from his command and replace him by Chiang's own man. This dismissal was not accepted by Chang Hsüeh-liang and on the night of December 11 to 12, Chang's troops moved against the small inn, outside Sian, where Chiang Kai-shek was lodged. They attacked and killed the small bodyguard unit which tried to cover Chiang's escape. In scaling a wall, Chiang fell, hurt his back, was incapacitated and soon captured by the mutinous troops, who brought him as a prisoner to Sian. Attempts by Chang Hsüeh-liang to negotiate with Chiang Kai-shek failed since Chiang, who was in pain and besides had lost his false teeth, at first refused to talk and later berated his captors as traitors.

The news of Chiang Kai-shek's kidnapping created naturally a great sensation internationally and within China and especially among the Communist leaders in Paoan. Mao Tse-tung called a public meeting and demanded in an excited speech the extradition of Chiang Kai-shek who should be placed before a public tribunal, presumably to be executed.[11] A telegram was sent to Moscow to seek advice.

Moscow's policy had been all along to build a broad united front in

China under Chiang Kai-shek against the danger of Japan. Now this policy was threatened. In the Soviet view, Chiang Kai-shek was the only leader able to unite a broad section of the people in China in the resistance against Japan. A telegram was therefore sent by the Comintern to the Chinese leaders at Paoan ordering them to protect Chiang, whose capture was described as a Japanese plot, and whose elimination would only play into Japanese hands. Moscow threatened that, if the Chinese Communists disobeyed this order, they would lose all support and be treated as bandits. The majority of the Chinese Communist leadership at Paoan accepted Moscow's order. Mao Tse-tung was reported to have stomped his feet and cursed the decision, but eventually he had to yield.[12] Moscow had come out with all its authority to save Chiang's life, and Mao gave in when he realized that this was Moscow's unshakable policy.[13] Chou En-lai was sent to Sian to bring about an agreement on the release of Chiang Kai-shek and, if possible, an end to the civil war and a united front against Japan under the leadership of the National Government. This was a major diplomatic feat.

It has been suggested that when Chou En-lai entered the room where Chiang Kai-shek was held, Chiang must have expected the worst since Chou, as head of the Communist Secret Service in Shanghai, had almost been captured by Chiang and would unquestionably have been killed. But Chou handled the situation with the suave diplomatic ability for which he later became known. Referring to the time when Chiang Kai-shek was president of Whampoa Academy and Chou was political commissar, Chou respectfully addressed his former boss by his full title, thus reversing the position of victor and captive, skillfully exploiting Chiang Kai-shek's known pride, and thus easing the way for the understanding which was reached.[14] The negotiations were soon joined by other Nationalist leaders: Madame Chiang Kai-shek, and minister of finance and chief troubleshooter T. V. Soong. What actually was agreed upon in these talks can only be surmised because neither side has fully revealed the substance of the discussions held among a small group of people. The outcome of the negotiations, however, was that Chiang Kai-shek was released on Christmas Day, 1936, and flew back to Nanking. Chou En-lai's diplomatic mission had been successful.[15] The losers were the leaders of the mutiny. Chang Hsüeh-liang went with Chiang Kai-shek to Nanking —on his own volition, according to Chou En-lai.[16] He was brought to trial, pardoned, but has remained ever since in the custody of the National Government, first in Nanking, then in Kunming, and, since 1949, on Taiwan; he has not, so far at least, provided a record of his knowledge and of his participation in the events of the incident. Chang Hsüeh-liang's officers regarded the Communist switch as a betrayal of their agreement on the fight against Chiang Kai-shek, and Chou En-lai appears to have had a hard time getting away from Sian after Chiang's release.[17] For the Communists, the civil war ended under conditions that enabled them to rebuild their shaken strength and raise the foundation for their eventual military victory.

What the negotiations carried on by Chou En-lai had obviously accomplished was not only the end of the fighting, but the acceptance by the National Government of Communist control over their occupied territory in Shensi as a quasi-independent administration within the framework of the National Government, and of the retention of the Communist military forces supposedly under Nationalist leadership. The presumed subordination of these forces under the Nationalist command and of the Communist administration under the National Government remained, however, a hazy and undefined relationship which was to become a matter of argument among the Communists themselves.

In January, 1937, Mao moved his headquarters from Paoan to Yenan. In Yenan the Communists remained until the end of the war, and this phase of the Communist history during the Second United Front has been described as the Yenan period. On arrival in Yenan the Communists issued a statement, agreeing on their part to give up the Soviet state—the name had indeed already been abandoned—and to incorporate their military units nominally in the Nationalist army under the official designation of the Eighth Route Army, a term which became well known in China and abroad.

December, 1936, marked therefore the beginning of the Second United Front in China, which differed fundamentally from the first one established in 1923 under the Sun-Joffe Agreement. Under the first United Front the Communists had joined the political and military organization of the Kuomintang, had individually become members of the Nationalist party and advisers and cadets in the Whampoa Academy. The aim then was to use the Nationalist movement and eventually to take it over from within—an attempt that had failed. The Second United Front was a link between an autonomous political and military Communist organization and the National Government under nominal Nationalist control, which in practice was never accepted by Mao Tse-tung. During the war with Japan, Mao's statements on cooperation veered back and forth according to Moscow pressure at any given time which, in turn, depended on the danger of the international situation as conceived by Moscow.

The outbreak of the war following the Japanese attack at Marco Polo Bridge near Peking on July 7, 1937, led to a more formal expression of cooperation than had resulted from the negotiations at Sian. In September, 1937, the Communist Central Committee issued a manifesto, officially abolishing the Chinese Soviet Government and the Red Army and accepting Sun Yat-sen's "Three Principles" as China's "paramount need" of the day. The manifesto called for the convocation of a people's congress and the enactment of a constitution. The National Government accepted the manifesto as fulfilling the essential conditions for a united war effort. In the place of the national people's congress, which could not be called under wartime conditions, a special congress of the Kuomintang was convoked in which Chou En-lai participated and which organized the People's Political Council. This People's Political Council was to be an advisory body to the National Government during wartime. It was to include Nationalist as well as Communist members and representatives of other groups. This was the main accomplishment of the United Front. It provided, however, no basis for a truly coordinated, much less a fused policy.

The course of the war provided Mao with ample opportunity to rebuild Communist power and extend Communist control over additional territory. This was the result of the strategy accepted by the National Government in the face of the Japanese aggressor who was vastly superior in equipment and firepower. Rather than confront the Japanese in major battles, the National Government followed the policy of trading space for time, retreating into the mountainous hinterland which could be more easily defended and sacrificing the coastal areas and the cities to the Japanese, whose extended lines could then be attacked in flanking movements and from the rear. After the heroic defense of Shanghai, the Nationalists abandoned the capital of Nanking and eventually retreated to the province of Szechwan. Surrounded by mountains and protected by the difficult access through the Yangtze gorges, Szechwan was ideally suited for the location of the wartime capital, which was established at Chungking. In its retreat the National Government and forces took along some of the industrial equipment needed for the war; the retreat was also joined by most of the higher academic institutions, which carried on their work in the western hinterland of Free China.[18]

This strategy of retreat and elastic warfare gave a great advantage to the Communists who had developed the tactic of guerilla warfare in their rural bases in Kiangsi and Yenan. The war against the foreign enemy permitted the full evolution of these guerilla tactics because of the national sentiment against the Japanese aroused by the invasion. Though they had failed to maintain their positions in Kiangsi against the strategy of the National Government, the use of guerilla tactics in the anti-Japanese war was a different matter. The Chinese population was united in the effort against Japan, and Communist policy of military organization of rural areas was much easier to carry out than before.

To make full use of the possibility of gaining broader popular support in the resistance against Japanese aggression, the Communists shifted from the policy of *agrarian revolution* to one of *agrarian reform* in line with their new United Front program. In the border regions, which they controlled, the new policy established administrations that were nominally made up of three different groups of representatives: one-third Communist party members; one-third non-Communist representatives of the peasants, selected by the Communists; and one-third reserved for representatives of the landlords of the respective areas. This form of government conformed with the Communist claim of sharing power under a united front representation. In practice it was entirely Communist controlled and in private Mao said so.[19] It was also difficult to find landlords for participation in these councils, because most of them had been caught in the cities occupied by the Japanese. They could, therefore, be treated as collaborators with the enemy and their land could be expropriated and distributed among the peasantry, which added to Communist popularity. In general the Communists changed the system of expropriating the land of rich peasants and landlords and accepted instead the principle which had been tried, though finally not carried through by the National Government in the lower Yangtze region before the outbreak of the war. According to this principle, a maximum of 37.5 percent of the main crop was fixed as the highest rent to be paid by tenants to the landlord.[20] The National Government's attempt in Chekiang province to enforce this maximum rent had failed to break the determined resistance of local landlords, but the principle had been established and would, therefore, have to be fully approved by the National Government when it was now introduced under the new Communist agrarian reform policy. It replaced the previous violent Communist actions under which they had exterminated landlords and their families, and was widely propagated by Communist propaganda abroad to prove the moderation of the Chinese Communists. It became the basis for the mistaken view of the Chinese Communists as *agrarian reformers* which circulated at that time in the United States and Europe.

The advantage which the Communists had in obtaining broader public support was increased by the fact that Mao did not honor the agreement of cooperation which the Communists claimed to have accepted at the outset. Though he had agreed to place the Red Army under the control of the National Government's Military Affairs Commission and had accepted a limitation on its size, Mao disregarded the substance if not the form of this accord. The understanding had been that the Red Army would be renamed the Eighth Route Army and would be composed of three divisions, with a total strength of 45,000 men. In renaming the armies into divisions, Mao did not reduce their size, but on the contrary enlarged them so that each of the divisions eventually formed a large field army. Two other armies were added—one of them in the lower Yangtze area. Of equal consequence was the fact that these armies remained independent of Nationalist military control or supervision.

The question of the Communist acceptance of Nationalist military direction was discussed at a politburo meeting at Loch'uan in northern Shensi in August, 1937. Here, as on later occasions, Mao Tse-tung favored independence of the Communist forces from any Nationalist control. Some of the Communist leaders like Chu Teh and Chou En-lai argued for integration of the Communist troops with the Nationalist armies in the interests of unity of command and integrated strategy, but Mao held his own. The upshot was a compromise under which the Communists did permit the stationing at Yenan of a small number of Nationalist officers for the purpose of liaison with Nationalist headquarters without permitting these officers to take any part in planning or witnessing any of the military actions. This token compliance with the agreement was typical of Mao's attitude during the war.[21] Mao's aim was to retain the greatest possible independence of the Communist forces and to emphasize the strengthening of the Communist position vis-à-vis the National Government over and above the defeat of the Japanese.

At times when Moscow became concerned with the Nationalist willingness and ability to stay in the war against Japan, Mao Tse-tung, under Soviet pressure, was quite willing to proclaim in the strongest terms his loyalty to Chiang Kai-shek and the acceptance of Chiang's leadership, but in action he did nothing to strengthen the National Government's position in the common war. In the political arguments among the leaders of the Communist Politburo, Mao maintained that, under the impact of the war, the Nationalist leadership would split and the Communists would be in a position to take over the leadership of the United Front and eventually would be able to defeat both the Japanese and Chiang Kai-shek. While on the surface acceding to the United Front policy, Mao therefore refused to support any action that would provide political or military substance to the Nationalist-Communist cooperation.

This was one of the reasons that throughout the war the Communists engaged the Japanese only twice in major military actions.[22]

Under the protection of the truce in the civil war and with the added advantage of comparative inactivity of the Communist armies in the war against Japan, Mao extended Communist control over a number of areas in north China. Several so-called border area governments were established and a number of smaller enclaves, nineteen in all, extended Communist infiltration across the north China plain from the mountains in

Shensi to the Shantung promontory, cutting off central China from Peking and Manchuria, a position that proved to be of utmost importance at the time of the revival of the civil war after the Japanese surrender. The four major border area governments established by the Communists were Shen-kan-ning (at the border of Shensi, Kansu and Ningsia) in 1937; Chin-ch'a-chi (at the border of Shansi, Chahar and Hopeh provinces) in 1938; Chin-chi-lu-yü (at the border of Shansi, Hopeh, Shantung and Honan provinces) in 1938; and Chin-sui (at the border of Shansi and Suiyuan) in 1939. In establishing his control in the rural areas of these provinces behind the Japanese line, Mao expanded Communist authority from the small region of Yenan in Shensi throughout the north China plain, claiming to control a population of 90 million people. The military forces consisting of some 30,000 regulars before the war, who in the agreement with the National Government were to remain limited to 45,000 combat troops, expanded into a force of over half a million men. The membership of the Communist party, according to Mao's claims, rose from 40,000 in 1937 to 1,200,000 in 1945. Before the war against Japan had ended, the balance of military and political power had begun to shift from the Nationalist to the Communist side. While the Nationalist political structure and economy were shaken under the continuing blows of Japanese offensives and economic warfare, the Communists in their decentralized and largely rural positions not only survived but flourished. Japanese aggression therefore undermined the very economic, social, military, political and moral foundations of the National Government and paved the way for the Communist victory in the civil war that followed Japan's surrender.

The Japanese occupation of the cities and lines of communication provided in practice a protection for the Communist organizational expansion, since it prevented the National Government from interfering in any way with the Communist advance. The Communists went even further. In areas close to Japanese-occupied centers, they cooperated with the enemy, or, in their words, "made deals with the enemy and took advantage of the little lawful protection under enemy rule to conserve anti-Japanese strength and protect the interests of the people."[23]

The period of Communist revival and growing strength was also the period of consolidation of power by Mao Tse-tung. This was the time when Mao Tse-tung created his own leadership team and concurrently established himself as the ideological leader of the Chinese Communist party. One by one, Mao removed competitors and opposing factions until he finally, before the end of the war, was clearly in full control. This intricate power struggle was closely linked to the events of the war and to the relationship with Moscow and Stalin.

Mao's hesitancy in accepting the full implications of the United Front policy caused Stalin to send back to China some of the leading Politburo and Central Committee members of the Chinese Communist party who had stayed in Moscow for training and as liaison between Moscow and the Chinese Communists. The most important among them were Wang Ming (Ch'en Shao-yü), one of the *Twenty-eight Bolsheviks,* or Internationalists, who had been in Moscow as Chinese representative at the Comintern, and K'ang Sheng, who had received his training in the Soviet Union in preparation for his intelligence and security work in China. These men arrived in October, 1937, to reassert Stalin's influence and policy in Yenan.[24] To strengthen this contact, Stalin also sent wireless equipment that would enable the Chinese Communist leaders to be in constant immediate communication with Moscow.[25]

These Chinese messengers from Moscow brought good news for Mao but also a new threat to his independence. From them Mao learned that Stalin had accepted Mao's leadership in the Chinese Communist party; but Stalin obviously intended to place at Mao's side a reliable Chinese who was loyal to Moscow and the Comintern, and who would be in a position to watch over Mao's action and check any inclination towards independence from the Soviet center.[26] Stalin wanted to educate Mao whose knowledge of the Marxist-Leninist doctrine he considered to be limited and whose procrastination in carrying out Moscow's orders would have to be overcome. Wang Ming, who had been a member of the Executive Committee of the Comintern and Stalin's principal adviser on Chinese problems, was supposed to entrench himself in the Chinese leadership in a position of authority that would give Moscow control over Mao and the Chinese Communist party.

One directive on policy that Wang Ming brought with him was the instruction that the internal strife between Mao and Chang Kuo-t'ao had to be de-emphasized.[27] The other move made on Stalin's directive as transmitted by Wang Ming was the removal of Chang Wen-t'ien, originally one of the Soviet-trained leaders, who had sided with Mao at the Tsunyi Conference and had since been politically Mao's supporter.[28] He was now removed from the position of party secretary, apparently to open the place for Wang Ming himself.

Wang Ming's obvious intent to challenge the monopoly of Mao's power soon led to a struggle between Wang and Mao. The confrontation began at a Politburo conference in December, 1937. The first issue to be dealt with was the form and substance of cooperation with the National Government in the war against Japan. At that time an attempt had been made by the German ambassador in China to negotiate a peace agreement between Japan and the National Government. After the presentation of the alleged Japanese position by Ambassador Trautman—which proved to be incorrect—Chiang Kai-shek saw the possibility of entering into negotiations with Japan without jeopardizing the Chinese Nationalist position. On this he consulted his generals. As it turned out, the Japanese had no intention of abandoning their goal of dominance over China and Trautman's effort was aborted. But the very attempt at negotiations raised for Moscow the grim specter of a settlement of the war in China which would have revived for the Soviet Union the threat of an onslaught by Japan against her eastern frontier. To prevent this danger, the Chinese Nationalists had to be placated at all costs. It again had to be made very clear to Mao and the Chinese Central Committee that Chiang Kai-shek was the only possible leader in the war against Japan and that the National Government was to be given all support by the Communists. To this directive, all Communist leaders, including Mao Tse-tung, had to agree.

To assert this policy and to strengthen his own influence over the direction of party affairs, Wang Ming demanded a reorganization of the party structure. In addition to the central authority in Yenan, regional party bureaus were to be established in north China, central China, and in southeast China in Nanchang. All of them were to be staffed by Wang Ming supporters, with Wang Ming himself assuming the position of heading the Central China Bureau located at Wuhan. Wang Ming had thus entrenched himself in the regional structure of the party, all the more important since the war forced a decentralization of authority in the Communist organization. To this, too, Mao had to agree.

As a last point Wang Ming tried at the conference to assert his power at the party center personally by moving into the position of party secretary. Here he did not succeed. The crucial struggle for control of the party organization ended in a compromise. Mao accepted the removal of Chang Wen-t'ien from the position of general secretary of the Party but successfully resisted the appointment of Wang Ming or of any of Wang Ming's men to the post. Instead, the position of general secretary was abolished and the function taken over by a nine-man committee in which Wang Ming maintained a precarious majority.

Wang Ming's new institutional power, however, also had important military backing. While Mao could be expected to retain the loyalty of the generals of his First Army Corps—now the Eighth Route Army—one of the new five armies created, the so-called Fourth Route Army in the lower Yangtze region under the command of generals who were not in Mao's camp, provided the military support for Wang Ming.[29]

As a result of this Politburo meeting in December, 1937, a balance of power seemed to have been established between Mao and Wang Ming. Mao retained his control of the Eighth Route Army and remained chairman of the Revolutionary Military Committee. He had also succeeded in having one of his chief supporters, Liu Shao-ch'i, appointed as head of the organizational department of the Party, which would give Mao decisive influence over appointments; and lastly, Mao was selected chairman of a preparatory committee which was to call a party congress, the seventh, to be held in 1938. Wang Ming became secretary of the Preparatory Committee, and Wang Ming's control of the regional party committees and of the Fourth Route Army, and his influence over the Politburo seemed to balance Mao's authority.

Events in 1938 and 1939 aggravated for Moscow the danger of a two-front war with Nazi Germany and Japan. In China, the Japanese established in March, 1939, a Chinese puppet government in Nanking to be headed by Wang Ching-wei, who defected from the National Government in 1938. In the summer the Japanese started a border incident at Changkufeng, a mountainous area at the border of Manchuria, north Korea and Soviet territory near Vladivostok. The incident led to severe fighting of large Soviet and Japanese armies with heavy casualties on both sides. The Soviets regarded this Japanese attack as a test of their strength. The Japanese claimed victory in the battle, but the Soviets turned back the Japanese attack and retained possession of the contested mountain area when the incident was settled in August. But the threat to Soviet territory in east Asia remained and was underscored by the Munich Agreement in September, in which the surrender of British and French resistance against Nazi encroachment in Czechoslovakia freed German forces for a possible attack against the Soviet Union.

Under this threat the Soviets provided military aid to the National Government in the form of airplanes and equipment — the latter coming over the Burma road — most welcome to the hard-pressed Nationalists. Simultaneously the Chinese Communists officially assumed a completely cooperative attitude towards the National Government. At the Sixth Plenum of the Central Committee from the end of September to the beginning of November, 1938, the Communists completely endorsed and accepted the Moscow directives. Of particular interest is the way in which Mao, who had been hesitant and recalcitrant in moving towards a true cooperation, stressed his willingness to accept the Kuomintang and Chiang Kai-shek's leadership.[30]   In his original speech Mao assigned the Kuomintang the leading role in the National resistance and spoke of the necessity of giving "unanimous support to Generalissimo Chiang Kai-shek" as the "supreme leader" of the resistance.[31] Mao even went so far as to predict that the China of the future would not be Soviet or Socialist but a democracy with universal suffrage and private ownership.[32] Mao expressed his expectation that the cooperation between the National

Government and the Communists would continue even after the war, leading to a Chinese state based on Sun Yat-sen's Three Peoples' Principles. It was the strongest demonstration of Mao's ability to accept politically inevitable stands at least on the surface.[33]

The link with the National Government in this United Front was formed by a group of Chinese Communist leaders sent as representatives to the National Government. The men selected represented a balance between the groups of Mao and Wang Ming. Wang Ming himself went to Hankow in 1938 and from there moved with the National Government to Chungking. It was indeed logical that the head of the pro-Moscow group himself took up residence at the wartime seat of the National Government, but it did place Wang Ming at a disadvantage vis-à-vis Mao Tse-tung, who remained in full control in Yenan. This disadvantage was somewhat modified by the fact that Wang Ming's main support was based on the party's regional offices, especially the Yangtze and south China bureaus; and Wang Ming used his post in Chungking to call in September, 1939, a Conference of the Communist leaders of the south China and Yangtze bureaus. Chou En-lai represented Mao's side in this Communist mission at the Nationalist headquarters.

This regional strength of Wang Ming was dependent, however, on Wang's backing by the Communist New Fourth Army in the lower Yangtze region; it ended when this army's leadership was destroyed and its forces taken over by Mao Tse-tung in January, 1941.

The New Fourth Army had been formed in the lower Yangtze area early in the war, in 1938, from the remnants of the Communist forces that had been left behind in Kiangsi at the time when the main Communist force went on the Long March. As the war went on, the National Government objected to this Communist entrenchment in the very region of the triangle between Shanghai, Hangchow and Nanking that had been the heartland of Nationalist authority before the Japanese attack. Under Nationalist pressure the Communists promised to remove this army to the provinces north of the Yellow River; when they procrastinated Chiang Kai-shek wired Yenan a deadline for the withdrawal and when it was ignored attacked the Communist troops. The main force retreated southward but the rear guard, including the commanders was annihilated.[34]

The destruction of an independent Communist army was very much in Mao's interests, as the loss of the New Fourth Army and its leadership was a fatal blow to Wang Ming, who lost his military base.[35] Instead of dissolving the New Fourth Army as Chiang Kai-shek had demanded, Mao sent a unit of 20,000 men of the Eighth Route Army to rebuild the New Fourth Army under Ch'en Yi as commander and Liu Shao-ch'i as political commissar, both Mao's men. Mao could now proceed to eliminate his political rival Wang Ming and Wang's faction and to assert his monopoly control over the Chinese Communist party and army. To do this Mao had to claim not only institutional but doctrinal authority over the Chinese Communist party.

The Thought of Mao Tse-tung

The authority of the leader of any Communist system is based on the claim of being able to understand the application of doctrine as a guide and justification of policy. When Mao had established his position in the Party and the army, he had still to gain this ideological leadership. Ideological sanction would give Mao the opportunity to lay down the political line and to condemn his rivals not only as political opponents but also as "deviationists" of the "right" or the "left." To do this, Mao had to be acquainted with the literature of Marxism-Leninism and to establish himself through his writings as an authority in the field of Marxist ideology.

Mao had begun his study of Marxism in Peking days by reading some secondary texts and learning from his peers. But he had never undertaken a systematic study of the Marxist-Leninist classics. In the caves of Yenan during the war years, Mao now had the time to read doctrinal works that would enable him to assume the role of ideological arbiter in the power struggles of the time and of years to come. On this material, Mao lectured in Yenan and, from 1938 on, he began to issue his major doctrinal essays and publications which were to form the ideological arsenal for his rise to power.

It is doubtful whether Mao ever read thoroughly the classical works of Marx and Engels or even of Lenin. Fragments of earlier Mao works show Mao's very limited knowledge of Marxism. An early study on dialectical materialism was apparently destroyed and is no longer available. Even in later days, however, Mao's familiarity with the Marxist classics appears to have been limited. Students of Mao's writings have pointed to these obvious limitations of Mao's knowledge of the Communist classics. What Mao's major writings in the Yenan period were based on were Soviet works, textbooks, and encyclopedia articles from which he seems to have copied, in some cases, almost verbatim, his major ideological formulations.[36]

These Soviet models Mao appears to have received from Stalin, and it is plausible to assume that they were sent to Mao as part of Stalin's effort to educate and bring into the proper Communist fold this Chinese revolutionary whose energy and vitality had commended him to Stalin as a leader for the direction of the Chinese Revolution.[37] It was on the basis of this reading that Mao produced at Yenan his major pieces, "On Practice" and "On Contradiction," and his program for China under the title "On the New Democracy."

"On Practice" and "On Contradiction" were companion pieces by Mao, important because they provided the first and indeed the main essays by Mao of Marxian philosophical content. Both these pieces have to be understood in the context of Mao's political power struggle against the Internationalists led by Wang Ming. But they also demonstrate that by that time, Mao had read his Soviet sources and could explain them to his Chinese audience as his understanding and interpretation of Marxism.

"On Practice" is Mao's emphasis of the point that "Marxism is not a dogma but a guide to action," a tenet that Marx had stressed, and that Lenin, whom Mao quotes, repeated. Mao describes the way in which man learns to understand nature's law through productive activity and human interrelations, especially by "class struggle." Through the "science of Marxism," the proletariat was to gain a comprehensive understanding of the objective world. The point of the whole essay was to demonstrate that revolutionary action had to be based on a thorough knowledge of given conditions to which the revolutionary leadership must be able to adapt. "Dogmatists" who failed to advance at the right time, and "adventurists" who wanted to move too fast for the objective conditions, followed a line of "rightist" or "leftist" opportunism and were therefore deviationist. By implication, it was Mao who understood conditions in China, the Internationalists did not. Showing his familiarity with the basic conceptual framework of the Marxist arsenal, Mao thus assumed the right to determine policy and to purge those who deviated from his line.

"On Contradiction," presumably part of the same lecture series as "On Practice," was Mao's more ambitious attempt to demonstrate his mastery of the proclaimed science of dialectical materialism. Contradiction, in Chinese *mao-tun,* is the essence of dialectics: thesis and antithesis, the opposites contained in each thing, the concept that in all phenomena and processes there are opposite forces that dictate development. The essay was Mao's attempt to define this concept. Mao did this in terms of simplified descriptions of Marxist theory of the development of the dialectical processes in natural and human life.

It is an incongruous combination of assumed opposites that Mao listed, linking Marxist concepts of class struggle with natural phenomena. Mao added the point that such contradictions need not be "antagonistic."[38] This distinction between simple, "non-antagonistic," contradictions and "antagonistic" contradictions closely followed Stalin's concept of essential and nonessential conflicts. Mao claimed that each form of society and each mode of thought had its particular contradictions which had to be fully known in order to decide which contradiction had to be dealt with at what time. Implying that he possessed a full understanding of the Chinese situation, Mao attacked the doctrinaires "who do not know this particularity because they live with abstract formulas and are too lazy to pay attention to the particular forms of Chinese contradiction which lead to national wars of liberation and democratic revolution."[39]

Referring to Marx and Engels, to Lenin and especially to Stalin, Mao claimed by implication that he had mastered the peculiarities and complexities of the various Chinese contadictions which had to be placed in proper perspective, and could not be understood by those "who get bogged down in abstract studies."[40]

Mao's purpose in this ideological treatise is to make a public demonstration of his understanding of the basic concepts of Marxism in order to apply it to his battle with the opposition. Mao stresses the fact that any ideological contradiction can become antagonistic. According to Mao, this was the case in the Soviet Union in the clashes of Lenin and Stalin with Trotsky and Bukharin, and in China in the conflict of the "correct leadership" with Ch'en Tu-hsiu and Chang Kuo-t'ao. He adds the ominous threat that, while at present the comrades in Yenan can still correct their mistakes, if they do not do so, the contradiction might become antagonistic and then one would have to "smash those doctrinaire ideas which run counter to the basic principles of Marxism-Leninism and are detrimental to our revolutionary cause. . . ." Not a theoretical piece, Mao's essay became a call to battle in which the concept of contradiction was used to judge his opponents and to find them wanting.

Mao's third major piece was "On the New Democracy," written in 1939 and published in January, 1940; it contained his description of the political situation. "On the New Democracy" was Mao's adaptation of the Leninist concept of national liberation movements for China. The period of 1939 was one in which the pressure on the Soviet Union had eased, and Mao could speak more freely about Communist strategy though still within the framework of the United Front.

The theoretical basis of "On the New Democracy" was the Stalinist and indeed Leninist theory that the "bourgeois democratic" and the succeeding "socialist" revolutions could be fused. As a joint revolution, it was to be carried out by the "joint dictatorship of all the revolutionary classes." In China as in other "colonial" or "semi-colonial" countries, this revolution was to be carried out in the main by peasants who made up "80% of the Chinese population."[41] But the workers were not to be left out in this allegedly proletarian revolution, so Mao, playing with figures, spoke of the workers who made up "several millions . . . as the leaders of the revolution." Mao further claimed that "the workers and peasants together make up more than 90% of the whole population," thus raising by his manipulation of figures the workers to some ten percent of the population or to a number of about 50 million. Aside from this statistical inflation of the workers number, there was nothing new in Mao's rendition of standard Communist doctrine of the United Front revolution in "national liberation movements."

Mao also followed the regular Communist doctrinal classification of China as a "feudal" or "feudal bourgeois" society in which the "capitalist" stage, which had not yet been completed, could be merged with the "socialist" stage in a joint revolution in which the capitalist aspect would slowly diminish until the socialist aspect had taken over. Since this thesis, however, was to be addressed not only to the Communists but also to the Nationalist partners in the United Front, Mao took care not to raise the fears of the "bourgeois" and intellectual members in the United Front; he reassured them by stating that this "new democracy" stage of the revolution was to continue in "a long-time cooperation." Aligning himself with Sun Yat-sen's Three Peoples' Principles, Mao proceeded to give Sun's slogans a new twist. Sun's principles of *Nationalism, Democracy, and Peoples' Livelihood* became in Mao's sloganized version an alliance of Sun's Nationalist party "with the Soviet Union," "with the Chinese Communists" and "with the workers and peasant class." This triple alliance had transformed the "old politics and old economy of the Nationalists into the new politics and new economy" of the anti-Japanese United Front. This was the reason that Mao's program was called "on the *new* democracy." In his section on economics Sun had included the possibility of combining private enterprise with the nationalization of large banks and industrial plants and had used the slogan of giving the "land to the tiller." Without offending his Kuomintang partners in the United Front, Mao could safely include in his "new democracy" the concept of a mixed nationalized and private industry and of Sun's land slogan in slight variation: "The tiller should own his land without a fear of affecting the wartime cooperation." To counter these concessions, Mao expressed confidence in the superiority of the "Communist culture" over that of the "flabby bourgeoisie." "This "anti-imperialist, anti-feudal culture of the broad masses of the people is . . . the new culture of the Chinese nation."[42] This was the "new China" which Mao asked his audience to hail and welcome.

Without compromising Communist doctrine, Mao Tse-tung had therefore explained the doctrine in popular terms within a framework calculated not to give too much offense to the Nationalist partners of the United Front. He thus preserved his independent position towards the

Kuomintang, proved himself faithful in interpreting the Moscow doctrine and prepared himself for the power struggle with the opposition within the Chinese Communist party.

The Cheng-feng Movement (Rectification)

It was under the guise of an educational campaign, the so-called Cheng-feng movement, that Mao purged Wang Ming and the Internationalist faction.[43] At the same time the Cheng-feng movement was used to indoctrinate the new members who joined the Communist party in Yenan in large numbers. This meant that the party members had to study Mao's Thought, that the party organization was to be centralized under Mao's control, and that the interpretation of the party line had to follow Mao's direction. Mao thus used the establishment of his new position as an arbiter in ideological matters to carry through a major purge in which he reorganized the party in his own image.

The timing of this major purge movement was skillfully chosen. The Soviet Union fought for its survival on the eastern front against the Nazi onslaught. With Japan, the Soviet Union had concluded in April of 1941 a neutrality pact in which the two countries pledged themselves to remain neutral in the event the other became "the object of hostility" on the part of one or several third powers. They promised to respect each other's territories and, in return for Japan's declaration to respect the territorial integrity of the Mongolian People's Republic, the Soviet Union was to do the same for Japan and Japan's position in Manchukuo. The pact was to be valid for five years. It was followed two months later by a Soviet-Japanese trade agreement for the same period of time, and by border negotiations which settled disputed border questions and reduced the tension in Japanese-Soviet relations. For Japan, the agreement meant freedom to intensify her war in China and to turn south with her plans of expansion. For the Soviet Union, it meant freedom to concentrate against the fearful attack by Nazi Germany, which was soon to follow. The Soviet pressure on the Chinese Communists to maintain a strict enforcement of the United Front with Chiang Kai-shek was therefore temporarily eased, at the very time when Stalin's representative and spokesman, Wang Ming, was losing his power in China.

The new freedom of action enabled Japan to mount a massive campaign in north China to destroy the Communist infrastructure. The Japanese offensive was ruthlessly carried out as the *Three-all Campaign (Kill All, Burn All, Destroy All)*. From the towns the Japanese soldiers moved out into the rural areas burning whole villages and killing the people to eliminate the popular support and organization that the Communists had established behind the Japanese lines over the last two years. This Japanese offensive was highly successful and resulted in serious Communist defeats and loss of territory, especially in the provinces of Shantung and Shansi. The shrinking of Communist territory facilitated Mao Tse-tung's decision to strengthen his central control. In April, 1941, he started a *rural survey campaign* which led to a purge of the leaders of Communist local organizations.

The massive Nazi attack along the entire European frontier of the Soviet Union in July, 1941, resulted in a renewed Soviet pressure for greater Chinese action against the Japanese. Mao, under duress himself, failed to act.[44] His attitude as well as the setbacks which the Communists had suffered created a restlessness among the Communist cadres in Yenan which provided Mao with the opportunity to stress party unity and loyalty, and issue political directives that heralded the later purge of the central party leaders.

The final opportunity, however, offered itself after the Japanese attack against the United States at Pearl Harbor in December, 1941, as the Japanese withdrew entire divisions from north China for their new campaigns in Southeast Asia, leaving the Chinese Communists free to settle their internal conflicts.

In its resolution of December, 1937, the Central Committee of the Party had proclaimed that a party congress be called and had named Mao Tse-tung chairman of the Preparatory Committee. Using this authorization, Mao called the leading cadres from all Communist areas and enclaves to Yenan, allegedly for the coming party congress. But instead of holding the congress, Mao used the presence of the large number of party leaders in Yenan to start the Cheng-feng educational campaign.[45] It was the first of Mao's major purge movements in which he followed an elaborate, carefully detailed plan, combining an assertion of ideological authority with an institutional attack against his competitors among the party leaders. Here for the first time Mao applied a political technique which reached its apogee in the Great Proletarian Cultural Revolution twenty-five years later. Beginning with a study program at the Central Party School in Yenan at which all the leading cadres were ordered to participate, the educational movement was extended to the party organization of the whole area, then shifted to a political reorganization of the party structure ending in Mao's complete control.

Mao's chief lieutenants in his rectification campaign were Liu Shao-ch'i and K'ang Sheng, men who from that time on remained Mao's close collaborators. Liu and K'ang had both very different backgrounds and personalities from that of Mao, and each in his way complemented Mao's great political ability. Liu Shao-ch'i joined the party in the late twenties in Shanghai; his chief experience was organizing labor unions, and he remained in urban underground work following the decimation of the Shanghai party structure by Chiang Kai-shek. He was therefore very familiar with organizational party work in the traditional sense, but also had a theoretical bent for Marxist doctrine and its practical application. He was an organization man and ideally suited to provide the methodical and mechanical detail work for which Mao had no patience. K'ang Sheng was the chief security agent in the Communist organization who had the training and gift for the kind of secret intelligence work that Mao needed to carry through his purges and establish his authority. Though trained in the Soviet Union and sent back to China together with Wang Ming, K'ang Sheng appears to have joined Mao's team immediately after arrival in Yenan.

Mao used his own speeches and those of his lieutenants as the material in which the party cadres were indoctrinated. Liu Shao-ch'i in his speeches placed major emphasis on party discipline and obedience to the leadership. Some of those speeches Mao had given earlier: a speech on "Reform our Study," in May, 1941. On February 1, 1942, at the opening of the Central Party School of which Mao became the self-appointed chairman, he lectured on "Rectify the Style in the Party." Mao included essays by Lenin, Stalin and the Comintern leader, Dimitrov, among the documents to be studied and discussed. All together these were twenty-two documents. In combining his own pronouncements and those of his men with those of the leaders of the Soviet party and the Comintern, Mao not only stressed his close relationship and loyalty to Moscow and the International Communist line but also raised his own status in this illustrious company.

The program consisted of study and discussion and later review and examination of the documents in question. The purpose was not an independent analysis or better grasp of Communist classics and of Mao's own contribution and that of his team, but rather the assertion of a particular line in which the cadres to be trained could be tested and classified according to their loyalty towards Mao. It was the first and prime example of the use of ideological justification for the buildup of personal dominance over a political team, a method unique to Mao.

Once this principle of ideological control was firmly established and the party cadres brought to its acceptance, Mao undertook the restructuring of the entire party organization. In September, 1942, the Central Politburo issued a decision on reestablishing "centralized leadership" and readjustment of relations among party organization in the anti-Japanese base area, abolishing the decentralized system of party, state and military organizations, and replacing it by party committees that were directly responsible to Mao in Yenan.[46]

This centralization was facilitated by the shrinking Communist authority in the various enclaves and border areas that had resulted from the Japanese offensive. It enabled Mao to remove from office Wang Ming's followers and all those whom he did not regard as his personal team. Since the previous structure was abolished and replaced by a new one, the actual purge was simplified. It was up to Mao to select the cadres for appointment to the new committees. In choosing the new staff, Mao, needless to say, promoted his followers, including among them a great number of army officers.

As with other purge movements in China, the Cheng-feng movement was, however, not simply a replacement of men outside of Mao's own team with Mao's own men; it was also a blood purge. Many of those found in disagreement with the proper ideology were not only politically eliminated but executed. The top opposition leaders were, however, not physically attacked. Wang Ming was removed from the Politburo though not from the Central Committee, and Mao appointed him principal of a girls' school.

One person who was most helpful to Mao in this purge was Kao Kang, the original organizer of the Communist soviet in Shensi province before Mao's arrival. His help was essential for the reorganization of the Chinese Communist party and administration in the border area. Because of his loyalty in the Cheng-feng movement, Kao Kang was later promoted to the Politburo and rewarded with a special administrative position in Manchuria after the establishment of the People's Republic. His purge would come ten years later.

Mao's Personal Life

In the midst of this political power struggle in Yenan, Mao formed a life-style which he continued in later times. For one thing, he established a personal image as a simple man who was close to the masses. Visitors commented on his plain habits and attire and his rustic life in his cave in Yenan.[47] Since Yenan was a barren area and the Communists had, by necessity, introduced the policy of planting their own food supply, the leaders participated to set an example. Mao, like the others, used his spare time to cultivate a garden and this occupation of his was well noted in China and abroad. The Western image of Mao as the peasant leader close to the soil and to the masses was at least partly based on this Yenan picture reported by several Western writers.

There was another connection formed by Mao during this time, his attachment to Chiang Ch'ing. She established a personal liaison with Mao which was to lead to a major political role in the Chinese Communist party much later on. The story, however, started as a scandal.[48]

As a student, Mao had fallen in love with and married Yang K'ai-hui, the daughter of his former teacher. She bore him two sons. After Mao organized the Autumn Harvest uprising in Hunan, both his wife and sister were arrested by the governor of the province and executed.

During the Kiangsi Soviet, at a meeting on party affairs, Mao became acquainted with a "pretty comrade," a secretary of the Communist Youth Organization, and formed a liaison with her. Her name was Ho Shih-chen (Ho Tzu-chen), the daughter of a bookstore owner in one of the towns of the Kiangsi Soviet area. Mao is said to have detained her after a political meeting and from that time on she lived with him as his wife. When the Kiangsi base was abandoned, she accompanied Mao on the Long March. Only thirty-five women were permitted to stay with the army and Ho Shih-chen, pregnant at the time, was one of them. All together she bore Mao three children, all believed to be girls, one of whom was born on the Long March. These children were left with peasants during the incredible hardships of the Long March. Much later Chou En-lai attempted to locate them, but they were never found.[49] The hardships of the march combined with the childbearing affected the physical appearance and strength of Ho Shih-chen, who in her early pictures appeared as a delicate beauty with a gay expression. In 1937, in Yenan, Mao found another female companion in Chiang Ch'ing.

Chiang Ch'ing's biographers do not present a very flattering picture of the lady who became the new wife of Mao Tse-tung. She was born in Chuch'eng County in Shantung province of a poor family named Luan. After her father's death the mother went with the child to join relatives in Tsinan and there the girl changed her family name and personal name to Li Yün-ho. According to one account, she moved on from primary school to lower middle school and is believed to have reached that level of regular education. At 15, she ran away from home and joined a theatrical troupe. Because of her interest in theatre, she later enrolled in a school for theatrical arts, whose principal, Chao Tai-mo, appears to have taken a special interest in her. When Chao became dean and later chancellor of National Tsingtao University, Li Yün-ho went with him and with his help became junior assistant in the university library. When her benefactor married a famous film star, Li Yün-ho met a cousin of the star, Yü Ch'i-wei, fell in love with him and lived with him until he left for Peking. Yü Ch'i-wei was an underground Communist party member and through him, Li Yün-ho had her first contact with the Communist organization.

At Tsingtao, she met a movie director from Shanghai, who arranged for her a job with a motion picture company in Shanghai. This company was a project of the Alliance of Leftist Writers, which included well-known Communist literary figures of the time. Li Yün-ho, who assumed the stage name of Lan P'ing, played minor parts in some of these films. In Shanghai, she soon married a motion picture figure, T'ang Na, and he promoted her career. Her affairs with other actors and directors reportedly drove T'ang Na to a suicide attempt, but they did not separate, and through her husband's help she was given supporting roles in some of his films. In August, 1937, when the fighting started around Shanghai, Li Yün-ho moved inland with the other actors and film companies to Hankow and Chungking, working for government films. Dissatisfied with the secondary role she was given, she left Chungking for the Northwest, tried unsuccessfully to get a position in Sian and traveled on to Yenan. Her sponsor in Yenan was K'ang Sheng, the head of the central intelligence and Mao's close associate, who came from the same district as Li Yün-ho and who now helped her obtain a job as instructor at the Lu Hsün Academy of Art.[50] In Yenan, Li Yün-ho took the name of Chiang Ch'ing (some suggest that it was Mao Tse-tung who selected the name for her) and under this name she has become widely known.[51]

In Yenan, as in previous times, Chiang Ch'ing was soon known for her aggressiveness in drawing attention to herself. Though not a beauty and not a gifted actress, she attracted attention to herself through sheer determination as much as by her willingness to use her physical endowments to attract people important to her. She came to Mao's attention when he gave a lecture at the Lu Hsün Academy and Chiang Ch'ing, as usual sitting in front, asked Mao a question which he liked. This led to further contact and eventually she moved into Mao's cave and in due course became pregnant. During the Yenan years, she bore Mao two daughters. To clear the way for Chiang Ch'ing as Mao's new wife, Ho Shih-chen was bundled off to Moscow.

Though affairs between Communist leaders and party girls were not at all unusual, Mao's affair with Chiang Ch'ing became a scandal, especially among many of the idealistic young people who had come to Yenan, and particularly in view of Chiang Ch'ing's past history. When Mao sent Ho Shih-chen to the Soviet Union and demanded officially to marry Chiang Ch'ing, there was strong objection among the leading Chinese comrades. Chiang Ch'ing's ambition and gall had not endeared her to many of the leaders, and these characteristics could be expected to become more pronounced in her position as Mao's wife. Mao's demand was therefore resisted by the majority of the leading party members, but Mao's strong will and threats as well as possibly the fact that Chiang Ch'ing was pregnant led to a compromise settlement.[52] The marriage was approved under the condition that Chiang Ch'ing would stay out of the limelight and out of political affairs; and so she did at the time. The very humiliation of this conditional approval and of the years she was forced to stay in the background may well have contributed to the aggressive and dominant political role that Chiang Ch'ing played in the Cultural Revolution and its aftermath, when she had the opportunity to step out into the limelight of affairs and to take revenge on those party ladies who had been prominent at the time when she was forced to remain in the cave. Madame Mao became one of the leading figures in the Great Proletarian Cultural Revolution and a most trusted political supporter of Mao's in this great venture.

During the Chinese Civil War
Top: Mao (right) confers with Chu Teh (center) and Chou En-lai.   *Wide World Photos.*
Bottom: Mao studying maps.   *Wide World Photos.*

CHAPTER

IV

Communist Victory

THE SECOND UNITED FRONT continued throughout the war with Japan, though below the surface a grim struggle, through skirmishes and assassination, was carried on behind the Japanese lines. Yet neither Chiang Kai-shek nor Mao Tse-tung had given up on the possibility of a negotiated settlement of the conflict. Discussions between representatives of both sides were begun in May, 1944, at Sian, and continued off and on. Neither side trusted the other and the Communist position shifted back and forth according to their evaluation of their own and the Nationalist's strength at any given time.

Negotiations and Renewed Civil War

Mao Tse-tung's attitudes toward the United Front with the National Government reflected the current international and domestic situation. At times he praised Chiang Kai-shek as the leader of China in the war. At other times he sabotaged the United Front, and exploited the war to expand the Communist territory and force at the expense of the Nationalists. He could therefore be expected to cooperate with the National Government only as far as he had to, given a situation of necessary compromise, without ever giving up his final goal of gaining a full Communist victory in China. Chiang Kai-shek was equally aware of the limitations of true cooperation with the Communist side, but knew that the realities of the situation required a political solution. In fact, he had already pointed out in several statements both before and after the Japanese surrender that the Communist issue in China was to be solved by political, not military, means in contrast to the prewar policy of annihilation campaigns.

At the outset the Communists demanded legal status in exchange for their willingness to reduce and reorganize their armies into twelve divisions, and to change the name of their Shen-Kan-Ning border government to an administrative area of the National Government. The National Government wanted to approve only ten Communist divisions and tried to avoid a formal acceptance of legality for the Communist party; it suggested instead the establishment of a constitutional government for China through a people's congress. During the summer of 1945, when a new Japanese offensive threatened the survival of the National Government in Chungking, Mao stalled further negotiations.

American participation confused the issue. General Stilwell, who had been appointed by President Roosevelt to a position of Chief of Staff to Chiang Kai-shek, Deputy to Lord Mountbatten, Commander of the Southeast Asia theater, and Theater Commander of American troops, recommended a strong stand by the United States Government to force Chiang to make an agreement with the Chinese Communists so as to enable the latter to participate in a counter-offensive against the Japanese. His recommendation led President Roosevelt to place great pressure on President Chiang Kai-shek to come to terms with the Chinese Communists—even adding the threat that in the absence of such a policy, the United States "might end its support of Chiang Kai-shek."[1]

Chiang believed that Stilwell, in his preoccupation with recouping his lost prestige in Burma, had "exhibited complete indifference to the outcome in East China," and had, therefore, damaged the overall strategy. Chiang also held that Stilwell had little understanding for the political situation in China.[2] Eventually Stilwell's recall led to a new American effort supporting the Government of Chiang Kai-shek and simultaneously working towards a reconciliation or unification between the National Government and the Communist opposition, carried out through the mission of Ambassador Hurley, the appointment of General Wedemeyer to succeed General Stilwell, and later the mission of General Marshall.

The most important dispute between the National Government of Chiang Kai-shek and the Chinese Communists under Mao was their respective interpretation of the form the future cooperation should take. In essence what was at stake was the continued existence of the National Government. What Chiang Kai-shek was willing to grant was admission of the Communists in one form or another into the existing government structure and its military forces, while Mao demanded the formation of a new government and army in a coalition that would replace the existing structure. The word *coalition* was loosely used by the American side and the decisive difference between the two positions was not fully appreciated. This failure to grasp the true issue rendered the American mediation effort futile and led to a defeat of American policy.

At the end of World War II, the United States' part in the fateful events that brought about the Communist victory in China was based on two assumptions which appear to have affected United States thinking on the China situation. One was President Roosevelt's belief that he had come to an understanding with Stalin regarding the settlements of any future conflicts in Asia as well as in Europe to guarantee peace and to make possible the establishment of the United Nations. The other was U. S. confidence that the government of Chiang Kai-shek was capable of holding its own against the Communists and that U. S. pressure on Chiang would bring about a compromise which the Chinese Communists would accept. Neither Stalin nor the Chinese Communists fitted these assumptions.[3]

The declarations at the Cairo and Teheran conferences held on November 26 and December 1, 1943, respectively, had laid the foundation for a postwar settlement in China. At Cairo, Roosevelt and Churchill promised Chiang Kai-shek that the war with Japan would be continued until Japan's unconditional surrender, and that Manchuria, Taiwan and the Pescadores would be restored to China. Roosevelt also promised the arming the training of nineteen Nationalist divisions and a common campaign in Burma that would be designed to reopen the Burma Road for China. In exchange, Chiang Kai-shek promised to bring the Communists into his government after the war. At the time the assumption was that Japan would be defeated through a major campaign in mainland China, enabling the United States to guarantee such a solution.

At Teheran, Roosevelt, Churchill and Stalin reached the understanding that the Soviet participation in the war against Japan would occur in Manchuria, resulting in a Soviet military presence in that part of China at the end of the war. On that assumption, Roosevelt was willing to grant the Soviet Union free port rights at Dairen, the chief port of Manchuria. This understanding was extended in the Yalta Agreement of February,

1945, when the defeat of Germany was close at hand, and the strategic planning of the Soviet Union as well as of the United States and Great Britain turned towards the war in Asia. As a price for Soviet participation in the war against Japan, the United States was willing to deliver the necessary lend-lease equipment for the Soviet east Asian forces which indeed was essential for the Soviet campaign. Beyond that, however, Soviet participation was to be based on a political agreement on the future Soviet position in Asia. Aside from such stipulations as the maintenance of the status quo in Outer Mongolia and the transfer of Sakhalin and the Kurile Islands to Soviet sovereignty, a major concession by the United States and Great Britain was a promise to establish Soviet privileges in Manchuria, after Chinese sovereignty had been reestablished. Such privileges included railroad rights, the internationalization of the port of Dairen and the lease of Port Arthur to the USSR as a joint Sino-Soviet naval base. Since these promises were given at the expense of China, they depended on the concurrence of Generalissimo Chiang Kai-shek who was not informed but whose eventual approval was to be obtained by the United States president as promised in the Yalta Agreement. In exchange for these concessions, Stalin promised that the Soviet Union was to deal only with the National Government in China with which the Soviet Union was to conclude a treaty of friendship and alliance in the war against Japan. The whole agreement, bringing the Soviet Union back into Asia and into Manchuria in particular was therefore based on a new treaty relationship between the National Government and the Soviet Union, which predicated that at the end of the war the National Government was to be in control of China. For both sides in the Chinese internal conflict, action was thus circumscribed by the policies of their respective allies and supporters, the United States and the Soviet Union.

For Mao the new Soviet policy was both advantageous and disadvantageous. It forced him to accept the continued existence of the National Government as the government of China and to agree to Chiang Kai-shek's position that the Communists would be permitted only a limited role in this government yet to be determined. Any challenge by the Chinese Communists to the authority of the National Government, any civil war in China, would clearly be in violation of this agreement. On the other hand, it provided a great opportunity for Mao to enter Manchuria under Soviet protection and develop there a new military-political position. This latter advantage proved to be the decisive factor in the eventual Communist victory in China.

In this fateful development in Manchuria, American policy played an important part. In pressing for negotiations between the National

Government and the Communists, President Roosevelt had sent the mission of Vice President Wallace to China in the spring of 1944, which obtained President Chiang's agreement to establish a United States observer group in Yenan so as to strengthen the American role in the cooperation between the two opposing sides in China. In the summer of 1944, in answer to a request by Generalissimo Chiang Kai-shek, President Roosevelt sent Major General Patrick J. Hurley to China as his special emissary.[4] In November, 1944, Hurley flew from Chungking to Yenan to talk with Chairman Mao about a reconciliation with the National Government.[5] Mao Tse-tung exploited Hurley's naiveté to discuss with him a five-point proposal which included a coalition government and unification of Communist forces under the joint control of this coalition government. This arrangement would, in practice, have provided the Communists with a decisive share in power as well as in the supplies provided from the outside.[6] This proposal was understandably turned down by President Chiang.

Mao must have learned of the Yalta Agreement at the latest in April, 1945. This was the time when the Chinese Communist party held its Seventh Party Congress. It was a congress of victory for Mao at which he formalized his newly gained control of the Party. The congress adopted a new party constitution, which included in its preamble the Thought of Mao Tse-tung together with Marx and Lenin as the doctrinal guide for Chinese communism. This ideological recognition of Mao was complemented by his institutional authority. The congress elected a new Central Committee and a new Politburo. The fifteen members of the Politburo belonged to Mao's team with two minor exceptions. They included Kao Kang who was in this way rewarded by Mao for his support in the fight against the Internationalists, by now completely excluded from power.[7]

At the congress Mao gave his main political report "On Coalition Government" in preparation for the coming negotiations with the National Government.[8] This whole lengthy report was aimed at undermining the position of the National Government—always referring to it as the "Kuomintang government" and replacing it by a coalition in which the Communist party would take a leading, if not the leading, position.[9] Vastly exaggerating the area and population under Communist control, Mao contrasted the alleged democracy and freedom of these "liberated areas" with the "suppression" of the peoples by the Kuomintang. He was careful enough not to burn the bridges to all Kuomintang members of the noncommitted and reserved his scorn for that party's "chief ruling clique" of the "feudal and facist . . . big landlords, big bankers and big compradores," carefully exempting not only "large numbers of the rank and file," but even "some of the leading figures" of the Kuomintang from his condemnation. And since he never mentioned Chiang Kai-shek by name, the door of negotiations with the Nationalist leader and president of the government was still left open.

To make this demand for a leading Communist role in the coalition more palatable, Mao combined it with a program taken from his *On the New Democracy*. According to this program the Communists were for the moment aiming not at socialism, but only at a bourgeois democratic revolution which "may last for several decades," and during which private capitalism would be developed, and corporative enterprises and private property would be protected. Indeed, the whole program was not "socialism," which was something for the distant future, but the true application of Sun Yat-sen's Three Peoples' Principles, referred to and quoted about two dozen times in Mao's report.

Mao's appeal was clearly directed not only to the domestic audience but also to United States opinion and his several references to an "independent and free, democratic and united, prosperous and powerful" China had their echo in President Truman's famous statement of a united, free and democratic China as a goal of American policy.

The whole point of this lengthy exercise in skillful propaganda was, however, Mao's attack against the National Government's proposal for the election of a national assembly which would draw up a new constitution to transfer the state power to an elected government. Instead of this "cloak of constitutionalism" Mao demanded the immediate establishment of a coalition government that in turn would convoke a national assembly. The issue was the continuity of the National Government versus the Communist attempt to gain power under cover of a newly established coalition.

Four months later on August 14, 1945, the Soviets concluded the Sino-Soviet Treaty of Friendship and Alliance with the National Government based on the Yalta Agreement. Mao's refusal to deal with the National Government on its terms was abandoned; on the basis of this Soviet move, Mao Tse-tung accepted an invitation by Chiang Kai-shek to come to Chungking for negotiations on the form of cooperation.

Mao flew to Chungking on August 28, after Ambassador Hurley agreed to fly to Yenan and bring Mao to Chungking and guarantee his safety for the period of negotiations. On his arrival in Chungking, Mao published one of his best-known poems, composed in the style of traditional poetry of the Sung dynasty. In the setting of a Chinese wintry landscape, Mao extolled the exploits of heroes long gone calling for a new hero for China today.[10]

In the negotiations at Chungking, Mao was, however, clearly at a disadvantage. The collapse of the Japanese resistance and the Yalta agreement had placed Chiang Kai-shek in the position of authority over all China, including the territory then occupied by the Japanese. While not giving up his determination to work towards eventual victory, Mao had to drop his present demand for a coalition government and accept the reduction of Communist territory and size of the military force. On this basis an agreement was reached between President Chiang and Chairman Mao, sealed by a proper toast between the two protagonists.

Ambassador Hurley thus helped to prepare the political compromise between Chiang Kai-shek and Mao Tse-tung which seemed at the time to fulfill the hope held both in China and the United States that civil war would be avoided and that a "democratic" solution would be found, fair to all sides. This view disregarded the Communist purpose and in particular Chairman Mao's determination to attain his ultimate goal of complete military victory whenever he was strong enough. On November 27, 1945, Hurley resigned as ambassador and returned to the United States.

Roosevelt's policy was inherited and continued by President Truman. To carry out this policy, Truman sent General Marshall on a special mission to China to assist in the negotiations between the National Goverment and the Communists. Marshall arrived in Chungking on December 22, 1945, and with his help the peace talks resumed. The Political Consultative Conference (PCC) was convoked on January 10, 1946, and the agreements reached there seemed to formalize successfully the compromise solution reached during Mao's visit to Chungking in August, 1945. They provided for both short- and long-range arrangements in the political, as well as in the military, field.

These agreements were urgently needed if civil war was to be avoided. Soon after the Japanese surrender both Nationalists and Communists began to contend for the areas from which the Japanese were now withdrawing. Whenever they faced each other in this race for territory, the two sides challenged each other in local battles which threatened to expand into a broad-scale civil war. To prevent this calamity the first agreement concluded at the PCC on January 10 consisted of a military truce. Both sides were to retain the territory which their troops were occupying at that time; to prevent further clashes, three-man truce teams were to be sent to each contested area; the teams were to consist of a Nationalist, a Communist and a neutral American officer who were to draw the lines between the opposing forces. This agreement proved at first successful, ending temporarily all local conflicts in north China.[11] Politically, this agreement accepted the Communist claim that they should remain the proper authority in the areas of the provinces in which they had established border governments during the war. Mao's exaggerated claims, however, were reduced to a more realistic interpretation of Communist power.[12]

For the future, a Western-type parliamentary system, based on general elections, was to overcome the present stalement. To end the military conflict between the opposing forces, the long-range agreement also provided that the Communist army was to be integrated into the Nationalist army. The agreement determined the actual strength and distribution of units of National Government and Communist forces, which were both to be reorganized, trained and equipped with United States assistance.

If carried out, these agreements might well have provided a working cooperation between the Nationalists and Communists, valid as long as the Soviet and United States sponsors were willing to support them. The problem of the PCC agreements was that they drew a line of truce in north China between the opposing Nationalist and Communist forces, but established no such delineation for Manchuria; and Manchuria was to become the key area of renewed conflict. At the end of the war Manchuria was in Soviet hands. Since the Japanese had succeeded in eliminating all Chinese Communist guerilla forces from "Manchukuo," Manchuria was politically a no-man's-land as far as the Nationalist-Communist conflict was concerned. The PCC agreements had provided for proportional Nationalist and Communist military strength in Manchuria in a relationship of five to one, but it soon became clear that the Communists were not to abide by these agreements. The Soviets had promised to deal only with the National Government and so it would have been the Soviet obligation to permit the transfer of authority in Manchuria to the Chinese National Government. The problem of Yalta, the Sino-Soviet Treaty, and the PCC agreements was not the limitations these various agreements imposed on the National Government, but the fact that they were not kept by the Soviets nor by their Chinese Communist protégés.

This breach of agreement was not anticipated by the American policy-makers whose goal had been a broad understanding with the Soviet Union to be underpinned by the PCC agreements between the Nationalists and the Communists.[13] General Marshall, believing that his mission had been successful, returned to the United States in February, 1946, with the intention of obtaining from the United States Congress the economic support needed for a successful peaceful development in China. Before leaving, Marshall made a tour of north China to inform himself about the viability of the PCC solutions. Wherever he went in north China, the agreements seemed to work and in Yenan Chairman

Mao assured General Marshall that the Chinese Communists would adhere completely to the promises which they had given. The reality was quite different and it was in retrospect fatal that Marshall could not obtain a firsthand knowledge of the situation in Manchuria.

The Manchurian struggle, it now appears, was decidedly influenced by Soviet political and military tactics, which were instrumental in giving the Chinese Communists control over this crucial area. While officially maintaining the proper diplomatic courtesies towards the Nationalist representatives who came to Manchuria, the Soviets illicitly provided the Chinese Communists with the opportunity to establish themselves militarily in Manchuria before the Nationalists could arrive by facilitating the movements of Communist troops overland into strategic positions in Manchuria while placing every obstacle in the way of Nationalist forces sent by Chiang Kai-shek to establish National control.

American policy at this point seemed strangely contradictory and indecisive. On one hand, the United States provided the ships to move Nationalist troops into Manchuria; on the other, at least at a later phase, General Wedemeyer, the American military adviser, attempted to dissuade Chiang Kai-shek from sending a major force into Manchuria. (In his secret report, Wedemeyer suggested a neutralization of Manchuria.)

The danger of conflict in Manchuria had been understood by the American side.[14] General Marshall had raised the issue of sending tripartite truce teams into Manchuria. Chiang Kai-shek accepted this proposal readily but Mao had no interest in having the Communist moves and preparations for a takeover observed and interfered with by such truce teams, and Marshall yielded. When the Soviets denied the use of Dairen for the landing of Nationalist troops from American ships, this denial was accepted.

In the first frustrated attempts of the Nationalists to enter Manchuria with American aid, weeks were lost which were used to good advantage by the Chinese Communist troops to establish themselves in Manchuria in strength before the Nationalist arrival. Mao Tse-tung's promise to Marshall clearly was not kept, nor did the Soviets abide by their treaty obligations. Even so, the Nationalists were still successful in moving their own forces into Manchuria overland; and they convincingly defeated Communist troops attempting to block their way.

Mao Tse-tung had ordered Lin Piao to assume command in Manchuria. The force that Lin Piao was taking from Shensi into Manchuria was only partly armed; the deficiency was to be made up by the equipment surrendered by the Japanese to the Soviets in Manchuria. This equipment, including heavy artillery and tanks, provided the Communist firepower that was to be decisive in later battles. Chiang Kai-shek sent to Manchuria his crack troops for what he understood to become a crucial showdown with his chief opponent. After the Nationalist move into south Manchuria had been successful, the Communists attempted to block their advance into northern Manchuria at the rail junction of Ssup'ingchieh. Here the two armies, each over a million strong, clashed in what could have been the decisive confrontation of the civil war. The battle of Ssup'ingchieh between May and June, 1946, ended in an overwhelming Nationalist victory. The Communists sustained massive losses, retreat turned into flight, and it appeared that the whole Communist position in Manchuria was broken. It was at this point that international intervention changed the course of military events.[15] Immediately after this Communist defeat, Stalin, obviously realizing the danger to the Communist position in Manchuria, sent an invitation to Chiang Kai-shek to come to Moscow for a discussion of the Manchuria situation.[16] Chiang Kai-shek replied that in view of the serious situation in China, he was unable to leave. This decision by Chiang to decline Stalin's invitation was to have far-reaching consequences. Stalin clearly was attempting to come to terms on Manchuria after the Soviets' appeared to have failed to secure their interests by military means.[17]

Both President Truman and General Marshall counseled Chiang Kai-shek to accept the invitation but apparently did not pursue the matter strongly, nor did they understand the consequences of Chiang's refusal. Chiang realized his refusal endangered any future agreement with the Soviet Union based on National control of Manchuria. What he did not realize was that the United States was not giving up on the coalition scheme and would not match the ensuing Soviet support to the Chinese Communists by U. S. support to the Nationalists in the continuing confrontation.

Returning to China while the battle of Ssup'ingchieh was still raging, General Marshall counseled Chiang Kai-shek to abandon Manchuria because of the Chinese Communist strength in that region. When the Communist resistance had collapsed, Marshall's advice was for discontinuing the battle and accepting the result of a division of Manchuria, leaving the northern part in Communist hands. The main means at the American's disposal to force Chiang Kai-shek into abandoning his successful offensive was the refusal of American military support needed by the Nationalists to carry on the fight.[18] An embargo was consequently placed on delivery of U. S. arms and ammunition to the National Government. Faced by the American refusal to provide the necessary ammunition and equipment to follow up the victory, Chiang Kai-shek made the crucial decision to shift from a pursuit of his advantage to a defense of his position. This decision may have been the most important factor in the

Nationalist defeat in China.

In contrast to United States' restraint on the Nationalist side, the Soviets provided all possible support to their Chinese Communist clients. This support included not only military equipment which was provided from Japanese stocks, but also the transfer of a large number of North Korean troops to boost the Chinese Communist military strength. This force could more than match in numbers and equipment the Nationalist troops whose line of supplies from China proper became more and more precarious. In addition, the Soviets also provided all vital cooperation in facilitating and building up the Communist infrastructure in the areas of Manchuria which they still occupied.

Mao Tse-tung realized the importance of this infrastructure and ordered Lin Piao and his staff to build up stable Communist bases in the hinterland in order to broaden the Communist position. Without such bases he believed the Communists could not succeed and might even fail.[19] At the same time, Mao sent Kao Kang to Manchuria as party secretary of the Northeast Bureau. The Soviets facilitated the Chinese Communist moves through technical advisers, assistance with communications, and economic and political planning. This cooperation between the Soviet occupation forces and the Chinese Communists enabled the latter to build from scratch the kind of political structure which enabled them to recruit more manpower for their growing armies, and train and equip them for the attack against the Nationalist forces that started about six months later in the spring of 1947.

The decisive battles in Manchuria that followed were won by the massive use of artillery and tanks provided by the Soviets. In February, 1947, President Truman, aware of the Soviet policy in disregard of the post-war agreements in Europe, changed American policy towards the Soviet Union under the so-called Truman Doctrine. The Truman Doctrine, however, referred only to Greece and Turkey and its applicability to China was expressly denied in the mistaken opinion that the Chinese National Government was not threatened by defeat as a result of the Communist attack. Two months later when the massive Communist offensive in Manchuria had gotten under way the United States decided to lift the embargo on arms support to the National Government. The actual delivery of arms provided in the China Aid Act of April, 1948, came too late, however, to affect the battle in Manchuria and north China. It provided mainly for economic aid, and what military aid was included was inadequate and delayed by several months. Some of the major battles in north China and in Manchuria were lost by the Nationalists through lack of equipment and ammunition. By the end of 1948, Manchuria was in Communist hands and the best trained and equipped

Nationalist divisions were lost. Militarily and morally the National Government did not recover from this decisive defeat.

The last battle for the fate of China was fought around Hsüchow in the Huai River area. Over 2.5 million men on each side were thrown into this gigantic struggle between November, 1948, and January, 1949. It was lost by the Nationalists after bitter and very costly fighting in which brilliant Communist strategy outgeneraled the confused Nationalist command. By that time demoralization had already affected the Nationalist troops. Some of the armies surrendered to the Communist side. Here too, however, the lack of ammunition may have contributed to the Nationalist disaster.

This military defeat of the Nationalist armies was compounded by the rapid economic, political and moral decline affecting the National Government and its whole position. The civil war began at a time when the strength of the National Government has considerably deteriorated. The prestige enjoyed by Chiang Kai-shek at the time of victory in 1945 had been largely dissipated by 1947. As a result of the war and post-war dislocation, inflation had grown out of control and widespread corruption and waste had led to a general decline of confidence in the government and of morale that affected the Nationalist army. The National Government had also alienated important sections of the politically articulate minority—the intellectuals, students, professional class, businessmen and even officials. Though very few of these turned to communism, they became indifferent to the outcome of the civil war; and Mao's propaganda, concealing the real intention of Communist goals, succeeded in successfully exploiting that neutralism.

Mao's triumph was not brought about by any "popular revolution." It was rather the result of superior military organization and strategy and of Mao's dogged persistence in never yielding more than temporarily when at a disadvantage, never settling on any compromise, and immediately exploiting any advantage to gain the eventual complete military defeat of the National Government, which lost the mainland and retreated to the island province of Taiwan.

The People's Republic of China

From the rostrum of the main gate of the Imperial Palace, Tienanmen in Peking, looking at an audience of over a million soldiers and followers crowded in the large square in front of him, Chairman Mao proclaimed the establishment of the People's Republic of China on October 1, 1949. Mao Tse-tung's chief goal was thus accomplished; after

23 years of war, the Chinese Communist party, under his leadership, had won a complete military victory and conquered all China—with the exception of the island of Taiwan.

On July 1, 1949, the eve of the conquest of mainland China and the twenty-eighth anniversary of the Communist party, Mao issued "On the People's Democratic Dictatorship."[20] In this essay he announced the form and policy the Communist state was to take. Conforming to the principles laid down in "On the New Democracy," the state was to be formed by a coalition of the working class, the peasant class, the petty bourgeoisie and the national bourgeoisie "under the leadership of the working class and the Communist party." Democracy was for the "people"—those who accepted Communist leadership; dictatorship was for the "reactionaries" —those who did not. Against them the state apparatus, "the army, the police and the courts" were to be the instruments of violent oppression. Under this dictatorship China was to be transformed from an agricultural to an industrial country. The grave problem was that of educating the peasants, who had to be induced to accept socialization of agriculture.

To prepare this program, Mao called in September, 1949, a People's Political Consultative Conference (PPCC) in Peking. *Peking* means northern capital; it had been renamed *Peiping,* northern peace, by the Nationalists whose seat of government had been in Nanking, the southern capital, in the Yangtze area where the strength of the Nationalist support was concentrated. This site, selected by Sun Yat-sen, was close to Shanghai, the commercial metropolis, close to the industrial and trade centers of the modern Chinese economic leadership, and to the outlet and contact with the West. Peking, in the north of China, was close to the Soviet Union, China's Communist ally. It also represented the great memories and traditions of the past, the Imperial Palace, called the Forbidden City, a most suitable backdrop for the new Communist power. It was the logical choice.

The representatives called by Chairman Mao to Peking included non-Communists, members of the Kuomintang who had come over to the Communist side, and members of the Democratic League who had been willing to accept Communist leadership, perhaps in many cases under the illusion that a united front would permit them to play a part under Communist leadership. In addition, there were other non-Party members, people selected by the Communists to represent different professional interests who were called "democratic personalities."

The People's Political Consultative Conference met from September 21 to 30. It approved two major documents, a Common Program and an Organic Law of the Central People's Government. The Common Program was a restatement of Mao's essay, "On the New Democracy," and his later "People's Democratic Dictatorship," which had elaborated the same theme of the joint revolution of the four classes which were forming the government. The flag of the People's Republic of China contained in the upper corner the four little stars which represented these four classes. Once again, the Common Program declared that the joint revolution was to be led by the Communist party. The Organic Law prescribed the government of the People's Republic of China. The highest policy-making body was the Central People's Government Council, the members of which were elected by the People's Political Consultative Conference. Mao Tse-tung became chairman of the Government Council, which had four vice chairmen and fifty-eight members. The actual administration was in the hands of a State Administrative Council, a cabinet which consisted then of twenty members, each of whom headed a ministry or committee. The premier of the State Council was Chou En-lai, who in this position of prime minister became the key executive in the governmental administration. The military affairs of the new Communist government were handled by the People's Revolutionary Military Council, which had been in charge of military affairs during the civil war, and was now formally charged with the governmental responsibility of military affairs. Mao Tse-tung was also the chairman of this military branch of the government, thus maintaining control of the army in his own hands.

Though it was Mao Tse-tung's team that now took over, the appearance of a coalition government was maintained by placing several prominent non-Communists in positions of prestige. The widow of Sun Yat-sen, former Kuomintang generals and leaders of the Democratic League and other democratic personalities became vice chairmen of the Government Council. Among them was Kuo Mo-jo, a well-recognized leader in the fields of literature and historical scholarship, who had formerly been a party member and was now given the position of chairman of the Cultural and Education Committee of the government. None of these non-Communists held a position of actual power; indeed the government was totally in the hands of Communists, with Mao himself clearly the dominating figure. Mao was at the same time chairman of the Central People's Government, chairman of the Communist party, and chairman of the Revolutionary Military Council. His title, Chairman Mao, expressed therefore a number of positions of authority. Mao's closest collaborator was Liu Shao-ch'i, the party theoretician, who from that time on was regarded as Mao's most likely successor, sharing the writing of major party statements and preparing concrete institutional planning. Chou En-lai as premier of the State Administrative Council was in effect the executive head of the government and thus one of the leading figures in the new Chinese political structure. Chou also was foreign minister and became therefore the most prominent Chinese Communist in international affairs and conferences. Chu Teh, Mao's chief commander since Chingkangshan, though not always in agreement with him, remained vice chairman of the Revolutionary Military Council and in command of the armies.

The establishment of the Central Government left unanswered the question of the new administration in the provinces and regions of the country. In most provinces no Communist infrastructure existed as yet that could have served as the framework of a regular civilian government. The armies which had conquered the country remained therefore temporarily in authority, and China was controlled by army commanders. The country was divided into six military administrative regions by the Organic Law of the Great Administrative Area Governments of December 16, 1949. Whatever civilian administration was set up was placed under army control. An interesting power structure emerged. During the civil war, Communist forces had been organized into five field armies named according to the regions in which they were formed, and now renamed the First, the Second, the Third and the Fourth field armies, and the North China Field Army, sometimes described as the Fifth Field Army. These armies and their commanders were to retain their organizational cohesion. Each was assigned a major role in one of the military regions with the exception of Manchuria, which was under the authority of Kao Kang, with a combination of military forces. After the Korean War the troop disposition was partly rearranged so that none of the field armies was to monopolize a region altogether and a system of checks and balances was thus established, which gave the Central Government, that is, Mao himself, central control.

With the government established, Chairman Mao went to Moscow in December, 1949, to obtain from Stalin the support which he needed for his government. The fact that the Communist party in China now had established its own state did not in any way affect the party lines between Moscow and Peking; it only established a new basis for cooperation in official state-to-state relations. It was this fact that Mao Tse-tung had in mind when he declared that the policy of the People's Republic was "leaning to one side," and that there was no other way but to rely on Moscow.[21] Nevertheless, the forms of this cooperation had to be worked out, and the importance of the support which Mao sought can be seen from the very fact that the leader of the new People's Republic went to Moscow right after the establishment of the new government when he was certainly needed in Peking, and remained in Moscow for a period of eight weeks, obviously a most crucial time for him. The length of his

visit can be used to measure not only the importance of the agreement reached, but also the difficulties which Chairman Mao apparently
encountered.

In September, 1962, at the height of the Sino-Soviet conflict, Mao
expressed in retrospect his dissatisfaction with the difficulties he had
encountered with Stalin during this first visit to Moscow. Even after the
success of the revolution, Stalin remained, so Mao claimed, suspicious
of Chinese potential Titoism. And so, when Mao went to Moscow, "we
had to go through another struggle. He was not willing to sign a treaty.
After two months' negotiation he at last signed." Only China's entry into
the Korean War ended Stalin's lingering doubts about Chairman Mao's
reliability.[22]

The Sino-Soviet Treaty of Friendship and Alliance between the Soviet
Union and the People's Republic of China, which Stalin signed in 1950,
was, however, a major turning point in Asian affairs. It provided for
Moscow's support and military cooperation to the Chinese People's
Republic in the case of any renewed attack by Japan or any country
supporting Japan. The alliance was therefore directed by implication not
only against a defeated Japan but also against any attempt by the United
States to act against China from its position as occupying power in Japan.
Clearly, the treaty established a political division in Asia and resulted in
turn in the peace treaty between the United States and Japan and the
Japanese-American Security Treaty. The political line was drawn in Asia
by these two treaties—two years after the cold war had started in Europe.

An equally important purpose of Mao's visit to Moscow was to obtain
Soviet economic support. In this and in other treaties that were to follow,
Moscow provided China—though not generously—with credits needed
to revive the Chinese economy, suffering from many years of war, and
furnished the capital, the equipment, the technology and the advice to set
China on the road to an accelerated industrial development.[23]

The first year in power was a time of relative political moderations.
After the disruptions and devastations of the war, the new government
had to reestablish the communication network, revive the economy, reestablish production and commence economic reconstruction. Those
who had thought that the Communists would establish a real united front
policy and that their Communist goals were far in the future could feel
reassured about their first experience with this new Communist government. Indeed, facing the necessity of continuing a political system which
they could not immediately replace with their own trained people, the
Communists maintained many officials of the former National Government in positions of local authority until they were eventually able to
replace them.

During the first three years of Communist rule, the revival of agricultural production was facilitated by a succession of three good harvests. But the most important problem of recovery was in industry where the pattern remained uneven. Iron, coal and electric power still lagged behind prewar levels. But there was an increase in the production of steel, vital for the restoration of the transportation system and for military purposes. The most important success was in the rehabilitation of railroad, highway and river transportation systems, on which all other economic development depended. Of special importance was the stabilization of the currency and the price level, putting an end to the inflationary spiral. The control established over the major commodities through state trading companies and the deflationary credit policy of the People's Bank were the instruments used to accomplish this. A national budget and a highly centralized taxation system which was strictly enforced made it possible to restore the economy. This was the work of the party administration, Chou En-lai, Liu Shao-ch'i, and the administrative cadres.

Social Revolution

After a year of Communist entrenchment in power and a policy of moderation and economic development, there followed a period of social revolution. Chairman Mao was about to destroy the old order and replace it with a Communist totalitarian system.

Immediately after the founding of the People's Republic, Mao abolished the existing legal order. The National Government had established a system of legal codes for civil and criminal law which was intended as the foundation for the new Chinese social order replacing the Confucian moral code of imperial time. The five books of the Nationalist civil code were in part taken directly from the Swiss and German civil codes, which in turn led back to the Code Napoleon. The criminal code was based on modern concepts of crime and punishment. The economic codes were fitted for a Westernized free enterprise system. The procedural codes had established a three-level system of courts from the district courts up to a supreme court whose decisions were of great interest in providing the guidance for the introduction of Western legal concepts into Chinese society. In some cases, like in aspects of family or inheritance laws, Chinese traditions continued, but the Nationalist laws provided a whole new system of norms for a modern Chinese society.

These were the laws Mao abolished; he did not replace them. Leaving aside codes that dealt with the new political structure, the only law that Mao introduced was the marriage law which was promulgated in

May, 1950, to regulate one form of private life for which norms had to exist. This Communist marriage law did not replace the traditional imperialist marriage system as was claimed by Communist propaganda, but the Nationalist family law which had in many ways been more detailed and more advanced than the Communist marriage law replacing it. Under the Communist law, the marital age was raised by one year to twenty for men and eighteen for women, with the obvious intent of delaying marriages and population increase through regulation. Monogamy and free choice of marriage partners had already been introduced by the Nationalist laws, but in practice the Communist system of party approval for marriages introduced a new limiting factor replacing the traditional parental authority with a much more ominous political element in approving or disapproving marriages as a matter of political reward or punishment. What was more important still was the introduction of the marriage law in connection with the land reform movement in the form of a drive, the very form in which the new Communist social transformation was to be implemented.[24]

Like all Chinese Communist major upheavals, Mao's attack against the exisiting order was carried out not by institution of laws, but by political drives that affected the whole society. Mao used a mixture of force and suasion, treating society and social groups as pliable bodies on which calculated social transformation could be carried through in carefully measured degrees. The chief method was terror, which was applied on a national scale to whole groups and classes. In his directives on the execution of the drives, Mao Tse-tung often dealt in percentage figures, setting quotas for all those who should be prosecuted, found guilty and treated in varying degrees of harshness or leniency. It was always the political purpose which determined the measures to be taken, not any abstract concept of law. Such drives could be started, interrupted and abandoned when they had accomplished their political goal. This flexibility and ruthlessness of the repressive campaigns distinguished from the outset the Chinese Revolution from its Soviet counterpart and appears to have been Mao's personal stamp on Chinese politics.

The drives to transform Chinese society started with the Agrarian Reform Act promulgated in June of 1950.[25] Designed to bring about land redistribution for all of China by the end of 1951 or beginning of 1952—particularly in those areas which the Communists had not controlled during or shortly after the war—it was first implemented with moderation. The peasants were divided into landless peasants, poor peasants, middle peasants, rich peasants, and landlords. The line was to be drawn between the landlords and the rich peasants, who were to be totally deprived of their property, and the middle peasants who were to be expropriated but permitted to retain a unit of land which a family could work for itself. The landless peasant and the poor peasant were to be given the expropriated land. This land distribution was carried out without compensation, but at first without violence.

By 1951, after the introduction of other social drives, this policy changed. The landlords were attacked as the representatives of *feudal* exploitation and the purpose of land reform became not only the distribution of land but a destruction and elimination of the leading upper social group in the rural communities. It led to a ruthless persecution of landlord and rich peasant families, who not only lost all their property but in many cases their lives. This was carried out through so-called public trials organized in the villages all over China. The trials were not judicial proceedings but public performances staged after previously conducted secret hearings for the purpose of involving the larger part of the rural population in the elimination of the traditional leadership of the communities. Witnesses were found and briefed to accuse the victims of these trials of crimes committed in the past against their fellow villagers through many forms of exploitation, misuse of women, bodily harm, or any other crime of oppression. These accusations were often not true, but behind the testimony of witnesses was the fear of reprisals against themselves and their families should they not comply with the directives given to them. Any denial of guilt by the victims would only aggravate the situation. These public trials led to mass verdicts by the crowds that attended the trials and were to shout the verdict of *sha*—kill. Millions were executed and an atmosphere of mass hysteria and fear was created which left its deep impression in the years thereafter.

Smaller in number of victims, but equally harsh, were the drives which followed shortly in other segments of the society. The Korean War, beginning in June, 1950, could be used as background for consolidating social control at a time of foreign hazard. A law promulgated in July, 1950, initiated a *counter-revolutionary suppression* campaign. All "war criminals, traitors, bureaucratic capitalists, and counter-revolutionaries" had their property confiscated and were subjected to punishment ranging from three years' imprisonment to death. In effect, this law served to eliminate all political opposition against the Communists by attacking anyone who could be accused of having cooperated with "American imperialism" or foreign economic interests. The campaign was climaxed by the introduction of public trials, which took place in the cities, including major cities like Shanghai, where they were held with mass participation in the former race course and transmitted by radio to the largest possible audience. While this campaign affected many foreigners, especially foreign missionaries who were imprisoned and in some cases lost their lives, its chief targets were the Chinese who had cooperated with foreigners in the past.

At the end of 1951, there followed the *Three Anti-Movement* and the *Five Anti-Movement,* each serving its social and political purpose. The Three Anti-Movement was directed in name against the three evils of "corruption," "waste," and "bureaucracy." Under the accusation of having committed such crimes, many of the former Kuomintang officials, who at first had been left in office but who could now be replaced, were found guilty and punished for their alleged past sins. The drive was also used to purge many members of the Communist party who had misused their power or who had been found wanting in party discipline. It demonstrated that the full power of the state would be applied to all those who were not fully trusted or who would not carry out unquestioningly the order of the new government.

The Five Anti-Movement was directed against the business class in the cities. The evils to be attacked were "tax evasion," "bribery," "cheating in government contracts," "theft of economic intelligence," and "stealing of national property." Under these slogans, the government could accuse practically any business firm and businessman of violating these principles during the preceding years of political confusion. In a period of corruption, dealing with government agencies had indeed depended on bribery in many cases. But as with the alleged crimes of other drives, the action itself did not matter; the purpose was to attack a class and destroy its position. As in other instances, Chairman Mao set a quota of ninety percent for those who would be found very guilty, guilty, or slightly guilty of crimes committed under these categories. The business group was terrorized by accusations over the radio directed at persons who were invited to come to the party offices and "confess" their crimes. Denial of guilt would only aggravate the situation; the only chance for the victim was to confess some actions calculated to satisfy the accuser and yet avoid the hardest punishment. The manipulation of this terror led to large numbers of suicides among the victims. The verdict in most cases, however, did not demand execution; rather fines were imposed as punishment for past actions alleged or true. Often the amounts involved covered or exceeded the total capital resources of the businessmen or firm involved. To pay them, the government was willing to advance credits at reasonable interests. As a result, this drive resulted in the practical expropriation of almost all the larger and many smaller business firms under the guise of criminal prosecution. The businessmen whose experience and skill were needed were for the time being permitted to continue the management of their respective enterprises but were provided with Communist supervision which prescribed their very actions.

The use of raw material, the type of production, the wages, prices, and sales were all determined by the government so that in practice free enterprise was abolished. The business managers were permitted to draw a limited interest income from their private accounts as an enticement to continue working in the system. This form of private enterprise was continued until it was formally abolished three years later. Though this drive was less costly in terms of human life, the terror served the purpose of breaking any resistance against the policy of confiscation.

The years 1950 to 1953 were thus a period of terror and major blood-letting as part of the strategy of social revolution. No exact figures are or may ever be available for the cost in human lives, but some careful estimates range as high as ten to twenty million liquidated in these major drives.[26]

More crucial perhaps than these drives against social groups or classes was the ideological campaign carried on during the same period. This campaign was designed to break any resistance against Communist doctrine among the population in general and the educated upper group in particular. In September, 1951, a *Study Campaign for Ideological Reform* was initiated by Chou En-lai speaking to a large group of educators; it was aimed at "reforming the teachers' minds." What the educators must learn was the "ideology of the progressive elements of the working class, that is to say, the revolutionary theories of Mao Tse-tung, a product of Marxism-Leninism, and the actual practice of the Chinese revolution."[27]

A special method was developed to accomplish the kind of "thought reform" which has been popularly called *brainwashing*. The method involved so-called criticism, self-criticism, and confession. The form was the arrangement of "struggle" meetings in which one person became the target of criticism by colleagues; the person in question had to respond by criticizing himself and confessing whatever errors were suggested. In practice, it resulted in a form of mutual control under the supervision and direction of Communist cadres. The goal was to expose one-by-one the errors committed by everyone, errors caused by parentage, by having studied abroad, or by other bad influences experienced in their past work and teaching. Under the influence of the "Thought of Mao Tse-tung" the person in question was to abandon his or her "feudalistic," "bourgeois" or "imperialist" background and accept the "real truth" of Mao's teachings. The process usually culminated in written confessions which had to be restated frequently before they became acceptable. Under these social and political pressures, each individual had to abandon all intellectual resistance, at least on the surface, and accept the official line of Mao's Thought. This campaign, first introduced in the field of education, especially higher education, eventually became a general method of control and pressure on deviating individuals in any group. The so-called struggle meetings in which examples were made of objectionable behavior became a widely feared means of establishing uniformity and acceptance of prescribed attitudes and behavior. Physical mistreatment and humiliation were often combined with this procedure, one of the most effective and highly calculated methods of creating political uniformity and eliminating any independence of thought, let alone action. The impressive uniformity of expression in China, maintained even under the often sweeping changes of the general line as directed by Chairman Mao, bears witness to the success of this simple, highly developed method of controlling human behavior.

The drives were carried out simultaneously with the Chinese participation in the Korean War. The claim of a national emergency and of the necessity for unity helped to buttress the argument in favor of eliminating all resistance and opposition. The drives lapsed when the Korean War ended and when the Chinese leadership was ready to establish a more permanent structure of government.

To organize this new structure a constitution was prepared and promulgated at the end of 1954. Preceding it, a census of the population taken during 1953 resulted in a figure of 582 million people for the People's Republic, and a total of slightly over 600 million Chinese people, including Chinese on Taiwan and overseas. This census was used at the end of 1953 to elect under Communist control representatives to people's congresses on the local level, which in turn elected representatives for a National People's Congress of over 1,200 members to meet in Peking in September, 1954. The election of representatives both on the local and national level was in the form of voting for lists of single candidates prescribed by the Communist party.

The Congress approved a draft constitution prepared by a Drafting Committee of the Central Committee of the Communist party of China chaired in person by Mao Tse-tung. Though there were many parallels between this Chinese constitution and the Soviet constitution of 1936, the People's Republic of China remained a "people's democratic state led by the working class and based on the alliance of workers and peasants," rather than becoming a "socialist state of workers and peasants," the official designation of the Soviet Union. Yet the new constitution described the progress made since 1949. The preamble stated that in the last years, the task of "anti-imperialism," "anti-feudalism," and "anti-bureaucratic capitalism," had been accomplished, and China was on the way to forming a "prosperous and happy socialist state." Though China was still in a period of gradual transition during which it carried out socialist transformation, the conditions for the establishment of a planned economy had been created.

The constitution established a regular form of Communist government, replacing that of the Organic Law of 1949. The National People's Congress was the highest organ of state authority in the People's Republic; its function, however, was simply the approval of Communist policies and the transmission of the Communist program to a broader public for acceptance and execution. The highest government position, according to the constitution, was that of chairman of the Republic, held by Mao Tse-tung; Chu Teh became vice chairman. The chairman of the State Council or prime minister was to be nominated by the Congress on recommendation of Mao Tse-tung. Chou En-lai continued to fill this position. A Council of National Defense directed military affairs and was chaired again by Mao Tse-tung.

Mao Tse-tung was thus confirmed in all his positions as leader of China. He had vast and undefined powers as chairman of the Republic, chairman of the National Defense Council, chairman of the Supreme State Conference, and, much more important, chairman of the Central Committee of the Communist party and head of its Politburo. Liu Shao-ch'i, Mao's right-hand man in political affairs, and Chou En-lai, the leading administrator and diplomat, were a part of Mao's team and would at this time post no challenge to Mao's power. Though the constitution continued the fiction of a united front government, no non-Communist had any influence on party or government affairs.

This reorganization of the center was paralleled by a major reorganization of regional and local government. The period of military rule, of a division of China into six military regions, had been completed and the Communist leadership was ready to establish regular provincial and local administrations. Regionally, China was divided into twenty-nine provinces, autonomous regions and large municipalities. Below these major units there were districts and other smaller subdivisions. Each of these administrative units had its own administrative council which at least in name was elected by local people's congresses, in turn charged with the election of the representatives to the National People's Congress. The people's congresses were modelled after the Communist party though they included non-party members. Direct elections were held on the local level but as always the voter could only vote for a candidate slate set forth by the Communist party.

This political system was paralleled by a new military organization providing the ultimate guarantee for Communist power. China was divided into thirteen military regions, each controlling one, two, or in some cases, three provinces and municipalities; and each military region was subdivided into military districts. With the abolishment of the six military regions of the first period of the People's Republic, Mao had therefore established centralized control over the whole country. Party and government apparatus were greatly expanded to carry on the new economic and administrative tasks, but the military remained the chief guarantee of power, and Mao's own power was anchored as much in the control of the military as in his position of party and state leadership.

Within the particularities derived from the strategy of national wars of liberation and the tradition of the civil war, the Chinese Communist system paralleled that of the Soviet Union and other Communist countries, in which the Party was in control of government, military and all other institutions. The supremacy of the Party over government and the interrelationships between the structure of the Party and government structure was expressed in an intricate system of appointments at the regional and local level. A fully developed party structure supervised the government in all its functions. The party secretaries and the members of the local party congresses possessed the professional qualifications and the authority to supervise their respective counterparts in the government's councils and organs of administration. There was, thus, a double hierarchy, one within the Party and one within the government, the Party serving as the watchdog over the administration.[28]

On both central and local levels, it was Mao's team and Mao's staff that filled the new positions. Many of the military men who originally combined military with political power transferred from the military to the political structure, so that indeed the large majority of Chinese political leaders derived their experience and their training from their military careers. Thus the military element remained as predominant in the Chinese political structure as it had been during the periods of the civil war. If the positions of the political commissars with the military forces are considered as a part of the military organization, the vast majority of Chinese Communist leadership, including Mao Tse-tung and Chou En-lai, must be regarded as political-military leaders. The character of the Chinese political structure remained thus heavily influenced by this tradition.

Though the united front aspect of the political structure was largely fictitious, the broader concept of the Chinese revolution as a multiclass and multiparty enterprise enabled Mao to create a much more pervasive system of penetrating all aspects of society than the Soviet system of political control promoted. No other Communist country experienced such a proliferation of mass organizations as that established by the Mao leadership. In order to mobilize the entire population for the Communist purpose, mass organizations were established in any functional group to reach every individual. Such organizations for the workers, the peasants, the teachers, the students and the employees in the urban sections of the Communist society were grouped not only professionally, but also by sex, age and location. Organizations of women, of children, organizations of local communities, of city blocks, organizations for specific purposes on a national basis, such as the Sino-Soviet Friendship Association, and many others, encompassed practically every individual except those who were outcasts of society. Of special importance were the New Democratic Youth League, with its offshoot, the Young Pioneers, which claimed to have nearly one-half million cells and twenty million members—children and adolescents between the ages of fourteen and twenty-five. The All China Democratic Women's Federation claimed about eighty million members. Fifty-eight million members were enlisted in the Sino-Soviet Friendship Association. The All China Federation of Trade Unions claimed to include about eleven million workers. All these mass organizations were controlled by the Communist party, and their organizations were set up on the basis of democratic centralism.

Krushchev and Mao propose a toast, 1954. *Courtesy of Ming Pao.*

Mao is greeted by Krushchev at the First Communist Intra-party Conference in Moscow, 1957. *Courtesy of Ming Pao.*

CHAPTER

V

Handling the Soviet Connection

$\mathbf{M}$AO'S RISE TO POWER had been within the framework of Moscow's support of the Chinese Communists. There had been moments when Mao asserted his own stand and when he defended the interests of the Chinese Communist party in the global framework of Moscow's Communist strategy. But never had Mao opposed the policy of the Comintern; whenever he realized that the issue was decisive for Moscow, he accepted the Moscow line, albeit reluctantly. Mao's sudden change of attitude toward Chiang Kai-shek during the Sian kidnaping or his praise of the leadership of Chiang Kai-shek at the moment of Soviet concern with negotiations between the National Government and Japan in 1941 are examples of Mao's compliance. There are many more. And the recent Soviet attempt to reconstruct Mao's early policy line as representing a Chinese nationalism and "peasant mentality" rather than true ideological communism must be understood in the light of the present conflict and the Soviet political purpose to discredit Mao as a leader who had never understood Marxism but rather had been all along a "petit bourgeois fanaticist."[1] This Soviet attempt is no more historical than was Mao's attempt to discredit his former Chinese Communist colleagues and supporters—men like Liu Shao-ch'i and Lin Piao—as capitalist roaders and traitors who had wormed their way into the Party and had therefore to be destroyed. Ideological warfare inherent in the intra-Communist conflict must not becloud the reality of history. Even though Mao may not have been a great Communist theorist but rather an ambitious, brilliant and imaginative leader in his rise to power, it was the Communist framework in which he operated and to which he was loyal.

This attitude of Mao was early recognized by Stalin. In spite of all conflicts on specifics, Stalin regarded Mao as an able and suitable leader of the Chinese Communist party, whose rise to power he had never tried to impede but rather had approved and assisted while maintaining a cautious policy of surveillance, a policy he practiced not only in China but within other Communist parties as well. Mao recognized Stalin's support and not only stayed in line but participated generously in the build-up of the cult of Stalin. Soviet support in making possible the Chinese Communist victory and Soviet backing of the economic and political growth in China after the establishment of the People's Republic prove this logical development.[2]

The Soviet Model Versus Revolution; the Purge of Kao Kang

If Mao followed the Soviet line in its main thrust, he nonetheless made sure that his own team was free of pro-Soviet Chinese leaders. In the last phase of the war against Japan, Mao had skillfully eliminated Wang Ming and the so-called Internationalists from the Chinese Communist leadership. Wang Ming's purge had been made possible through the help of Kao Kang, and Kao, though he had joined Mao, was, strictly speaking, not Mao's man. He had been a political leader in Yenan before Mao's arrival and, though Mao had helped Kao Kang when he was in trouble with the Party Central, Kao Kang regarded himself as the man who had given Mao protection when he arrived with the survivors of the Long March —as "beggars in rags," as Kao Kang is reported to have said. As a reward for his assistance in the defeat of the Internationalists, Kao Kang was appointed, after the establishment of the People's Republic, head of the North East Bureau of the Party and its top administrator in industrialized Manchuria.

In the autumn of 1952, Mao set up a State Planning Committee in Peking and appointed Kao Kang as chairman. Jao Shu-shih, a second committee member, held a similar position in the east China region, which included the industrial and commercial center of Shanghai. Jao Shu-shih was also appointed as the new head of the organization department of the Party in the same year.

This was the time when a draft constitution was being prepared, to be accepted a year later, and when the military phase of the conquest of China was to give place to an organized political Communist system. This was also the time when Mao, the revolutionary, first came into conflict with his comrades in the Party over the methods of policy to be followed. The party leaders believed it was time to reestablish norms and administrative order for the coming economic development of the People's Republic. They were inclined to move cautiously both in agricultural and industrial policy planning to maintain and increase production. Serious thought was given to the introduction of criminal and civil legal codes into the political system.

The years from 1950 to 1953 had been years of mass movements. The law codes of the National Government had been abolished and had not been replaced by any Communist laws with the single exception of the marriage law. Now new codes were to be prepared; the chairman of the Political and Legal Committee of the government, Tung Pi-wu, one of the original founders of the Party, suggested this at the time. Tung, who had studied law in Japan and was now a deputy prime minister, declared that after the constitution was adopted, the Chinese Communists would no longer live by movements but by law. The adoption of legal codes would also be in line with the Soviet example where a legal system, albeit not in the Western concept, had been introduced to establish social cohesion in Communist society. At issue was the question whether the time had come to institutionalize the social and economic system created by Mao's revolutionary drives, or whether the revolution was to continue as a perpetual revolution. The orthodox Communist administrators wanted to see the country settle down into productivity and social order. Mao dreamed of a new China based on intermittent, continuing revolutionary drives, as part of a universal continuing struggle, forever reshaping human society. These conflicting goals were to characterize Chinese internal politics throughout the rest of the era of Mao Tse-tung.

Mao prevailed; no codes were written. The argument shifted to agriculture. The chief goal of the land reform drive was the elimination of the upper class landlords and rich peasants and the distribution of their fields to landless or impoverished peasants. Next, the Communists began to set up agricultural cooperatives in which labor and tools were shared by the members. When these arrangements did not work too well, resulting in decreased production, many of the cooperatives were dissolved again. Liu Shao-ch'i believed that the next step, collectivization, had to be postponed until mechanization, which alone would make collectivization feasible, was introduced. This order of precedence of mechanization over collectivization followed the model of the Soviet Union. Liu Shao-ch'i even declared that land reform was to go slowly, the disruption of the villages through agricultural drives was to cease and a rich peasant economy was to be preserved as a long-term measure. Liu Shao-ch'i stated in August, 1952, upon completion of the original land reform drive, that "big movements are not possible again hereafter. The main thing is to concentrate energy on economic constructions."[3] The assumption by Liu and other party leaders was that after the first major revolutionary measures had been accomplished, law and order and the increase of agrarian production were to be the immediate goals of Communist policy.

This was not Mao's view. Mao was particularly incensed when the first steps towards cooperatives were abandoned by many regional administrators. When Mao insisted on a continued policy of radical transformation of society and economy, he found not only passive resistance, but open opposition, among some of his colleagues who were going so far as to try to force Mao out of his leading position.[4] This group reportedly turned to Kao Kang, then still in Manchuria, who, after initial reluctance, indicated his willingness to join the opposition to Mao at the price of becoming either general secretary of the Party or prime minister, or both. In aspiring to these posts, Kao Kang threatened not only Mao but key members of Mao's team, Liu Shao-ch'i and Chou En-lai, who held these positions. Mao could therefore divide the opposition, singling out his most dangerous opponent, Kao Kang, and turn the issue from a conflict between his radical revolutionary tactics and the party leaders' belief in law and economic planning to one of personal rivalry and ambition. Kao Kang was also suspect for his independence of actions in Manchuria where, on his own, he had negotiated and signed agreements with Moscow for regional economic support and development. This challenge to Mao could therefore be interpreted as Moscow's influence in Chinese party struggles.

The conflict appears to have been fought out at a meeting in Peking shortly after Kao Kang and Jao Shu-shih had arrived to join the Planning Commission, and were therefore separated from their power bases in Manchuria and Shanghai.[5] The actual purge of these leaders which followed the conference took place behind the scenes and its details are not known. At the beginning of 1954, the case was taken up in a meeting of the Politburo and then of the Central Committee. Both Kao Kang and Jao Shu-shih were accused of having disregarded Mao and his leadership and Kao Kang was accused of having attempted to build an "independent kingdom" in Manchuria. At the time, the purge became known only to party cadres. In the spring of 1955 it was officially announced that both men had been removed from their positions and expelled from the Party and that Kao Kang had committed suicide. According to the announcement: "Kao Kang not only did not admit his guilt to the party, but committed suicide as an ultimate expression of his betrayal of the party."[6]

The purge of Kao Kang was the opening move of another reorganization of the political structure by Mao, who during 1954 and 1955, abolished the regional bureaus of the Party and the regional government administrations to strengthen his control through a centralization of government and party structure. The new constitution which provided the interlocking relationship between specialists in the party hierarchy and in the administration was also designed to prevent future provincial leaders from gaining the kind of dangerous autonomous power which Kao Kang had held in Manchuria. The prevention of the dangers of regionalism was all the more urgent since there had been "certain high ranking cadres," besides Kao Kang, who were accused of regarding "the region or the department under their leadership as their individual inheritance or kingdom." When the new constitution was proclaimed in 1954, Mao established central control of Party and government.

As a final guarantee of political power, Mao also assumed direct command of the People's Liberation Army (PLA).[7] Chu Teh, who was never regarded as a serious threat to Mao, was simply removed from his position as commander-in-chief of the PLA's and in practice was retired. P'eng Teh-huai became minister of defense. Mao thus survived the challenge to his leadership and strengthened his control; but the conflict between Mao's revolutionary concept of political movements and his colleagues' desire to institutionalize the economic and administrative system was to continue.

In the purge of Kao Kang, Mao removed a competitor not only of his political power within the Chinese system, but also a man who could become particularly dangerous because of the Soviet backing he had received in Manchuria. In his struggle for independence from Soviet control, Mao had considerably strengthened his position, without endangering the support on which Chinese industrialization depended.

Five-Year Plan and Soviet Support; Mao's Pressure for Acceleration

In the first three years of Communist rule, from the end of 1949 to 1953, Mao Tse-tung set up the major institutions of the new political system. Now he was in a position to create a new economic order. Thousands of Chinese Communist cadres had been trained in the Soviet Union, not only in tactics of military warfare and political organization, but also economic planning. As in the Soviet Union, they were ready to adopt the economic system beginning with a Five-Year Plan. The advance towards this stage had been faster in China than in the Soviet Union. The First Soviet Five-Year Plan was initiated in 1928, more than ten years after the Bolshevik Revolution, and the Soviet constitution was promulgated in 1936. In China, the Soviet-type consitution and Five-Year Plan were introduced in 1953 and 1954, four and five years respectively after the military victory in 1949. This accelerated progress was made possible by Soviet help, as well as by drawing on the models and experiences provided in the Russian case.

The Sino-Russian Treaty of Friendship, Alliance and Mutual Assistance of February, 1950, promised support to China in every field—political, military, economic and cultural. First, the military stipulations were designed to modernize the PLA through the introduction of modern weapons accompanied by large numbers of Soviet military advisers and technicians. Indeed, the Korean War served to transform the Chinese army from a guerrilla force into a professional army equipped with modern weapons which were provided by the Soviet Union in great quantities.

Next, the treaty dealt with "economic and cultural ties," and promised every possible assistance and the "necessary economic cooperation" by the Soviet Union. To pay for Soviet deliveries of industrial equipment and materials, the treaty provided a five-year credit, the equivalent of 300 million United States dollars; as with other Soviet aid, this was not to be a grant, but rather a loan to be repaid through Chinese exports of tea and raw materials. These credits were badly needed to revive the Chinese economy suffering from World War II, the civil war and the Korean War and to introduce the capital, equipment and technology, and the advisers to put China on the way towards an accelerated industrial development.

In 1953, with the initiation of the First Five-Year Plan, additional Soviet assistance was needed. After prolonged negotiations, a second agreement concluded in Moscow in September, 1953, provided Soviet equipment and technical aid for the construction of 141 large-scale industrial enterprises as contribution to the Chinese Five-Year Plan.

The first Chinese plan was announced worldwide by Chou En-lai in December, 1952. A State Planning Commission was set up at the time. As its chairman Mao Tse-tung selected Kao Kang, then still the head of the administration in Manchuria. The choice of Kao Kang to head this commission was another indication of the dependence on the Soviet Union for the new economic start. As administrator of Manchuria, Kao was in control of the region that was closest to the Soviet Union and Soviet means of communication. Manchuria also had the greatest concentration of known natural resources, and because of its development as the Japanese puppet state of Manchukuo, was the most highly industrialized area in China. It was therefore the logical place to begin the implementation of industrialization under the Five-Year Plan.

The announcement of the plan by Chou En-lai was not followed immediately by a list of particulars; indeed, it appears unlikely that at that time a fully detailed economic plan had been prepared. The public announcement listed a limited number of production goals for the first year only; this list proved to be tentative since the actual production results were drastically changed several times later. One of the reasons for the haphazard approach to economic planning was the fact that at the time of the takeover the Communist leaders had removed the whole statistical bureau established by the National Government. It was not to be replaced for some time. For that reason alone, Soviet help not only in economic aid, but through technical advisers and blueprints, was crucial for the start of this development.

The general aim was to build up heavy industry in China as rapidly as possible. The first 141 industrial projects to be delivered by the Soviets were mainly in the fields of electric power, mining, chemicals and metal. The emphasis remained the same when this Soviet aid was later increased to over 400 major industrial plants. To handle this vast program, over 12,000 Soviet technical advisers were sent to China. Chinese education had to be attuned to this Soviet aid; the Russian language became the primary foreign language taught in China, and Russian techniques were studied both in China and by Chinese technicians and engineers sent to the Soviet Union.

The capital for this development was to be provided from the main section of the Chinese economy, that is, agriculture. The Chinese peasantry had to provide both the labor and the tax on which the new economic development depended. In addition to drafting peasant corvée labor used in China since times immemorial, the Communists gained an additional labor force from the prisoner camps set up following the various drives of the preceding years. The use of this labor, limited to building and extending agricultural irrigation works and dikes and major construction of industrial plants, could not, however, provide the goods nor the capital needed to repay the Soviet government. This capital was to be obtained through the same method as applied in the Eastern European Communist states, a system of grain rationing and forced grain deliveries at prices fixed by the government imposed on the peasants by Mao in the fall of 1953. These deliveries were in addition to the already heavy grain taxes; they remained the basic source of income for the Chinese Communist state.

Enforced collection from individual peasants is, however, a difficult and costly enterprise. With the new Five-Year Plan, the time had come for agricultural collectivization. Under the administration headed by Chou En-lai and Liu Shao-ch'i, this collectivization was to be approached more gradually than had been the case under Stalin in the Soviet Union. At first, collectivization was to be voluntary and the peasants were to be "guided and helped" into accepting it. The initial stages were to consist of so-called mutual aid teams and peasant cooperatives. Without abolishing private ownership of land which had just been strengthened through the Communist land distribution, Peking arranged through the "mutual aid" teams for collaboration among peasant families in planting and harvesting crops. From this stage the cooperatives advanced to the establishment of joint ownership or use of implements, the cooperative buying of seeds and marketing of products, and joint administration of farmland in villages. The most advanced type of agricultural cooperative provided for the pooling of land by the farmers who shared in the income according to a scale in which their labor counted for more than their land, without abolishing actual land ownership. This gradual transformation from private ownership to collectivization was to test peasant acceptance and peasant resistance respectively, before introducing full collectivization.

By the end of 1953, Peking claimed that about half the toal peasant population was organized into cooperatives, but the transformation had encountered considerable peasant resistance; in many cases producer cooperatives had to be changed back into mutual aid teams. By the end of 1954, Chou En-lai stated that the transformation to collective farming would be slow and that by the end of the First Five-Year Plan in 1957, only about half the peasants would be organized into producer cooperatives. This was the policy as directed by Chou En-lai with the political support of Liu Shao-ch'i. It turned out to be not to Mao Tse-tung's liking. In July, 1955, Mao declared that full collectivization would have to be completed by the end of China's First Five-Year Plan and that industrial development could not be accomplished without full collectivization of agriculture. He accused his colleagues of being slow in carrying out the revolution, ridiculing Liu Shao-ch'i, though not by name, as "walking on bound feet" like old women of traditional China.[8]

As a result of Mao's pressure, individual farm units were transformed into cooperatives much more rapidly, and the number of cooperatives reached about a third of Chinese family farms by the end of 1956. Under this system, the land was contributed by the peasants and jointly worked by them, but a residual ownership was indicated in the pay which was calculated on the basis of work hours contributed as well as the value of the land of the individual peasant. This system, called *semisocialist,* was to precede the socialist stage of full collectivization in which the pay would be calculated according to work time only. The gradual approach used in reaching this stage facilitated the transition and eliminated the danger of opposition such as had occurred in the Soviet Union and in Eastern European countries.

What lessened the resistance to Communist policy in China, however, was not so much the gradual transformation as the fact that the potential leadership of any opposition had been eliminated during the land reform drives of 1950 to 1953, when the bloodletting in the countryside occurred. In the Soviet Union this had happened during the collectivization itself with the physical extinction of about five million *kulaks* by Stalin.

The lack of opposition encouraged Mao to accelerate the process, aiming at complete collectivization in 1955. Here he appeared to have overreached himself; from early 1956 on, there were reports of peasant resistance against collectivization. Such opposition could not be expressed by the defense of ownership of land, possible only through organized open rebellion, but rather through sabotage in affecting the handing over of farm animals and equipment. Rather than surrender their animals to the new collectives, the peasants engaged in "wanton slaughter," substantially reducing the animal population in large areas of the country. Directives limiting slaughter or sale of animals, equipment or products, by demanding approval of local governments, came too late and in March and April, 1956, reports spoke of a "spring famine" and of peasant unrest. As a result, the pace of collectivization slowed and rules against private production were eased. Pigs, chickens and fruit trees could again be privately owned and corvée labor for public construction of roads and buildings was reduced; these measures did not have sufficient impact on the agricultural difficulties caused by the collectivization program.

The main emphasis of the First Five-Year Plan, however, was on industrialization. As in agriculture, the takeover by the state of the industrial capital was arranged in stages. The *Five Anti-* drive had resulted in financial control of private enterprise throughout the country through fines imposed on business. In 1956 under Mao's pressure, the government moved on to the next step. The industrial enterprises, already controlled for all practical purposes by the Communist state, were now formally nationalized. Since their experience was still needed, Chinese businessmen were retained as managers at a salary; to induce them to use their full ability to further develop the industries and firms they formerly owned, they were promised a dividend of five percent on their private capital in addition to their salaries. To celebrate their "liberation," they were made to dance in the streets of cities like Shanghai in honor of the measures of Mao Tse-tung. Indeed it may have been easier for many of them to be released of the burden of responsibility without authority during the intermediate twilight stage before full takeover of their firms. The image of "liberated" capitalists was also propagated abroad, and a number of foreign visitors were given the impression that this was a voluntary and happy situation for the entrepreneur class now deprived of any vestige of previous ownership and authority.[9] The five percent dividend was supposed to be abolished in 1961, but was then continued in order to retain the services of a group of business managers during a critical economic situation. It was finally abolished during the Cultural Revolution.

The emphasis on industrialization was expected to continue under the coming five-year plans and was to be furthered by close cooperation with the Soviet Union. Some of the geographical planning depended particularly on a close link with Soviet economy. To make up for the deficit in agricultural production, plans were initiated to reclaim undeveloped land in outlying areas and Chinese dependencies and to resettle large numbers of Chinese farmers in border areas in such regions as Chinese Turkestan, northern Manchuria, Inner Mongolia and the provinces of the Northwest. Some 140,000 peasant families were settled in the northernmost area of Manchuria, and 200,000 demobilized soldiers were transferred to Sinkiang to undertake irrigation work and cultivation and to lay the foundation for additional Chinese immigration.[10] Another settlement was planned for the island of Hainan where Peking claimed that over two million acres could be used for special crops such as coffee, cocoa, coconut and hemp. In all, more than 250 million acres, according to Peking's claim, were available for agricultural development, provided capital support could be obtained; and since much of this development was along the Soviet frontier, Soviet support was obviously hoped for.

The same was true for plans to develop natural resources for industry. Extensive geological surveys were made in Tibet, particularly the Tsaidam area, and in Chinese Turkestan, where large resources of minerals as well as uranium and oil were discovered. To strengthen the physical link between Soviet central Asia and the new Chinese industrial areas of the Northwest and the West of China, two major railroads were to be constructed, one through Outer Mongolia towards Tatung and Peking, and one through Chinese Turkestan and the Kansu corridor to central China. They would connect the Soviet central Asian industrial center of Kuznetsk and the Russian Turksib Railroad, a triangle of heavy industrial development, with the new Chinese industrial regions. The line between Alma Ata in Soviet Kazakstan to Tihwa, the capital of Chinese Sinkiang, and from there to Lanchow in Kansu, connecting with the Tsaidam area in Tibet, would, when carried out, link the Chinese and Soviet industrial regions of central Asia in a joint development program. Until the Sino-Soviet conflict interrupted these plans, Mao's economic thinking was still perceived in the framework of Sino-Soviet cooperation.

Even in the assertion of his authority over the world of Marxist writers, Mao did not attempt to disturb relations with the Soviet Union. In October, 1954, the first attempts were made to discipline Chinese Marxist writers to accept the official line, now established by Mao's team. A book on the history of Chinese literature published in 1954 formulated the official standards for judging writers from the whole range of Chinese history. All writers of the past were to be classified according to Marxist-Leninist doctrinal interpretation of intellectual history. For the student of Chinese history it was odd to find the classical authors forced into the straitjacket of Marxism-Leninism with demerits and merits distributed according to alleged conformity with or violation of the doctrine of today. Confucius and Confucianism were found to have possessed some positive aspects. Confucius was described as "over-conservative, over-cautious, and not radical," but was believed to have "exercised a certain function according to his determined historical stage." The Confucian disciple Mencius was condemned as an "idealist" who believed in God and protected the reactionary aristocracy but was praised for his willingness to give more weight to the people than to the rulers and for his dialectical revolutionary style. Taoist and other schools of thought were also classified according to doctrinal pattern.

With this official tabulation of the past came the assertion of control over literature and its proper interpretation by the group around Mao which suppressed literary rebels, who tried to continue the satirical criticism that had become standard practice of writers in the last phase of the National Government. The case of the writer Hu Feng is the main example of this literary warfare.[11] Hu had been one of the favorite younger protégés of Lu Hsün, the literary hero of the Chinese Communists, who died in 1936 still a freewheeling social critic. Mao would not tolerate continued literary criticism of the new social order, and Hu Feng's group was broken up and he himself purged. Mao's group headed by the well-known leftist writer and scholar, Kuo Mo-jo, condemned Hu Feng as a representative of "the undercurrent of organized and capitalist-sponsored, anti-party, anti-people, anti-revolutionary movement."

This attack against dissidents was still in line with Soviet policy and when Mao's party writer Chou Yang spoke to the Soviet Second Writers Congress in Moscow in 1954, he asked that Chinese authors "should be allowed to be your [the Soviets] young brothers and disciples." Though Mao had begun to go his own way and to strengthen his own team and central control, he did not attack the basis of Sino-Soviet cooperation under which he had risen to the top.

The cooperation with the Soviet Union was written into the preamble of the Chinese constitution of 1954: "China has already built an indestructable friendship with the great Union of Soviet Socialist Republics and People's Democracies."[12] The Soviet backing, which had made possible Communist victories in China, guaranteed victory against future attack by the West by the Security Treaty of 1950. Soviet support was also crucial to the economic development of the five-year plans and was regarded as a logical part of the relationship of fraternal Communist parties and the practical foundation of Chinese Communist policy.

However, this relationship was not without its tensions, even during the first years of the People's Republic. The treaty of 1950 which Mao concluded in Moscow after hard bargaining implied a Soviet dominance in Chinese economic development. Though Stalin was willing to limit the rights gained in Manchuria on the basis of the Yalta Agreement and the Treaty with the National Government of August, 1945, and promised to return the railroad rights and the naval base in Port Arthur at the conclusion of a peace treaty with Japan or at the latest at the end of 1952, this concession was matched by an agreement for the establishment in Manchuria and Sinkiang of joint Sino-Soviet economic enterprises, indicating Stalin's attempt to retain a measure of control in the economic development of these vital industrial areas.[13] After Stalin's death when the new first secretary of the Central Committee of the Communist party, Nikita S. Khrushchev, came to Peking to negotiate a new aid agreement, he was surprised to discover Mao's hostility to the arrangement of joint enterprises, and, instead of expanding them, as he had hoped to do, agreed to relinquish them altogether. Under Khrushchev, the Soviet-Chinese cooperation was thus placed on a more equal basis than it had been before.

Stalin's death in 1953 removed from the Communist bloc the most important senior leader. His Soviet successors could not claim the same seniority or authority over other Communist parties and governments that Stalin had held. Indeed, the process of decentralization of control which had already begun during Stalin's last years was bound to continue and to lead to a new internal relationship within the Communist system. Greater autonomy developed than was held by the non-Soviet Communist parties when the Soviet Union was the only "fatherland of Communism" and when, through the Comintern and the Soviet police system, Stalin wielded almost unlimited power over Communist party organizations the world over. The change that was unavoidable with the establishment of new Communist governments, first in Europe and then in Asia, would perhaps have transformed the intra-Communist relationships in any event; but it need not have led to the deep and bitter conflict that characterized more and more the Sino-Soviet relationship since 1956, had it not been for a shift in the policy by the Moscow leadership that deeply affected the whole Communist world and particularly the relationship between Moscow and Peking: Khrushchev's de-Stalinization policy.

De-Stalinization in China; the Hundred Flowers and Poisonous Weeds

Despite the assertion of his own policy and occasional reluctance to carry out Moscow's directives, at times bordering on defiance of Stalin's orders, Mao had never broken with Stalin or challenged Stalin's position in the Communist world. There may have been an ambiguity in Mao's attitude based on an apparent jealousy of Stalin's power. When Mao later criticized those Chinese artists who, in their pictures of Stalin and Mao, painted Mao always "a little bit shorter" than Stalin, a common practice throughout the Communist world, it apparently was an irritation that grated still on Mao in the post-Stalin years.[14] Yet Mao's participation in the adulation of Stalin and his many statements in praise of Stalin appear to have been not simply matters of expediency and political necessity; as an admirer of historical heroes, Mao seems to have had a real appreciation of Stalin's ability to establish himself as an unchallenged leader in the Communist world and to have somewhat patterned his own role after that of Stalin. The praise of Stalin in which Mao joined is clearly related to the later build-up of the cult of Mao who became the "red sun in the people's hearts." On Stalin's death Mao wrote an essay dedicated to Stalin entitled, "The Greatest Friendship."[15] Khrushchev's attack against Stalin in his secret speech at the end of the Twentieth Soviet Party Congress came therefore as a shock to Mao and was contrary to Mao's whole concept of the role of leadership whether within or outside of the Communist system.

Khrushchev's "de-Stalinization" affected not only the Soviet Union but the whole Communist world. Several of the Communist leaders in Eastern Europe who had followed Stalin's policy and were now attacked as Stalinists were toppled from their positions and some lost their lives. Mao was vulnerable to the accusations of a "cult of personality," and of the excesses in the massive purges in China which were similar to those of which Stalin was accused in Khrushchev's secret speech.

There is no indication that the Chinese Communist leader had been consulted or even forewarned of Khrushchev's move.[16] Khrushchev's sudden attack against Stalin and the de-Stalinization campaign that followed came therefore as an embarassing surprise to Mao Tse-tung who to the very last moment had praised Stalin and built up his power in China in line with Stalin's Moscow model. Khrushchev's accusation that Stalin had terrorized the comrades in the Party, had caused the death of many innocent victims and had created the "cult of personality" could also be applied to China.

Indeed it came at the time when Mao's insistence on continuing revolution versus orderly economic development had met opposition from within the party leadership. It suddenly seemed to accentuate a potential domestic conflict for which there had not been any preparation by either of the opponents. Reaction in China was therefore cautious. After a period of silence, the *People's Daily* reprinted, in March, 1956, a Soviet editorial attacking Stalin and Stalinism. In April, the Chinese press began to write its own editorials downgrading Stalin.[17] But the tenor of this criticism was somewhat different from that used in the Soviet Union. The condemnation of Stalin never reached the proportions of the Soviet attacks. Stalin had made mistakes, but they were still outweighed by the great merits of the leader of the Communist world movement. Stalin's image was never destroyed and it was later revived in the People's Republic when Mao had regained the leading position that was threatened through de-Stalinization.

Even more cautious were the attempts to apply the lessons of de-Stalinization to the Chinese scene. Articles in the leading Chinese daily newspapers acknowledged that serious mistakes had been made in China too, but, at first, confined the accounting of mistakes to the period preceding Mao's leadership. After all, Mao could not, as Khrushchev, blame the mistakes of the past on a predecessor; Chairman Mao could obviously not de-Mao himself. Yet Mao could not avoid the impact of de-Stalinization on the Chinese leadership and escape the ensuing intra-Party struggle.

The new political course in China was taken up at the Eighth Party Congress of the Chinese Communist party in its first session held in Peking in September, 1956. Mao's role at the congress was clearly diminished—he gave no major speech—and the shift in policy towards the new Soviet line became visible. The most obvious change was expressed in the new party statutes adopted by the Congress.[18] In contrast to the previous statutes of 1945, the preamble omitted any reference to the Thought of Mao Tse-tung, limiting itself to Marxism-Leninism pure and simple. It stressed the importance of "collective leadership," by implication criticizing Mao's one-man rule. The statutes presumed to strengthen the position of the Party vis-à-vis its chairman by prescribing that the Congress, elected for five years, was henceforth to meet every year, thus, at least on the surface, to play a major role in the manifestation of Chinese

Communist policy. The Central Committee was to be enlarged to more than double the previous number, including many new members who owed no loyalty to Mao. The speeches made at the Congress proposed policies that followed the more liberal line initiated by Khrushchev and the Twentieth Soviet Congress. The president of the Chinese Communist Supreme Court, Tung Pi-wu, reiterated the suggestions he had informally pressed in 1953 and proposed in his speech the acceptance of basic laws such as a criminal code, a civil code, a law of procedure, a labor law and a law on utilization of land, which should be urgently introduced and be binding on the Party as well as the government. Criminal law was to be regulated, making possible the defense of the accused. This important move was indeed the only time that a proposal of this order was openly made in the People's Republic to herald, if accepted, a shift from the flexible policy of political drives to that of binding laws even though within the limitations existing under all Communist governments. The trend towards Communist legality was paralleled in the discussion on economic development with an emphasis on the production of consumer goods and on raising the standard of living. The Minister of Defense P'eng Teh-huai proposed a reduction of the armed forces and an upgrading of professional specialization, an improvement of technical equipment and the development of special branches, especially the air force. Most interesting was the attempt to reconcile the Chinese intellectuals to the Communist system and to counter the damage done by the thought-reform drive. Chou En-lai announced a program to build up the academic level of Chinese scientists in competition with world scientific development.[19] More respect was to be shown to the "upper level intellectuals," who were to be given better work facilities, higher material rewards and special professional treatment; some were to be recruited into the Party. In the statistical language of the Chinese Communist, the intellectuals were classified into forty percent who were "progressive," forty percent who were "middle-of-the-road," and twenty percent who were "backward elements." The aim was to reduce the number of "backward elements," transform as many as possible of the "middle-of-the-roaders" into "progressives," and to change all "progressives" into full "socialist intellectuals." To provide the climate in which the "intellectuals" would be permitted to contribute to Communist development, directives were issued indicating that it was "erroneous" to judge scientific theories entirely under doctrinal labels. Western-trained intellectuals were not to be denounced out-of-hand for their "bourgeois" thought and science but were permitted participation in academic debate as long as it was held within the "Marxist viewpoint, system and method." A "march on science" was to involve Western-trained scientists in the new Communist program. This attempt to draw the Chinese academic elite into the Communist program was combined with offers to Chinese intellectuals abroad, who had either been away during the revolution or fled after the Communist victory, to return and participate in the rebuilding of their motherland. They received letters from relatives in China or were approached by Communist contacts with offers of good positions if they returned to the mainland. At a meeting of the People's Congress in July, 1956, a domestic policy of "peaceful coexistence" was proclaimed and the Chinese Communists even admitted that in the preceding years during the drives against counter-revolutionaries, "wrongful" arrests were made and innocents were executed. In the future, the policy was to be one of "persuasion" and of "coexistence" with non-Communist individuals and parties.

This less-restrictive attitude toward the people at large found dramatic expression in the so-called Hundred Flowers movement. The turn about from repression towards more lenient means of control was clearly in line with the shift in Soviet policy. The removal of restrictions in the Soviet Union under Khrushchev had introduced the so-called thaw; *The Thaw,* the title of a book by Ilya Ehrenburg, became therefore the name of an era which was to end the ruthless policy of Stalin and presumably initiate a time of greater tolerance. The Chinese Hundred Flowers period appeared to be a similar attempt to shift from the repressive and brutal time of the great drives to a phase of greater tolerance and leniency. This new line was initiated in 1956 by the Eighth Party Congress.

The Chinese policy of *let a hundred flowers bloom* and *let the hundred schools of thought contend* differed, however, in character from the Soviet *thaw.* The *thaw* in the Soviet Union initiated a genuine literary protest against the atrocities of Stalin's time. Solzhenitsyn's famous book, *One Day in the Life of Ivan Denisovich,* was the first of a series of writings which, temporarily tolerated by the Soviet party and government, was eventually curbed when the criticism appeared to become too dangerous. In China such a literary protest never occurred.

The Hundred Flowers drive in China was a government attempt to introduce controlled criticism as a means to let off steam without affecting government control. No writers dramatized the sufferings of the past, no Chinese Ehrenburg or Solzhenitsyn stirred the conscience of Chinese intellectuals.

The slogan, *let the hundred schools of thought contend,* referred to an early age of Chinese history between the sixth and third centuries B.C. when contending schools of thought dealt with the problems of creating new ethical beliefs and loyalties during a chaotic period of transition from earlier feudalism to what became the bureaucratic order of imperial

China. For the Communists the slogan simply meant permissible and regulated criticism of lesser ills within the system. Together with another historical slogan, *let the hundred flowers bloom,* it was to serve a phase of lessening the pressure as a safety valve for accumulated discontent. These slogans were first introduced by the director of the propaganda department of the Central Committee, Liu Ting-yi; speaking in May, 1956, to a group of intellectuals in Peking, he proclaimed:

> *The Chinese Communist Party advocates [that] a hundred flowers bloom for literary works and a hundred schools of thought contend in the scientific field . . . to promote the freedom of independent thinking. Freedom of debate, freedom of creation and criticism, freedom of expression, one's own opinion. . . .*[20]

In this claim there seemed to be unlimited possibilities for a broadening of China's Communist policy, broader even than that permitted at the time in the Soviet Union.

Quickly Mao took the lead in applying the new policy. At a Central Committee meeting in November, 1956, he introduced the first application by welcoming criticism from "democratic party" members and other non-Communists of mistakes made by the Party, mistakes of "subjectivism," "factionalism," and "bureaucratism," held responsible for the repressive aspects of party policy in the previous period. At a Supreme State Conference in February, 1957, Mao publicized this policy to an audience that included non-Communists, in a speech entitled "On the Correct Handling of Contradictions Among the People," later called the Hundred Flowers speech, because it gave the widest publicity to the slogan. Mao admitted that mistakes had been made in the past and that there had been "excesses." The ideological remolding had been "carried on in a somewhat rough and ready way" and the "feelings of some people had been hurt." But these excesses Mao ascribed to the zeal of lower cadres, certainly not to his own policy and they were excused by the fact that "the main thing is that we have achieved successes." He promised, however, that there would be a survey of the past and where necessary "exoneration and rehabilitation,"—though the spirits of the functionaries should not be dampened.[21] For this purpose Mao invited criticism within the framework of the Communist system. The reason for this new policy was apparent from Mao's references to the Hungarian Revolution. It was obviously the purpose of the Hundred Flowers policy to deflect any similar resentment that might exist in China into controlled channels.

A major emphasis in Mao's speech was the distinction he drew between "antagonistic" and "non-antagonistic" contradictions.[22] The "non-antagonistic" contradictions were those which could be resolved peacefully and by persuasion among the "people"; the "antagonistic" contradictions were those with the "enemy" which could be resolved only by force. According to Mao such "non-antagonistic" contradictions were possible within the working class, the intelligentsia and the national bourgeoisie, and between these classes, and even between "the government and the masses." The possibility that the Communist party itself, the vanguard of the proletariat, could be alienated from the masses and could be wrong, to be found in this startling admission of the causes of mistakes made under Communist leadership can, in retrospect, be seen as Mao's theoretical justification for his later attack against the Party when it refused to follow him.

The concept of two types of contradictions permitted a flexible policy, for it was up to the Communist leaders, that is, to Mao, to decide which contradictions were "non-antagonistic," and which were "antagonistic"; in other words, who were the "people," and who was the "enemy"; and, what was more, any "non-antagonistic" contradictions if not properly treated could turn into "antagonistic" contradictions. In other words, anybody who was "people" today could be "enemy" tomorrow—at the discretion of the leader's decision. In Mao's words, at this stage of socialism, "all classes, strata, and social groups which approved, supported, and worked for the cause of socialist construction belong to the categories of the people, while those social forces and groups which resist the socialist revolution, and are hostile to and try to wreck socialist constructions are enemies of the people." The first type of contradictions among the people "are not antagonistic. But if they are not dealt with properly, or if we relax our vigilance or lower our guard, antagonism may arise." Whatever leeway Mao was willing to give to criticism, was, therefore, not only circumscribed but was flexible enough to crush such opposition whenever the opportunity arose.[23]

If Mao had hoped to reflect criticism and to control dissatisfaction, the result of the Hundred Flowers speech would rapidly disillusion him and other leaders. At first, remembering the terror of the drives, people were distrustful and hesitant to speak openly and critically of Communist policy. But when a few hardy souls made critical statements published in the daily news and no dire consequences occurred many others began to trust the promises of no retaliation. A wave of criticism and demonstrations exploded in protest against the Communist party itself and its leaders and policies. If Mao had hoped to prevent any large meetings and permit only limited criticism in small groups under supervision of Communist cadres, he was soon disappointed. The new protest took on the character of a mass movement. In at least two universities, mass demonstrations were avoided only by suspension of classes, but soon non-Communist academic and political leaders were openly expressing their disillusionment. Strikes and peasant riots occurred in several parts of the country, large student protest meetings climaxed in attacks against the Party and its officials. Communist cadres were physically attacked and some were killed. Even Communists participated in the rash of criticism that spread nationwide. It was this unexpected development which forced Mao in June, 1957, shortly after publication of his Hundred Flowers speech, to retract his policy.

At the end of June, 1957, Mao Tse-tung issued a new directive to the Communist police to deal with counter-revolutionaries and preserve public order and security; he also forbade the criticism meetings at the local level. A wave of repression followed. A month later the obvious failure of the policy of controlled criticism was explained away in the *People's Daily* as a trap to entice potential enemies to reveal themselves so that they could be destroyed. The Hundred Flowers campaign had been a means of bringing out the "poisonous weeds" so that they could be eradicated. Speeches and articles denounced counter-revolutionary traitors who were accused of having collaborated with American imperialism. A campaign of criticism and self-criticism, of denunciation and humiliating confessions followed. The most outspoken critics were purged and some were executed. A new *Anti-Rightist drive* was introduced. In addition to non-Communist political figures, such as members of the Democratic League, and some university professors, the anti-rightist drive became directed against students and indeed against Communist party members themselves who had shared in the criticism, eventually even involving some military leaders. The massive campaign to weed out all those guilty demonstrated something about the extent of the discontent. According to the minister of public security, over a million and a half people were investigated and more than 100,000 were discovered to be counter-revolutionaries. Among those found guilty were 5,000 members of the Communist party and 3,000 members of the Communist Youth League. The major form of purge for the dissidents was the *hsia-fang* movement. Those to be reformed were sent to the countryside to be educated through manual labor. The drive began as a movement against teachers and students who lost their positions at universities. In this way, forty percent of the students of the People's Communist University in Peking were sent to rural areas to work on collective farms.

This *hsia-fang* movement became for some a permanent removal from studies, the end of their career and a condemnation to rural labor. For others, it was a temporary assignment, usually for indefinite periods, which meant that the threat or permanency and of transfer to the status of agricultural worker could be used to coerce pliant behavior. The fiction was maintained that the transfer to rural labor was voluntary. The tens of thousands, and in fact millions, of young and sometimes older people who eventually were sent to join the peasants were sent off at the railroad stations with flowers and musical bands and had to express their happiness about the change in their fortunes. In November, 1957, Peking claimed that some three million students and teachers had been sent to rural sections to work on collective farms.

Even the most enthusiastic students were soon dismayed by the primitive living conditions that awaited them and the poor reception often given by the peasants to youngsters untrained for hard physical work; in turn the peasants were often unwilling to share their limited food supply with the soft hands from the city who could not even speak the peasants' language. The resulting disillusionment was so severe that it led to suicides, to secret escapes to the cities and large-scale alienation of this section of the younger generation that was to trouble the government for years to come.

This was clearly not foreseen by the government for whom the *hsia-fang* movement served a double purpose. In addition to intimidating the intellectual and future intellectual leadership of the country, it was obviously meant to bolster agricultural production and agricultural life by bringing educated people to the rural areas. Among them were party cadres and others, many of them anxious to earn their return by faithful execution of Communist policy. By placing them in the rural areas to "work and live with the masses," Mao hoped to establish a two-way link which was meant to facilitate Communist policy in the countryside.

The *hsia-fang* movement continued after its first political purpose was fulfilled.[24] In years to come, students, communist functionaries, and military men were "sent down" as a matter of discipline and warning. Physical labor in agriculture or other manual work was to prevent this leading group from becoming "alienated from the masses," and to retain perspective of their dependency on the Party. A special effort was made to undermine the self-respect of self-conscious academics by humiliating manual labor, such as carrying manure and similar tasks. *Hsia-fang* remained a major part of Mao's program of maintaining control over the social and political hierarchy. It led to the permanent institution of what amounted to forced labor for a large section of educated Chinese.[25]

With the change in policy from the Hundred Flowers to the Anti-Rightist movement, the program of modifying Communist policies was abandoned. The promises of the introduction of a legal system, for instance, were never mentioned again.

In the summer of 1957, Khrushchev called an intra-party Conference of all Communist parties to Moscow to discuss Communist policy in light of the new Soviet line.[26]

Mao himself journeyed to Moscow to participate in the intra-Communist meeting and to assert his position. This was the time when Soviet prestige had been raised by the success of space exploration. The Soviet *Sputnik*, which had such impact in the United States because of the realization of the tremendous technical gains made by the Soviet Union, impressed the Communist world with the strength of Soviet leadership. It was used by Mao to demand in Moscow a harder political line towards the United States and the West. In a five-hour speech in November, 1957, at Moscow University, Mao claimed that the Communist world had gained the upper hand in competition with the West and could force the Western powers to major concessions; in Mao's words: "The East Wind prevails over the West Wind."[27] In expressing this harder political line, Mao tried to establish a claim to a leading role in international communism as a participant in the framing of overall Communist policy. This demand for a harder Communist policy towards the West ran directly counter to Khrushchev's new strategy of "peaceful coexistence" and was therefore simply ignored. Mao had no luck either with his demand that, as a senior Communist leader, he should become a participant in the framing of overall Communist policy. If he took part in the decision making, Mao would not be again surprised and threatened by sudden policy shifts as he was by Khrushchev's de-Stalinization. Mao demanded therefore from Khrushchev "real" not only formal consultation. But Mao was ignored by Khrushchev and returned to Peking from Moscow with the realization that his position in China and in international Communism could only be asserted by challenging the present political leadership in Moscow. This challenge led to the Sino-Soviet conflict.

The Great Leap Forward

Top: Backyard steel furnaces.   *Courtesy of Ming Pao.*
Middle: Workers in a commune labor behind their rifles.   *Courtesy of Ming Pao.*
Bottom: Night labor.   *Courtesy of Ming Pao.*

CHAPTER

VI

The Sino-Soviet Conflict

Mao tse-tung's policy in China had been based on cooperation with the Soviet Union and on Soviet support. The expansion of Chinese economic development under the First Five-Year Plan depended on Soviet credits, factories, blueprints and technical advisers. It was obvious that this Chinese dependence on Moscow could be exploited by Khrushchev to force the Chinese leadership into line. A successful challenge to Khrushchev could only be undertaken if the People's Republic could become independent of Moscow's help. It was this realization that was instrumental in introducing Mao's next spectacular move—the Great Leap Forward.

The Great Leap Forward

The Great Leap Forward was Mao's rather fantastic attempt to move China directly to the stage of communism through a superhuman effort in massive organization. In Moscow, Mao had failed to persuade Khrushchev to admit him to the highest council of Communist policy making for cooperation on the overall political line. After having been turned down Mao could expect that Khrushchev would use every economic leverage at his command to force Mao and the Chinese leadership into line with Soviet decisions. Mao was vulnerable and if he was to survive under the new Communist international line against the "cult of personality" and for the introduction of collectivized leadership in China, he had to become independent from this Soviet economic support. In his effort to defy the de-Stalinization policy as applied to him in China, the Great Leap Forward was Mao's attempt to become self-sufficient economically by dint of China's own effort.

Mao's position was aggravated by his conflict over economic policy with his colleagues in the party leadership. His demand for rapid collectivization had met some passive resistance and had resulted in the decline of agricultural production. A retreat from this policy because of popular resistance would have further weakened Mao's position vis-à-vis the party leadership. Mao could not afford to give up his agricultural goals without adding internal defeat to the outside threat. Had it not been for this danger, Mao would have had a choice in domestic policy; he could have again permitted more private farming, as had been done in other Communist countries. The other, more risky, policy was to move ahead by enforcing even stricter control over all agricultural production. Under the circumstances, Mao almost had to choose the latter path and move towards all-out Communist transformation, a policy which may have been in any case more in accord with Mao's temper.

The Great Leap Forward therefore was Mao's attempt to speed up the Chinese advance towards communism on the basis of the development of China's own resources and complete control of labor in large-scale, quasi-military organizations in order to increase rapidly China's production, to solve the growing agricultural crisis, to offset capital shortages and to replace Soviet aid on which, as Mao realized, he could no longer rely. It was Mao's most decisive move to free himself from Soviet control.

This extraordinary venture was the first demonstration on a grand scale of Mao's almost mystic revolutionary conception of his own leadership ability in organizing and driving "the masses" towards his visionary goals. Here Mao broke for the first time with the structural tradition and economic strategy of the Communist party system to engage in a quasi-military mass mobilization effort through which he could, in his belief, accomplish an immediate social, economic and indeed ideological transformation of China towards an instant Communist order.

Mao did not yet exclude the Communist party from his fantastic plan of action, but it was "the people" who, in Mao's faith would become the dynamic force who, led by him, could accomplish the near impossible.

In a famous passage of an article published in April, 1958, Mao wrote: "The decisive factor, apart from the leadership by the Party, is our six hundred million people. The more the people, the more the views and suggestions, the more intense the fervor, and the greater the energy."[1]

It was Mao, however, who was to initiate and direct this energy according to his plans: "Apart from their other characteristics, China's 600 million people have two remarkable peculiarities. They are, first of all, poor and secondly, blank. This may seem like a bad thing, but it is really a good thing. Poor people want change, want to do things, want revolution. A clean sheet of paper has no blotches, and so the newest and most beautiful words can be written on it. The newest and most beautiful pictures can be painted on it." Mao would fill in the blanks.

In May, 1958, at the second session of the Eighth Party Congress, Liu Shao-chi announced for Mao the program of the Great Leap Forward, which was then already under way.[2] It was sloganized under the *Three Red Banners:* the *General Line,* the *Great Leap Forward,* and the *People's Communes.* Popularly it became known under the second slogan, as the *Great Leap Forward.*[3] The idea behind the whole program was to use militarized manpower instead of capital equipment to speed up and increase economic production.

The most radical part of this program was the establishment of a system of *communes* throughout China. The communes were intended to group large numbers of collective farms combined with local towns into huge centralized systems which would direct the work in agriculture, in local industry, and indeed in any other field of human life. Where the collective farms had organized the villages into work teams comprised largely of local village communities, the communes consisted of from several tens of thousands to about 200,000 people in a massive organization of human labor. All China was to be organized into some 26,000 communes, at the beginning encompassing rural areas and townships, and eventually larger cities as well.

Under this plan all private labor, effort and indeed private life were to be replaced by the collective community. All people in a commune were organized in quasi-military fashion for work and life. The people of each commune were to live together in barracks; family houses were to be demolished, the material to be used for construction of community barracks. Commune members were to eat together in the barrack mess halls, fed by communal kitchens, and were to be organized in work teams whose labor could be applied alternately to rural or industrial work.

In this extreme form, which was described in the Central Committee's resolutions and in the leaders' speeches and glorified in newspaper articles, communes were to replace the family. Husband and wife were assigned to labor teams which might be allotted not only separate tasks, but different areas in which to work. The communal kitchen replaced family cooking; pots and pans of families were collected in scrap drives and melted for the use of metal. Children were to be cared for in communal nurseries and schools, and live in dormitories. Old people were assigned to *old peoples' happy homes,* where they were to work according to their ability. Since husbands and wives could be assigned to different teams, family life would be broken up, and the separation of children and older people would indeed destroy the family unit.

With the establishment of the communes, the remnants of private property which had survived collectivization, such as garden plots, and ownership of small animals, were to be abolished. Labor was to be paid for largely in kind; all people were provided with clothing and with food from the communal kitchen. Health, education, and other needs, including burial expenses, were to be taken care of by the communes. In the propaganda of the time, communal life was the introduction of a stage in which everyone was to be provided for *according to his need,* the final goal of the Communist millennium.

Commune organization was quasi-military in character. The members were assigned to squadrons, formed into companies, battalions, regiments and divisions, and in addition to the organization of labor in this form, these units were also to provide regular military training—for women as well as for men—in a people's militia. The population's whole life was to be regimented in military exactness. At six o'clock in the morning there was reveille and then the units marched in military formation to and from work. The rest of the day was organized in similar fashion. Evenings were filled with indoctrination and communal recreation.

The organization of the communes corresponded in size to what had been the smallest administrative unit of government in Chinese tradition, the *hsiang.* In some cases, commune organization and direction was actually taken over by the party organization at this level; and, in a sense, a social organization under party leadership could be expected to replace the formal government by the state, a development that could be interpreted as the Communist goal of the *self-regulating collective* and the *withering away of the state.* These claims, the possibility of giving to everybody according to his need and the transformation of the social structure in the form of a self-regulating collective, were the bases of Mao Tse-tung's claim that in this way China, indeed, was reaching the stage of communism.

Mao Tse-tung's economic goal was to achieve, through such intensive labor organization and control, a massive increase in production without the need of outside support. Commune labor teams were given assignments that far surpassed the time and effort spent on production under normal life. Production goals were set that could be attempted only through whipping up a spirit of competitive labor that demanded the utmost effort and time. Actually, even at night, there was little time for rest. The resulting weakness, illness and death eventually necessitated a regulation that at least eight hours of rest should be provided during the twenty-four hours of the day.

In this effort, spirit was to be maintained by military élan. The whole Great Leap was described in military terminology; labor became a military campaign; production was accomplished through "victories." The purpose was the massive increase of both agricultural and industrial production. The assignment of the same labor teams to agricultural as well as industrial production was apparently influenced by the belief of Marx that *socialist man* would be an all-round person who could extend his work efforts to many fields: the idealized future man in this Marxist-utopian view took the place of professional or class specialization of the capitalist world. Thus, in Mao's plan, the members of the communes could one day plant crops, fertilize the fields, or build dikes or irrigation systems in agricultural labor, and the next day work in steel production or other industrial fields.

If, under Mao's new economic vision, China was to replace capital by labor as far as that would be possible, it had also to replace the economic centralization provided for in Soviet planning through a program of decentralized economic development based on the labor intensive system of the communes. In industry that meant that emphasis had to be shifted from construction of a small number of major industrial plants to the building of a vast number of small enterprises to be established all over the country with little capital investment. This was the work of the communes and of the communal labor teams.

The most sensational aspect of this diversified and small-scale type of industrial development was the *backyard steel furnaces*. These much-publicized, small-scale production units were built all over China, both in the rural communities and in the cities. In the cities, such furnaces were to be worked by office staff and clerks who were to produce steel during their lunch hours and other off-work time. The claim was that in October, 1958, fifty million people were engaged in this way in iron and steel production in over 600,000 backyard steel furnaces. Scrap iron from pots and pans and other material goods collected from individual households would provide the increased need of raw materials. Large scrap drives were carried out in every city and rural community which were to facilitate the concentration of life in the communes. The plan was to raise steel production rapidly to more than double its current figure, to an expected total of 10,800,000 tons in one year, and in the following year to increase it again to eighteen million tons.

For almost a year the plan of Mao Tse-tung was propagated as a tremendous success. This was the time of statistical inflation. Claims were made that agricultural production had risen in one year from about 185 million tons of grain to 375 million tons. The production of steel, coal and many other commodities had been increased in similar fashion. At first, the leadership itself seemed to believe in this extraordinary increase in output. The reason that the government fell for its own propaganda was not hard to find.[4] At the time of the Communist takeover in 1949, the new government had abolished the statistical organization of the National Government but had not been able to replace it. When Mao issued the orders about increase of production quantities to the provincial authorities at the time of the Great Leap, the provincial authorities simply divided and transmitted their assignments to the local authorities, raising the quantity somewhat to make certain the prescribed amount would be forthcoming. On receiving the orders, the local cadres assumed that their positions and indeed careers would depend on fulfillment of these allotments, and, not trained in statistical methods, simply estimated very crudely the production of grain in the field and of factory goods and reported back to their superiors that they could fulfill and indeed over-fulfill their quotas. When the provincial authorities in turn reported this to Peking, the government authorities there believed that they had underestimated the productive capacity of their own new method and published the inflated figures. The claim was that by new methods in agriculture, such as intense labor application, deep plowing, increased collection of mud from streams and ditches for fertilizer, and other means, and by the labor effort in industry, this miracle had been accomplished. Thus higher authorities, men like Chou En-lai, carried away for a time by their own propaganda enthusiasm, accepted and published these statistical fictions. A year later, early in 1959, the disillusionment set in and the figures were reduced.[5] But the hope remained that the new, intensified labor effort could produce that affluence on which doctrinally and practically the change from socialist production with payment "according to labor" to Communist production with payment "according to need" could be accomplished.

It was not until a year later that the full catastrophe of Mao's utopian economic planning sank in. Instead of the affluence, there was misery caused by a serious economic crisis; instead of an increase in production, there was actual decline, and soon shortages of food led to strict rationing, to privations and eventually to famine. The same was true in the industrial production drive. The products of the backyard steel furnaces were found useless, a waste of labor and material; and similar waste and miscalculation occurred in almost all industries, so that by the end of 1959 the exisiting plants and factories began to stand idle and a production breakdown occurred leading to economic disaster. Poor agricultural techniques, such as wrongly applied methods of deep plowing, led to salinization, irrigation systems constructed in unsuitable areas, senseless deforestation or poorly planned reforestation caused damage to soil and water levels affecting production on a large scale.[6]

Mao never admitted his mistake. The disastrous decline in agricultural production and the necessity for introducing strict rationing was ascribed to natural calamities, such as droughts, floods and other natural misfortunes which were supposed to have occurred all over the country. Quietly, however, the whole policy of the Great Leap was abandoned, even though the retreat was never publicly admitted.

This retreat began with a Central Committee meeting in December, 1958, resulting in a statement on December 10 which restated the aims of the new economic program in greatly modified form. Replacing previous directives of August, 1958, which have never been mentioned since, the new policy statement transferred the administration of the commune to the work teams, which corresponded to the village collectives that existed before the Great Leap. The title *communes* was maintained, but their function was limited to coordination and overall direction. Within the collectives, workers were paid for work done rather than according to need. Working hours were reduced and pay increased; private garden plots and private ownership of domestic animals were again permitted; family life was restored so that "old and young could live together," and it was clearly implied that government and party administration were not to be merged. Under these changes, the communes were no longer the instruments of total regimentation of people's lives, but only the administrative units for the coordination of planning. Nothing much remained of the Great Leap except the slogan. Even in the collectives, more private production was allowed because of the necessity to stimulate agricultural production. As the famine began to take its toll, from January, 1960, on, the economic emphasis was shifted from industry to agriculture. But the agricultural crisis took its course and both direct and indirect losses through famine and disease are believed to have led to a very high death rate in the period between 1959 and 1962, for which no statistical data exist. The magnitude of the agricultural crisis in itself aggravated the disarray of the industrial development caused by the Great Leap. Experts believed that by 1962 only about one-third of the existing Chinese industrial plants were working.

This economic catastrophe could be laid at the feet of Mao Tse-tung, who had been chiefly responsible for the plan itself and for forcing its execution. The complete failure of the program would have led to the downfall of any government with less total control over the country; even in the Communist system in China, it had to affect the position of Chairman Mao. At the very meeting in December, 1958, at which the program of the Great Leap was reformulated and a calculated retreat was decided upon, Mao's leadership position was challenged. The year before at the last session of the Eighth Party Congress in 1958, Mao had been able to regain much of the position lost two years earlier at the opening of the Congress of 1956. Not only was he in control of the Party; he was able to enforce his ideas on the new economic program. When he returned from the intra-party conference in Moscow in 1957 and decided that China should do without Soviet support, there must have been concern among his colleagues in the Chinese Communist leadership; but on the surface, at least, though with some indications of reluctance, his key men, such as Liu Shao-ch'i and Chou En-lai accepted Mao's program. Less than a year later, at the December meeting in 1958, when the program's failure had become obvious, Mao had to resign from his position of chairmanship of the Republic, the highest executive position in the country, which he had held up to that time. Officially, Mao abandoned this position, now proclaimed to have been largely ceremonial, in order to have more time for planning and formulating basic policies. In practice, the position which he relinquished was of primary importance and was not abandoned willingly. Mao's place was to be taken by the number two man in the Party, Liu Shao-ch'i, but Mao retained the leadership of the Party.

To save his face, Mao's resignation from the chairmanship of the Republic was described as voluntary and Liu Shao-ch'i became chairman officially at Mao's request. He was, in the words of the time, Mao's "closest comrade in arms." Mao's remaining position as chairman of the Central Committee of the Party became more emphasized; from that time on, Mao was always to be called *Chairman Mao*.

Mao explained his resignation as a retreat to the "second line"—in his view, a position of policy- and decision-making—leaving the "first line" of actual administration to Liu Shao-ch'i and, as second in command, Teng Hsiao-p'ing, a man who was from now on to play a major role in Chinese government. All the greater was Mao's bitter resentment, when the new leaders of the first line, Liu Shao-ch'i and Teng Hsiao-p'ing, completely reversed the trend of Mao's policy towards full communism and did this without consulting Chairman Mao.[7]

Mao's domestic radicalism had been matched by a policy of foreign adventure. In August, 1958, Mao prepared what was obviously a plan for the invasion of Taiwan. After concentrating a force of over 300,000 men in Fukien province, Mao began a massive bombardment of the islands of Quemoy and Matsu off the coast of Fukien as a first step in an amphibious venture that would remove the island obstacles to an attack against Taiwan. It was a test of American willingness to defend Taiwan and the off-shore islands. In its propaganda statements, Peking asserted its ability to cut off the off-shore islands from all supply and demanded the surrender of the Nationalist garrison. The supply line, however, was maintained with American naval and air support and when the Soviets, unwilling to risk nuclear war, refused to back Mao against the United States, Mao had to give up the venture. This failure weakened Mao's position further, but it also hardened his feeling against the Soviet Union which had been unwilling to share what the Soviets regarded as a reckless venture. It was reportedly on this occasion that Mao claimed that the Soviet unwillingness to go the full measure of risking nuclear war for China's sake sealed, in his eyes, the break between the two Communist partners.[8] The defeat of this venture contributed to the weakening of Mao's domestic position, though perhaps it was less important than the catastrophic disaster of the Great Leap Forward whose failure remained the chief cause for Mao's demotion.

Liu Shao-ch'i abandoned the Great Leap Forward in substance if not in form. His new economic policy was aimed at restoring production to the minimum level. Out of sheer necessity, a considerable amount of private production by individual farmers had to be permitted to reestablish a level of agricultural production sufficient only to feed the population and overcome the famine, which was at its worst during the year 1960-1961. Private markets of privately produced goods had to be tolerated and the recovery from this economic catastrophe in the main should be ascribed to the initiative of the Chinese farmers, once they were permitted to use their own efforts for their own benefit. The increase of agricultural production became a primary goal of Communist economic policy and, from January, 1960, on, agriculture was described as the "central link in developing the economy of the country."

At first there was official hesitancy to abandon plans for industrial production, especially in steel; but when the agricultural crisis reached its most serious proportions by early 1962, an emergency secret session of the National People's Congress accepted a new ten-point economic program which contained a complete reversal of the former economic policy. First priority was now given to agriculture; second, to consumer goods industry, and only third to heavy industry. Even so, the economic catastrophe could not be curbed quickly. When many of the existing industrial plants had to be closed, large numbers of people became unemployed and when millions of people were shifted to the rural areas, which were short of food, this massive crisis led among other things to a stampede of some 200,000 refugees mainly from Kwangtung province who crossed the border to Hong Kong.[9]

To modify the consequences of the famine, Liu Shao-ch'i's administration bought in 1961, 1962 and 1963, large amounts of wheat and other grains from Canada, Australia and other countries. Though only a small percentage of the Chinese population's total need, these imports were crucial in providing the most urgent necessities, especially feeding the government's administrative staff and its military forces. Eventually Liu Shao-ch'i succeeded in bringing the Chinese economic ship back on an even keel, and by 1965 the Chinese agrarian and industrial production was believed to have reached the level of 1957, the year before the Great Leap Forward.

If Liu Shao-ch'i thus succeeded in overcoming the disastrous economic consequences of Mao's Great Leap Forward within China, the political consequences on the intra-Communist scene were not removed. What had started as Mao's defense against Khrushchev's de-Stalinization policy became a conflict between the Soviet Union and the People's Republic over policy and leadership of the Communist camp.

Who's Ahead on the Way to Communism?

Mao's failure in the Great Leap Forward was more than a domestic defeat. Mao had not only meant to become independent of Soviet economic support, he also mounted a counter-offensive against Moscow's leading position in world communism.

Before World War II, Soviet leadership of the Communist movement had been based on the fact that the Soviet Union, as the only country under control of a Communist government, had become the "fatherland" of communism. Moscow indeed determined the policy line, not only for the Soviet Union, but globally for the Communist movement. At first the Comintern was Moscow's tool to direct the movement, and even after its dissolution in 1943, Stalin's secret police determined the policies and the purges in the Communist parties the world over. After World War II, the Cominform (Communist Information Bureau), established in 1947 in Warsaw, had served the same purpose even though China, not then Communist, had not been included in its membership. In 1956, Khrushchev dissolved the Cominform in line with his *peaceful coexistence* policy. Since then there has been no longer any institutional framework for world communism; and the question as to the direction of world Communist policy and of leadership in the Communist camp and movement has become acute.

With the conquest of power by Communist parties in Eastern Europe and in Asia, the monopoly of the Soviet Union as the only Communist state ended and the issue of central control and direction of Communist global policy would probably have become topical in any case; indeed already under Stalin moves toward decentralization of Communist decision-making were under way. But an entirely new dimension was added to this problem of central leadership of communism by Mao's challenge to Moscow's position that resulted in the Sino-Soviet conflict.

The only remaining organizational form by which overall Communist policy could be determined and a common strategy line established after the end of the Comintern and the Cominform was through the convocation of intra-party conferences. The first of these conferences was called in Moscow in 1957 shortly after the dissolution of the Cominform. It was at this conference that Mao appeared and where his attempt to claim a new role as participant in overall Communist policy-making failed. The conference ended with an acceptance of the Moscow Declaration of 1957, which contained a consensus on Communist strategy partly arrived at by compromise. The second such meeting took place in Moscow in 1960, resulting in the Moscow Statement of that year, again an attempt to provide through compromises a common agreement on overall policy. These intra-party meetings and the two that followed set the pattern for the new form of intra-Communist cooperation. Conflicts would have to be fought out in the intraparty conferences and it was unavoidable that eventually the conferences themselves became a part of the conflict. The question of participation in the conferences called by Moscow determined the position of Communist parties in the intra-Communist rivalry. At the conferences the debates and the maneuvering behind the scene dealt with the Communist doctrinal line and strategy, but also with the issue of leadership of the movement and the bloc, under the new looser framework of Communist cohesion.

Even under the Comintern, Moscow leadership had been practical rather than theoretical because the Comintern was organized by Lenin as an international Communist party that happened to have its seat in Moscow. The Soviet leadership was accepted not as a matter of theory, but out of actual respect due to Soviet authority because of Soviet superior experience stemming from the Bolshevik Revolution and the subsequent establishment of a Communist government and state. The Soviet leaders had set an example which the others had to follow. With the establishment of other Communist regimes, however, the Soviet monopoly of being the only Communist government had ended and the question of leadership became more complicated, as Tito's defection

Two views of mass labor during the Great Leap Forward.   *Courtesy of Ming Pao.*

Steel mill, Anshan, Manchuria, 1958. *Henri Cartier-Bresson, Courtesy of Magnum Photos.*

Mao with Krushchev (left) and Ho Chi Minh at a banquet in Peking celebrating the 10th anniversary of Communist rule in China, October 1959. *Wide World Photos.*

demonstrated. After the end of the Cominform there was no longer any permanent organization which Moscow could use to manipulate its leadership of the Communist movement.

In challenging the Soviet leadership, Mao at first attempted to institutionalize Moscow's role by having the Soviet party designated as the "center" of the Communist movement, a potentially vulnerable position which, once established, could be institutionally attacked by the Chinese later. To avoid this exposed status, the Soviets preferred to rely on their practical leadership. They alone allegedly had reached the true stage of "socialism" in their development and were therefore ahead on a path which must eventually be followed by all Communist parties; they were "ahead on the way to Communism."

The common road to a common goal did not preclude, however, the freedom of other Communist parties to apply their own tactics on the way to the Communist future. According to the Moscow Statement of 1960, all Marxist-Leninist parties were independent and had equal rights.[10] They were permitted to shape their policies according to the specific conditions in their respective countries, and the Moscow statement specifically mentioned different means, including "parliamentary means," through which Communist victory could be obtained according to "concrete historical conditions" in each individual country. But all these different tactics were naturally to be applied within the framework of Marxism-Leninism and "socialist internationalism." The statement specifically stressed that no "undue emphasis" should be placed "on the role of national peculiarities," and expressed the belief that the interests of development of any "national economy, culture and statehood" were identical with those of the entire world socialist system in which the national interests were presumably "harmoniously combined"; "national egoism typical of capitalism" had been superseded. A certain fear of the danger of a revival of "bourgeois nationalism and chauvinism" in the socialist camp could be discerned in the wording of this statement, which permitted different tactics to be used on the way to socialism as long as they remained in the common framework of the socialist camp that was to safeguard every member against "encroachment by imperialist reaction."

The final Communist goal for society remained unaffected by the diversity of methods which could be applied to reach it. The final guarantee for unity was still maintained by Soviet leadership resting on practical accomplishment rather than on institutional safeguards. In the words of the Moscow Statement of 1960, cosigned by the Chinese party: "The Communist workers' parties unanimously declare, that the Communist party of the Soviet Union has been, and remains, the universally recognized vanguard of the world Communist movement being the most experienced and steeled contingent of the international Communist movement." The Soviet vanguard position was thus a matter of experience and of development. It was up to the others to reach the stage of the Soviet development by their own transformation including the growth of industrialization and productive capacity which alone, in the Communist belief, would provide the affluence necessary for entering the stage of communism.

This economic development, however, depended not only on capital accumulation and production increase within the respective Communist countries but would also be affected by whatever aid was given to them from the outside. Since they were members of the Communist camp, this aid would basically have to come from the Soviet Union. With their economic advantage the Soviets possessed thus a leverage of power in providing or withholding aid from the other fraternal socialist countries and thus determining how rapid or gradual would be their advance towards a socialist economy. By slowing down or speeding up the economic development in the fraternal socialist countries, the Soviet Union could affect the rate of advance enabling them to draw even with the Soviet Union on the way towards the ultimate goal of socialism, and thus end the Soviet leadership monopoly. China, under Mao, was clearly in this dependent phase, and the economic leverage which the Soviets maintained was the main means by which they could not only affect the Chinese domestic situation and power struggles but also curb any ambition of the Chinese leader, Mao Tse-tung, to play an equal or indeed leading role in the Communist world movement.

The Soviet policy towards economic aid, to be given as a matter of "fraternal assistance" in this race for communism, was ambiguously expressed in the Moscow Statement. The statement said: "Gradual elimination along these lines, of historical differences on the levels of economic development, and the provision of a material basis for a more or less simultaneous transition of all the peoples of the socialist system to Communism" was the necessary prerequisite for the successful development of the world economic system of socialism towards the Communist future. The stipulation of a "more or less simultaneous transition" left the Soviet Union in authority to maintain its head start whenever and to whatever degree it decided to do so by giving or witholding economic aid. This was then the major means by which the Soviets would maintain dominance within the camp. In severing his economic dependence from Moscow, Mao by implication and later in expressed policy, challenged this Soviet leadership.

The Great Leap Forward was therefore a challenge to Moscow's position at the head of the movement which the Soviet leaders could not take lightly. In the exaggerated claims of the time, the Chinese propaganda emphasized this challenge by professing that China under Mao was "bypassing the Soviet Union on the way to Communism." Khrushchev's dismay became obvious when the Soviet press ridiculed the idea of the Chinese communes. The Soviet Union, after all, had attempted this move towards instant communism after the Bolshevik Revolution and had failed. This attempt at a short cut to communism was regarded as naïve, leftist adventurism, an "infantile" interpretation of Marxist economic development, which as the Soviet well knew would obviously have to fail. How serious this matter was to Khrushchev could be gauged by the fact that he criticized and ridiculed the Chinese commune policy as egalitarianism "without material incentives" even to a foreign visitor, Senator Hubert Humphrey, during his visit to Moscow in December, 1958.[11]

By this challenge to the claim of factual Soviet leadership through the Chinese commune system, Mao had therefore combined the goal of asserting the Chinese People's Republic independence from Moscow and his own defense against Soviet attack with a challenge to Moscow's leadership. It was this move that transformed the latent conflict into an open confrontation which would be further aggravated over the years to come. Much was at stake for Mao in the Great Leap Forward when he moved from the defensive to an attack on the whole Soviet position. It was at this moment that the conflict, begun in 1956, became a bitter battle for leadership in which the Soviet Union had to reassert its position as pathfinder on the way to communism.

When the Great Leap failed, the conflict between Mao and his colleagues in the Chinese party leadership became linked with the problem of Sino-Soviet relations. Mao's demotion in December, 1958, may have been not only an internal matter within the Chinese Communist leadership but may also have been connected with an understanding between the Chinese party leaders and Moscow. In January, 1959, after Mao had given up the chairmanship of the Republic, Chou En-lai journeyed to Moscow to obtain another, albeit limited, agreement on Soviet economic support crucial in staving off some of the worst consequences of the Great Leap. In February, 1959, at the Twenty-first Congress of the Soviet Party, Khrushchev reasserted his policy of peaceful coexistence and extended his claim that the industrial development of the Soviet Union would, in peaceful competition, lead to a victory of communism over the Western world. This policy formulation was later to become a major issue of ideological attack by Mao against Khrushchev's leadership.

In China, the attack against Mao continued. At a Central Committee meeting at Lushan, the mountain resort in central China, in July, 1959, a critical move was made to remove Mao from his leading party position.

The leading military member of the Central Committee and of the Politburo, P'eng Teh-huai, then minister of defense, led the accusation against Mao by condemning the policies of the Great Leap Forward and its failure. P'eng Teh-huai had visited the Soviet Union and Eastern Europe from late April to mid-June, 1959, as the head of a Chinese good-will mission. On May 28, he met with Khrushchev in the Crimea and is be-lieved to have discussed there the Chinese domestic situation. His attack against Mao could, therefore, have been carried out on Khrushchev's instigation or at least with Khrushchev's previous knowledge.

P'eng's attack was open. He submitted at the Lushan Conference to Mao and the members of the committee a letter in which he condemned the Great Leap Forward as "petit bourgeois fanaticism," a deadly sin in Communist eyes, the sin of which Mao was both then and later accused by Moscow.[12] P'eng not only attacked the use of Chinese military forces for public labor during the Great Leap Forward, demanding instead profes-sionalization of the army and its equipment with modern weapons which would have to come from Moscow, but extended his criticism also to the whole policy of the Great Leap with its disastrous economic conse-quences, and is said to have demanded Mao's resignation. In a fierce rebuttal, Mao claimed that he would not yield to criticism and if the army deserted him, he would return to the rural areas, organize his own military forces and challenge the present leadership.[13] With his defiant stand, Mao appears to have gained the support of the majority of those present and carried the day.

The extent of opposition can be gauged from the number of leaders, both military and administrative, who were at this time removed from their positions and later purged as a direct result of the confrontation and of Mao's victory. At the time, Mao had to be content with replacing the minister of defense, P'eng Teh-huai, the chief of staff, and some forty other leaders with people more acceptable to himself. Otherwise, they were not punished and, as Mao later complained, did not even have to confess their mistake and accept self-criticism. But though he had to compromise, Mao gained the replacement of P'eng, his leading opponent, by Mao's most loyal paladin among the military leaders, Lin Piao, who became the new minister of defense and who was to be instru-mental in Mao's final victory over the recalcitrant and hostile party leader in the Great Proletarian Cultural Revolution.

Mao not only survived but was able to maintain his position of chal-lenging Moscow, a position on which his power in China depended. From 1960 on, the Sino-Soviet conflict became further aggravated by mutual ideological incriminations between Moscow and Peking, leading even-tually to the threat of military confrontation.

Mao's Return to Power

On October 1, 1959, the Chinese Communists celebrated the Tenth Anniversary of the establishment of the People's Republic. Having defeated the opposition's attack led by P'eng Teh-huai and having retained his position as party leader, Mao played a preeminent part in the celebrations, aiming at reestablishing his position in the Communist movement. Among the thousands of visitors who came to Peking were representatives of all Communist parties and all Communist governments. Ignoring the actual economic crisis caused by the Great Leap, the speeches by Chinese leaders and foreign visitors eulogized the tremendous success of the Chinese Revolution. The Great Leap and its disasters seemed forgotten but there was a distinction in the speeches with regard to the role that Chairman Mao had played in the Chinese success story. For the Chinese speakers, Mao had reestablished his political if not his administrative authority and was "the leader of the Chinese people" to whom all credit for the success story was due. In the official Soviet version as expressed by Moscow's representatives it was the Chinese Communist party which had gained the success under the direction of its Central Committee and its chairman, Mao Tse-tung. In view of the fact that the Party and Mao, though standing together on this occasion, were still in conflict over policy, this distinction in the speeches showed a strengthening of Mao's domestic position and the continued opposition to Mao expressed by Moscow. The speakers of the other international Communist parties sided with one or the other interpretation, neatly revealing the line of alignments in the potential Sino-Soviet conflict. Khrushchev, who was one day late for the occasion, coming from his talks with President Eisenhower at Camp David, used the Soviet formula, but, as a compromise, added some general praise of Mao Tse-tung.[14] The conflict, only thinly concealed by the ceremonial proceedings, could be gleaned from the cold attitude shown by Mao towards Khrushchev from the moment of his reception at the airport to his departure. This treatment contrasted sharply with previous occasions of Khrushchev's visits to Peking and indicated Mao's hostility as well as his control over the leadership in Peking.

During this period Mao's major concern was to reestablish his authority both at home and abroad in the field of ideology. From the end of 1959 on, the Chinese press again began a glorification of Mao Tse-tung and his leadership which had been interrupted by the de-Stalinization period and the attack against the cult of personality. The new campaign to heroize Mao soon went far beyond the idolization of the past and came to equal the cult of Stalin in its latter years, and eventually surpassed it.

The build-up of Mao's image was not limited to the chairman's position in China. It soon extended over the Communist movement as a whole. When the Chinese Communist press proclaimed in January, 1960: "Comrade Mao Tse-tung is the most outstanding representative of the proletariat in our country, and the greatest revolutionary leader, statesman, and theoretician of Marxism-Leninism in the present era," the message was clearly a challenge to Soviet leadership over the Communist movement. In strident tones the Chinese press began to attack the policy of Soviet leaders. The "peace strategy" of Khrushchev misjudged American imperialism and aggressiveness; it overestimated the American "paper tiger" and demonstrated an exaggerated fear of nuclear war. Nuclear war, if it occurred, would not bring the annihilation of mankind but would destroy imperialism on whose debris "the victorious people would create very swiftly a new civilization thousands of times higher than the capitalist system and a beautiful future for themselves."

This statement became the basis of the Soviet accusation that Mao's policy was to provoke nuclear war between the Soviet Union and the United States which would enable China, in the position of "the man sitting on the mountain to watch the tigers fight," to profit from the mutual destruction of the nuclear powers. Indeed Soviet sources traced Mao's attitude back to his reaction towards their unwillingness to support his confrontation with the United States during his attack on the off-shore islands in 1958.[15]

Mao's attempt to attack the Soviets in their leading position continued throughout 1960. He found a target in the "neo-revisionist" policy of the Yugoslav leader, Tito, towards whom Khrushchev had initiated a rapprochement. In answer to the Chinese attacks, the Soviets recalled their technical advisers from China and reduced Soviet aid and trade, aggravating the catastrophic economic crisis caused by the Great Leap Forward. Peking in turn withdrew most Chinese students from Soviet institutions.

The interparty meeting in Moscow in November, 1960, and the Moscow statement "papered over the conflict but was in fact a Soviet victory."[16] For a while the Sino-Soviet conflict abated. To soften the effect of Chinese omission from the Communist Council for Economic Assistance (COMECON), established for the economic cooperation between the Soviet Union and Eastern Europe, the Soviets claimed in a *Pravda* article in October, 1960, that the assistance given to China in the previous years was part of the development plan of COMECON, which served the purpose of furthering economic advancement and leveling the distinction between the per capita income of the socialist countries. This reaffirmation of Soviet obligation to contribute to the development of fraternal socialist countries indicated a Soviet willingness to resume economic aid to the People's Republic of China provided understanding could be reached on the political conflict between Moscow and Peking.

In the spring of 1961 a Soviet delegation came to China to negotiate renewed Soviet economic assistance, and Peking papers printed statements of the importance of previous Soviet aid. An agreement was concluded in April, 1961, for additional Soviet deliveries, mainly on half a million tons of sugar, and for a settlement of the repayment of 300 million dollars in loans and credits which China owed from previous Soviet deliveries. Delivery was also continued on the most important item on which the Chinese economy depended, namely oil.

This renewal of economic relations was of short duration. At the Twenty-second Soviet Party Congress in Moscow in October, 1961, Khrushchev stressed two policies which were anathema to Mao. The first one was a renewal of de-Stalinization policy—Stalin's body was removed from its tomb in the Kremlin next to Lenin—and the second was a renewed attack against the Stalinist leaders of Albania, the only Communists who had sided with Peking in the growing conflict. This was the time during which the full debacle of the Great Leap Forward was felt in China and Khrushchev's hardening of his line was apparently connected with his belief that there could be no Chinese resistance. But the Chinese representative at the congress, Chou En-lai, sharply answered Khrushchev's actions and flew back to China where he was personally welcomed by Mao Tse-tung at the airport.

The new phase of the Sino-Soviet conflict led to a sharpening of the attacks against Moscow's *revisionism* in general and Khrushchev in particular. While officially Moscow was attacked by proxy through a condemnation of Yugoslav revisionism, an unofficial personal attack against Khrushchev was organized throughout China. It led to the publication in China of five volumes of Khrushchev's speeches identifying the Soviet leader with Stalin in order to demonstrate the hypocrisy of his whole policy. In 1962 and 1963, the so-called ideological conflict between Mao and the Soviet leaders heated up. Seeking an opportunity for broadening the attack against Khrushchev, Mao requested a new biparty meeting to discuss the differences. Both sides agreed to meet in July, 1963, but before the Chinese delegation left for Moscow the Central Committee of the Chinese Communist party sent and simultaneously published a letter to the Central Committee of the Soviet party which formulated in the sharpest form the denunciations against the policy of Khrushchev who was pictured as an appeaser who had surrendered to imperialism and had abandoned the support of the revolution and of national liberation movements. This 50,000-word letter was answered during the talks in

Moscow in an open letter of the Central Committee of the Soviet party. The two letters together documented the mutual recriminations in their strongest form. The Soviets were accused by Mao of having violated the 1957 Moscow Declaration and the 1960 Moscow Statement, of having abandoned the world revolution and departed from the doctrine of Marxism-Leninism; Moscow had betrayed the interests of the proletariat and the national liberation struggles. This Chinese attack was not only a challenge to the Soviet leadership but was also an obvious distortion of the Soviet line. It was answered by the Soviets in their letter accusing the Chinese of promoting a policy aimed at atomic war. Both the Soviet and Chinese accusations grossly distorted the positions of the other side, which indeed were not too far apart. But the so-called ideological conflict seemed to be a necessity in providing the justification for the hostility of the two Communist opponents.

The Chinese accusations were pursued further in a series of nine pamphlets published beginning in September, 1963, attacking, point-by-point, the Soviet position. These Chinese pamphlets dealt with the general line, with de-Stalinization, with Yugoslav revisionism, with Soviet alleged support of neo-colonialism, with the question of war and peace, with the issue of peaceful coexistence, with the splitting of the Communist movement, with Khrushchev's alleged revisionism and his so-called phony communism.[17] These well-done doctrinal attacks and others that followed, though not signed by Mao, showed Mao's style and obviously contained Mao's arguments.[18] They served the purpose of presenting Mao's leadership as the only revolutionary Communist line worth following and laid the groundwork for Mao's later attempt to seek his followership not only in China but in the world Communist movement.

While maintaining and building up his position within the Communist movement in this verbal battle with Khrushchev, Mao attempted to regain the control over the Chinese Communist party which he had lost as the result of his failure in the Great Leap Forward. Though officially still the chairman of the Central Committee, Mao was not in actual control of the party machinery. Liu Shao-ch'i, who had replaced Mao as chairman of the Republic, also had become the dominant figure in party decision-making. And though Mao had succeeded in defeating the final attempt to unseat him in 1959 and to purge the leaders of the opposition, he was not able to exercise practical control over the Party and, as he later complained, was not even consulted on major decisions. His ideological battle with Khrushchev, though tolerated and even supported by his colleagues, did not reflect Mao's actual position within the country. To regain the power that had slipped from his hands, Mao attempted between 1962 and

1964, in the so-called Socialist Education movement, to regain authority over the cadres from Liu Shao-ch'i.

At the Lushan meeting in 1959, Mao had succeeded in having P'eng Teh-huai removed as minister of defense but not as a member of the Politburo. The majority of party leaders who had yielded to Mao's pressure over the issue of P'eng's dismissal continued to sympathize with P'eng, who had expressed openly what many of them felt and who had been sacrificed. In 1962 P'eng Teh-huai formally asked that his case be reopened. Mao used this opportunity to call the Central Committee in September, 1962, again into plenary session which he would, of course, chair. Disregarding all attacks against him, Mao continued to belabor what he called "right opportunism and revisionism" of his comrades. He not only prevented the reinstatement of P'eng Teh-huai but also succeeded in replacing members of the secretariat disloyal to him with leaders whom he regarded as men on whom he could rely, among them his secret police chief, K'ang Sheng, and the new army chief-of-staff, General Lo Jui-ch'ing.[19] The communique issued after the session warned against so-called bourgeois elements who were attempting a comeback to power. It took note of the difficulties that had been created as an aftermath of the work stoppage following the Great Leap Forward; the responsibility of these setbacks, however, was ascribed to the "incompetence of leading cadres, some production teams, some factories, and some business establishments," whose production had declined and whose work should be improved.[20]

It was this rectification of the cadre's work which became known as the *Socialist Education movement.* This movement was an attempt to reeducate and reindoctrinate the party cadres not only on the central but also on the local level and to make up for the demoralization and slackening of discipline that had resulted from the catastrophe of the Great Leap Forward. Mao Tse-tung and Liu Shao-ch'i engaged in a tug-of-war, each issuing a spate of directives on the policy to be followed in improving the party's work.[21] Since no specific policies could be implemented, the movement created only uncertainty and confusion among the administrative cadres in the provinces without affecting the policy of Liu Shao-ch'i. Thus, the Socialist Education movement resulted in a draw between Mao and Liu, leaving Liu in practical administrative control. Mao had failed in this attempt to wrest party control from his rival in order to reestablish his radical line.

Mao now abandoned the struggle for control of the Party. If he was to regain full command of Chinese politics, he had to use other means of power; thus, when the Party no longer followed his order, Mao turned to the People's Liberation Army (PLA) to attack the Party and the government controlled by it. This was truly a revolutionary defiance of a basic part of the Communist system itself. The Communist party claimed to be *the vanguard of the proletariat* and as such it expressed historical truth. Individuals could deviate from the true line and could be purged; the Party could not be wrong. No other Communist, not even Stalin with his vast purges of party comrades, had attacked the Party itself. To attack the Party was a grave challenge of a basic concept of Marxism-Leninism.

If the Party was wrong, a superior source of truth had to be found that would justify such revolutionary action. To Mao, this new source of truth was Mao himself. In the conflict between the Party and Mao, Mao was right; the Party was wrong. From a leader of the Party, working within the framework of the Marxist-Leninist system, Mao changed thus to a leader in his own right who alone was able to determine the correct line for the proletarian revolution. In this assertion of his infallibility, Mao became a leader in the manner of the German and Italian totalitarian systems of the 1930s and 1940s in which the word of the supreme leader was the final source of authority. This was the beginning of the Cult of Mao Tse-tung, which was to take the place of the Party in the orthodox Communist system.

In Yenan days Mao had first established the authority of his interpretation of the doctrine after the Leninist-Stalinist model, as did all Communist leaders. The Thought of Mao Tse-tung had been included in the party statutes drawn up at the Seventh Congress in 1945, as part of the Marxist-Leninist guide for the Chinese party. Now the Thought of Mao Tse-tung was to become the supreme guide to action independently of the Party and in conflict with the party leadership.

The man who did more to build up the new Cult of Mao than anybody else was Lin Piao, since 1959 minister of defense and vice chairman of the Military Affairs Committee under Mao, and Mao's most loyal supporter. In a number of escalating speeches, Lin Piao stressed Mao's role first as leader within the Party but eventually by himself, independently of the Party. Others joined in preparing Mao's new role, especially Mao's secretary and ghost writer, Ch'en Po-ta. In retrospect, the lengthy article published by Ch'en Po-ta on July 16, 1958, in *Red Flag* under the title "Under the Banner of Comrade Mao Tse-tung" was an initiatory move in the new Maoist strategy. The article, celebrating the thirty-seven years of the Chinese Communist party, was a eulogy to Mao Tse-tung. Ch'en proclaimed that it was Comrade Mao alone who had supplied Communist theory to China by integrating his work

... with the creativeness of the masses. He puts faith in the masses, relies on the masses and respects the intelligence of the ordinary masses, thereby to increase the invincible power of Marxist-Leninist theory under new conditions and in new surroundings.[22]

The "banner of Mao Tse-tung's *Thought*" provided the solution.

However, it was chiefly Lin Piao who during that period and later during the Cultural Revolution created the slogans and phrases of the exaggerated Cult of Mao. The People's Liberation Army was the vehicle through which this belief in Mao as the supreme leader and the Thought of Mao as the answer to all questions was to be spread. The PLA was to fulfill a double function. On one hand it was the leverage of power in Mao's attack against the Party; on the other hand, it was the tool of indoctrination in the belief in Mao's Thought for the whole of China.

The first of Lin Piao's acts when he took over was the indoctrination of the PLA in the belief in Mao. Under Lin Piao's predecessors, the party structure and the political indoctrination within the army had been neglected. Now a new effort was made to politicize the military, this time in the belief not of the Party but of Mao. For the purpose of this indoctrination, Lin Piao selected from Mao's writings popular and easily remembered phrases grouped under major themes and had them published in red bindings in a booklet which became known as *The Little Red Book of the Sayings of Chairman Mao*. These sayings could be easily memorized by the semieducated, and shouted in slogans as a statement of faith in the leader. They were issued with a preface by Lin Piao in which Lin asked the readers to study Chairman Mao's writings, follow his teaching, and be good soldiers of Chairman Mao. The *Little Red Book* became widely used first in the army and then by the population at large. Printed by the hundreds of millions and translated into English and other languages, this *Little Red Book* of Lin Piao became the catechism not only for Maoist China, but also for Maoist groups the world over. Its sayings and slogans made their impact, especially on the young, in many countries beyond China.

In China the indoctrination of the PLA was only the first step of propagandizing the Chinese people. To do this the PLA was soon held up as a model for all Chinese under the slogan of *Learn from the PLA*. While the Socialist Education movement was still under way, Lin Piao began to organize an infiltraton by the military of the Party, the administration and the social and economic institutions of the whole country. To strengthen the military authority over the Party, commanders of military regions were appointed party secretaries in five of the six regional party bureaus. At the same time party secretaries were concurrently appointed to positions of political commissars in the military districts, becoming thus part of the military structure commanded by Lin Piao. Next, and on a much larger scale, the army invaded all institutional structures; army personnel were detached to local party and government offices, to communes, factories, educational institutions and all other organizations of the economic-social-political system of China. These army men were to spread the spirit of the sanctification of Mao Tse-tung, in which they themselves had been indoctrinated. At the same time, they served as a supervisory and controlling group over the political, economic and educational structure. The extent to which the army was used by Lin Piao under Mao's direction as a means of propaganda and control can be deduced from the fact that over 200,000 officers and men of the People's Liberation Army were so employed, raising a question as to the combat capability of the People's Liberation Army during the time of this revolutionary assignment. In fact, Mao was replacing the Party with the PLA in the control of the country.

To prepare the PLA for such a revolutionary task, Lin Piao initiated a movement to strengthen the "democratic tradition" in the PLA, aiming at rebuilding the party structure within the army. As a result of this movement, one-third of all soldiers and all officers became members of the party organization in the army under the discipline not of the Central Committee of the civilian party but of the party structure within the army—under the control of Lin Piao through the army's political department. In May, 1965, Lin Piao under Mao's orders decreed that all titles and insignia of rank were abolished, presumably to reintroduce the wartime spirit of equality and comradship of officers and men and to weaken any possible opposition of the emerging professional officer class within the PLA against the army's politicization. In view of the history of the fusion of Party and army during the civil war and the war against Japan, it was not farfetched, nor difficult for Mao to reestablish this system of a party-army as a tool in his comeback to power. This time, however, it was not directed against the National Government, let alone the foreign enemy, but against the Communist government and party structure itself.

Welcoming Liu Shao-ch'i as Chairman of Standing Committee, Third National People's Congress. *Courtesy of Ming Pao.*

Students protest American interference in Congo, 1964. *Rene Bu Courtesy of Magnum Photos.*

Mao's famous swim in the Yangtze, July 1966. *Wide World Pho*

Voting for Liu as Chairman of Standing Committee. *Courtesy of Ming Pao.*

Mao and Lin Piao attend rally in Peking, August 1966. *Wide World Photos.*

Chiang Ch'ing during Great Proletariat Cultural Revolution. *Wide World Photos.*

Mao working in his residence, circa 1966. *Wide World Photos.*

CHAPTER

VII

The Great Proletarian Cultural Revolution

MAO'S ATTEMPT TO place himself above the Party as the source of ideological authority alarmed his party comrades. His endeavor to dictate party policy without accepting any critical opinion from Politburo members was particularly galling after the failure of Mao's Great Leap Forward, and to have party policy determined under the banner of the Thought of Mao Tse-tung was unacceptable to those brought up in Lenin's party system of *democratic centralism.*

Who Control's the Truth?

To counter Chairman Mao's claim of superior doctrinal position, Liu Shao-ch'i in 1962 republished his book *How to Be a Good Communist.* The earlier version, approved by the Party and by Mao, had been used as a textbook for all new candidates for membership in the rapidly growing Party. The new edition refuted the claim of anyone who might want to place himself above the rest of the party leaders. Without attacking Mao by name, Liu criticized those who "regarded themselves as 'China's Marx or China's Lenin . . . and had the impudence to require that our Party members should revere them as Marx and Lenin are revered. . . .' " These self-appointed "leaders" had issued orders and punished party members.[1] When Liu claimed, "We should not break with comrades who have committed errors but who are nevertheless loyal . . . should not castigate or expel them unless they persist in their mistakes and prove incorrigible," he was not only attacking Mao Tse-tung's autocracy in general terms, but in particular was taking up the defense of the former defense minister, P'eng Teh-huai.[2] What must have been all the more roiling to Mao was the fact that Liu's booklet printed and sold about ten times as many copies as the four-volume set of the *Selected Works of Mao Tse-tung.*[3]

This attack in the official party literature was complemented by a concerted effort of a group of party writers to ridicule Mao's new claims. This attack had been instituted by one of the leading members of the Party, P'eng Chen, who was mayor of Peking, a member of the Politburo and the second-ranking secretary of the Central Committee of the Communist party. In 1961, P'eng Chen had organized a group to study party documents for the last two years with the obvious intent of investigating the high-handed directives that Mao had issued during the years without checking with members of the Politburo or the Central Committee. The head of this group was Teng T'o, who had been an editor of the *People's Daily* in Peking and was one of those purged by Mao in 1959. Though the study of these documents did not at the time lead to the initiation of procedures in the Party against Mao Tse-tung—Liu Shao-ch'i obviously did not feel strong enough—it was useful material for journalistic attacks against Mao's exaggerated claims. Together with two others—Wu Han, a well-known party writer who at the time was vice-mayor of Peking, and Liao Mo-sha, an official of the Peking Party Committee—Teng T'o formed a threesome which published a number of satirical essays under the heading, "Notes From the Three-Family Village," and "Evening Chats on Yenshan," that by implication made fun of Mao's claim of omniscience. Though Mao was not mentioned by name, the initiated reader could well recognize him in the person of the boastful athlete who bragged of his former record, or of the child that preferred the East Wind over the West Wind, or of the victim of amnesia who had spells of anger and fits of temper that eventually might end in insanity. Anyone, so Teng T'o wrote in his satire, who was suffering from these symptoms should take a complete rest, and do nothing in order not to come to grief. The treatment had to be handled by outside doctors and the patient must not interfere.[4]

This general critical satire, in which Mao was obviously the target, though unnamed, was climaxed by a historical play written by Wu Han, under the title of *Hai Jui Dismissed from Office*.[5] Hai Jui had been a loyal official who was dismissed by an emperor of the Ming dynasty because of his honest criticism of the emperor's wrong policies, and, even more pertinently, of the emperor's laziness and self-imposed removal from responsible participation in government at practical levels. This transparent parallel to Mao Tse-tung's dismissal of the Defense Minister P'eng Teh-huai, together with the rest of the satires, was directed not only against Mao's autocracy but against the very attempt of Mao to build up his image of being able to replace the Party as the infallible source of correct policy decisions. Chairman Mao's ideological claim on which his whole strategy was based was undermined by this propaganda campaign conducted against him under the direction of the party leadership.

Mao understood this form of power struggle only too well. Had he not used it himself? The use of novels and historical similes as means of political attack were nothing new to him and would be used by him and his followers in years to come. Mao fully understood the technique of what is called in modern terms *psychological operations*. In his words: "In order to overthrow a political power, it is always necessary to create public opinion, to do work in the ideological sphere."[6] He was soon to have his revenge on his disparagers.

The conflict between Mao and the Party was thus focusing on the field of the media, on the use of literature and historical models for a challenge to Mao's claim to ideological infallibility. It was soon also carried into the field of cultural tradition, especially the field of theater, of so-called Chinese opera or ballet. It was in this arena that Mao's wife, Chiang Ch'ing, was to make her debut as a new political figure.

Traditional Chinese opera consisted chiefly of plays that dealt with the society of imperial China in which emperors, officials and beautiful women made up the dramatis personae of stories that were placed in historical settings, and whose content was well known to the audiences. The stage action included both spoken sequences and songs accompanied by musical instruments. In dress, makeup, and deportment of the actors, a stylized tradition had developed ever since the drama had become popular in Mongol time; and the operas themselves, the texts, the personalities and even the actors became well known to Chinese of all walks of life. The Communist leaders who had grown up in this tradition continued to appreciate it.

It was this tradition that was attacked by Mao's wife, Chiang Ch'ing, as early as in Yenan times. In her past, she had been a minor actress in modern Chinese plays; perhaps for that reason she was keenly interested in abolishing the traditional Chinese opera and replacing it with some new, revolutionary forms and themes. Her attempt to influence or defeat the Ministry of Culture under whose auspices the Chinese stage tradition was continued, failed at first. But when the conflict between Mao and the party writers came to a head, particularly after the fight over Wu Han's play, Mao took his wife's side and encouraged her to use the theater as an additional means of propagating the success of his military and political strategy. With this encouragement and support, Chiang Ch'ing sponsored the writing of modern plays that contained revolutionary themes.

Chiang Ch'ing's revolutionary operas dealt with events of Communist guerilla warfare and the liberation of the peasants from the oppression which, according to Communist account, they had suffered. During the time of the civil war one of the most effective Communist propaganda plays had been the story of *The White-Haired Girl,* a woman who had been attacked and raped by a landlord and whose hair, as a result of her suffering, had turned white. Now other similar plays were written to take the place of the operas of the past. In 1963 and 1964, several such plays were staged. Though still called *operas* because the action was presented in the form of dance and songs reminiscent of the past, these plays introduced totally new theatrical inscenation and choreography. In all, eight such operas or ballets were created; the best known of them, produced not only in China but also abroad, was *The Red Detachment of Women.* The story was a typical one of a landlord who had oppressed his tenants and was overthrown by a group of peasant women, formed into a Red Army detachment with the help of Red Army troops. In this as in other plays, the content was melodramatic. Revolutionary songs took the place of the Chinese opera singing of the past, and a piano became the main accompanying instrument. These ballets or operas were propaganda pieces whose technique of dance and gymnastics was impressive but whose artistic value was debatable.[7] In fact, some of the Chinese Communist leaders were highly critical of this new form of revolutionary theater. They included the secretary general of the Party, Teng Hsiao-p'ing, and his second in command and mayor of Peking, P'eng Chen.[8] The conflict between Mao and his supporters and the Party leadership was thus extended to the field of journalism, literature and theater, thereby constituting the "cultural" aspect of the Great Proletarian Cultural Revolution.

To counter the attack against his ideological authority, Mao demanded at a Central Committee work meeting in September, 1965, that the "capitalist" and "reactionary" thought should be criticized and that this criticism in particular must apply to Wu Han, whose play had been most damaging in challenging Mao's authority. The session was reportedly stormy. Mao did not prevail. After this defeat, and feeling no longer safe in Peking, Mao retreated to Shanghai and Hangchow from where he was to direct his countermoves to the challenge to his authority.

To reconcile the clash between Mao and themselves, the party leaders agreed to the establishment of a Cultural Revolution Committee of five persons headed by P'eng Chen, the man most responsible for organizing the literary group that criticized Mao. The selection of P'eng Chen to head this group may have been forced upon Mao by the party leaders, but it could also have been Mao's attempt to force P'eng Chen into the open where he would have to choose a position either in support of Mao or against him. The only member of P'eng Chen's group clearly on Mao's side was K'ang Sheng, the secret police chief, who could be expected to keep Mao informed on the deliberations and actions of the committee.

In Shanghai, Mao used in his attack against the literary opposition the support of two leftist writers brought to his attention by his wife, Chiang Ch'ing. Chang Ch'un-ch'iao and Yao Wen-yuan, both products of the Shanghai literary world and of proven flexibility, had been used before to denounce fellow writers in conflict with the prevailing line. Yao Wen-yuan now became the author of an article written under Chiang Ch'ing's and Mao's supervision, published under the editorship of Chang Ch'un-ch'iao in a Shanghai paper on November 10, 1965. This article condemned the play by Wu Han, with its implicit attack of Mao's purge of P'eng Teh-huai. On the strength of this article, Mao attempted to have Wu Han dismissed from his position of mayor of Peking.

P'eng Chen's committee attempted to blunt Mao's protest of the attack against him by issuing on February 22, 1966, a circular draft which defined the conflict between Mao and his critics as a "non-antagonistic" theoretical and academic debate in which historical interpretations could differ. This was, of course, totally unsatisfactory to Mao whose opponents were left in the position to continue the attack against Mao as a theoretical and academic exercise. In answer, therefore, Mao Tse-tung issued on May 16, 1966, from Shanghai a circular letter of his own, repudiating P'eng Chen, abolishing the five-man Cultural Revolution Group, and describing the issue as a "battle" between the two lines — the proletarian and the bourgeois lines — placing the opposing writers and their party sponsors in the "enemy" camp. The May 16 circular was later regarded by the Maoists as the beginning of the Cultural Revolution. In it Mao attacked P'eng and his committee for distortion of the "Cultural Revolution."[9] His basic accusation was:

While feigning compliance, the outline report actually opposes and stubbornly resists the great cultural revolution initiated and led personally by Comade Mao. . . .

P'eng Chen had channeled "the political struggle in the cultural sphere into so-called pure academic discussion, as frequently advocated by the bourgeoisie." He had attacked the wrong target and protected the intellectual enemies of Mao. P'eng's aim was:

> to label the Marxist-Leninists "scholar-tyrants" and thus to support the real, bourgeois scholar-tyrants and prop up their tottering monopoly position in academic circles. As a matter of fact, those Party people in authority taking the capitalist road . . . do not read books, do not read the daily press, have no contact with the masses, and know nothing at all.

In short, P'eng Chen had committed the crime of opposing Mao's Cultural Revolution, attacking the "proletarian left" and shielding "the bourgeois right, thereby preparing public opinion for the restoration of capitalism." P'eng Chen's circular letter was therefore to be replaced by Mao's new directive.[10]

Mao's counterattack against P'eng Chen was followed by military action in Peking, through which P'eng Chen was removed from office. It was the first open action of the People's Liberation Army (PLA) under Lin Piao's command attacking party leaders opposed to Mao. After the removal of P'eng Chen and the dissolution of his Cultural Revolution Committee with the support of Lin Piao, the attack against Wu Han and the three-village group now led to the purge of Mao's critics. Chiang Ch'ing, Chang Ch'un-ch'iao and Yao Wen-yuan were to form the core of a Maoist group in Shanghai which later moved into key positions in the new Maoist controlled Chinese party, as a new Cultural Revolution Committee.

The fall of P'eng Chen initiated a battle for control of the news media that ran parallel to the political battle against the party leadership throughout the summer of 1966. The importance of this battle was later admitted in an editorial of the *People's Daily* of January 19, 1967, under the title, "Let the Thought of Mao Tse-tung Occupy the Newspaper Battleground."[11] Mao's shift from Party to mass support was clearly indicated.

> . . . our Party newspaper is the important instrument of proletarian dictatorship. It enables us to influence the spirit of the masses, to influence the beating of the pulse of the masses, and to influence the ideological feelings and the politics of the masses.

In the newspaper takeover, three stages can be discerned. The first stage was marked by a purge of anti-Maoists in every newspaper agency. During the summer of 1966 many chairmen, editors and deputy editors were eliminated and the organization and personnel were revamped. During the second period, the last quarter of the year 1966, some leading newspapers were either suspended or totally reorganized. The third period began with the power seizure of important Shanghai papers in January, 1967. By the end of May, 1967, more than twenty newspapers in provinces and cities had been seized by the Mao-Lin group and the decisive takeover was completed.[12]

The victorious emergence of the Thought of Mao Tse-tung in this battle can be followed in the issues of the *Peking Review* from June to August, 1966. Of special importance was Lin Piao's letter, "Chairman Mao Has Elevated Marxism-Leninism to a Completely New Stage with Great Talent."[13] During the summer of 1966, in the months leading up to the Eleventh Plenum of the Central Committee to be held in August, the press, by now in Maoist hands, fiercely propagated the Thought of Mao Tse-tung.[14] Mao was raised to the status of Marx, Engels, Lenin and Stalin, and the Thought of Mao Tse-tung was given the all-encompassing role of

> ... *the sole correct guiding principle in the different stages of the Chinese revolution and a powerful ideological weapon of revolution in the hands of the oppressed people and oppressed nations against the imperialism, modern revisionism and all reactionaries.* ... *Mao Tse-tung's thought is Marxism-Leninism inherited and developed with genius, creatively and in an all-round way in the era in which imperialism is approaching complete collapse and socialism is advancing to victory all over the world; it is the acme of Marxism-Leninism in the present era; it is living Marxism-Leninism at its highest. Comrade Mao Tse-tung is the greatest Marxist-Leninist of the present era.*

To back up his ideological attack against the party leaders, Mao needed now the support of the military. This support was uncertain because the number two man in the military command structure, Lo Jui-ch'ing, the chief-of-staff, had begun to turn against Mao. The issue was extraneous to the ideological battle with the party leadership but of crucial importance to Mao Tse-tung.

The year 1965 was a decisive year in Vietnam. After the assassination of the South Vietnamese Prime Minister Ngo Dinh Diem, South Vietnam seemed to fall rapidly into Communist hands until President Johnson decided on full-scale American intervention. The build-up of American forces in South Vietnam deprived the Communists of an almost certain victory. This serious setback soon led to a Soviet appeal to the Chinese Communist leaders to forego the Sino-Soviet conflict in favor of a united support of Hanoi's policy of victory in South Vietnam. This Soviet call for unity found a favorable echo among party leaders in China; Liu Shao-ch'i accepted it and Lo Jui-ch'ing supported it. In Februry, 1966, the *People's Daily*—not yet taken over by Mao—carried an article "Struggle to Safeguard Soviet-Sino Unity," and on May 10, the same paper published an article by Lo Jui-ch'ing entitled "Carry the Struggle Against Fascism to the End," appealing for Communist unity. Clearly such a shift in Chinese policy towards cooperation and unity with Moscow over Vietnam further threatened Mao's position. This was the time when a number of articles in the Chinese press, obviously inspired by Mao, renewed the attack against "Khrushchev revisionism," and when under Lin Piao's orders the indoctrination of the PLA in the Thought of Mao Tse-tung and against Soviet "revisionism" was accelerated.

On September 3, 1965, two important essays, one by Lin Piao, the other by Lo Jui-ch'ing were published simultaneously in the *Peking Review,* indicating the opposed positions toward the Soviet offer. Lin Piao's article "Long Live the Victory of People's Wars" restated the well-known thesis of wars of national liberation as a means to defeat the capitalist powers in the nonindustrial countries. Lin Piao stressed that these wars of national liberation had to be fought by the peoples concerned without outside intervention, clearly a negative answer to the Soviet appeal for united action in support of Vietnam.

Lo Jui-ch'ing's essay under the title, "The People Defeated Japanese Fascism and They Certainly Can Defeat United States Imperialism Too," belittled the Sino-Soviet conflict calling it only a "debate," and stressed the advantage of interaction between Soviet and Chinese policies. In Lo's words:

> *One aspect of the historic significance of the debate of the last few years between the two lines in the international Communist movement is that it has enabled Marxism-Leninism to spread on an unprecedented scale and has promoted the integration of the universal truth of Marxism-Leninism with the concrete practice of the people's revolution in every country.* [15]

On this basis, Lo favored Sino-Soviet cooperation. It was Lo Jui-ch'ing's last published statement. Sometime later, probably in November, 1965, he was purged from his powerful position. [16] With Lo's capture the way was free for Mao and Lin to use military force in breaking down all obstructions to Mao's authority.

Nineteen sixty-six was then the decisive year for Mao's reassertion of his authority and his move to attack the Party that had been disobedient to him. However, to assert himself Mao had to counter the belief that he was physically incapacitated by a stroke and no longer capable of resuming the leadership. Pictures of Mao indicated a physical handicap presumably caused by a stroke which had left his right arm partly paralyzed. To counter these rumors and demonstrate his physical fitness, Mao organized on July 16, 1966, a swim in the Yangtze River. Mao's feat was advertised and broadcast nationwide and even abroad, in a fashion that reached ridiculous extremes of exaggeration. The claim was that in his swim Mao broke all olympic records and had, in superman fashion, wrought all kinds of miracles. Indeed the stories attached to Mao's feat in the *People's Daily* and other papers spoke of Mao's deed in a way which can only be compared to simplistic forms of religious deification.[17] These accounts of Mao's swim were only the beginning of a massive promotion of a quasi-religious Cult of Mao, whose Thought was alone the source of all inventions, discoveries, and the solutions to all problems incurred by his followers. "Thanks to the Thought of Mao Tse-tung" became the standard phrase used to explain all accomplishments, from scientific advances to the sale of cucumbers or successful operations on hopeless cases of worker patients.

THE RED GUARDS: *Young Generals of the Revolution*

One of Mao's most brilliant inspirations in the Great Proletarian Cultural Revolution was his use of high school and college students whom he mobilized to assault the party and government organizations in the provinces. Mao appears to have sensed the restlessness of youth in the educational institutions and knew how to exploit it for his political purpose. That this was no improvisation, but a well-planned program, can be surmised from Mao's comment to his secret service chief and confidante, K'ang Sheng, to whom he entrusted his idea and the organization of its execution in March, 1966.

A famous folktale read by most Chinese youngsters in their early years, and well known to Mao, was the story of a monkey, Sun Wu-k'ung, who used a magic golden stick to transform himself into many shapes.[18] The hero of the tale emerged from an old rock which had eroded through rain, wind and sunshine, and took on life in the form of a monkey who became a major mischief maker. Sun Wu-k'ung broke into Hell to erase his name from the record of the living and the dead; he entered

Paradise and ate the peaches of immortality and even tried to overthrow the heavenly emperor. He could leap a thousand miles and travel to the ends of the world. To help him in his battles the monkey would pull out some hairs, spit on them, cite the magic word, and each hair was transformed into hundreds of small monkeys who fought for Sun Wu-k'ung. When victory was won, Sun Wu-k'ung would use another magic word to turn the little monkeys back into hairs on his body. It was this magic story to which Mao referred when he told his trusted intelligence chief: "We must overthrow the king of Hell and liberate the little devils. For that purpose we need more Sun Wu-k'ungs from various localities to disrupt the heavenly palace.[19] These little devils were the Red Guards.

Actually the preparation for this venture of exploiting youthful discontent had been carried on since the fall of 1965 when Mao had sent the young officers and soldiers of the indoctrinated People's Liberation Army into the colleges to recruit Maoist followers. This effort was now to be backed by K'ang Sheng, who provided the professional intelligence organization behind the army's role. It did not take long for the party leaders to become aware of Mao's infiltration into the colleges and universities. To answer Mao's threat, Liu Shao-ch'i and the party leaders set up their own work teams in the colleges to support the party committees and administrators that were the targets of Mao's student organizations. The conflict within the educational institutions between the young work teams of Liu and the Party and the recruits of the Maoist student organizations had its origin in the social antagonism of the opposing student groups. Liu's work teams were composed mainly of children of the new party and administrative elite, who were also in many cases educationally better prepared for their college education than were their opponents. The Maoist youngsters, mostly recruited from a new type of student—the children of poor peasants, workers and soldiers, admitted to the schools on the basis of their political loyalty—were frequently poorly prepared for the studies which they had to pursue.[20] They were, therefore, at a disadvantage in the examinations and hostile to their more privileged and successful fellow students. This conflict translated into a political battle between Mao and the Party for the control of college and high school students.[21]

In this confrontation the Maoist student groups were supported by Mao's Cultural Revolution leaders. In June, Chiang Ch'ing, Chou En-lai and Ch'en Po-ta appeared in person at a meeting at Peking University to criticize the student leaders of the opposition for failure to attack the university president and the party authorities within the institution. Chiang Ch'ing claimed that Mao Tse-tung had forbidden the establishment of work teams by the Party, but had been disobeyed. She made it clear that "the question is not the form of working teams, but their direction of policy."[22] As a result of this backing by Mao, radical student groups in Peking and at other universities nationwide began to attack both the university administrations and their student supporters. At Nanking University a student group attacked by wall poster the university administration for failing proletarian students in the examinations. The result of these posters was a change in admission examination requirements; and students were praised for standing up against their teachers.

On July 28 Mao issued a directive abolishing all the party work teams in the universities and schools and ordered that in their place should be established mass organizations: "Teachers, students, and staff of all schools must separately elect and set up mass organizations at various levels." This expressly included the secondary schools.[23]

The formation of these Maoist student groups were the result of Mao's directive of June 2, 1966, in which he suspended admission to higher schools for six months and promised a proletarianization of education itself. Actually the schools and universities remained closed in the fall of 1966 and were not to reopen for over a year, so that students had ample opportunity and time to establish student organizations and to engage in their political work. A multitude of student organizations now sprang up in high schools, colleges and military cadet schools, and were given wholehearted support by the troops of the People's Liberation Army, especially in Peking.[24] At first numerous names were given to these organizations in the various institutions; eventually they became known as the *Red Guards.*[25]

With the organizational help of the People's Liberation Army and under its direction, the Red Guard movement rapidly became a mass movement that encompassed tens of millions of students. It was here that Mao's strategy to go directly to the masses could be applied—with the support of the PLA. Indeed, the Red Guards were Mao's main force used to attack and destroy the party and government administration in the first phase of the Great Proletarian Cultural Revolution. The students were flattered by the designation *revolutionary little generals,* which had first been applied to a class in a Canton middle school which had objected to Wu Han's play attacking Mao Tse-tung. Now, according to wall posters, "the little generals of the revolution were very excited" and soon enjoyed to the full their new privileged political role.

In August, 1966, the Eleventh Plenum of the Central Committe of the Party met in Peking to provide the official blessing for Mao's Great Proletarian Cultural Revolution. Liu Shao-ch'i had wanted to call the Central Committee earlier when he held full authority of the Party and control over the situation in Peking, but Mao had delayed this meeting until he was in secure command of Peking with the help of Lin Piao, who had shifted some loyal military units into the capital city. The Central Committee meeting was held in a hall which was surrounded by Lin Piao's forces. Less than half of the regular and alternate members were permitted to attend, and the galleries were filled with Mao's Red Guard representatives. Under this pressure, on August 8 the session accepted a sixteen-article resolution that contained the main goals of Mao's authority over the Party, phrased as "the victory of the proletarian revolution over the open and hidden representatives of the bourgeoisie, the reactionaries and capitalist roaders, as represented by the leadership of the Party." The Red Guards, Mao's revolutionary masses, were to carry out this revolution. Article Two of the sixteen-article resolution spoke of "large numbers of revolutionary young people, previously unknown, who had become courageous and daring path breakers" and who had through their character posters and attacks become the "main current" of the revolution. As a reward they were promised in Article Ten an educational reform with shorter courses, simplified teaching material, and the fusion of their studies with other activities.

This formal sanction and acclaim given to their new role led to an immediate nationwide rising of Red Guard organizations.[26] Millions of them came to Peking on trains and buses provided and placed at their disposal by the People's Liberation Army that organized the logistics of the student mass movement. Between August and November, 1966, nine mass student rallies were held at the Great Square of Tienanmen in Peking where eleven million revolutionary students were assembled to see their leader and to listen to speeches of Lin Piao, Chou En-lai and others. These mass meetings, held in an atmosphere of great excitement, galvanized frenzied emotions that were to propel the Red Guards into their work for the revolution. Behind the scene, it was the People's Liberation Army that organized and directed the rallies, transported the students to and from the square and arranged their marching order and placement; and behind it was the hand of K'ang Sheng's secret police.

Before they were directed to attack Mao's party opposition, the Red Guards were to get an experience in social revolution. They were instructed to attack the *Four Olds:* old customs, old habits, old thoughts and old culture.[27] They were also to attack the *Five Black Elements:* landlords, rich peasants, counter-revolutionaries, rightists and bad elements. They were to "pick up one by one the blood sucking worms, the enemies of the people . . . and change the whole aspect of our society."[28] Rampaging in the cities, they changed the street names and traffic signs — red became the signal for "go" — broke into middle-class houses to loot, smashed furniture and belongings, and attacked in the

...ng University students organize into Red Guard Units during Cultural Revolution.   *Courtesy of Ming Pao.*

...ng Ch'ing, Chou En-lai, and Chang Ch'un-ch'iao review the Red Guards, ...   *Courtesy of Ming Pao.*

Wall posters.   *Courtesy of Ming Pao.*

...tory workers (left), agricultural students (right), and nursery school children (below) read Mao's *Little Red Book*.   *Courtesy of Ming Pao.*

Young women at work in a quarr
Courtesy of Ming Pao.

Red Guards demonstrating. *Courtesy of Ming Pao.*

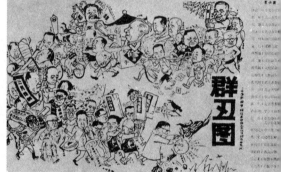

People's Militia at daily morning drill.
Henri Cartier-Bresson, Courtesy of Magnum Photos.

Wall poster attacking victims of the Cultural Revolution.
Courtesy of Ming Pao.

Young students at work with the peasants.
Courtesy of Ming Pao.

Students on a farm reading from the *Little Red Book*. *Courtesy of Ming Pao.*

University students at work in the countryside. *Courtesy of Ming Pao.*

street passers-by who attracted their hostility by dress or demeanor. They attacked, imprisoned, tortured and sometimes killed their teachers.[29] There are many eye-witness accounts including those of foreign diplomats who saw elderly people beaten to death on the streets or in trains. There are accounts of the destruction of irreplaceable ancient art objects in museums and homes, and the terrible story of the famous Chinese pianist Liu Shih-k'un, a runner-up to Van Cliburn in the Moscow competition of 1958, who had his wrists twisted so he could not play again.[30]

The violence was obviously intended to have the effect of creating an atmosphere of fear through a reign of terror. Neither the police nor the military interfered with these Red Guards. Mao Tse-tung clearly approved of the violence and brutalities, which he appears to have regarded as a necessary battle-hardening of his storm troopers of the Proletarian Cultural Revolution.[31]

These brutalities may well have been Mao's calculated operation to prepare the Red Guards for their main role as an attack force against the entrenched party and government authorities in the provinces and localities of China. For this purpose the Red Guards had been organized not only in Peking and other key cities, but in the provinces as well, where they at first followed the same routine as applied in Peking, attacking the Four Olds. From there they were drawn to Peking, indoctrinated, their units linked to the Peking Red Guards and then returned from the capital to the provinces to carry out their assignment. This was the period of Red Guard travel between Peking and the countryside called *an exchange of experiences.*[32]

In November, 1966, the Red Guards officially learned who the real targets of their attack were: "the power holders in the Communist party who followed the capitalist road." Until that time, the attack on the party's top echelon had been camouflaged. No one knew for certain what was meant by *capitalist roaders* or who were the *power holders* announced as the target of the attack.

The new phase of the attack was marked by Mao's speech of October 26, 1966, in which he gloated over his enemies and their fears and boasted about his initiative in starting the Cultural Revolution, which his enemies regarded as a great calamity. After seventeen years of the socialist revolution, one blow by him had placed his enemies in a "fine mess" and put things on the right track. By November, it became official that Liu Shao-ch'i and Teng Hsiao-p'ing were themselves the main culprits. Red Guards were permitted into the enclosed compound in the center of Peking where the party leaders lived to drag them out and submit them to "struggle meetings." On December 4, P'eng Chen was arrested and Liu Shao-ch'i and Teng Hsiao-p'ing were attacked in wall posters in Peking which soon became known nationwide. On December 16 and 17, secret meetings were held in which Chou En-lai, Chen Po-ta, K'ang Sheng and Chiang Ch'ing participated, planning the destruction of the party leaders. Finally, on December 26, a wall poster published Liu Shao-ch'i's self-criticism allegedly expressed already at the end of October.[33] Teng Hsiao-p'ing similarly confessed on October 23. Mao's opposition in the central leadership of the Party was eliminated.

At the provincial and local level, however, the party and government cadres attempted to deflect and counter the Red Guard attack with an organizational move of their own. There was no attempt directly to oppose Mao's strategy of forming Red Guard units to carry on the revolution. The answer was rather to turn Mao's strategy against him by gaining support from worker and commune peasant groups to whom the party leaders made concessions in the form of wage raises, distribution of grain and the permission of private production that would improve the standards of living of workers and peasants. On this basis representatives of worker and peasant organizations were paid to go on *exchange of experiences* of their own to neighboring localities and to Peking to present their grievances there. This countermove was naturally extremely popular with the workers and peasants, tired of the economic stringencies of their life. It had to be countered by Mao.

Anticipating the conflict between Red Guard teams sent out from Peking to the provinces and the workers and peasants from the factories and the communes, Chou En-lai ordered the Red Guards in September not to move into the factories, communes and villages.[34] When the workers and peasants themselves took to the road, their move was immediately condemned by the Maoist group as antirevolutionary *economism* which put private interests over that of the collective.

The party's use of the workers and peasants seriously embarrassed the Maoists. Economism not only affected production and government control of economic resources, it severely disrupted the transportation system which had already been overstrained by the travels of the Red Guards. The Maoists therefore distinguished between students who could travel and who had the time, since the schools were closed, and workers and peasants who were not permitted to leave their work, but were told to promote the Cultural Revolution on the job. The new slogan was *Grasp Revolution and Promote Production.*

The exclusion of factories, communes and local party and government agencies in the agricultural and industrial institutions from revolutionary takeover was, however, only temporary. If the Red Guards could not break down party control in local areas and moreover were divided by the establishment of pseudo-Red Guards under party protection, a new force would have to be formed to bring about the seizure of power by the left. The Red Guards were therefore expanded and transformed into *revolutionary rebels*. The question for Mao was how to break down the resistance of the party-backed workers and peasants against the leftist takover. The method chosen appears to have been a combination of infiltration and military force. As had been the practice in the schools, the lowest element of the workers and peasants, those with complaints against management, were drawn to the Maoist side. Any conflict between management and workers was turned into a class struggle; workers were not to be punished for attacking managers who had taken the so-called capitalist road. The managers were told that they were not permitted to fire workers, dock wages or revoke contracts with either regular or temporary employees.[35]

This development within factories and communes was complemented by roving teams of young Red Guards, their numbers possibly padded by local dissidents who were now sent into the factories and communes, "in an organized and planned fashion," accompanied by military personnel.[36] On December 19, a ten-point regulation on the Cultural Revolution in industry was announced on wall posters.[37] In essence, this regulation decreed that workers within the factories and peasants within the communes should elect their own Cultural Revolution teams or committees. It also guaranteed the protection of those who had demonstrated against managers or cadres within the factories and communes, and it related this local organization of the Maoist left to the well-planned and orderly student participation. All this, however, should be done without any interruption of work, and without any conflicts or fighting.

The Red Guard teams of the schools and colleges were thus to be complemented by the so-called Revolutionary Rebel teams in the factories and communes. That this was not accomplished without bitter resistance could be seen from the *People's Daily* editorial of December 26, which complained about the "capitalist, revisionist and even feudalist influence" of leadership and management which had "impeded revolutionary fervor of the workers' masses." To counter the benefits given to workers and peasants by the party leaders—condemned as *economism* —the Maoists promised an eight-hour workday and at the same time restored the rehabilitation and wages to those workers whom the party leaders had dismissed as *counterrevolutionaries* because of their anti-management activities.

The organization of the new revolutionary rebels was by no means a clear-cut affair. While the local party and government leadership was in many cases toppled, the second echelon had been able to effect the formation of new power groups. The opportunity to organize new political leadership led to a mushrooming of organizations, each of which claimed to represent the correct Maoist line, and accused the others of being counterrevolutionaries. To distinguish politically between them was all the more difficult since political claims were often only a thin disguise for vested interests. Whether backed by the Maoist center or local party and People's Liberation Army interests, all these groups claimed to carry out the Cultural Revolution in the name of Mao Tsetung. Revolutionary rebels or revolutionary upheaval groups throughout the country supported by the People's Liberation Army issued the same ten-point regulations that were the bases for the new local political structure. The emphasis was on local teams and on the entrance of revolutionary teachers, students and intelligentsia in a "planned, organized way to the factories and to the villages to work with and learn from workers and peasants, and discuss with them questions of the Cultural Revolution.[38] The result was a mixture of numerous worker and Red Guard groups formed into revolutionary upheaval organizations.[39] On December 13, an editorial in the *People's Daily* and in *Red Flag* declared that the "broad masses of revolutionary workers" had joined the movement, and from that time on the working class was described as the leading force and most active factor in the revolution.

On January 1, a *Red Flag* editorial confirmed that the Cultural Revolution had moved into the factories and villages of all provinces and that the "masses" were ready to control the party committees. By now there was a "left" in the local areas which could take over and establish a new authority in those administrative areas where the Red Guards had failed. This was the time for an all-out attack against the party control in the provinces and localities.

"Seize Power"

On January 9, 1967, the call went out to all revolutionaries to "seize power," a call repeated by radio and newspapers all over the country. Having attacked, abused, in some cases killed, the "local power rulers," Mao's revolutionaries were now to take over the government in the localities themselves. Obviously, the Red Guard and revolutionary rebels could not do that by themselves. They needed the backing of a superior force, not only to overcome local resistance at all levels, but also to establish the new power structure. This force was to be provided by the People's Liberation Army.

On January 21, 1967, Maoist headquarters called on the People's Liberation Army to give active support to the revolutionary masses of the "left."[40] This directive explicitly ordered the army to give such support when "genuine proletarian leftists ask the army for help" in their struggle to seize power. The army was no longer to be an "air raid shelter for the party power holders taking the capitalist road and diehards who persist in the bourgeois reactionary line."

The People's Liberation Army had, of course, been behind the organization and transportation of the Red Guards but had, in the majority of cases, supported a "conservative" element in the provincial takeover. No longer permitted to remain in the background or to remain neutral, the People's Liberation Army must now take a major part in the revolution on the side of the Left.

The move to throw the military actively into the power struggle must have been made by Mao out of necessity and, as it appears, without previous plan or preparation. At this very moment, new leadership purges were undertaken in the People's Liberation Army to weaken any opposition to the application of the new directive. To undertake purges at this time only served to aggravate the internal and external risks of the embroilment of the People's Liberation Army.[41] The dangers were obvious. An army involved in a major political battle would scarcely be capable of defending the country against outside attack. Internally the new role of political action would provide a test of loyalty for the People's Liberation Army (PLA), a test crucial not only for the Cultural Revolution but for the very survival of Mao's leadership.[42] The measures now taken to counter these dangers indicate by their substance and timing the improvised character of the whole operation.

On January 28, only five days after the PLA was called in to "support the left," a new directive and another order of the Military Affairs Commission of the Central Committee were issued simultaneously circumscribing and limiting PLA action both geographically and organizationally.[43] The new directive proclaimed that: "the great cultural revolution in military regions should be carried out stage by stage and group by group according to the instructions of Chairman Mao and Vice Chairman Lin Piao." Action should be postponed "in the military regions on the first line of defense against imperialism and revisionism (Tsinan, Nanking, Foochow, Canton, Kunming and Sinkiang) and the Wuhan Military Region."[44] The pretext of this postponement was national defense, and it may well have been important to prevent political turmoil in areas militarily so sensitive.

The use of the PLA as a controlling force in this power seizure was a highly dangerous undertaking. The Red Guards had begun to penetrate units of the PLA themselves and to propagate their revolutionary attack against the "power holders." This led to "excesses" inside and outside the PLA, which endangered the discipline. Mao therefore ordered that: "In armed force units where the Great Cultural Revolution has been launched, the big contending should be done by reasoning." No more "assaults on military leader organizations," were permitted in order to safeguard military discipline. Even in those provinces that were not excluded from revolutionary action, a vital distinction was drawn between command organizations and troops. In the former, the Great Cultural Revolution was to be carried out according to discussions but "armies, divisions, regiments, battalions, companies and special units designated by the military commission . . ." were not to do any contending but only to engage in positive "education" while retaining their preparation for national defense.[45] Only the leading organs above the army level were therefore subjected to the revolutionary purges, while the troops were to remain a disciplined force to guard against outside attack as well as to be used to back up the action of the revolutionary left. Mao was to retain control over the military and, therefore, instituted a double limitation of the PLA's action in the Cultural Revolution on a geographical, vertical basis as well as on an institutional, horizontal basis.

This was all the more crucial since the breakdown of the political system forced Mao to use the military as a form of local government where no other existed by establihsing military control commissions during February and March, 1967, in most provinces of China. These military control commissions were to be temporary authorities until Mao could establish his new political system.

It appears doubtful whether Mao had from the outset a grand design for all the steps taken in this revolutionary drama. He may have had to improvise as new situations and emergencies required. But when he decided to turn against the Party, Mao had to have a plan for a new institutional framework which was to take the place of the Party that he was to overthrow. His slogan of leading *the masses* had to be given some new form. Since most of his *little revolutionary generals,* the Red Guards, did not belong to the Communist party, Mao had to create a non-party revolutionary organization responsive to himself. This new "mass" structure was, so Mao said, to be modeled after the Paris Commune of 1871.

During the siege of Paris by the Prussian armies in 1871, the French *proletariat*—at least this is what Karl Marx had called the French popular forces—had taken up arms and had directly engaged its enemy in a struggle to seize political power. Describing this French history, a *Red Flag* article of March 24, 1966, later reproduced in the *Peking Review,* first mentioned the Paris Commune of 1871.[46] According to this article, the Paris Commune represented a pure model of the proletarian revolution. The article dwelt with great emphasis on the link between the "proletariat" and the armed forces. Next, the article stressed what may have been the main reason for Mao's interest in the Paris Commune, the fact that this was a proletarian revolution without a Communist party. In spite of "reactionary slanders" criticizing the Paris Commune because of the absence of a Marxist political party, the commune had been a working class movement, as stated by Marx himself. By introducing a type of organization which Karl Marx had once regarded as a proletarian mass organization, Mao pretended to stay within the framework of Marxism — though he quietly abandoned Lenin's party concept.

The description in the article of the functions of the Paris Commune reveals Mao's own ideals for his proletarian revolution: The "masses" were the real masters in the Paris Commune; they elected the members of the commune by universal suffrage, subject to recall at any time; the masses were organized on a wide scale, and discussed all important matters; they carefully checked on the work of the commune, and the commune members paid close attention to the views of the masses, and attended mass meetings. All this was in contrast, so it was claimed, to the privileged system established by the "leading clique of Khrushchev's revisionists," who had completely ignored the important experience of the Paris Commune.

If this article laid the theoretical foundation, the political basis for the acceptance of the Paris Commune system was established in Article 9 of the sixteen-point decision of the Cultural Revolution of August 8, 1966.[47] This fitted Mao's strategy of a direct approach to the masses through a fanatical indoctrination in the Thought of Mao Tse-tung. When the time to seize power appeared to be at hand, a *Red Flag* editorial of January 1, 1967, called for the establishment of people's communes after the Paris model. The communes were to be controlled by the proletariat, which would elect its representatives and could recall them. In this way, Mao's "proletarian" revolutionists could indeed replace the Party.

This attempt at a Paris Commune type of political system was the one occasion at which Mao attempted to institutionalize his vague concept of relationship between the leader and the masses. Mao had played with hazy ideas of anarchism in his youth. His earlier trend towards voluntarism may have been based on Mao's genuine belief that rule by the people themselves without a bureaucratic structure would be possible if the people were properly directed. These ideas were, however, clearly in contrast with Mao's autocratic nature which led him to refute all compromise and cooperation threatening the establishment of his one-man rule under which he brooked no opposition. His attitude towards rule by the masses had always been more a dream than a reality. Mao only accepted the masses that followed him; if they did not, they were the "misguided masses." The action of the masses was never to be decided by *them* but by the leader, by Mao. The position of the masses was, in any case, never to be influenced by the will of the majority. If the majority was against him, Mao relied on those masses that would go "against the tide." Those masses who were with Mao were the "proletarian masses," those who were against him were on the side of the "bourgeoisie." After all, the masses had been compared by him to a sheet of white paper on which he could print his will. The Paris Commune was for Mao this type of mass organization and was as close as he ever came to finding an institutional formula for his utopian concept.

A number of attempts were made in January and February, 1967, to establish such Paris Communes. On February 7, an attempt was made in Honan province to establish such a Commune but it was opposed by the PLA. On February 13, wall posters in Peking announced the establishment of a Peking People's Commune, but nothing seems to have come of it. The Harbin radio announced on February 16 the establishment of a Paris Commune in Harbin. However, the Shanghai Commune, formally set up on February 5, 1967, was the most important and instructive test case for evaluating the attempt. [48] Here the Shanghai People's Commune was established at a mass rally of one million "rebels, revolutionary people and the PLA," only to be abandoned with considerable embarassment on February 24 at another "Oath-taking Rally for holding high the Great Red Banner of Mao Tse-tung Thought and further developing the Struggle for Seizure of Power." [49]

The key figures in the revolutionary takeover in Shanghai were Chang Ch'un-ch'iao and Yao Wen-yüan. After their attack on the anti-Maoist party writers, they had participated in the August Central Committee meeting in Peking and in January, 1967, were entrusted with the revolutionary takeover in Shanghai. The Maoist takeover was made possible with the support of the Shanghai Garrison Commander and his officers, and of commanders of naval and air force units stationed in Shanghai. They were backed up by two additional PLA units sent to the Shanghai-Nanking area. The main problem appears to have been that of insufficient support from the workers in Shanghai. The Maoist workers were only a small minority of several thousand, while the *Workers' Red Militia,* organized by the Party Municipal Committee with military aid, numbered 800,000. The Workers' Red Militia cut off water, electricity and communications and created chaos until Chang Ch'un-ch'iao brought it into line with military support by occuping the party offices and removing the leaders. Mao's men had won.

When the Shanghai Commune was set up, however, the Maoists had apparently overreached themselves. Whether a system based on a mass movement could be established by such a small minority of the so-called masses may be very questionable. More questionable still was the assumption that the officers of the PLA who had been instrumental in establishing the new revolutionary authority and who had now become a dominant force could be expected to abandon their newly gained role in favor of a hazy concept of authority that promised continued anarchy.

The decision on the Paris Commune system appears, however, to have been of utmost importance to Chairman Mao. Before abandoning his dream of the Paris Commune, Mao invited Chang Ch'un-ch'iao and Yao Wen-yüan to Peking to question them and to review the commune problem. According to Red Guard papers and Chang Ch'un-ch'iao's report, Mao was asking for Chang and Yao before they had arrived at the Peking Airport and was then waiting for them at the door of his residence. He had several lengthy talks with them and was "highly concerned about and understood Shanghai." Subsequently Mao summoned and presided over meetings of the Central Committee, at which the question of Shanghai and other work was discussed and a series of decisions was issued. Then Mao again received Chang and Yao on the eve of their return to Shanghai.

When Chang and Yao returned to Shanghai on February 23, the decision had been made by Mao to discard the Shanghai Commune organization and transform it into a *Revolutionary Committee,* the structure then adopted for the entire country as the new political system. The argument which Chang Ch'un-ch'iao used to explain the shift from the Paris Commune to a new form of administration, the Revolutionary Committees, indicates something of the reasons for the failure of Mao's plan. Chang noted that the real takeover was not a matter simply of occupying buildings but of establishing a functioning government, which required the expertise of cadres and the backing of military power. From this explanation one may imply that the military and presumably Chou En-lai, as head of the administration, concerned about the establishment of a workable administrative system, appear to have balked at Mao's commune plan and at the authority given to the Red Guards and the revolutionary rebels as the revolutionary leaders of Mao's masses. The excuse which Chang Ch'un-ch'iao used to explain the shift was simply that it was a change of name from Paris Commune to Revolutionary Committee, which was necessary because if the former name was to be retained, the whole of China would have to be called a Paris Commune and this would hardly be proper. It seemed a rather lame argument to cover the retreat from Mao's radical program. Perhaps it was more to the point when Chang Ch'un-ch'iao said: "With the commune inaugurated, do we still need the Party? I think we need it, because we must have a hard core, whether it is called the Communist Party or a social democratic party. . . . In short we still need a party."[50]

Thus, Mao's attempt to introduce a Paris Commune-type political structure was abortive wherever it was made.[51]

The failure of establishing the system of Paris communes could be regarded as a decisive defeat of Mao's major purpose in the Great Proletarian Revolution. Mao had succeeded in overthrowing the party administration and structure which was opposed to him, but he had not been able to realize his utopian plan, the introduction of a non-party system of mass organization under his leadership.

Its failure demonstrated the need of reestablishing authority; and this could only be done if the military were moved from the supporting role which they had played into the front position. Mao had used the strategy of removing the authority of his opponents and letting loose the Red Guard genii. He had created havoc and introduced a reign of terror which obviously was inspired and approved by Mao, who had spurred them on, who approved of them, and whose interpretation of Marxism-Leninism was defined by him in the one sentence: "To rebel is justified."[52] When the Red Guards had fulfilled their purpose and proved not disciplined enough to follow Mao's orders, they had, however, to be recalled, and the Paris Commune project had to be abandoned.

The result of the failure of this experiment was the establishment of a new structure as a compromise between the need for authority, for expertise and of Mao's revolutionary purpose. The new structure, called *Revolutionary Committees,* was formed by three elements: the military, the "liberated" cadres and the revolutionaries—known as the *three-in-one combination.* The military was to provide the power leverage and the controlling force; some cadres who submitted to the Cultural Revolution were to contribute the professional expertise; and the Maoist revolutionaries—the Red Guards—were to make up Mao's leftist political ingredient.

The shift towards Revolutionary Committees was to the advantage not only of the military, who became the dominant element in the new government structure, but also to Chou En-lai's group which would supply the administrative cadres and experts essential for a new working structure. Chou became, therefore, next to Lin Piao the leading figure in the new system.

Chou En-lai's new authority was the result of his skillful handling of the politics of the Cultural Revolution. During the revolutionary upheaval Chou En-lai sided from the outset with Mao and Lin Piao against the party leadership of Liu Shao-ch'i. For Chou as prime minister this stand was facilitated by the fact that the attack was primarily directed against the Party, not the administration at the center. Chou therefore did not oppose the political drives of the Cultural Revolution but attempted to give them his own direction. His primary concern was the defense of the basic administrative structure at the center and the maintenance of his own role as well as the reestablishment of a reasonably stable administration in the provinces. In Peking, Chou En-lai succeeded in January, 1967, in exempting the Capital Construction Engineering Corps from the penetration of Red Guard revolutionaries. This organization had control over a broad range of military and civil production, including strategic weapon facilities, and was therefore vital for an orderly continuation of the production in this area. Chou En-lai also manipulated the *seizure of power* in the key ministries of machine building, dealing with nuclear weapons and other military equipment, and protected their personnel. While sacrificing some ministers and staff of lesser ministries to satisfy the revolutionary appetite of the Red Guards, Chou maintained control over the basic aspects of administration, of military production and economic affairs. He also took a leading part in selecting the personnel for the restructuring of the administration of the twenty-nine provinces, municipalities and autonomous areas of China. In the process of the complex negotiations and compromises necessary for the rebuilding of the administration, Chou En-lai was successful in protecting former military leaders and others against Red Guard excesses and therefore gained the support of many of these leaders who became beholden to him.

The most difficult problem was to bring about the necessary compromises between the many Red Guard groups that had mushroomed into existence and were competing among each other for the turf of their respective areas of control. The power struggle among these groups led to much fighting and loss of life, and the eventual compromises were not only a matter of skillful negotiations but also of the use of power which could be provided only by the PLA. It was up to the army to knock heads together among the leaders of the various revolutionary rebel groups and to unite them in what was called the *great alliances*. The problem was that the party opposition would also organize great alliances among its revolutionary rebel groups; and, though declaring these illegal, Mao could not stop a flourishing organizational development of many different political colors. It was therefore obviously not easy to negotiate the political agreements necessary for the great alliances and for the three-in-one combinations, which had to be formed before the Revolutionary Committees could be established. These agreements had to be worked out by compromise in prolonged sessions in which Chou En-lai came to play a major role.

It was a slow process. The Red Guards, infatuated with their new role, remained intractable in many cases and continued their zealous internecine fighting. Only six acceptable provincial Revolutionary Committees were established between January and April of 1967. Others were regarded by Mao as "false" or "fake" power seizures in which the party followers of Liu Shao-ch'i were able to maintain themselves by making full use of the Red Guard chaos and disunity.

To deal with the Red Guards and the revolutionary rebel organizations an attempt was made to stop their travel and send them home. In February, no more free meals were provided for the young travelers and all reception centers were ordered closed but with little effect on the student peregrinations. As late as September, a joint appeal was made by Chou En-lai, Ch'en Po-ta and Chiang Ch'ing to the students to return home immediately.

What was more serious, the young radicals continued their attempts to penetrate the PLA and overthrow army authority and discipline. When the army defended itself against this attack by "ruthless armed suppression," killing a number of rebels in several incidents, it was told in April, 1967, by an order of the Military Affairs Commission on Mao's direction, that "in dealing with mass organizations, be they revolutionary or controlled by reactionary elements . . . shooting is forbidden."[53] It was this order which forced the PLA to accept abuses and even physical attacks without being able to retaliate. Mao's adventure in permitting his radical organizations to attack the very military force that was his mainstay of power was playing with fire. It was dramatized by a major incident that occurred in the city of Wuhan in mid-July of 1967.

Victory for the People's Liberation Army

The year from the spring of 1967 to the fall of 1968 was a chaotic and stormy period. The Red Guard and revolutionary rebel forces, which Mao had conjured up for his Cultural Revolution, did their best to make a clean sweep of the old order. They dragged out the party leaders opposed to Mao and toppled them. To remove them officially from their positions, Mao still needed the approval of the highest Politburo members. In a meeting of the Standing Committee of the Politburo in March of 1967, held in a building that was surrounded by violent street demonstrations of his Red Guards, Mao succeeded in mustering the necessary majority—six to five—to have his enemies removed from their positions of authority.

However, this was not enough for Mao, who meant to realize the utopian concept of his leadership of the masses by carrying the Cultural Revolution as far as it would go into the Central Government and even into the military forces. By threatening what was left of the Chinese

Central Government structure, and of the military discipline itself, Mao brought the country close to a breakdown of all order. Beginning in February, 1967, news from all parts of China spoke of Red Guard units that had attacked military command organizations, seized military men, beat them up, took arms and ammunition from military depots and armories, and even broke into security systems, occupying secret file rooms. Conditions in some military units could be judged from the wording of emergency orders to contain the radicals: "The style of killing at one stroke can never be encouraged" or "We cannot advocate anarchism, radical democratization" or "From now on nobody is allowed to storm and attack military leadership organs. . . . Attacking of armed force units, local war preparation systems, confidential systems, and the security systems . . . are also forbidden from now on."[54] But these orders were to little avail. When the army began to defend itself against these attacks, the order of "No shooting" had been issued. This order, too, was not obeyed and incidents occurred in which a number of rebels were killed or wounded.[55] As a result of this threatening situation, a number of government leaders, such as Chou En-lai, and some of the prominent military figures, attempted to counsel Mao on constraint of his radical policies—with limited success; the clashes continued and in mid-July, led to the Wuhan incident.

Centrally located in the Yangtze area at the point where a major tributary, the Han River, joins the Yangtze, the metropolis of Wuhan is a complex of three cities: Wuchang, the provincial capital of Hupeh province; Hanyang, the site of one of the largest steel works in China; and Hankou, north of the Yangtze River, a former treaty port and major commerical and industrial center. Its location at the heart of the navigation system of the Yangtze and its chief tributary, and as a railroad crossing point of the main north-south line from Peking to Canton and the east-west railroad system, makes Wuhan the foremost economic, communications and strategic center in central China. Because of this strategic location, military control of Wuhan was an especially sensitive issue for the leadership in Peking.

In the spring of 1967 Wuhan's military regional commander, General Ch'en Tsai-tao, had backed a mass organization called *a million heroes,* formed by the people's armed militia with the cooperation of the former public security bureau, which had maintained order and opposed radical Red Guards sent in to overthrow the local party authorities, but attacking the military leaders as well. A number of these radicals had been killed in local clashes. Mao sent two representatives from his Cultural Revolution headquarters in Peking to investigate the incidents.

The two emissaries were Hsieh Fu-chih, minister of public security and member of the Politburo, one of the key figures of the Peking leadership, and a strong supporter of Mao in the Cultural Revolution; and Wang Li, one of the original members of Mao's Cultural Revolution group, established by Madame Mao and Ch'en Po-ta. In their approach to the Wuhan incident, these two emissaries acted more like grand inquisitors than as men inclined to settle a serious conflict by compromise. They openly sided with the attacking Red Guards and offended the military commanders who tried to present their account of the incident. Consequently, the two Maoist leaders were seized by the militia leaders, beaten, tortured, and then marched through the streets with dunce caps on their heads. They were only freed when Chou En-lai—backed by naval and air units under Lin Piao's command—intervened in person and secured removal of Ch'en Tsai-tao from his position and a purge of the military leadership in Wuhan.[56]

Rather than serving as a warning, this incident led to a short period of intensified attack against the PLA under the slogan of *Dragging out the small handful of powerholders in the army.* By now the army was no longer permitted to carry out its own Cultural Revolution purges. The "powerholders in the army" were mentioned almost daily in all national, regional and local newspapers with the demand to "strike them down and make them stink," the typical phrase of denunciation by Mao's Left during this phase of the Cultural Revolution.[57] Mao's wife, Chiang Ch'ing, fanned the flames by making a statement advising the Red Guards to "attack with reason, but defend with force" which resulted in further Red Guard raids on army arsenals and escalated the fighting.

It was the military's discontent with their impossible role as supporters of the radical Left which remained free to attack and purge them, that eventually forced Mao to rein in his attempt of carrying the Cultural Revolution into the PLA. The army fought back, and Mao had to retreat. From the end of July on, there appeared in the *People's Daily* and other newspapers a new slogan, *Support the army and cherish the people,* which was printed for several days side-by-side with attacks against the "army powerholders."

The confrontation between the PLA and the Maoist radical Left ended in August with the victory of the slogan, *Raise high the great banner of supporting the army and cherishing the people,* which then became the dominent theme. The defeat of the Maoist Left was marked by a speech by Chiang Ch'ing on September 5 in which she referred to the "mistaken slogan" to drag out the small handful of powerholders in the army, condemned all attacks against the PLA, and only pleaded with the military not to be too harsh on the Red Guards who had been overenthusiastic in their revolutonary zeal.

The Red Guard attacks against the PLA had their counterpart in their assault on the foreign ministry and their attempt to expand the Cultural Revolution from the homegrounds to the field of international ventures. At the end of 1966, Mao recalled all his foreign ambassadors—with one exception, that of Egypt. The embassy staffs remaining abroad began to wear Mao buttons and use every occasion to affront the government and peoples of their host countries, disrupting all normal relations. This move towards self-established isolation and the introduction of seeming irrationality into the field of diplomatic relations was frequently regarded abroad as a peculiar kind of madness, characteristic of the whole Cultural Revolution. Some of the actions that followed appeared indeed to fly in the face of all civilized conduct and could only serve to alienate foreign countries and their public opinion. Yet, breaking off foreign relations at the time of domestic revolutionary upheaval could intentionally or instinctively also serve to protect the chaotic domestic situation from exploitation by foreign intervention; the isolation might well have been intended.

However, the Red Guard actions toward the foreign representatives in China led to such vulgar and sadistic extremes that more sophisticated leaders like Chou En-lai, though siding with Mao, made every effort to neutralize these excesses. The attacks began with an assault against the foreign minister, Ch'en Yi, Chou En-lai's close collaborator and protégé, who was several times "struggled against." In the course of the Red Guard seizures of government agencies, several radical, discontented staff members of the Foreign Ministry organized their own mass organization and attempted several times to seize the Foreign Ministry during the period from April to August, 1967. Much of the time during these months, Ch'en Yi's and Chou En-lai's control of the foreign ministry was greatly restricted until in August Ch'en Yi lost his post of foreign minister all together to be temporarily replaced by the leader of the radical revolutionaries. The months leading up to this seizure of power were a period of demonstrations abroad and assaults on foreign embassies and their staffs in Peking.

It began at the end of January with demonstrations against the Soviet Embassy. The pretext was an incident in Moscow at which Chinese students, called home by Mao, had staged a demonstration at Lenin's tomb and were removed by the Soviet police. Exploiting this incident and distorting the facts, the Chinese press transformed the incident into a bloody and savage fight, and when the students came home they donned bandages on the plane and were received with demonstrations of outraged sympathy for their suffering. As anticipated, this led to attacks on the Soviet Embassy, which was harassed by continuous mass demonstrations of Red Guards, troops and peasants. When the Soviets sent their dependents home, the wives and children were humiliated at the airport before being allowed to leave. The Czechs followed the Soviet example and so did the Poles and East Germans. At this point, Chou En-lai interfered, demanding in a public appearance that foreign diplomats be protected from the demonstrations, and, for a while, the incidents ended. They were resumed in April, coinciding with the new leftist trend in Red Guard behavior as encouraged by Mao Tse-tung. At the time the Chinese charge d'affaire in Indonesia, Yao Teng-shan, returned to Peking after having been expelled from Indonesia as a result of Chinese demonstrations there. He soon became a leader of the foreign office radical Left. In May, his group invaded and occupied the Foreign Ministry, smashed doors and windows, beat up officials and broke onto the confidential archives raiding secret documents and files.

In the summer and fall of 1967, during the height of Red Guard violence in China and abroad, the British became a special target of attack. The immediate cause of the British being singled out for special attacks was the spread of Red Guard activities to Hong Kong, the British crown colony on the south China coast.[58] Hong Kong, originally established by the British as a free port and entrepôt for international trade in Asia, developed into a booming trading and industrial center whose population, almost entirely Chinese, greatly increased after the Communist victory in China. Large numbers of refugees fled then from the mainland, many of them highly skilled and educated and some succeeding in transferring their capital resources to the British colony.[59] Under the stimulation of this influx, by 1976 Hong Kong reached a population of about four and a half million people and became a thriving industrial center whose economy remains in many ways linked to China.

There is no doubt that the armies of the People's Republic of China could have taken Hong Kong at any time with little or no resistance, but it appeared unlikely that this would have been to the advantage of the People's Republic. As a result of British policy aiming at providing full trade opportunities to the People's Republic of China, Hong Kong had become the main economic link between Communist China and the non-Communist world. Its industry depended to a large degree on raw material from the mainland; its Chinese population, like overseas Chinese elsewhere, provided a large financial contribution to the People's Republic, through food parcels and later through subsidies to their relatives within China. Hong Kong had therefore become for Peking the chief source of foreign exchange to the amount of about $600 million per year. Any Chinese military takeover would end this independent economic role of Hong Kong, and would kill the goose that lays the golden eggs. Indeed at the time when Mao Tse-tung accused Khrushchev of appeasement and lack of support for revolutions and wars of national liberation, Khrushchev retaliated, pointing to Mao Tse-tung's unwillingness to take action against Hong Kong.[60]

Hong Kong remained thus unaffected by any direct military threat. During the Cultural Revolution, Chinese Communists in Hong Kong began, however, to create disturbances and street demonstrations in an attempt to force the British administration to submit to a series of humiliating demands which, at the very least, would have led to Chinese Communist domination within the British colony. The British remained firm, however, and they received the wholehearted support of the Chinese population of Hong Kong, which clearly preferred the British administration to Communist domination. The majority of them had escaped from the mainland and understood the situation in the People's Republic only too well. They could, therefore, not be intimidated, and Hong Kong's trade and industry went on as usual.

British defiance of the Communist threat in Hong Kong, however, left the British Embassy in Peking especially vulnerable to attacks by the radical Red Guards when they had succeeded in taking over the Chinese Foreign Ministry in August 1967. On August 22, the British Embassy in Peking was surrounded by a mob that broke through a line of unarmed Chinese troops, entered the embassy and set it afire. When the charge d'affaire and the embassy staff came out to escape the fire, they were savagely beaten and humiliated. Eventually they were saved by Chinese secret police.[61] The shock that this and other lesser incidents caused among the diplomatic community led to the recall of a number of foreign representatives. It also resulted, however, in a reassertion of control over the Chinese foreign ministry by Prime Minister Chou En-lai, who ejected Yao Teng-shan from his position as self-appointed minister of foreign affairs and issued a directive prohibiting any mistreatment of foreigners, foreign diplomats or interference with their work. With the reassertion of Chou En-lai's authority in foreign affairs, this violent Red Guard phase of China's foreign relations came to an end, as did the Red Guards domestic attacks against the military.

Lin Piao, Mao's main supporter in the Cultural Revolution, had played a somewhat ambivalent part in reconciling the interests of the military with those of the Maoist Left. He had been willing, under Mao's direction, to give the order to the PLA not to shoot at attacking Red Guards, but he could not ignore the disaffection among the army forces, particularly those that were originally under his command.

The PLA was still compartmentalized in five field armies that had been formed during the civil war. Though no longer officially designated as such, these field armies had retained their cohesion after the establishment of the People's Republic. In each of these former field armies career advancement had taken place in the main within the respective army group, so that by now the former field armies formed what could be regarded as separate military factions. It was this division of the military forces that forced Lin Piao to be concerned with the attitude among the leading commanders, particularly those not belonging to his former Fourth Field Army group.[62]

The armies that cooperated with Mao, but were not originally part of Lin Piao's command, were the former Second and Third field armies, whose most important leaders, Ch'en Hsi-lien in Manchuria and Hsü Shih-yu in the Shanghai-Nanking area, had gone along with the Cultural Revolution and had at times been singled out by Mao Tse-tung for special honors. They had, however, maintained a disdain towards the Red Guards. Ch'en Hsi-lien had been somewhat hesitant at first to join the revolutionary drive of the Left and Hsu Shih-yu, had, in his comments, made fun of the students, whom he considered weaklings compared with the combat soldiers.

When the PLA was permitted a free hand in dealing with the Maoist Red Guards and revolutionary rebels, Lin Piao reportedly called, on August 9, a meeting of a small group of military leaders, counseling them to make their peace with the Left and play a role in reconciling the two opposing camps of the revolutionaries and the PLA. This advice did little to restrain the military commanders who now could put the Maoist revolutionaries in their proper place.

The new restrictions imposed on the revolutionary Left gave the military the decisive role when the establishment of Revolutionary Committees, interrupted by the power struggle during spring and summer, was resumed. At first, progress was slow; but at the beginning of 1968 committees were set up in rapid succession until, by September, 1968, all twenty-nine Revolutionary Committees for the provinces and major administrative units were organized and China was, in the words of Peking's propaganda, *All Red.*

The second series of Revolutionary Committees, which were established during this new phase, however, did not represent the original Maoist revolutionary goal—seizure of power by the revolutionary Left, duly supported by the PLA. In the new committees, set up between November, 1967, and August, 1968, almost all positions of chairman and vice chairman were held by officers of the PLA or, in a few cases, former party officials. The revolutionary rebels were almost completely excluded from leadership and contributed no more than a quarter of the committees' membership.[63]

However, the establishment of the Revolutionary Committees by the PLA and the reduction of the authority of the Red Guards did not prevent nor end the internecine warfare between rival revolutionary groups represented in the new administrative bodies. Even the fact that the army was in control did not enable it to hold the rebels in line. A system of political alliances developed among the various revolutionary groups in the provincial and local committees. In many provinces and localities a fierce competition among radical groups and leaders led to bloody factional fighting. Unable to eliminate each other, small factions inclined to coalesce into two large opposing organizations. Though this simplified the conflict, it also enlarged it. It was this confrontation of two large, often confederated groups, which led Mao to issue his operational directive of September, 1967: "There is no basic conflict of interests within the working class. There is even less reason why the working class must be split into two opposing factional organizations." But the factions continued to exist and to grow. They formed their own action columns and armed fighting corps, first outside and then within the committees. The very disappearance of the party and government structure forced people in the communes and factories to join one or the other of these factions, if for no other reason than for self-protection. The representatives of these radical factions in the Revolutionary Committees had only been forced together under bargained agreements, usually after long negotiations. It was to no avail to tell the new ambitious and opportunistic leaders of these groups to "read the Thought of Mao Tse-tung" and to "forget self." News items from all over the country indicated continued fighting, officially denounced as *factionalism.*

A typical situation, best known abroad because of the closeness of Hong Kong, developed in Kwangtung province where during the latter part of 1967 and the first half of 1968 major battles ocurred between two opposed rebel groups, the *Red Flag* and the *East Wind.* These clashes resulted in large numbers of dead and wounded on both sides.[64] The fighting was not limited to the combat of Red Guard organizations against each other; it soon led to a revival of old clan and village rivalries, reaching such proportions that the military regional commander was called to Peking by Mao Tse-tung and ordered to restore law and order by August at the latest, with authorization for the PLA to shoot to kill when encountering armed Red Guards.[65]

To prevent open division while transforming the committees into pliable tools for Maoist leadership depended, however, on more than power, and so the PLA was asked to invite the leaders of the various groups for discussion and to apply "the living use of the Thought of Mao Tse-tung" as it had been practiced within the armed forces. In this position of arbiter, the army was to act strongly against any opposition to its leadership. Those who continued "to create a cleavage between the army and the people" and to accuse "the troops of supporting factions and not the Left" were to be "smashed like flies on the wall."

The Red Guards and the revolutionary rebels were bitterly disappointed with the emerging new power structure. They would not accept an administration dominated by the army in which key positions of power were held by those cadres whom they had tried to replace. They hoped to continue the Revolution and seize power for themselves. Among them were leaders who had more than an average knowledge of Marxist doctrine and who tried to apply it for their utopian plans. One such group, formed of several rebel organizations in Hunan province, was the *Sheng-wu Lien.* It consisted mainly of middle school students, but included also some former military officers and even government officials.[66]

The *Sheng-wu Lien* was established on October 11, 1967, and outlined its program in three major documents, of which the longest under the title, "Whither China?" consisted of 10,000 words. For these radicals, the Revolutionary Committees were only another kind of "bourgeois" rule. What was needed was a radical change that had to start in the army itself, through a revolution from below. These rebels recalled Mao's original directive of May 7, 1966, in which Mao had spoken of the new all-around Communist person with proletarian political consciousness. Mao had indicated that this original proletarian ideal could be realized through a revolutionary shortcut, and now his followers refused to abandon Mao's concept. They wanted to return to the Paris Commune of those early weeks in 1967, which in their view had proven that they could live without bureaucrats. Groups similar to the *Sheng-wu Lien* existed in other provinces and there were connections between these different rebel associations of the extreme Left. There was even talk of *underground revolutionary committees.* The dream of a new society of instant communism died hard.

To answer this threat from his own revolutionary supporters, Mao initiated two policies. The first measure was his authorization to the PLA commanders to use military force in suppressing recalcitrant Red Guards. To assist them, local security forces which had been destroyed in the attack against the local party and government leaders were now rapidly being reorganized under a different name and placed under the direction of the PLA. The second reaction to the leftist discontent was a new attempt to relate the Revolutionary Committees to the masses. Leading cadres were told to spend a large part of their time working side-by-side with workers and peasants to demonstrate their proletarian attitude and their distinction from the old bureaucracy. Purges continued in the committees themselves under the label of reducing membership and simplifying administration. There was to be an investigation of the bureaucrats by the masses. There was also a new attack against scientists and technical experts who were suspected of being "bourgeois reactionary" technical authorities who could not be "separated from foreign textbooks or be free from the restrictions of foreign conventions."

A new leftist trend thus entered the educational institutions again, and on July 22, 1968, Mao issued a new directive:

> *It is still necessary to have universities; here I refer mainly to colleges of science and engineering. However, it is essential to shorten the length of schooling, revolutionize education, put proletarian politics in command . . . Students should be selected from among workers and peasants with practical experience, and they should return to production after a few years' study.*[67]

This directive was hailed all over the country in editorials and letters to newspapers as a weapon for destroying the *bourgeois educational system.* The basis of the new curriculum that was introduced with this new form of college education was to be the "living study and application of the Thought of Mao Tse-tung." With it there was introduced into the schools a course entitled "Salute to Chairman Mao," which consisted of daily ceremonies under which the students assembled in the morning before a picture of Chairman Mao to "ask the Chairman's advice" and again in the evening to report to him on the day's events.[68]

Such a frontal attack against education itself would take time, however, and the battle of the discontented Left against the committees and the PLA remained acute. To reassert his authority and give new direction to his revolutionary drive, Mao issued, on August 15, a directive replacing the Red Guards and revolutionary rebels with a new political force. The directive declared that the "working class is the leading class" and this class was to have the leading role in the Great Proletarian Cultural Revolution.

The new force of workers and poor peasants established by this directive consisted of teams sent to educational institutions to propagate the Thought of Mao Tse-tung. They were to be strengthened by revolutionary cadres and backed by the PLA. In effect, this establishment of Worker-Peasant Mao Thought Propaganda teams was a repeat of the earlier formation of revolutionary rebel forces in the factories and communes. Only this time the teams, newly formed, were sent into the educational institutions to break the defiance of the Red Guards and

Maoist radicals on their home ground.

Mao's new initiative was demonstrated on July 28 when Mao called five Red Guard leaders to his home at 3 A.M. In an emotional, five-hour session Mao complained bitterly about the factionalism in the educational institutions and among the Red Guard organizations throughout China and demanded that it cease immediately or he would turn to full military control. Actually this last threat was already being implemented. Mao Thought Propaganda teams by that time had entered universities in Canton and Peking to suppress the factionalism within these institutions. At Tsinghua such a team had reportedly been so successful that Mao sent it a gift of mangoes given to him by a foreign delegation.[69]

The purpose of these Worker-Peasant Mao Thought Propaganda teams was obviously to confront the educated or quasi-educated groups of students and teachers with strong-arm tactics by workers and peasants who were sent as "teachers" into the schools. These worker teams, which would replace the rule by educated people in "universities, middle schools and primary schools in literature and art, science, legal work, propaganda, medicine, and public health" consisted of uneducated and often illiterate people.[70] "Many of them were entering the university for the first time." The method applied by these teams was "struggle, criticism, transformation" and, according to reports, they succeeded in "promptly eliminating the differences among the opposing factions, performing studies and establishing a revolutionary order."

In January, 1967, when the PLA supported the Organization of Workers and Poor Peasants in the factories and communes, the Red Guards were the leading force in the Revolution; now the Red Guards had to "integrate themselves with the main force, the workers, peasants and soldiers armed with Mao Tse-tung Thought." They had to accept the workers as their teachers and study together with Mao Thought "the world outlook of the working class." Their reeducation was to deprive the Red Guards permanently of a leading position in the coming order. With the exception of a few who made good, the Red Guards were sent to the countryside to join the peasants — not temporarily but for the rest of their lives. A new *down to the countryside (hsia fang)* movement was under way and, as before, this movement was to continue during the years to come, masked as a voluntary action by the students who were supposedly enthusiastically joining the peasants in carrying on Mao's revolution there. In practice, of course, they had no choice. And their drastic demotion was only thinly disguised by the faint praise given them by their leader, Chiang Ch'ing, in her speeches of September 5 and 7 in which she combined praise for her wards with the plea that they should not be punished for the mistakes they had committed but rather helped in correcting them. In a lengthy speech on the same date of September 7 at a rally in Peking, Chou En-lai, celebrating the completion of the process of establishing Revolutionary Committees throughout China, said that "youth must respond to our great leader, Chairman Mao's call and turn towards the lower levels, the masses and production, go to the hilly areas and countryside and work in factories, mines, and rural areas." It could almost be regarded as irony when Chou ended his speech with the salute: "Long live the Chinese Red Guards." From now on the Red Guards "must learn from workers, peasants, and the People's Liberation Army." They had proved that they could not lead the Revolution and had to suffer the consequences.

The new policy and the change in the system of education had a devastating impact on the students and teachers who were, in the words of the press, panic stricken and so discouraged that they were unwilling under any circumstances to continue working in education, literature or art in order to avoid any further danger. Condescendingly they were assured that if they were willing to serve the workers, peasants and soldiers there was hope for them and they might have a future.

Actually, the movement did not proceed smoothly. Students were "hesitant" to go to the countryside. Their attitude was interpreted as an indication of having been influenced by the "revisionist line on education" and "bourgeois individualism." The student reaction was, however, more than hesitation. News came from many parts of the country about violent clashes between worker teams on one hand and Red Guards on the other.[71]

As the Red Guards were sent into the wilderness, so were their opponents, the party cadres. According to Chairman Mao's instructions, "sending the masses of cadres to do manual work gives them an excellent opportunity to study once again. This should be done by all cadres except those who are too old, weak, ill, or disabled. Those who are now working as cadres should also go in groups to do manual work." That such hard labor for cadres was used not only to promote the merger with the masses but as a form of forced labor and as a matter of disciplining the cadres is evident from a model school established in Manchuria and given the name of *The Seventh May Cadres School* after the date of Mao's directive. This was a labor farm that was to serve to transform the spirit of those cadres that had not been in line with the "socialist economic base." They were to be reformed through fierce class struggle and intense manual labor that would "touch them to the core." The May Seven Cadre Schools were soon established all over the country and served several purposes. Some cadres were sent to this "reeducation" because they were purged from their jobs. Others were sent for a period of time, usually indefinite, to temper themselves through labor. Others again were "class enemies" who had been "dragged out" of the administration and had become "live targets" for the revolutionaries in their struggle against class enemies. Members of each group often had their families transferred with them so that the picture emerged of a forced labor camp with varying categories of intimidation and terror. As in all such institutions the treatment was graded according to the history, behavior and pliability of the inmates. The forced labor education of the cadres was a mirror image of the treatment of the Red Guards and of later students graduating from the schools that were to be sent to the countryside to carry on Mao's Revolution there. Ruthless as it was, this system carried the stamp of Mao Tse-tung's style in remolding the masses in his revolutionary image.

The victors in this power struggle between classes and class groups as manipulated by Mao Tse-tung were the leaders of the People's Liberation Army whose forces were needed to carry out and guarantee the new social upheaval, and who came to fill the new positions of authority. At their head was Lin Piao, who seemed to emerge as the chief winner next to Mao Tse-tung in this grandiose revolutionary scheme and who, as Mao's most loyal comrade in arms, was to be designated as Mao's sucessor.

CHAPTER

VIII

Mao and the Succession

M AO'S GREAT PROLETARIAN CULTURAL REVOLUTION had to be aborted before Mao's purpose could be fully accomplished—if indeed it ever could be. While the disruption of the Chinese political structure was still at its height, a major outside threat forced Mao to change his plans. This was the build-up occurring over a period of a year and a half of forty-nine fully equipped Soviet divisions—close to a million men—along the Chinese borders of Manchuria, Mongolia and Sinkiang, clearly raising the threat of Soviet intervention in the internal Chinese struggle.

The Soviet Threat

The Soviet concern with internal developments in China was readily understandable. Soviet alarm at the course of events in China increased in 1967 when Mao in effect destroyed the Chinese Communist party with the original intention to replace it was a non-party structure and, when that failed, with a form of military dictatorship. Mao's challenge to orthodox communism soon went farther. The deification of Mao Tse-tung during the Cultural Revolution was carried beyond Chinese borders to the Communist parties in Asia, Europe, Africa, Australia and other parts of the world. Mao's extreme revolutionary program appealed chiefly to a younger generation of Communists, impatient with the policy of the Soviet Union and of Communist parties acting under Soviet direction. These younger radicals who turned against the regular party leaderships were in many cases expelled, and formed their own Marxist-Leninist (pro-Mao) party organizations leading to a division of the Communist movement. As many as thirty such pro-Maoist Communist groups all over the world were listed by Peking in May, 1969, at the time of the Ninth Chinese Communist Party Congress. The *Little Red Book,* which had been used in China to indoctrinate the military and then inflame the youth, became a propaganda tool abroad affecting students far beyond the membership of the Communist political organization. In many non-Communist countries, radical Maoist student groups supported what were characteristically simplistic and sloganized expressions of their hazy revolutionary thoughts. The Soviets were naturally very concerned with this Maoist challenge which threatened the Soviet world role as the leading Communist power and even challenged the orthodox Communist system itself in an attempt to build a worldwide Maoist leader cult. In reaction, propaganda emanating from Moscow more and more maligned Mao as a "petit bourgeois fanaticist," a type of anarchist who had never truly understood Marxism-Leninism. In describing Mao as the culprit behind the whole mistaken Chinese policy, the Soviets sided at the end of 1966 with the purged Chinese party leaders, clearly attempting to maintain a constituency in the People's Republic for their brand of world communism. Therefore when the Soviets began to concentrate their military forces along the Chinese frontiers from Manchuria to Sinkiang, this military threat clearly became a leverage of power behind the possibility of intervention in the event of open conflict among Chinese leaders.

This Soviet threat grew even more ominous after the Soviet intervention in Czechoslovakia in September, 1968, when the Soviets demonstrated that they would take open military-political action once they believed their vital interests were at stake. The Czechoslovakian intervention was combined with what in the West was called the *Brezhnev Doctrine* according to which a socialist country had not only the right, but indeed the duty, to intervene in a fraternal socialist country, if socialism there was threatened from within or from the outside. In Soviet interpretation that was clearly the case in the People's Republic of China. The Czechoslovakian action had not been a war between two countries but rather a political-military intervention. The military aspect of this intervention was carried through so well that it startled the commanders of the NATO powers into replanning their alliance strategy. The political action was bungled, and only after prolonged military occupation did the Soviet leaders succeed in establishing in Prague the type of Communist leadership suitable to them. China was indeed a much more difficult problem. The country was too large to be occupied by Soviet tanks and the political intervention would be more complex and difficult.

In December, 1968, the Soviets announced that they were holding military maneuvers in their east Asian border region, clearly a parallel to the maneuvers held in Eastern Europe before the Czech invasion. The danger became more ominous early in 1969 when a series of frontier incidents along the Manchurian and Turkestan borders led to Sino-Soviet clashes. It began with demonstrations by Chinese frontier guards who insulted their Soviet opposites in vulgar fashion. On the Manchurian border these conflicts focused on territorial arguments over ownership of islands in the Amur River and its tributary, the Ussuri. The first clash occurred at a small uninhabited island in the Ussuri River, *Damansky* in Russian, *Chenpao* in Chinese, in which the Chinese side ambushed a Soviet patrol killing its officer and several dozen men. The incident led to more serious clashes in Manchuria and in Turkestan where several thousand men and tanks were involved in both sides and in which the Soviets killed hundreds of Chinese troops, and, for a time at least, occupied some Chinese territory.

This grave situation led Chairman Mao to put an end to the Cultural Revolution and reestablish unity in the country, by now essential in the face of the Soviet threat. In November, 1968, the Twelfth Plenum of the Central Committee of the Party was secretly convened, the first such session since the beginning of the Cultural Revolution. At this rump session, Mao succeeded in formally expelling his opponents, Liu Shao-ch'i and Teng Hsiao-ping, plus their factions from the Party and from all their positions; then he introduced the draft of a new party constitution that was to reorganize the Communist system in China. This draft, passed at the Central Committee meeting, was then accepted at the Ninth Party Congress in April, 1969, a congress significantly called the *Congress of Unity*.[1] It was clearly the fear of Moscow intervention, indicated by the Soviets' demonstration that they might be in earnest in their determination to maintain both Communist orthodoxy and their world leadership, that induced Mao to abandon his goal of a full victory in the Cultural Revolution.

The forced tempo in the establishment of Revolutionary Committees during the latter part of 1968 was to the advantage of the commanders of the People's Liberation Army (PLA) who became the chairmen and deputy chairmen of the new political structure. By the time of the Ninth Congress in April, 1969, the PLA and particularly Lin Piao, who had organized and directed the Cultural Revolution, were at the height of their power. The new party statutes confirmed the new power structure. Mao was the leader again. His Thought was reintroduced into the party statutes as the guiding beacon of Chinese communism together with Marxism-Leninism. Mao had to accept, however, Lin Piao as his partner in power. According to the constitution, Lin Piao, "Mao's closest comrade in arms," became Mao's designated successor.[2] Everywhere propaganda posters and pictures depicted Mao Tse-tung together with Lin Piao, who was described as the most qualified interpreter of Mao Tse-tung's Thought. The critical Soviets viewed this constitution that designated a successor as a "monarchical," rather than a Communist, system.

Under the shadow of the Soviet power build-up, Mao was thus forced to accept an outcome of the Cultural Revolution which, in retrospect, he had clearly not intended. Mao had made use of Lin Piao to organize the Mao Cult and the Cultural Revolution; but when Lin Piao pushed his personal ambition too far, Mao appears to have decided to rid himself of this competition, as he had done with previous number two men who came too close to Mao's own power. However, the final confrontation had to wait until the ominous danger of Soviet intervention had become less acute.

A new foreign policy was mandatory. It began with a meeting between Soviet Foreign Minister Kosygin and Chou En-lai at the Peking Airport in September, 1969, which initiated Sino-Soviet negotiations. Mao's purpose in the negotiations was to remove the Soviet threat by proposing a mutual withdrawal from the border area and an agreement on border issues. The Soviets strove for broader negotiations encompassing the basic aspects of the Sino-Soviet conflict—the question of the policy line and leadership of the Communist movement. The Chinese side refused to compromise on the basic aspects of the conflict which would have involved Mao's position. The negotiations continued off and on during the next several years. Though officially there was little progress, the very fact of negotiations between Peking and Moscow took some of the immediacy out of the conflict.

To reduce the danger of Soviet encirclement, Chou En-lai visited Pyongyang in April, 1970, to initiate in close consultation with Mao a new cooperation with Kim Il-sung in North Korea, and then called a conference of Communist leaders from Hanoi, Vientiane, Pnom-Penh and Saigon "somewhere in South China," to reassert Chinese support for the "peoples of Indochina."[3] China became host to the deposed Cambodian leader, Sihanouk, increased her support to Hanoi and offered to be the "reliable rear area" for the Communist revolutionaries on her northern and southern flanks. In retrospect these moves to reestablish contact with North Korea and Indochina and to begin negotiations with Moscow were only the first part of a new Chinese foreign policy that would eventually establish diplomatic relations with the West, leading to *normalization* of relations with the United States and the entrance of the Chinese People's Republic into the United Nations as a move away from isolation in view of the Soviet threat. This startling turn in Peking's foreign policy was clearly undertaken on Mao's initiative, making use of President Nixon's attempt to exploit the Sino-Soviet conflict for the benefit of the United States. Mao initiated a new global role for the People's Republic which was meant to de-emphasize the predominance of the relation with Moscow and to place China eventually in a leading role in the Third World of the developing countries. This dramatic change of course lessened the possibility of Soviet action to bring China back into the orbit of the socialist commonwealth. While the Sino-Soviet conflict continued, the immediate danger of Soviet intervention appeared removed. At the very time at which the United States' willingness to "normalize" relations with Peking was taken up by Mao, the purge of Lin Piao began.

The Purge of Lin Piao

When Lin Piao began to promote his position as successor of Chairman Mao, he prepared his own fall. Mao's suspicion of Lin Piao as another challenger to his supreme power may well have been raised at the beginning of the Cultural Revolution. In 1972, Mao published a letter to Chiang Ch'ing, allegedly written on July 8, 1966.[4] In this letter, Mao accused his "friend"—Lin Piao—of having built up the Mao Cult beyond all reason. Mao even stated that "they," obviously the Lin Piao group, wanted "to overthrow our party and myself."

Whether such a letter to Chiang Ch'ing was written by Mao at that time remains uncertain; the letter seems to provide a *post facto* proof that Mao realized the wickedness of Lin Piao all along. However that may be, Mao's suspicion that Lin Piao was using Mao for Lin's own ascent to power may well have dated back to the outset of the Cultural Revolution. The letter, whether written in 1966 in this form or at all, seems to represent Mao's thinking then and later. Its whole tenor is based on a weltanschauung that assumes continuous conspiracies and purges, and endless struggle. Like Stalin, Mao appears to have become more wary as he grew older. What characterizes this worldview of Mao's is that he himself remained as the stable center in this continuing series of upheavals and turmoil. Nothing could demonstrate better than this letter that Mao, despite his denial that he had any "fantastic magic" of his own, regarded himself as the only source of truth. To Mao the battle with Lin Piao was but a continuation of other power struggles of the past which he recounts with the satisfaction of a winner.[5] There was always a struggle between the two lines, the proletarian line and the bourgeois line, Mao being the infallible defender of the proletarian faith and his enemies the bourgeois spoilers. In Mao's view this was a never-ending battle which recurred in regular cycles.

If Chairman Mao regarded the minister of defense as another challenger to his supreme power, he may have had reason to suspect Lin when the Cultural Revolution did not take the course Mao had wanted. The failure of the Paris Commune system in Shanghai and elsewhere in January of 1967, perhaps caused by opposition to it by Lin Piao and the People's Liberation Army, may have sharpened Mao's suspicion during the first phase of the Cultural Revolution. At that time there was no other choice. The use of the PLA for the promotion of the Cult of Mao and as the leverage of power had been the main facet of Mao's strategy for the Cultural Revolution; if the instrument which he used got out of hand, Mao would bide his time and discard it later. With the Cultural Revolution brought to an end and the Soviet threat at least temporarily deflected, the time had come for action. Mao's first move was made at the Second Plenum of the Ninth Central Committee at Lushan in August, 1970. At this plenum the new structure of the Chinese state was being discussed.

The Ninth Party Congress in May, 1969, had dealt with the reestablishment of the Party. Now a new meeting of the National People's Congress was being prepared to accept a new state constitution; when the draft of this new constitution was taken up at the Second Plenum, the chief point of contention was the position of chairman of the Republic. This was the position which Mao Tse-tung had held at the establishment of the People's Republic in 1949 and according to the constitution of 1954. In December, 1958, after the failure of the Great Leap Forward, Mao had been removed from this supreme post, and Liu Shao-ch'i had taken over. Mao was never to seek this position again, connected as it was with his earlier defeat. But this was not the idea of Lin Piao, who drafted the new constitution. Lin attempted to reinstate the chairmanship of the Republic, and place Mao in the position, hoping, one must assume, that he would become Mao's successor as chairman of the

Republic as he was already Mao's successor as chairman of the Central Committee of the Party. Lin Piao's mistake was that he drafted this stipulation without consulting Mao and in disregard of Mao's wishes. In Mao's words: "Someone is seeking the state chairmanship and attempting to split the party and seize power."[6] That someone was Lin Piao.

Lin had acted through Ch'en Po-ta, Mao's long-time supporter and secretary, who backed Lin Piao in this attempt to prepare for the successorship. In shifting his loyalty to Lin Piao, Ch'en Po-ta had badly miscalculated. Mao, obviously infuriated by this betrayal, directed his fire first against Ch'en Po-ta who was purged as a surrogate of Lin Piao. While Ch'en became the first victim, the main attack was directed against Lin Piao and his military supporters who had attempted to force Mao's hand without consulting him. Since he could not be openly accused of seeking the state chairmanship, Lin's sin was the constant use of the word "genius" in describing Mao Tse-tung. Extravagant in his build-up of the Cult of Chairman Mao, Lin had claimed — according to Mao — that a genius had appeared only once in the world in the last several hundred years and in China in the last several thousand years. Mao, properly modest, pointed to Marx, Engels and Lenin on the global stage, and to Sun Yat-sen, Hung Hsiu-ch'üan (the Taiping leader) and other great men in China to refute such an exaggerated claim. Appearing to disclaim the application of the term "genius" to himself, Mao on the other hand did not want the term "genius" dropped. It should rather be connected with the Party on which "a genius must rely."[7] This formulation indicated a retreat by Mao, who had during the Cultural Revolution defied the idea of working within the framework of the Party which he then attacked. Now he returned to it.

It was of course a different party from the pre-Cultural Revolution organization; it was Mao's party accepting Chairman Mao as the leader and the Thought of Mao as guide to action. Yet the process of rehabilitating party cadres purged during the Cultural Revolution but needed for their expertise, had already begun under the direction of Chou En-lai. When Mao decided to act against Lin Piao, he had to gain the support of this recreated party and of Chou En-lai. Mao's willingness to place his position as "genius" within the structural context of the Party was thus designed to strengthen this party's support. To pacify the party cadres further Mao added that only one percent of all cadres had been bad and no more than three percent questionable and that not all "good cadres" had yet been rehabilitated after the Great Proletarian Cultural Revolution. In his attack on the military clique of Lin Piao, Mao thus had to seek the support of the rehabilitated cadres under Chou En-lai's administration. Later Mao was to renew the attack against these rehabilitated "revisionists."

There is no indication even in the material circulated by Mao to other members of the Party that Lin Piao had demonstrated any intention of challenging Mao's role, let alone overthrowing him. He was rather trying to place himself into position for successorship; but that in itself was clearly unacceptable to Mao. Lin's strength even at the height of his power was rather shadowy and shallow. Though he manipulated the Mao Cult, Lin's own charismatic appeal was more than questionable, his language dull and cold. While he commanded the loyalty of most of the officers of his former Fourth Field Army, the leading generals of the other field armies were not beholden to him. In the end, therefore, it was more a game of military and secret police action than an organizational power struggle that caused Lin his life.

The tactics that Mao used were described in his characteristic style: "I attempted three measures: one was to cast stones, one to blend with sand and one to dig up the cornerstone."[8] By "casting stones," Mao referred to the purge of Ch'en Po-ta in the Second Plenum. While Lin Piao and his lieutenants were not attacked then, they were criticized for their "ideological mistakes" in allegedly following the bourgeois line. The "blending with sand" was Mao's jocose reference to his packing the Military Affairs Committee (MAC) with men more dependent on him than on Lin Piao. This he could do because of the divided loyalty of the leading officers of the former field armies. The "digging up of the cornerstone" referred to Mao's reorganization of the Peking military region. The latter was accomplished at a north China meeting in December, 1970, when Mao had obviously obtained enough support within the Military Affairs Committee to remove the commander and the political commissar of the Peking military region.[9] They were presumed to be Lin supporters and were replaced by men on whom Mao could rely.

Only now when the Lin Piao faction had already been castigated for its ideological mistake, deprived of its military support at the center and openly threatened with a purge did Lin and his supporters act to counter the danger. For Lin's countermove, we have two fragmentary documents later circulated by Mao to justify his actions in the blood purge of Lin Piao and his group. According to this account, Lin, his wife Yeh Ch'ün and his son Lin Li-kuo, met in Soochow in February, 1971, to "map a counter-revolutionary plot."[10] According to the documents, Lin Piao ordered "a plan" drawn up. A proposed military action, apparently outlined by Lin's son, assumed different scenarios ranging from an attempted open takeover of military power in Shanghai to a retreat to the nearby mountains for guerilla warfare in case of failure. This military action was to rely mainly on the support of air force units commanded by officers from Lin Piao's former Fourth Field Army

…emonstration against Lin Piao and Confucius, 1974. *Courtesy of …g Pao.*

Chou En-lai at 10th Party Congress, 1973. *Courtesy of Ming Pao.*

…posters criticizing Lin Piao, 1974. *Courtesy of Ming Pao.*

Mao greeting President Nixon during 1972 China visit. *Courtesy of Ming Pao.*

…retary of State Kissinger conferring with Mao at Chungnanhai, February 1973. *Wide World Photos.*

President and Mrs. Ford look on as Mao greets daughter Susan, December 1975. *Wide World Photos.*

Teng Hsiao-p'ing, acting Prime Minister. *Courtesy of Ming Pao.*

Party and state leaders before the bier of Mao Tse-tung. *Wide World Photos.*

and some other trusted units of the army. The plan allegedly included an attempt to assassinate Mao.

There is no way to check the reliability of these documents and their incrimination of Lin's faction. That some attempt at resistance was prepared appears plausible enough and what makes the authenticity of the plan credible is the bitter denunciation of Mao contained in the document. Indeed, Mao's willingness to circulate among his supporters the conspirators' accusations is most surprising in view of the damning content of the statements. They accuse Mao of

> *always playing off one side against another, today using this group to attack that group, and tomorrow vice versa. Today he is saying sweet things to one group and tomorrow he condemns them to death for a non-existent crime; today he treats them as honored guests, and tomorrow they are cast into prison. For the past several decades, has anyone whom he has pulled up not been sentenced to a political death later on?*

and Mao's major policies are bitterly attacked:

> *The send-down program for intellectual youth is nothing but labor reform under another name.*
> *The Red Guards were hoodwinked, utilized, and turned into cannonfodder during the first half of the Cultural Revolution, and were the scapegoats during the second half.*
> *In the simplification of government agencies, sending cadres to the May 7 cadre schools was equivalent to compulsory unemployment.*
> *Freezing the wages of workers (especially young workers) is nothing more than exploitation in disguise.*[11]

To destroy Lin Piao, Mao had to be in full control of the PLA units in the decisive strategic locations. By September, 1971, Mao was certain of this control. Lin's support in the Fourth Field Army was weakened by the fact that he had appointed most of his army commanders to leading positions in Peking; they thus had been removed from command of their units. Huang Yung-sheng, the former regional commander of Canton, for instance, had become chief-of-staff in Peking; and he and the deputy chiefs-of-staff, all Lin Piao men, were purged when Lin fell. In his characteristic way, Mao taunted Huang Yung-sheng, Lin's leading supporter, about Huang's inability to enlist military support: "I do not think our army will rebel nor do I believe that you, Huang Yung-sheng, can command the Liberation Army to rebel. There are divisions and regiments under the army; there are also commanding headquarters, political and logistics departments. Will they all listen to you?"[12]

The purge itself which had its dramatic climax at a meeting of the Central Committee on September 11 or 12, 1971, is still shrouded in mystery. The official explanation was that Lin Piao attempted to escape with his wife in a plane towards the Soviet Union and that the plane crashed in Mongolia. Lesser participants allegedly attempted to flee by helicopter from north China and were intercepted on the flight to Canton. The plane crash in Mongolia has been confirmed by Mongolian and Soviet statements, which maintained, however, that the burned bodies found at the crash site belonged to younger persons than Lin Piao and his wife. This claim was never withdrawn and it is possible that Lin's son or some other younger members of Lin's faction were on the plane which was shot down or crashed in Outer Mongolia and that Lin Piao himself may have been killed in Peking. Wherever and in whatever way, it appears certain that Lin Piao died at the time and that the members of his group were either arrested or killed.

How Mao accomplished this purge is still a matter of speculation. Wang Tung-hsing, the former head of Mao's personal bodyguard and head of Mao's security staff, who figured in many of Mao's purges, may have played a key part. Mao also had, as he later stated, the support and cooperation of Chou En-lai.[13] The chief credit for the flawless action of this purge of a major military figure and contender for power must be given to Mao himself, another demonstration of his superb ability as a political strategist and infighter. Mao's timing was also more than a matter of good fortune. The Sino-Soviet tension had abated, frontier incidents had ceased, and while the Soviet military build-up remained in place on the frontiers, Mao's attack against the alleged propagators of extremes of the Mao Cult could not easily be disapproved by Moscow. This may explain the inability of the Soviets to exploit the rapidly evolving crisis to their advantage. Lin Piao was later charged with "illicit relations with a foreign power," and accused of having intended to "surrender to the Soviet social revisionism, uniting with the Soviet Union and the United States and opposing China and Communism"; he was also denounced for importing a large number of secret service tools from foreign countries.[14] But the very role which Lin Piao had played in building up the Mao Cult and attacking the Soviet Union made a quick shift of alignment difficult for Lin as well as for Moscow, while the speed of Mao's maneuver left little time for Moscow to back Lin's faction, if indeed Moscow wanted to do so. At the same time, the move for normalization of relations between the People's Republic and the United States was carried on, resulting in a greatly strengthened international position for Mao. Thus, a dangerous game was played successfully by skillful exploitation of a complex domestic and international situation.

Chou En-lai's Position

The purge of Lin Piao carried out with the help of Mao's radical supporters—and no doubt the secret police—and with the backing of Chou En-lai, was only a surface manifestation of a basic change in the post-Cultural Revolution structure that deeply affected the Chinese political order. As the military element was weakened, Chou En-lai gained the immediate advantage. He was the man of the hour; both domestically and in foreign affairs a new policy was charted under Chou's direction. This new policy, clearly related to the growing Soviet military and political threat, led to a normalization of relations with the United States, to the entrance of the People's Republic into the United Nations and to the visit to Peking by the United States President Richard Nixon.

Domestically, more emphasis was placed on production and economic stability. Incentive was reintroduced by permitting private plots in agriculture and payment by work points according to labor performed. If Mao Tse-tung can be assumed to have charted this policy, who could have better implemented it than the efficient and experienced Chou En-lai? As Lin Piao was essential to Mao for the Cultural Revolution, Chou En-lai was the man for the postrevolutionary course.

The most astounding shift in this new policy was the *normalization* of relations with the United States, a complete departure from previous policy not only for Mao but also for the American government. In July, Dr. Henry Kissinger, the president's foreign policy adviser and head of the National Security Staff, went on a secret trip to Peking from which he returned with an invitation from Chou En-lai for President Nixon to visit China. The visit took place in February, 1972. For the United States, this move indicated a fundamental change in foreign policy based on the assumption that the Sino-Soviet conflict had made it possible and advantageous to the United States to deal separately with both Moscow and Peking in a balance of power system that would be part and parcel of a policy of negotiations to ease the danger of confrontation between the Communist and the Free World. For Mao Tse-tung this new relation with the United States ended the self-imposed isolation of the Cultural Revolution, and enabled China to strengthen her international position vis-à-vis the Soviet menace. An immediate benefit of the new relationship was the admission of the People's Republic to the United Nations combined with the expulsion of the Republic of China. A last-ditch American effort to keep the Republic of China in the U.N. failed, and Chairman Mao had won a significant victory in the early stages of the new Sino-American relationship. At hardly any cost to itself, Peking had secured membership in the United Nations and weakened any possibility of recognition of the Republic of China as a separate entity.

The Shanghai Communique concluded at the end of the president's visit was constructed in such a way as to state separately the position of the United States and China on those points on which there was no agreement. On the crucial issue of Taiwan, the Chinese side stated that there was only one China and that the "liberation of Taiwan" was a Chinese internal affair. While acknowledging that all Chinese agreed that there was but one China, the United States reaffirmed its interest in the peaceful settlement of the Taiwan question between the Chinese themselves and stated that she would ultimately withdraw all American forces from Taiwan "as the tension in the areas diminishes." While the United States commitments to the National Government remained intact, diplomatic missions were exchanged between Washington and Peking. The question of "full normalization" of relations between the People's Republic of China and the United States at the expense of "de-recognition" of the National Government and of Taiwan's security remained an unresolved issue.

The new course in Chinese policy carried out under Chou En-lai's management appeared to strengthen greatly the premier's position. Chou was the leading negotiator in the arrangement of the new foreign policy line and the rebuilding of the Chinese administration. In rebuilding the provincial Revolutionary Committees Chou had played a decisive role in arranging compromises and selecting candidates. During the Cultural Revolution, he had protected a number of military leaders against Red Guard attacks so that they became beholden to him. In the period following the purge of Lin Piao, Chou had rehabilitated a growing number of former party cadres purged during the Cultural Revolution who could be expected to support him. Thus he clearly became the chief architect and symbol of Peking's new policy and was regarded as such abroad. Many observers thought that this new course indicated the end of the revolutionary radicalism in China.

Soon, however, it became clear that the new policy had been only another tactical move and that Mao had not veered from his ultimate purpose, first demonstrated in the Great Leap Forward in 1958 and more clearly in the Great Proletarian Revolution—the purpose of transforming Chinese society into a true socialist order as he saw it through a continued, indeed a perpetual, revolution. A new shift in policy, back to the goals of the Cultural Revolution, was initiated in the latter part of 1973. A most unusual campaign was begun to attack the Chinese sage, Confucius, for his allegedly reactionary role in Chinese history two thousand years ago. The drive was all the more surprising since in previous Communist characterizations, even by Mao, Confucius had not been altogether condemned. Now Confucius was maligned not only as a reactionary of his time, but also as a man whose views were still maintained by present-day capitalist roaders. On several occasions in the past, Mao used historical allegories to open an attack against adversaries who at first remained unnamed; the question, therefore, was who was the target in this new drive.

The attack began in Canton with an article by Yang Yung-kuo, a professor of Chungshan University. It appeared in the *People's Daily* on August 7, 1973, and was later reprinted in the *Peking Review*.[15] Heavily spaced with quotations from Confucian writings and doctrinal interpretations of the past, the article accused Confucius of having attempted to "turn back the wheel of history," and prevent progressive forces of that time from establishing a new order. Confucius now became the prototype of a reactionary and a revisionist. When this claim was taken up by the media, the center of the attack moved to Shanghai where a new journal under the title, *Study and Criticism,* appeared. To indicate its political color, the journal carried a Mao masthead and quoted statements by the chairman at the head of each number.

Leaving aside the question of doctrinal Marxist-Leninist interpretation of the role of Confucius in Chinese history, the attacks by implication could be understood to condemn all the new policies in the economy, in politics, and in education, in the rehabilitation of cadres, and, indeed in foreign policy, that were initiated by Chou En-lai in the post-Cultural Revolution period. Some specific hints seemed to identify Chou further as the target of attack. When the Duke of Chou, a founder of the Chou dynasty in the twelfth century B.C., once highly praised by Confucius, was singled out in the attack, it was striking that his name happened to be the same as that of Chou En-lai. When the original anti-Confucian article was reprinted in Peking in the *People's Daily* and the *Peking Review,* the reference to the Duke of Chou, together with some of the most embarassing parallels to recent policy, were omitted from the reprinted text indicating that a propaganda battle was under way.

While this new propaganda drive was spreading, the Tenth Congress of the Chinese Communist Party was called in Peking from August 24 to 28, 1973. An obvious reason for calling a new congress was the need to give formal recognition to the change in leadership that had taken place as a result of the purge of Lin Piao. In the party statutes adopted at the Ninth

Congress, Lin Piao had been proclaimed as Mao's successor; this had to be corrected. To make it clear, however, that the fall of Lin did not infer a change of the political line, Mao used the congress to assert again the goals of the Cultural Revolution.

The congress met in utter secrecy and lasted only four days, an unusual procedure. The main statements, published afterwards, were the reports by Chou En-lai and Wang Hung-wen, a new member of the Politburo. Wang, a man in his late thirties, was a rapidly rising star in the Maoist group in Shanghai; at the congress, he was elected to the third-ranking position in the Politburo immediately after Chairman Mao and Chou En-lai, providing a new younger leadership for the Maoist group. Wang reported on the new party constitution while Chou En-lai delivered the statement on the general situation.[16] The tenor of these statements clearly demonstrated Mao's renewed shift towards the Left.

The new party constitution deleted the paragraph of previous party statutes proclaiming Lin Piao's successorship but otherwise reemphasized the Maoist character of the previous document.[17] Renewed stress was placed on the need for revolutionary Maoist successors and the role of the "masses" in criticising and supervising the Party. The new constitution, as well as Wang's report, expressly stated that cultural revolutions were "to be carried out many times in the future." Wang quoted Mao's words: "Great disorder across the land leads to great order and so once again every seven or eight years monsters and demons will jump out" and will have to be defeated. As Wang put it, there were still cadres, especially leading cadres, who would not accept the "views from the masses inside or outside the Party." Wang's stress on the slogan that a "true Communist must dare to go against the tide" indicated that the attack by the Maoist radicals against "revisionist" party leaders might at any time be resumed.[18]

Chou En-lai's statement was a surprise to those abroad who had believed him to be a "moderate." Rather than reporting on the accomplishments of his administration as prime minister both in domestic and foreign affairs, Chou chose to give a litany in praise of the Cultural Revolution and a bitter condemnation of Lin Piao and what Lin had allegedly stood for. The radical tone of Chou's speech appeared to indicate that he had to yield to pressure resulting from the new turn in the domestic power struggle. In essence, Chou joined the mainstream of the Cultural Revolution argument. In his paean to revolution, all that he had to say about domestic and foreign policies was compressed into two paragraphs. Chou stated that the economy in China was flourishing; China had maintained her revolutionary friendship with fraternal socialist countries and genuine Marxist-Leninist parties, had established new diplomatic relations with an increasing number of countries and had broken through her isolation by joining the United Nations. The normalization policy with the United States was mentioned in half a sentence: ". . . Sino-United States relations have been improved to some extent." To cover himself against any criticism of this policy and to contrast it to the Soviet-United States negotiations which the Chinese denounced as "collusion," Chou quoted Lenin on the difference between two types of dealing with a bandit. In Lenin's words: "One must learn to distinguish between a man who gives the bandits money and firearms in order to lessen the damage they do and facilitate their capture and execution, and a man who gives bandits money and firearms in order to share in the loot," the former Chinese, the latter, the Soviet purpose. This explanation of the Chinese policy of normalization as serving to destroy the U. S. imperialism was later to be extended by explaining to the Chinese public that the approach to the American president, a "temporary" figure, was a means to reach the American people in order to provoke revolution in the United States.[19]

Most of Chou's speech was given to an attack against the Soviet Union and a praise of Mao and the Maoist Revolution, particularly the revolution in literature, art, education and public health, the areas in which Chou's policies might have been objectionable to the Maoist radicals, to Madame Mao and to Mao himself. By implication, these statements sounded like a retreat from some of Chou's domestic policies. Chou quoted Mao extensively on the importance of leadership of the proletariat and on his prediction that other cultural revolutions would have to be carried out after several years. "The struggle between the socialist road and the capitalist road" would continue and there was always the danger of capitalist restoration and subversion, and of agression by imperialism and social imperialism. In Chou's words, "for a long time to come there will still be two-line struggles within the party reflecting these contradictions and such struggles will occur ten, twenty or thirty times." All of Mao's slogans—the "going against the tide"; the "great disorder on the earth," which is a "good thing"; putting proletarian politics in command; the ever-continuing class struggle even after classes have disappeared; and revolution is the main trend in the world today—can be found in Chou's speech. His greatest venom Chou reserved for Lin Piao, the "bourgeois careerist, conspirator, double-dealer, renegade, and traitor," who had attempted a counterrevolutionary coup-d'etat "in a wild attempt to assassinate our great leader, Chairman Mao, and set up a rival Central Committee."

If Chou En-lai wanted to deflect the anti-Confucian drive from his own person and find a new target, it clearly was Lin Piao. Whatever

Chou's purpose, at this time the anti-Confucius drive became fused with the anti-Lin Piao drive as a new major political campaign which was taken up by the media and in mass meetings in Peking as well as in the provinces.[20]

This transposition of the attack against Chou to another target was apparently only partially successful. The veiled argument against Chou continued after the Tenth Congress and the division in the leadership could be sensed from contradictory editorials that appeared in leading newspapers in rapid succession. A play written by a group in Shansi and performed at a festival in Peking with the approval of the authorities came under attack as a hidden implied criticism against Chairman Mao's policy of the Great Leap Forward. In April, 1974, an article was published in the *Red Flag* describing the case of a minister in the state of Chin who had given wrong advice to his ruler to be friendly with far-away countries and to challenge neighboring states.[21] The minister had been advised to resign from his position, the obvious implication being that Chou En-lai, who had directed the policy of normalization with the United States, should see that it was time for him to resign.

Throughout this time, two contradictory lines could be discerned in all the arguments that took place behind an ideological screen. One side called for unity and stability and the other for struggle and violence. The call for unity had been stressed by Chou En-lai ever since he used the slogan of "seeking the common ground and reserving minor differences" at the Bandung Conference in 1955. The Maoist radicals on the other side stressed the need for continuing struggle and "revolutionary violence" to bring about the new order. This emphasis on the Cultural Revolution, on its revival and its continuation for a long time to come appeared to reflect Mao's purpose. From Mao's point of view, any retreat in domestic or foreign policy could only be temporary. The relentless drive toward the Maoist goal had to be resumed whenever temporary concessions had removed immediate danger.

Only later did it become known that during all this time Chou En-lai was ill. When Chou died in January, 1976, it was officially stated for the first time that his illness had been cancer. If so, he himself may have known his illness was terminal. The apparent decline of Chou's role from 1973 on could therefore be explained by his growing physical disability. In 1974, Chou entered a Peking hospital, where he still received occasional visitors, but which he left only at special occasions. More and more, he was absent from major functions which used to be under his personal supervision, and, when he was present, Chou no longer played the starring role that had been his after Lin Piao's purge. Whether this was due entirely to his illness or whether Chou was also politically demoted was a matter of speculation.

The man who took over much of Chou's work was Teng Hsiao-ping. Teng had been the number two target of the Cultural Revolution, next to Liu Shao-ch'i, a chief culprit, revisionist, and follower of the capitalist road. His rehabilitation in April, 1973, was a major surprise. Before his purge, Teng was an experienced administrator who held many important positions in the Party and the government. In his earlier career, Teng had been political commissar of the Second Field Army and he had retained his contacts with his former military colleagues. If one man could replace the irreplaceable Chou En-lai, Teng had the ability and experience.

The question was—who was responsible for Teng's rehabilitation? One assumption was that Chou En-lai brought Teng back after persuading Mao Tse-tung that Teng was needed when Chou could no longer carry the full load. On the other hand, Teng may have been Mao's choice when Mao wanted to replace Chou for whatever reasons. When Teng reappeared first at a reception, he was led to the room by Mao Tse-tung's niece, a sign of Mao's special favor; in view of the continued implied attacks against Chou En-lai and his policies, Teng's selection may have been arranged by Chairman Mao himself.

Teng soon rose to new and major prominence. On January 16, 1974, Teng was co-opted into the Politburo and soon was given the position of first deputy prime minister. In April, 1974, he represented China at the United Nations, and visited Washington, D. C. This was the time when Chou En-lai's power seemed to decline, when news about his illness became official and Chou entered a Peking hospital. Chou En-lai's last public appearance was at the National People's Congress, January 13-17, 1975, at which he gave his last report on the work of government. Apparently no longer able to deliver a long speech himself, Chou En-lai sat on the podium while the report was read in his name by someone else.[22]

It is of interest to compare this last statement by Chou En-lai with the report given by him to the Tenth Party Congress a year and a quarter before. If Chou ever attempted to stress his own role and introduce his own political ideas into the stream of Chinese policy, it could be discerned perhaps in this last account of the state of Chinese affairs. In contrast to his previous report, Chou detailed the economic accomplishments of his administration. He claimed the overfulfillment of the Third Five-Year Plan which ended in 1970 and promised the fulfillment of the Fourth Five-Year Plan in 1975. He spoke of good harvests for each of the last thirteen years and of an increase in agricultural output which rose fifty-one percent during the last decade. He maintained that a population increase of sixty percent since "liberation" was matched by an increase in

grain production of 140 percent and a cotton increase of 470 percent, so
that the needs for food and clothing had been secured. In the industrial
area, he claimed similar successes, contrasting the balance between
national revenue and expenditure in China with the economic turmoil
and inflation of the capitalist world. He asserted a Chinese role in the
tremendous "victories" in the struggle against imperialism and colonial-
ism, success in smashing imperialist and social imperialist encirclement,
the "restoration" of the Chinese seat in the United Nations, and the great
increase of diplomatic relations with foreign countries. It was a proud
account for Chou En-lai to give even if some of the data might have been
questionable. As for the future, Chou envisaged the development of a
Chinese national economy in two stages; the first stage to build an
independent and relatively comprehensive industrial and economic system by 1980, and the second to "accomplish a comprehensive modernization of agriculture, industry, national defense, science and technology
before the end of the century so that our national economy will be
advancing in the front ranks of the world." Without stepping out of line
regarding the purposes of the Cultural Revolution and while repeating
Mao's slogans, Chou thus placed a major emphasis on economic development as a basis for strengthening China. He stressed unity rather than
conflict. Most important perhaps was the form in which Chou addressed
himself to the Soviet Union. Compared to his report to the Tenth Party
Congress, Chou's tone had changed. He still accused the "Soviet leading
clique of having betrayed Marxism-Leninism," but some of the abusive
vocabulary used previously was omitted. More important, in describing
the Sino-Soviet conflict, Chou used the word "debate," rather than conflict and stressed that "this debate should not obstruct the maintenance of
normal state relations between China and the Soviet Union." Complain-
ing about the obstinacy of Soviet leaders who refused to sign border
agreements and used deceptive maneuvering, Chou called for these
leaders "to sit down and negotiate honestly, do something to solve a bit
of the problem and stop playing such deceitful tricks." This invitation to
unconditional negotiations combined with the use of the word "debate"
in describing the conflict was clearly an offer to improve Sino-Soviet
relations, an offer that may have been crucial for international as well
as domestic Chinese affairs. It was Chou's last published statement.
Chou En-lai died January 8, 1976, officially mourned by the country and
eulogized by Teng Hsiao-ping.[23] Chairman Mao did not come to the
memorial services nor did he make any statement in praise of Chou. His
attitude toward Chou and Chou's management of policy during 1973 and
1974 remained a matter of speculation, especially when in April, 1976,
massive anti-Mao demonstrations on Tienanmen Square in Peking were

triggered by the removal by police of large bouquets of flowers placed at the square in memory of Chou En-lai.[24]

The Struggle for Succession

In his Great Proletarian Cultural Revolution movement, Chairman Mao had not only succeeded in purging the party leadership opposed to him and in reasserting his dominant position, he had also affected the relationship between the institutional hierarchies in the People's Republic. In an orthodox Communist country, the Party is the dominant structure controlling both the government and the military. Power struggles among the leaders in the Soviet Union, for instance, are fought out in the Central Committee and the Politburo or Presidium of the ruling party. With the destruction of the Party during the Cultural Revolution and the elevation of the military to the dominant role, this system in China was brought into disarray. When Mao's plan of direct rule by the masses, the so-called Paris Commune system failed, Mao reestablished a party structure. But the new party, Mao's party, did not regain the authority over the government or the army, prescribed in its constitution. As a result, the conflict for power in post-Cultural Revolution China was carried out not only on the basis of personal rivalry or factional sparring in the Politburo or Central Committee of the Party, but between leaders basing their power on separate institutional structures. Of the three institutional hierarchies, the Party, the government, and the military, the military became most powerful in the Cultural Revolution and its head, Lin Piao, was the logical heir to Mao Tse-tung. After Lin Piao's purge, no military leader remained who was strong enough to step into Lin's position, and the People's Liberation Army was reduced to a supporting role in a potential rivalry between the leaders of the new Party, predominantly controlled by Maoist revolutionaries, and those in government reorganized under the direction of Chou En-lai, the leading administrator. The post-Lin Piao political struggle in China became in essence a conflict between the administrators, promoting an orthodox Communist policy of economic development and the Maoist radicals, championing a continuing revolution in the pursuit of Mao's goal of creating the ideal socialist order in a never-ending struggle. Distrustful of any stabilization of the political and economic system, Mao retained with his slogan of "going against the tide," the possibility of calling on the masses from within or without the Party to keep the cadres in government and indeed in the Party constantly on their toes.

In the Cultural Revolution Mao had used the People's Liberation Army as the main revolutionary force. As a result, the military commanders became entrenched in regional power positions. In many cases the chief commanders of the military regions had become chairmen of the Revo-lutionary Committees and concurrently first secretaries of the Party in their region, combining their military with political and administrative power. Some of these men, Ch'en Hsi-lien in Mukden and Hsü Shih-yu in Nanking had been commanders in their regions for twenty and fifteen years, respectively. With the additional gain of political and adminis-trative power, they became in fact satraps in their region, posing the danger of regional defiance to central authority. To strengthen the power of his radical followers in the Party, Mao's next step was to break this military monopoly of regional power. This was done by ordering an exchange of positions among the regional commands. In December, 1973, eight of the eleven regional commanders were rotated; the regional commander of Nanking changed place with the commander of Canton; the one in Mukden with the one in Peking; the one in Fuchow with the one in Lanchow; the one in Tsinan with the one in Wuhan. While not demoted in rank, the commanders, in their new positions, were not given chairmenship of the Revolutionary Committees nor did they become secretaries of the Party committees, so that their military authority was separated from administrative or political power.

This game of musical chairs was a major step in reducing the regional power of the military commanders. Its success could only be explained by linking it with a jockeying for position between the political factions. It occurred at the time when Teng Hsiao-p'ing as deputy prime minister had assumed a major role in directing administration. As political commissar of the former Second Field Army, Teng had been closely connected with this military faction. Its leading commander, Ch'en Hsi-lien, was trans-ferred to Peking, greatly strengthening Teng's local military backing. The most important of the military factions could therefore not complain about the rearrangement of power. Nor could the Maoist radicals. Their major political bases were in Manchuria and in Shanghai and the removal of the two most influential military commanders, Ch'en and Hsü, from the commanding positions in these areas freed them from their potential military dominance. In addition to breaking up the danger of regionalism, Mao had thus succeeded in arranging a compromise that would give the administrative group of Teng Hsiao-p'ing an advantage in Peking in exchange for the strengthening of the Maoist radical factions in their main base areas of Shanghai and Manchuria.

With the fading of Chou En-lai from leadership in government during 1974, Teng Hsiao-p'ing appeared to move into Chou's shoes. Domes-tically Teng continued Chou's policy of rehabilitating expert cadres who had been purged during the Cultural Revolution and appointing them to positions in the provincial administration. Since his closeness to the former Second Field Army leaders gave Teng his own group of military backers, he appeared to be in the process of establishing his own power base.

Teng also assumed a leading role in Peking's foreign policy. At his appearance at the United Nations in April, 1974, Teng described China's new interpretation of the world situation and her position among the conflicting power groups of the world as conceived in Mao's interpretation of the advance of world revolution.[25] Since Mao had lost the fight with Moscow for leadership in the socialist camp, Teng simply denied the camp's existence: "As a result of the emergence of social imperialism, the socialist camp which existed for a time after World War II, is no longer in existence." Instead, the global configurations were to be divided into three worlds. According to Teng:

> *Judging from the changes in interrelationships, the world today actually consists of three parts, or three worlds, that are both interconnected and in contradiction to one another. The United States and the Soviet Union make up the first world. The developing countries in Asia, Africa, Latin America and other regions make up the Third World, the developed countries between the two make up the second world.*

The United States and the USSR, the two superpowers of the First World, were attempting to establish hegemony in an interrelationship of collusion and conflict and were the main threat to world peace. The lesser capitalist countries of the Second World, Europe and Japan, were considered to be oppressed by the superpowers and could therefore be supported in the coming fight against the control of the world by the superpowers; but the true revolutionaries were the countries of the Third World, the chief revolutionary motive force of our time. In Teng's words: "China is a socialist country and developing country as well. China belongs to the Third World." The battle cry for this new phase in world affairs was the oft-repeated Mao slogan, "Countries want independence, nations want liberation, and the people want revolution—this is the irresistible trend of history." In this new role, China supported the revolutionary trend in the Third World in several international conferences. This shift from socialist camp to Third World leadership may be interpreted as a retreat from Mao's challenge to Moscow's leadership in the socialist camp to the new theater of operations, the Third World—according to Mao the most promising stage for world revolution. As spokesman for this policy, Teng Hsiao-p'ing demonstrated on the international scene his leading position in China and was therefore regarded abroad as the logical successor to Chou En-lai as head of the Chinese government under the direction of Chairman Mao.

Actually, the conflict for power between the orthodox Communist administrators and the radical Maoists continued and became more pronounced as Mao Tse-tung's health declined. The position of the PLA remained dubious; whether after Mao's demise a majority of the commanders of the PLA and of the leaders of the military factions would support the Maoist radical group or the orthodox Communist faction remained a matter of speculation. All the more crucial was a new move by Mao in the period after the purge of Lin Piao to build another instrument of power: a quasi-military force, a Chinese militia. Chairman Mao's first known directive concerning the strengthening of a Chinese militia was issued on September 29, 1958, when Mao ordered the build-up of militia divisions on a large scale; the purpose was quick mobilization of manpower to assist in the production drive, the main goal of the Great Leap Forward. In 1967, during the Cultural Revolution, the militia, then under the control of Lin Piao and the People's Liberation Army, was part of the force that was to "support the left" in its attack against the Party structure, and in 1969 the militia was used under the control of the PLA as a force to guard the Chinese border, especially against the Soviet Union.

After Lin Piao's fall the policy towards the militia and their role changed radically. From a production force and a border guard the militia was transformed into a force to maintain Maoist authority within the cities as well as in the communes. The militia became a police force trained in the study of "Chairman Mao's Instructions" about the dictatorship of the proletariat, and assigned the task of "dealing hard blows at the class enemies" and keeping the young in line. In a joint editorial of the *People's Daily* and the *Liberation Army Daily* on September 29, 1973, celebrating the fifteenth anniversary of "Mao's Instructions" on the militia, the militia's task was redefined as participation in class struggle and police duties. Most important was the revelation that party committees had assumed leadership of the militia. References to the existence of municipal militia commands in Peking and Shanghai showed that the militia in the cities were "under the direct leadership of the Party Committees." The same appears to have been attempted in the rural areas where the armed militia was subordinated to the commune party committees. Since these party committees were headed by a Maoist faction, the purpose was obviously to provide a new quasi-military support for the Maoist faction when the loyalties of the PLA had become uncertain.

This new party-controlled militia was divided into three categories: ordinary, backbone and armed militia. The armed militia was equipped with tanks, mortars, light artillery and with anti-tank and anti-aircraft weapons as a quasi-military force. Wang Hung-wen, in direct control of the Shanghai militia, assumed a major responsibility for the development of the militia, a force perhaps intended to become analagous to the Soviet Secret Police divisions under Stalin, or for that matter, the quasi-military party forces in pre-World War II Italy and Germany. In his final struggle for the survival of his policy, Mao seemed to attempt the introduction of this militia as another guarantee of power for his supporters.

During 1975 the renewed emphasis on revolution became apparent from the resumption of accusations against unnamed capitalist roaders through the tried and proven method of using historical parables to discredit policies and leaders not acceptable to Mao. One such attack was contained in the criticism of a Chinese historical novel known in English under the title of *Water Margin.*[26] This novel dealt with a peasant rebel, Sung Chiang, a legendary bandit of the twelfth century who had fought a corrupt local administrator and had eventually been pardoned by the Sung emperor and appointed to official position to suppress other rebellions in the lower Yangtze area. Sung Chiang had become a famous hero in Chinese tradition, a Chinese Robin Hood. Now, Sung Chiang's role was reinterpreted as that of a traitor who in his acceptance of the emperor's pardon and service had betrayed the cause of peasant rebellion. His name became synonymous with unnamed Communist leaders who had strayed from the revolutionary path, had become "revisionists," and might even be tempted to turn to Moscow.

The main conflict between the Maoists and the orthodox administrators recurred in the field of education. In the view of some of the leaders in education in the universities and in the administration, the politicization of education in the Cultural Revolution resulted in a most serious decline of standards that, in the long run, would damage China's whole development and undermine all efforts to build a strong and leading nation by the end of the century. With the reestablishment of an orderly government under Chou En-lai, Chou Jung-hsin, purged during the Cultural Revolution, was rehabilitated and appointed minister of education. In this post, Chou Jung-hsin reestablished examinations for admission to higher education and for graduation. The reintroduction of standards of learning and of tests was, however, bitterly opposed by the radical Left that regarded such measures as a reestablishment of bourgeois science and a betrayal of the goals of the Cultural Revolution. The opposition was taken up by students at some of the major institutions and propagated by the media in a revival of ideas of the Cultural Revolution.

In March, 1975, Madame Mao stepped out of her specialized role as patron of the performing arts and of student rebels of the Cultural Revolution and began to extend her activities to the field of Chinese foreign policy. Speaking to a group of Chinese diplomats called back from overseas to become reacquainted with the political thinking of Peking, Madame Mao presented an outline of Chinese Communist foreign policy, as seen by Mao Tse-tung, to the assembled Chinese ambassadors.[27] She admonished the senior Chinese diplomatic representatives to pay more heed to the study and promotion of political campaigns and to maintain close links with the Central Committee and its directives in order to "catch up with the pace of the entire country so that even while staying abroad they could also throw themselves into the campaigns, enhance their own awareness, oppose imperialism, and revisionism, and become Red diplomatic personnel both in name and in reality." Critical of some diplomatic representatives who dealt too much with day-to-day operations and technical diplomatic work, Chiang Ch'ing singled out the embassies in east and central Africa as having been negligent in their political study. Those diplomats who refused to cooperate would be replaced by orders of departments of the Central Committee under Chiang Ch'ing's control. In her comments, Chiang Ch'ing was critical of Secretary Kissinger, an "adventurist and also a defeatist," whose theory of balance of power "recognized the contradictions" but had no solution; she stressed the importance of exploiting the opportunities in the "great epoch of social changes" and supporting the national liberation struggle in south Africa, the Middle East, Latin America and Indochina and the revolutionary struggles in Eastern Europe as the "spark of revolution." She stated that the old-timers who were mission chiefs had to make certain concessions to diplomatic formalities, and must not be attacked for them publicly; irregularities could be exposed by letters home, "bypassing the regular channels." Inserting herself thus in the field of foreign diplomacy, Chiang Ch'ing attempted to stress the need for more revolutionary vigilance by the Chinese diplomatic staff and greater loyalty to the chairman's directives. In September, 1975, Chiang Ch'ing was one of the three chief leaders making a statement at an important conference in Shensi province dealing with the development of the agricultural economy after the pattern of the Tachai Commune, the outstanding model of the chairman's agricultural ideas.

Chiang Ch'ing's public appearances were paralleled by those of the other leading figures of the Maoist faction. In January, 1974, Wang Hung-wen, the youngest of the Shanghai Maoist group, who had been appointed a second vice chairman of the Party at the Congress in August, 1973, gave a secret speech to the "Reading Class" of the Party's Central

Committee.[28] At this gathering, which represented a part of the continuing educational process of the Central Committee members from all provinces and municipalities, Wang illustrated the struggle of the Cultural Revolution group against the administrators who still "do not understand the Great Cultural Revolution today." Defending the successes of the Cultural Revolution as a rebellion against imperialism, feudalism and bureaucratic capitalism, Wang criticized the old cadres for discriminating against new cadres who had made mistakes; he referred particularly to "obstruction among army units against the appointment of younger revolutionary loyalists." Naming certain alleged rightists who had recently been removed, Wang complained that there were "still capitalist roaders," even in defense plants, who blocked the policy of the Great Proletarian Cultural Revolution. In March, 1975, an article by Yao Wen-yuan appeared in *Red Flag* followed in April by an article by Chang Ch'un-ch'iao, both attacking the "bourgeois right" and "those people like Lin Piao" who were still causing a "danger to China to turn revisionist."[29] These rightists were not only leftovers from the past, but "new bourgeois elements are being engendered daily and hourly as Lenin put it." Chang used the slogan of "the evil bourgeois wind" which was hostile to "the newborn things," and predicted that the class struggle in the ideological field between the "proletariat and the bourgeoisie will continue to be long and tortuous."

Hua Kuo-feng, a new star on the Maoist side, rose to prominence during this same period. Hua, born February 15, 1922, in a small town in Shensi province, made his career as party secretary in Mao's district in Hunan where he gained Mao's attention for his good record in organizing water conservancy projects. The real break for Hua came when Mao visited his home village in 1959 for the first time after over 30 years. Hua did not leave Mao's side during the whole visit, showing what he had built in Mao's honor. In appreciation, Mao personally appointed Hua as first secretary of the province. As deputy governor of Hunan province, Hua joined the Cultural Revolution and became first deputy and then chairman of the provincial Revolutionary Committee. As such he was elected to the new Central Committee of the Party at the Ninth Party Congress in 1969, and was elected as member of the Politburo at the Tenth Party Congress in 1973. In 1975, at the Fourth National People's Congress, Hua was appointed deputy prime minister in charge of public security. Since the public security system included not only the secret police but also the control of the whole judicial system under the procurator general, as well as the intelligence apparatus, Hua was given by Mao Tse-tung as powerful a position of trust as had been held in the past by Mao's close supporter, K'ang Sheng, who had died in 1974. Together with Wang Tung-hsing, chief of Mao's bodyguard and key figure in the secret police control of Peking, Hua was regarded as the police arm of Mao's faction. In September, 1975, Hua became known through two speeches, one in Tibet where he was sent as representative for the celebration in Lhasa of the tenth anniversary of the Tibetan autonomous region and where he stressed Tibet's strategic position, and the other at the same Tachai conference at which Madame Mao had made an important statement.[30]

Tibet had become important as a new Chinese nuclear base in the confrontation with the Soviet Union.[31] The transfer of much of the nuclear and missile production from the Turkestan corridor, where it was exposed to Soviet attack to Nagchuk fifty miles north of Lhasa, and the establishment of missile launching sites on the high plateau of Tibet was a major strategic move to counter the Soviet build-up of military power on the Chinese northwestern border and to threaten the Soviet link with India and the Soviet naval position in the Indian Ocean. The construction of year-round open roads and a major radar communication system underlined the importance attributed by Mao to this Tibetan position. It was only natural that the new head of the security system was given the opportunity to survey in person the Chinese position in Tibet.

The second appearance of Hua as speaker at the Tachai conference was in line with his experience as an agricultural specialist. Hua termed agricultural production a great "militant task" in which proletarian politics and Mao Tse-tung's Thought had to be placed in command. In forseeing the transformation of the people's communes to a system of ownership by the whole people, Hua stressed Mao's concept of proletarianization of the agricultural production under which private plots and private incentive would disappear.

At the end of 1975, in the last weeks before Chou En-lai's death, the conflict between the orthodox administrative group under the acting leadership of Teng Hsiao-p'ing and the Maoist radicals appeared to become polarized. In essence, the orthodox group stood for "stability and unity" to strengthen China's economic development and her international position. The Maoists advocated continued revolution and attacked the "revisionists and capitalist roaders," who had abandoned Mao's revolutionary concept. In the joint New Year's editorial the *People's Daily,* the *Red Flag* and the *Liberation Army Daily* attacked those who had confused Chairman Mao's latest instructions "by combining Mao's emphasis on continued class struggle with the slogans of stability and unity and economic construction as three equally valid principles." This was a falsification of Mao's concept according to which class struggle came first, preceding the principles of stability and unity and the boosting of the national economy. According to the editorial, the downgrading of the principle of class struggle was directed against the "new-born things" of the Cultural Revolution. What was more, "the recent farrago on the educational front representing right deviationist wind . . . is a conspicuous manifestation of the revisionist line . . . to approve or negate the Great Cultural Revolution is in essence a struggle between continuing revolution on the one hand and restoration and retrogression on the other." The article appealed to every member of the Communist party to "fervently support the new revolutionary things and continue the class struggle in all fields."

The conflict had ramifications in international policy. The release in December, 1975, of the Soviet helicopter pilots captured a year and a half earlier by the Chinese at the Turkestan border and accused of a spying mission, was an extraordinary gesture of friendliness towards the Soviet Union; it was followed immediately by a renewed bitter attack in the *People's Daily* and *Red Flag* against the revisionist Soviet leadership. Teng Hsiao-p'ing was now attacked by name in wall posters at Peking University, raising the question whether the release of the Soviet pilots was under his order and without Mao's approval. If so, was the conflict between the orthodox administrators and the Maoist radicals being extended into the crucial issue of relationship with the Soviet Union? Was an attempt being made for a rapprochement with the Soviet Union even before Mao's death? Chou En-lai's last speech, the rehabilitation of Lo Jui-ch'ing, and now this extraordinary gesture of releasing the helicopter pilots pointed in that direction. Chairman Mao's bitter opposition may have been expressed in the ensuing revival of media attacks. The group most likely to come to seek a realignment with the Soviet Union in a Communist partnership was, after all, that faction of so-called moderates, the administrative bureaucracy of the government, who believed in an orderly, staged, planned economy after the Soviet model—provided the Soviets were willing to grant the Chinese Communists a true partnership.

It is understandable that such attempts toward reconciliation would be intolerable to Chairman Mao. On January 8, 1976, Chou En-lai's death removed from the scene the patron of the orthodox group, the so-called moderates. On January 15, Teng Hsiao-p'ing delivered the eulogy in the memorial service for the late prime minister. Chairman Mao neither appeared nor voiced any expression of mourning at the death of his old comrade who had so ably carried out his policies for so many decades.

The chairman's disapproval of Teng's policy became manifest to the world on February 8, when he appointed Hua Kuo-feng as acting premier to succeed Chou En-lai, rather than the man whom Chou En-lai appeared to be grooming for the position, Teng Hsiao-p'ing. The appointment of Hua Kuo-feng, head of the secret police and the judiciary department, now to be placed in charge of the day-to-day working of the government, clearly meant that Mao wished to guarantee the succession of his radical faction. Daily news media attacks against Teng Hsiao-p'ing mounted to a new crescendo.

Then something extraordinary happened. On April 4, Chinese memorial day, a large group laid wreaths at the big square of Tienanmen in memory of Chou En-lai. When these flowers were removed overnight, over 100,000 people surged into the square on the following day in a massive protest over the neglect of the memory of the late prime minister. The crowd attacked and burned several vehicles belonging to the police, invaded an occupied part of a building that housed the headquarters of the secret police, shouting slogans, demanding the end of the rule of the first emperor (Mao's hero), and of the empress dowager, a clear reference to Madame Mao, and demanding the restoration of genuine Marxism-Leninism. Throughout the day the crowd milled about, beating up police and some nearby soldiers, without interference from any unit of the Peking Garrison of the PLA. By evening, order was restored by militia forces, who were brought in from neighboring cities.

This demonstration, which had counterparts in several other cities throughout the country, was the first organized massive anti-Mao demonstration in the history of the Chinese People's Republic. It was suppressed, though with some difficulty, and was followed two days later by equally massive rallies and meetings organized in Peking and throughout China in support of Chairman Mao and the "criminal conspiracies" of Teng Hsiao-p'ing and his alleged attempt to usurp control of the Communist party. Wall posters in Shanghai demanded the death sentence for Teng.

Chairman Mao, or the Maoists, had reasserted a precarious authority over the country; but with Mao's certain approaching death on September 9, 1977, the end of an era had arrived, leaving China in an uncertain and unstable condition. In Peking, the group surrounding Mao appeared in control. On their political survival after the chairman's death would depend the fate of the concept of perpetual revolution.

CHAPTER

IX

The Verdict of History?

BY THE END OF 1976, after Chairman Mao's death, the verdict of history began to come into focus. That Mao was one of the great revolutionaries of all time cannot be questioned. It was his good fortune to live in a period of great turmoil and of transition in social and economic institutions. This gave his the opportunity to place his stamp on the history of his nation in line with the changing ideas of the time.

He had the great ability to project an image of his own role, to create an aura that gave him that undefinable charisma on which his leadership was based. Although an elitist, he set about to undermine the traditional status of the educated in China by sending the students and his cadres back to the countryside to "merge with the peasants" and loose their status consciousness, but also for discipline and control. The egalitarianism which he tried to instill seemed strangely incongrous with the need of a trained bureaucratic management of a totalitarian society. These measures, as did his ideas, seemed utopian in their ruthless disregard for human nature, and the permanency of their impact remains dubious, indeed.

Throughout his lifetime, the political role of Mao Tse-tung created wide controversy among China specialists and casual observers; and an idolized image of Mao had its impact worldwide on a diverse group of youthful anarchists who saw in him a prophet meaningful to them in terms of their own utopian dreams. The basic difference of strategy between the Communist Revolution in China and the Bolshevik Revolution in the Soviet Union led early to an attempt to see in Mao Tse-tung the propagator of a different "Chinese" revolution which Mao was credited with creating. During World War II when the Chinese Communists first came to Western attention through Edgar Snow's *Red Star Over China,* the heroic campaigns of the Long March and the obvious differences in the revolutionary methods between the Chinese and the Soviets led to a widely held belief in a Chinese model of revolution—a "peasant revolution," rather than a "proletarian revolution" in the orthodox style of the Soviet precedent. At that time, the Chinese Communists, because of their United Front with the Nationalists in the war against Japan, had modified their policy from "agrarian revolution" to "agrarian reform." This policy was misunderstood and misinterpreted in the West, and the Chinese Communists became "agrarian reformers." Diplomats, government leaders and intellectuals in Europe and the United States widely accepted this belief, which meant that Mao and his team were regarded as a moderate agrarian reform force that should be supported. Since this image of Mao as the leader of agrarian reform was combined very often with a growing disapproval of the Nationalist leader Chiang Kai-shek and his government as being corrupt and inefficient, there emerged a school of thought that favored the support of the Chinese "agrarian reformers" and of Mao as a promising leader for a democratic future for China. A whole literature of that period and even for the postwar period dealt with Mao as the "peasant leader."

Postwar events, the renewal of the civil war, the Communist victory, and the realization of the ruthlessness of Chinese communism eventually dispelled this idyllic image of the Communist rural and moderate setting. But the issue of the assumed difference between Chinese and Soviet communism remained. From "agrarian reformer" and "peasant leader," Mao was elevated to the position of the inventor of a different kind of communism based on agrarian revolution. Disregarding Lenin's role as initiator of the strategy of national wars of liberation and Stalin's support of the Chinese agrarian revolution, a school of thought held and still holds that it was Mao who shifted from urban uprisings to rural revolution in China against Lenin's concept and in conflict with Stalin, who in this view did not understand the Chinese situation.[1]

Another debate over the issue of Mao's assumed heresy from the Soviet line of Stalin focused later on the question of the role of the

Chinese Communist leader, Li Li-san, who was purged for his pursuit of a policy of urban revolution in disregard of Soviet directives. The defenders of Mao's originality maintained that Li Li-san, in following his urban strategy, had only carried out Stalin's orders and was sacrificed as a "scapegoat" when the policy failed. Others maintained that Li Li-san was indeed a deviationist and that Mao was closer to Soviet, and in particular Stalin's, line than his Chinese competitor, Li Li-san.[2]

Related to this argument was the issue of Stalin's view of the potential of the Chinese Revolution. We know from several sources that at the end of World War II Stalin was unconvinced of the feasibility of a success of all-out military action by the Chinese Communists. According to Mao's testimony and Stalin's admission, Stalin had clearly misjudged the strength of the Chinese Communists, or perhaps rather the weakness of the National Government and, even more crucially, the determination of the American government to support its ally. But then, it appears that Mao himself was not aware of the immediacy of the Communist victory, predicting a long-drawn-out struggle. The only question is whether Stalin's view was merely a mistaken assessment of the military and politcal power factors or whether he indeed was hesitant to promote a Chinese Communist victory and with it the rise to power of a Chinese Communist rival. There is no proof for this latter interpretation in Chinese or Soviet statements.

Many of these arguments have faded with the emergence of a Chinese communism that was very different from the notions of agrarian revolution maintained abroad during the early stages of the civil war and Chinese Communist victories. The peasant issue, while ideologically relevant, has been recognized as a marginal aspect of Chinese communism and of Mao's rise to power, and has been replaced by an understanding of the military character of Chinese communism. There has been no argument about the fact that the concept of the *revolutionary army* came from Moscow, from Lenin and from Stalin, and that Mao Tse-tung, riding to power on his use of this military factor, was a successful practitioner of this strategy. The link between Mao's well-known slogan, "Political power grows out of the barrel of a gun" and Stalin's "revolutionary army" has been admitted by Mao himself.

Another issue related to the interpretation of Mao's special role in world communism is the question of the originality of Mao's Thought. One of the most outstanding of Mao's biographers in the West, Stuart Schram, has attempted in his various writings to find and explain Mao's intellectual originality and contribution to Marxist-Leninist Thought.[3] It is this author's view that while Mao was ingenious in popularizing Marxist-Leninist concepts in slogan form and easy formulations for his Chinese audiences, he was not a creative contributor to the concept of dialectic materialism and of Marxist-Leninist Thought.[4] Indeed Mao's simplistic extrapolations of the tenets of the doctrine have done more to reveal the limitations of Mao's Thought than to establish him as an intellect among the classical writers of the Marxist faith.

That does not preclude a recognition of the great influenc which Mao asserted particularly at the height of his most radical experiment, the Cultural Revolution, over some of the emotional, idealistic and demonstrative youth in the Western world. The *Little Red Book* was read, quoted, and its formulas chanted in unison by demonstrators in Europe and the United States. Yet within a few years, the Maoist worldwide movement was in disarray and the survival of the cult appeared questionable. Whether the cult, more emotional than intellectual, will long survive the leader, or whether Mao, like Stalin, will be discredited through de-Maoization is a matter yet to be decided.

*   *   *   *   *

Beyond the arguments of the day, a final assessment of Mao's role after his death can be made only after an interval of regroupment, redirection or conflict. One thing may be said. Mao Tse-tung, since his rise to power, held China in continuing turmoil in working towards a goal which was to serve two purposes: one was Mao's own sole authority and power, and for this end he was capable of carrying out dramatic shifts in policy; beyond that, however, Mao aimed throughout toward the fulfillment of his concept of a utopian revolution. In the first purpose he succeeded; so much could be said by 1977. In the second, the struggle continues and Mao's revolution has not been institutionalized, if it ever is to be.

In surveying the specifics of Mao's personality, his successes and his failures, one comes to the conclusion that his concepts and methods, as with any historical figure, evolved with the history of the Chinese Communist movement. This is no surprise. But there can also be discerned in the man certain proclivities and attitudes which found their expression at different phases of the story of Mao's rise to power and of his leadership role.

Some of these characteristics can be seen already in the young student Mao. His penchant towards admiration for historical "heroes," men who made history, the Napoleons and a misinterpreted George Washington, together with some of the heroic figures of the Chinese past, especially the first emperor, Ch'in Shih Huang-ti, formed his early pantheon. This hero worship is not too different from that of many a youngster in every country. But with Mao it was more than a youthful phase. He clearly believed in the mandate of great men to shape history, and was determined to become one himself. This had little to do with socialist revolution or the doctrinal theories of Communist totalitarianism scarcely known to him then, and never sufficiently grasped to replace that leadership concept formed in his early years.

The leader was there to lead, and Mao thought of the people needing strong leadership. In later terms, Mao's whole emphasis on the "masses" was the counterpoint to the concept of the leader. To him, the people were not individuals in the humanist tradition whether in the West or in China, but a group that could be inspired by their leader, clearly an elitist concept. His populist penchant enabled him not only to fit into the Marxist-Leninist framework but to go beyond it and to justify in his mind that form of totalitarian leader cult which is the most important phenomenon of our time. These attitudes appear to have been there according to his own account in his early life, but were to be brought out later in his struggle to remain on top of the political pyramid.

The ladder to reach that top, however, was clearly the Communist—or rather Maxist-Leninist—organization, introduced to China by the Soviets through the agents of the Comintern who became not only organizers but teachers to their Chinese disciples. It was Mao's good fortune that through his minor position in the library of Peking University, he came into personal contact with a group of intellectuals who had played with socialist-Marxist ideas and became disciples of the Soviet agents. The concept of the Communists as the *vanguard of the proletariat* provided a justification for that elitism of a few who were always in control of the so-called democratic centralism proclaimed by the Communist faith. The young Mao was at the outset a member of the organization of this Chinese group, and there found the starting point for his rise to power in an elitist structure that would enable him to apply his great talents for contending for power in a small leadership group. Mao was at first in a secondary position within this group led by his seniors, and he understood well the power relationship within the group as much as the dependence of the group on Moscow. He was always capable of accepting authority, including that of Moscow, and particularly that of Stalin, whom he greatly admired. But he also was able to use any opportunity to assert himself and to remain recalcitrant to superiors as far as it was in his view safe to go, and he appears to have had a good instinct for that limitation. In this context Mao's innate sense of timing enabled him to exploit all openings that offered themselves in the complexities of the political power struggles.

The advantages of complex leadership situations for any member of the elitist group were broadened by Lenin's policy of the United Front which in practice permitted Chinese Communist participation in the leadership organs of the Kuomintang. Mao used this opportunity to the hilt, and saw it strategically rather than with much concern for the doctrinal basis. Whether his willingness to stay with the Kuomintang after the split longer than any other Communist leader was motivated by a temptation to try another course within the power game, or whether he simply felt that there was still more mileage in this organizational set-up, can only be surmised. Mao's skill in exploiting complex leadership situations and conflicts may have been sharpened by this experience which turned out to be so disastrous for the fledgling Chinese Communist party. The split with the Kuomintang and the turn to agrarian revolution provided, however, a decisive opportunity for Mao because the shift of Communist strategy towards rural-based military organization introduced that military factor which Mao learned to use for his rise to power.

That Mao was chosen to play a part in this strategy was again a fortunate circumstance, but it was also a matter of Mao's own background and inclinations. Already in Canton while working with the Kuomintang in close contact with top leaders, Mao had been singled out for special training and organizational participation in the strategy of *agrarian revolution.* He had listened to lectures by the chief Soviet adviser, Michael Borodin, and had been charged with the administration of the training of rural functionaries, many of whom were, in fact, Communist party members working within the Kuomintang. Because of his rural origin from Hunan province, Mao was thus trained in the agitation of the peasant population for revolutionary purposes. In his travels at the time between Canton, Shanghai and Hunan, Mao followed party policy rather than a penchant of his own, until the Party determined his future career by sending him back to Hunan first for an investigation and report and later for a leading role in the Autumn Harvest uprising.

Mao's Hunan report demonstrated his limited understanding of the agrarian situation. Evidently hoping to please his sponsors, Mao greatly overrated the revolutionary capability of the peasantry. In describing them, however, he also revealed his populist inclination. Mao's emphasis on the point that the so-called Lumpen peasants, who had been equated with the "Lumpen proletariat," which Marx had despised, were not really bad elements but rather would be the mainstay of the rural-based revolution, was at variance with the Marxist revolutionary concept. What Mao misjudged was the potential of this revolutionary force which, according to him, would rise like a tempest sweeping away the establishment. His optimistic report found favor in the party leadership and also in Moscow and may have contributed to the tactical failure of the so-called

Autumn Harvest uprising which Moscow initiated.

In his first military assignment to organize in Hunan the rural population for this uprising, Mao disobeyed the directives of the Party Central. After the uprising failed, Mao was demoted not for too much, but for too little, peasant organization, an error he soon learned to rectify. He became the tough, ruthless leader needed in this rural battle for survival. The willingness of the dedicated Communist to disregard values and relationships of a humanist tradition and accept brutality as a necessary method to reach the sublime goal of the new social order is a given fact which any successful Communist leader has to understand. It is perhaps particularly so in a rural setting where sophistication cannot be a modifying factor if it ever was. A willingness to kill large numbers of people, men, women and children, translating class hatred into physical elimination of those regarded as class enemies, originated in this rural setting. It was applied by Mao on a large scale during the years of the civil war and the great drives of the early 1950s after the seizure of power. While Mao was in command, the partisans of the Kiangsi Soviet lived on loot and destruction, the killing of landlords and well-to-do peasants, and the seizure of their funds. That such indiscriminate action may have disturbed the conscience of even hardened Communist leaders can be seen in a short conversation between Mao and his rival Chang Kuo-t'ao, referred to in Chang's memoirs.[5] The human feelings existed, but there was no question but that they would have to be suppressed. Mao had learned the harshness of this type of warfare.

The other element that Mao experienced in this early setting of rural-based military organization was military action. The fusion of the remnants of his riffraff group of rural recruits with the trained military forces of Chu Teh provided the setting in which a new type of military warfare had to be conceived. The creation and use of a *revolutionary army* may have been Mao's greatest accomplishment. His great gift of indoctrination is unquestioned. Yet he has become better known as the assumed inventor of a new strategy of guerilla warfare. This strategy was proclaimed by Mao in his numerous military writings, a strategy which influenced many would-be revolutionaries outside China. Mao became the propagator of a military theory which became perhaps more important as a myth than as a strategic reality. Furthermore, Mao had learned the crucial importance of military power not only against the enemy but also within the contest for leadership among competing leaders within the Party. The practice of guerilla warfare as then carried on was actually strangely similar to Mao's manipulation of political power struggles, and if he was not an inventor of either strategy, he became a master in handling both of them.

Again it took time before Mao could assert himself in this setting. When his rural force in the Kiangsi border area grew in size and became the most important of the three or four Communist rural bases, the party leadership took an interest in the direction of this part of the Communist Revolution. The destruction of the party infrastructure in Shanghai forced the Communist leaders to flee to the military protection of this rural center and to take over its direction. Though shunted aside, Mao still remained on the spot.

The destruction of the Kiangsi Soviet by the Nationalists in the fifth campaign in 1934, forcing the Communists on the Long March in search of another base, gave Mao his new chance to regain leadership. He made his move in the early stage of the Long March. It was a desperate time for the Communist organization which, outmaneuvered by the National Government, had abandoned its base and fought its way into the open towards an uncertain future. Under these conditions, arguments within the leadership were bound to become grim and reproaches heavy. Mao obviously used the discontent among junior commanders to attack and dislocate the existing ledership and assume the decisive military command himself. At the Tsunyi Conference, which he called in January, 1935, Mao, acting in the absence of some of his competitors and with the backing of the younger commanders, plucked the leadership from a pliant Chou En-lai. He was never to relinquish it again. Mao's innate grasp of the use of the military as the key leverage of power, not only in the civil war but also in the conflicts to come after the establishment of the People's Republic, was fortified by this first success.

Mao's ability to use men and factions only later to discard them demonstrated his extraordinary sense of the potential of factional divisions and their use in the establishment and retention of his commanding position. Lin Piao's plaintive account of Mao's tactics of always playing off one side against the other and favoring one group today only to destroy it tomorrow is still the best characterization of Mao's ability and inclination to use Machiavellian tactics in his battle for maintaining the leading position.

Leadership in a Communist system demands not only organizational and, in Mao's case, military control, but more important still ideological sanction. As *vanguard of the proletariat,* the Communist party is presumed to represent the proper historical truth of the moment, and this historical truth has to be interpreted by the leader. One of the major sources of the leader's authority is based on this ability to determine "the line" as well as "deviation" from it. This authority has to be clothed in the Marxist-Leninist framework of doctrine and requires therefore an understanding of this framework and of its manipulation. When he assumed the leading position in the Party which he finally consolidated in Yenan, Mao also assumed this ideological mantle.

A great deal has been said and written about Mao's Thought, and attempts have been made to find in his various writings and statements philosophical contributions not only to Marxism-Leninism but sometimes on a broader basis to a new philosophical weltanschauung. Checked against the fundamentals of Marxism-Leninism as expressed in the classics of that faith, there are as indicated earlier few, if any, such philosophical contributions in Mao's writings. They play, however, an inherent role in the establishment of Mao's image and his leadership. Most of them, as far as theoretical pieces are concerned, date from the period during World War II and from the period shortly thereafter.

In the caves of the mountain fastness of Yenan, Mao was supplied with Soviet literature on Marxism-Leninism and had the leisure to study. Then he explained his newly acquired theoretical knowledge to his largely illiterate audiences, popularizing the concepts through slogans and images, and these lectures became the basis of his writings.

Mao understood both his theoretical shortcomings and the necessity for a Communist leader to manipulate the ideological power skillfully. At the end of 1949 after the establishment of the Chinese People's Republic, Mao is reported to have requested in correspondence with Stalin that the first Soviet ambassador sent to China be a man well-versed in Marxist philosophy. Stalin picked the former head of the Comintern, Yudin, who became one of the few Soviet or other foreigners to gain the confidence of Mao Tse-tung.[6] As Stalin regarded Mao all along as an effective activist and strategist but a weak theoretician, this Soviet assistance was unquestionably gladly given. Its importance was never publicized by either Moscow or Peking for obvious, though different, reasons. It was on this basis of Soviet texts and tutelage that Mao wrote his major theoretical pieces, few of which deal directly with doctrinal matters of Marxism.

The important point, however, was not that Mao did not add theoretical contributions or innovations to Marxist-Leninist teachings, nor that he neglected to produce a cohesive discourse on Marxism-Leninism; what was to him and to the outside world crucial was that he had written these essays and that they could be used to sanction his decisions and actions. Once the reputation of ideological qualification was assured, the Communist leader could justify his authority to establish the correct political "line" and to condemn his opponents as "deviationists" of the right or left without any challenge, because any attack against Mao's decisions would have impugned the authority of the ideological system itself as represented in the person of the leader. Mao understood this very well, and the purges of the so-called Cheng-feng movement during 1942-44 at Yenan show his masterful application of the monopoly of doctrine as a weapon in getting rid of his opponents.

Mao's Thought, then, though not a profound intellectual or philosophical program, was a very effective weapon for his political power-play. He handled it superbly. The importance of ideological manipulation, popularly known as *propaganda,* or in modern terminology *psychological operations* was well understood by Mao as apparent in his often quoted statement: "To overthrow a political power, it is always necessary first of all to create public opinion, to do work in the ideological sphere."[7] The claim that Mao possessed deeper insight into the essentials of the historical moment has not only been accepted in China in the peculiar form in which the Thought of Mao Tse-tung became the source of all wisdom, but also outside of China where many attempts were made to analyze the Thought and discern its philosophical ingredients.

Of all Mao's political writings, his directives received the most practical and widest use. In these directives, Mao focused on certain issues without, however, defining them too closely, placing the burden of mistakes on those who acted on the basis of misinterpretation of Mao's intent. Mao's Thought was therefore a somewhat elastic framework under which action could be taken, and the great variety of Mao's expressions made it possible to requote at different times different statements by Mao which when held side-by-side would have appeared often contradictory. This could be explained by the so-called dialectics. Seen in this light Mao's Thought and its application is a superb example of the ideological monopoly held by a Communist leader and used as sanction for his authority.

In Mao's Thought is thus reflected his political story. As a great admirer of the heroes of history, Mao had a genuine admiration for Stalin and his paeans of praise of Stalin, "the sun," were not only sung for reasons of political expediency. It may be significant that in the building up of his own cult, Mao himself was described as "the Red Sun in the people's hearts."

Mao's attitude towards Stalin appears to have been ambiguous. On one hand, he obviously admired Stalin as he indicated in many of his expressions; but on the other hand, he appears to have been jealous of Stalin's power.[8] Later, Mao also felt free to point to Stalin's mistakes in understanding the potential of the Chinese Revolution. But with this exception, Stalin was still a great Communist leader and "the correct side of Stalin" justified the cult. When Mao was threatened by de-Stalinization, he abandoned not the concept of hero which he believed himself to be, but he stepped out of the framework that had brought him to power but now threatened him. Stalin was attacked only after his death. During his lifetime, Stalin had played havoc within the party system through his purges that eventually turned the Party against its deceased leader. Mao had to challenge the Party itself to survive and needed a new conceptual framework to serve his own ends.

In establishing this conceptual framework, Mao went beyond the Marxist-Leninist system. The reason for Mao's "deviation" from Marxism-Leninism may not have been so much a matter of theoretical disagreement as of practical politics. After de-Stalinization, when Mao found himself deserted by the majority of the Chinese party leadership who were willing to accept the concept of *collective leadership,* Mao decided not to accept the party's verdict and see his position diminished. Instead, he threatened to bypass the party organization and go back to the rural areas, build his own military organization, and start all over.[9] It was this threat which led the party leadership to yield to Mao, sacrifice the minister of defense, who had led the attack, and have him replaced by Mao's most loyal standard-bearer among the military, Lin Piao, in order to avoid a split. Yet Mao did not then or later again regain control of the Party, so he built up his ideological leadership into a Cult of Mao outside the Party and directed against the Party. When the Party was reestablished after the Cultural Revolution, it had become Mao's party, a party which accepted the leadership cult. This leadership principle which emerged in China from that time on not only affected Mao's attitude towards the institutional system of Lenin, but also stimulated Mao to roam in his Thought far beyond the confines of the Marxist-Leninist beliefs as accepted by the current Communist organization.

Up to the period of the conflict, Mao had simply popularized Marxist-Leninist orthodoxy for his Chinese audience. Now he became a utopian visionary proclaiming his own rather simplistic concept of the revolutionary advance of mankind. Instead of the stages of the Marxist-Leninist doctrine which would progress step-by-step to the Communist ideal that remained undefined but final, Mao innovated two concepts which more and more came to define his weltanschauung. For one thing, the gradual transition of socialism to communism gave room to the idea of imminent accomplishment of the Communist order through willpower and organization. The accomplishment of instant communism, of the economic and social miracle that could be wrought by the leader, was the basis of the policy of the Great Leap Forward which ended in such disaster.

This concept, however, with its uncertain outcome was to be matched by the theory of *perpetual revolution.* Mao's penchant for this concept was apparent at an earlier time. As a revolutionary organizer and strategist, Mao was never at home with the task of building a viable government structure and program after the victory of revolution over the old order. The day-to-day work of administering a program of progressive development was alien to his nature. As he himself admitted, Mao was not familiar with the economic problems of planning or reorganization. No wonder he had little patience with routinization of government. In its place, he accepted the idea of constant struggle and disequilibrium. After the Revolution had succeeded, its results still would be challenged, and from this conviction Mao derived a concept of permanent struggle that would be carried on ideologically as well as in the material world. This concept of continued conflict and continued contradiction between the two lines—the "proletarian revolutionary" and "bourgeois reactionary" line—was first expressed by Mao in the very year of his jeopardy, 1956, when the new Soviet de-Stalinization policy endangered Mao's position in the Chinese party. It continued ever since. It was no longer possible according to Mao's view to end contradictions in the Communist social order but, even after the establishment of communism, the struggle between the two lines would continue forever. China could easily revert to capitalism and the cycle from equilibrium to disequilibrium would never end. From 1958 on, Mao clearly stated that communism once it has been accepted must also be transformed and that the struggle would go on even after the disappearance of mankind in a continuing conflict in the universe. Indeed, Mao's later pronouncements about the course of humanity and of the universe appear to express the belief in just one surviving faith, the faith in struggle as the ultimate value end in itself.

Speaking in August 1964, on "Questions of Philosophy," Mao expanded on a popular type of Darwinism in developing his own philosophy about the future of the universe.[10] Starting from the reference to man as a "tool-making and social animal," taken from Marx and relating that to the concept of evolution, Mao held that "in the future animals will continue to develop." Believing that monkeys were not the only animals that could evolve, Mao raised the question whether "horses, cows, sheep and insects will all change," and indicated that he did not believe that man alone was "capable of having two hands." In this amateurish way, Mao stressed the need to study the history of natural science, giving other examples of the story of evolution.

It is essentially this sort of primitive expansion of Darwinism, of the concept of *survival of the fittest,* that in Mao's view dictated a continuation of the class struggle beyond the Marxist goal of proclaimed elimination of exploitation in the postulated Communist society of the future. This concept led Mao to believe in struggle as the goal in itself, a belief responsible for the hostility to all institutionalization which characterized the tumultuous years of Mao's leadership.

Mao then was a unique embodiment of the concept of revolution for revolution's sake, a proof of H. G. Well's prescription that utopia can never be static. He was a remarkable man with a genius for creating social upheavals that is perhaps unmatched in history. It remains to be seen what can possibly survive of the cult, the concepts, and the chaos that Mao tried to impose on a society that was at the same time struggling continuously to regain some order, whether under more orthodox Communism or by salvaging or regaining some of the humanist values of the past.

Courtesy of Ming Pao.

Courtesy of Ming Pao.

Courtesy of Ming Pao.

Courtesy of Ming Pao.

Wall Posters attacking the Gang of Four.

Epilogue

M AO TSE-TUNG died on September 9, 1976, at 12:10 A.M., in the first minutes of the new day. He had been steadily declining in health and strength for over a year. On June 15, the Central Committee announced that the chairman would no longer receive foreign visitors as he had been doing during the last month in ever shorter audiences. The last such meeting was on May 29, when Mao received the Pakistani President Bhutto for a brief fifteen minutes. The films of these visits document for the viewer the steady decline of the old man, eventually no longer capable of lifting his head from the depths of his armchair. The visible paralysis of his mouth impaired Mao's speech, limiting him to gutteral sounds. Yet, at the last visit of Secretary of State Kissinger earlier in the year, Mao had forced himself to express ideas ranging over all phases of world policy, for two hours, despite this terrible handicap, "in the most stupendous demonstration of will I had ever seen," as Secretary Kissinger later stated. Information from Peking indicated that just two days before his death, Mao had expressed the wish to meet Dr. James Schlesinger, former secretary of defense of the United States, who was then visiting the People's Republic of China on invitation from

Peking. In the joint message issued at Mao's death, the Chinese leaders indicated that Mao "waged a tenacious struggle against his illness." We can thus assume that almost to the end, Mao was part and perhaps the key figure in the decision-making process on the most crucial domestic and foreign Chinese policy issues.

The final departure of this extraordinary, dynamic revolutionary leader, though long expected, came as a shock, and it was at the time impossible to foretell how the void left by his disappearance could be filled. The news of Mao's death was delayed for sixteen hours, and when finally announced the message contained plans for eight days of elaborate memorial services. During the period from September 11 to September 17, mourning services were to be held at the Great Hall of the People in Peking, with all leading members of the Party, the government, the army and the Peking Municipality, as well as representatives of workers, peasants, soldiers and the masses paying their respects to the chairman's bier. No foreign leaders were invited to Peking. Similar memorial services would be held throughout the country. On September 18, a memorial rally was held at Tienanmen Square, transmitted nationwide by television and radio. At the beginning of this service, all activities ceased throughout China for a three-minute period of silence in tribute to the chairman, while sirens sounded from trains, ships and factories.

The original death announcement broadcast by loudspeakers was given in the name of party and government leaders. The sponsors included the Military Commission of the Party, indicating the important role of the People's Liberation Army (PLA) among the successors. The funeral committee list included practically every name of importance, whether radical or orthodox, demonstrating the unity that the leadership wanted to manifest at this critical time. At the top of the list, singled out, were the four surviving members of the Standing Committee of the Politburo. These four were expected to form a collective leadership until the new chairman was determined. The first of the four was Hua Kuo-feng, the new prime minister, first deputy of the Party, and minister of public security in control of all police and security agencies, clearly the most powerful figure of the new leaders, at least for the moment. Of the other three, Yeh Chien-ying, the minister of defense, though 78, was the senior military leader and proved to be a key figure in the coming power struggle. Wang Hung-wen and Chang Ch'un-ch'iao, the Maoist radical leaders from Shanghai, came to the top during the Cultural Revolution as protégés of Madame Mao. Wang had a meteoric rise to power from labor organizer in a cotton mill in Shanghai to second-ranking leading member of the Politburo. A main organizer of the Maoist militia, Wang was often mentioned as a coming leader because of his youthful age.

Chang Ch'un-ch'iao, deputy prime minister and director general of the political department of the PLA, was frequently described as the most able of the radical leaders and a potential successor to Mao. In addition to these four men, speculation centered around Madame Mao, Chiang Ch'ing, the *dark horse* of some hypothesists, who achieved the power she had always apparently sought, as creator of the melodramatic revolutionary theater and sponsor of the Red Guards.

The placement of these leaders was the outcome of Mao's final power struggle, which began in 1975 in typical allegorical fashion through an attack on the hero of the historical novel *Water Margin,* who was now condemned as an early "revisionist" and traitor to the revolutionary cause. The contemporary target of this historical parable turned out to be Teng Hsiao-p'ing, then the first deputy prime minister acting for the seriously ill Chou En-lai. Though Teng was at first not attacked by name, it became ever cleared that it was his policy, carried out by his administrators, rehabilitated and reappointed to important provincial and central posts, that came under furious attack. It was Teng who opposed the new educational trend that rewarded political activism at the expense of scholarship and knowledge. It was Teng who advocated economic progress over continued revolutionary upheaval, who wanted to raise wages as production incentive instead of relying on ideological fervor. In fact, Teng has issued a general program dealing with the importance of science for speeding up China's industrial production. Honoring professors and scientists, he openly disapproved of Madame Mao's new revolutionary operas and ridiculed the rapid rise of radical revolutionaries to high political posts, whose advancement he termed *helicopter careers.* On their side, the young radicals objected to the reappointment of cadres purged during the Cultural Revolution, to positions to which they aspired.

When Chou En-lai died, in early January, 1975, following a prolonged illness, Mao bypassed Teng Hsiao-p'ing, the first deputy prime minister, to the surprise of many, and appointed Hua Kuo-feng as acting prime minister, advancing him from his position as sixth deputy prime minister. With Hua's appointment, Teng's policy was aborted.

The open backlash became apparent to the world at a massive anti-Mao rally at Tienamen Square on April 5 (Chinese All Souls Day), when over 100,000 demonstrators honored Chou En-lai and clashed with the security police, condemning Mao and Madame Mao with placards and slogans, chanting anti-Mao poems. The suppression of this outburst, echoed in provincial cities, gave Mao and his followers the opportunity to solidify control. Teng was held responsible and purged from all offices; he came under mounting vilification in an anti-Tang drive. Hua Kuo-feng formally became prime minister and first deputy chairman of the Party.

The great earthquake that shook north China in late July, completely destroying the city of T'angshan, leveling parts of Peking, Tientsin and other cities and causing over a million casualties, was one of the greatest human tragedies of this decade. It also had political implications. For the superstitious, these and other lesser quakes that preceded and followed it in other parts of China, may have been a reminder of the ancient belief that such natural disasters were portents of the imminent fall of dynasties, a popular superstition enhanced by the general knowledge of Mao's impending death. To counter it, party leaders counseled the people not to listen to rumors and superstitions spread by "a small clique of class enemies." As noted by foreign observers forced to leave Peking, the earthquake provided the new leadership an opportunity to assert control in devastated areas while effectively managing relief and rehabilitation. These actions were celebrated in Peking on September 1 as a great victory over the earthquake which had given rise to many miracles of heroism. A picture of this celebration, distributed nationwide, showed the four leaders and Madame Mao standing together, indicating the unity of this new leadership at the time of the triumph over natural adversity. Two weeks later, at the bier of the chairman, the same leader group was depicted, leading the nation in mourning for the Great Leader and Great Teacher, Chairman Mao Tse-tung.

Less than a month after Mao's death, on October 7, the power struggle for succession came into the open. In an obviously well-prepared move, Hua Kuo-feng, who claimed to have been appointed as successor by Chairman Mao, arrested the four leading Maoist radicals, Madame Mao, Chang Ch'un-ch'iao, Wang Hung-wen and Yao Wen-yuan. From that moment on, the four were accused of having attempted a coup of their own and were condemned as the "gang of four" or the "four pests" or by similar epithets for having committed numerous crimes in the past, of having been "capitalist roaders," subverting Mao's will and Communist policy. This extraordinary move appeared to shift the balance of power, as well as the political line, away from the Maoist policy of perpetual revolution. The new policy was to be carried on in the name of Chairman Mao whose many and often contradictory sayings could be selectively used by his successor. But the situation remained uncertain and unstable. Potential opposition from Maoist radicals, though deprived of their leaders, was clearly a concern, as was the possible rivalry among the new leaders. Of equal concern to the leadership must have been the decline of discipline during the last months before Mao's death, in such contrast to the complete rigidity of total control previously maintained in the People's Republic. Incidents of undisciplined behavior, gang fighting, shoplifting, even bank robberies came to the notice of foreign observers; and a great deal of looting appears to have occurred after the earthquake. Was the *socialist morality* so constantly hammered in by Maoist propaganda, beginning to evaporate by the time of chairman's death?

There continued the impending Soviet threat on the border, receiving new momentum from Moscow's hope that Mao's death might open an opportunity for new relations with Peking. In several ways, relations with the Soviet Union seemed to improve; but soon new statements were issued by Mao's successors, clearly meant to nip in the bud such Soviet expectations and to reassert Mao's anti-Soviet line. The long-range outlook in Sino-Soviet relations remained ambigious after Mao's orbit, adding to the uncertainty of the domestic scene to which it was so obviously related. Mao's statement, "The current international situation is one of great disorder under heaven and one in which the wind sweeping through the tower heralds a rising storm in the mountains," quoted time and again by his successors who saw their great revolutionary opportunity in the chaos of world affairs, might instead come to apply to China herself, heralding a crisis that would jar the world.

After his seizure of power, Chairman Hua Kuo-feng built a colossal mausoleum at Tienanmen—much larger than Lenin's tomb—for Mao Tse-tung, where the dead leader's body was enshrined in a crystal sarcophagus.

From July 16 to 21, a secret Central Committee meeting was held in Peking where, as a result of prolonged pressure by military leaders and party cadres, Teng Hsiao-p'ing was rehabilitated and restored to all his former positions for the second time. The new leadership was confirmed by a new party congress, the Eleventh, from August 12 to 18, 1977, which elected a new Central Committee, a new Politburo, and a new Standing Committee of the Politburo with a heavy emphasis on the military and the rehabilitated party cadres. It also drafted a new party constitution.

Under the new leadership the People's Republic was ruled by a Troika consisting of Hua Kuo-feng, Yeh Chien-ying and Teng Hsiao-p'ing. Teng appeared to be the chief administrator in this new ruling constellation. While claiming to follow the will of Chairman Mao, the new leaders appeared to promote the economic program of Chou En-lai. The new party congress also proclaimed the final end of the Cultural Revolution. Indeed, the era of Mao Tse-tung appeared to have come to an end.

Nevertheless, the revolution that Mao created has set in motion forces that may not yet have run their course. Mao kept China in a state of turmoil to further his revolutionary goals, and has left a heritage of perpetual revolution—without a known successor of equal and single-minded revolutionary zeal. China's new leadership has used quotations from Mao Tse-tung selectively to reinterpret the history of the era of Mao Tse-tung. The excesses of the Cultural Revolution and the years since have been blamed on the "gang of four," but the image of the late Chairman remains unblemished, sanctioning the policies of Mao's successor.

Appendix

SNOW

Mao's best known poem, "Snow" was published on August 28, 1945, on Mao's arrival in Chungking for negotiations with Chiang Kai-shek. Both the occasion and Mao's purpose in writing the poem are discussed in Chapter IV, p. 80 and footnote 10.

This is the scene in that Northern Land;
A hundred leagues are sealed with ice,
A thousand leagues of whirling snow.
On either side of the Great Wall
    One vastness is all you see.
From end to end of the Great River,
    The rushing water is frozen and lost.
The mountains dance like silver snakes,
The highlands roll like waxen elephants,
As if they thought to vie in height
    with the Lord of Heaven.
And on a sunny day
See how the white-robed beauty is adorned with rouge,
Enchantment beyond compare.

Lured by such great beauty in our landscape,
Innumerable heroes have rivalled one another
    to bow in homage.
But alas, Chin Shih Huang and Han Wu-Ti
    Were rather lacking in culture,
T'ang Tai-tsung and Sung Tai-tsu had little
    taste for poetry.
And Genghis Khan
    the favorite son of heaven for a day
Knew only how to bend his bow to shoot great vultures.
Now they are all past and gone.
To find heroes in the grand manner,
We must look in the present.

From *Mao Tse-tung,* ©1966 by Stuart Schram. Reprinted by permission of Simon & Schuster, Inc.

ON CONTRADICTION

(August, 1937)

This essay was part of a lecture series, given by Mao in Yenan in 1938, and later edited and published in the first volume of Mao's selected works.* On Contradiction was Mao's most ambitious attempt to demonstrate his mastery of dialectical materialism and to explain it to his Communist audience and readers, closely following his Soviet material. Its substance and importance is described in Chapter III, pages 65 and 66.

The law of contradiction in things, that is, the law of the unity of opposites, is the most basic law in materialist dialectics. Lenin said: "In its proper meaning, dialectics is the study of the contradiction within the very essence of things".[1] Lenin often called this law the essence of dialectics; he also called it the kernel of dialectics.[2] Therefore, in studying this law, we cannot but touch upon a wide range of subjects, upon a great number of problems of philosophy. If we can clear up all these problems we shall arrive at a basic understanding of materialist dialectics. These problems are: the two world outlooks; the universality of contradiction; the particularity of contradiction; the principal contradiction and the principal aspect of a contradiction; the identity and the struggle of the aspects of a contradiction; the role of antagonism in contradiction.

Great interest has been aroused among us by the criticism levelled at the idealism of the Deborin school in Soviet philosophical circles in recent years. Deborin's idealism has exerted a very bad influence in the Chinese Communist Party, and it must be admitted that doctrinaire ways of thought in our Party have something to do with this school's style in work. Thus the principal objective of our philosophical studies at present should be the eradication of doctrinaire ways of thought.

I. THE TWO WORLD OUTLOOKS

In the history of human knowledge, there have always been two views concerning the laws of development of the world; the metaphysical view and the dialectical view, which form two mutually opposed world outlooks. Lenin said: "The two basic (or two possible? or historically observable?) conceptions of development (evolution) are: development as decrease and increase, as repetition, and development as a unity of opposites (the division of the one into

---

*Originally published as the first piece in the second volume, *On Contradiction* was later transferred to the first volume, where, according to Peking's claim, it chronologically belonged.

Selection from *Selected Works of Mao Tse-tung*, vol. 1 (Peking: Foreign Languages Press, 1965), pp. 311-347.

mutually exclusive opposites and their reciprocal relation)".[3] What Lenin was referring to is these two different world outlooks.

For a very long period of history both in China and in Europe, metaphysics formed part of the idealist world outlook and occupied a dominant position in human thought. In the early days of the bourgeoisie in Europe, materialism was also metaphysical. The Marxist materialist-dialectical world outlook emerged because in many European countries social economy had entered the stage of highly developed capitalism, the productive forces, the class struggle and the sciences had all developed to a level unprecedented in history, and the industrial proletariat had become the greatest motive force in historical development. Then among the bourgeoisie, besides an openly avowed, extremely barefaced reactionary idealism, there also emerged vulgar evolutionism to oppose materialist dialectics.

The so-called metaphysical world outlook or the world outlook of vulgar evolutionism consists of looking at the world from an isolated, static and one-sided viewpoint. It regards all things in the world, their forms and their species, as for ever isolated from one another and for ever changeless. Whatever change there is, means merely an increase or decrease in quantity or a transplacement in space. Moreover, the cause of such an increase or decrease or transplacement does not lie inside things, but outside them, that is, propulsion by external forces. Metaphysicians hold that all varieties of things in the world, as well as their characteristics, have remained unchanged ever since the moment they came into being. Any subsequent change is a mere quantitative expansion or contraction. They hold that a thing can only be repeatedly reproduced as the self-same thing for ever and cannot change into something different. In their eyes, capitalist exploitation, capitalist competition, the ideology of individualism in capitalist society, and so on, can all be found in the slave society of antiquity, or even in primitive society, and will exist for ever without any change. They trace the causes of social development to conditions external to society, like geography and climate. They naively seek outside the things themselves for the cause of their development and repudiate the theory advanced by materialist dialectics that it is the contradictions inside things that cause their development. Therefore they cannot explain the multiplicity of the qualities of things; nor can they explain the phenomenon of one quality changing into another. In Europe, this mode of thought existed as mechanistic materialism in the seventeenth and eighteenth centuries and as vulgar evolutionism at the end of the nineteenth and the beginning of the twentieth century. In China, the metaphysical mode of thought that "Heaven changes not, and the Way too changes not",[4] was for a long time suppported by the decadent feudal ruling classes. Imported from Europe in the last hundred years, mechanistic materialism and vulgar evolutionism have been supported by the bourgeoisie.

Contrary to the metaphysical world outlook, the materialist-dialectical world outlook advocates the study of the development of things from the inside, from the relationship of a thing to other things, namely, that the development of things should be regarded as their internal and necessary self-movement, that a thing in its movement and the things round it should be regarded as interconnected and interacting upon each other. The basic cause of development of things does not lie outside but inside them, in their internal contradictions. The movement and development of things arise because of the presence of such contradictions inside all of them. This contradiction within a thing is the basic cause of its development, while the relationship of a thing with other things—their inter-connection and interaction—is a secondary cause. Thus materialist dialectics forcefully combats the theory of external causes, or of propulsion, advanced by metaphysical mechanistic materialism and vulgar evolutionism. It is evident that purely external causes can only lead to the mechanical motion of things, that is, to changes in size and quantity, but cannot explain why things are qualitatively different in a thousand and one ways and why things change into one another. As a matter of fact, even a mechanical motion of things propelled by some external force is also brought about through their internal contradictions. Mere growth in plants and animals and their quantitative development are also chiefly caused by their internal contradictions. Similarly, social development is chiefly due not to external but internal causes. Many countries exist under almost the same geographical and climatic conditions, yet they are extremely different and uneven in their development. Tremendous social changes take place even in one and the same country while no change has occurred in its geography and climate. Imperialist Russia changed into the socialist Soviet Union and feudal, insulated Japan changed into imperialist Japan, while no change has occurred in the geography and climate of these two countries. China, for long dominated by feudalism, has undergone great changes in the last hundred years and is now changing in the direction of a new China, liberated and free; yet no change has occurred in her geography and climate. Changes are taking place in the geography and climate of the earth as a whole and in every part of it, but they are very insignificant when compared with changes in society; in the former the changes manifest themselves in terms of tens of thousands or millions of years, while in the latter they manifest themselves in mere thousands, hundreds, tens, or even a few years or even months (as in times of revolution). According to the viewpoint of materialist dialectics, changes in nature are chiefly due to the development of the internal contradictions in nature. Changes in society are chiefly due to the development of the internal contradictions in society, namely the contradiction between the productive forces and the relations of production, the contradiction between the old and the new; it is the development of these contradictions that impels society forward and starts the process of the supersession of the old society by a new one. Does materialist dialectics leave external causes out of account? Not at all. Materialist dialectics considers external causes to be the condition of change and internal causes to be the basis of change, external causes becoming operative through internal causes. In a suitable temperature an egg changes into a chicken, but there is no such temperature as can change a stone into a chicken, the fundamentals of the two things being different. There is a constant interaction between the peoples of different countries. In the era of capitalism, especially the era of imperialism and the proletarian revolution, interaction and mutual stimulation, political, economic and cultural, between various countries have been extremely great. The October Socialist Revolution ushered in a new epoch not only in Russian history but also in world history, exerting an influence on the internal changes in all countries of the world and, in a similar and yet particularly profound way, on the internal changes in China; such changes, however, arose from an inner necessity in those countries as well as in China. Two armies engage in battle; one is victorious and the other defeated; both victory and defeat are determined by internal causes. One is victorious either because of its strength or because of its correct command; the other is defeated either because of its weakness or because of its incompetent command: it is through internal causes that external causes become operative. In 1927 the Chinese big bourgeoisie defeated the proletariat, operating through the opportunism existing within the Chinese proletariat itself (within the Chinese Communist Party). When we liquidated this opportunism, the Chinese revolution resumed its advance. Later, the Chinese revolution again suffered severe blows from the enemy, because adventurism appeared within our Party. When we liquidated this adventurism, our cause once more resumed its advance. Thus, to lead the revolution to victory, a political party must rely upon the correctness of its own political line and the consolidation of its own organisation.

The dialectical world outlook had already emerged in ancient times both in China and in Europe. But ancient dialectics has something spontaneous and naive about it; being based upon the social and historical conditions of the times, it was not formulated into an adequate theory, hence it could not fully explain the world, and was later supplanted by metaphysics. The famous German philosopher Hegel, who lived from the late eighteenth century to the early nineteenth, made very important contributions to dialectics, but his is idealist dialectics. It was not until Marx and Engels, the great men of action of the proletarian movement, made a synthesis of the positive achievements in the history of human knowledge and, in particular, critically absorbed the rational elements of Hegelian dialectics and created the great theory of dialectical materialism and historical materialism, that a great, unprecedented revolution took place in the history of human knowledge. Later Lenin and Stalin have further developed this great theory. Introduced in China, this theory immediately brought about tremendous changes in the world of Chinese thought.

This dialectical world outlook teaches man chiefly how to observe and analyse skillfully the movement of opposites in various things and, on the basis of such analysis, to find out the methods of solving the contradictions. Consequently, it is of paramount importance for us to understand concretely the law of contradiction in things.

2. THE UNIVERSALITY OF CONTRADICTION

For convenience in exposition, I shall deal here first with the universality of contradiction, and then with the particularity of contradiction. Only a brief remark is needed to explain the former, because many people have accepted the universality of contradiction ever since the great creators and continuers of Marxism—Marx, Engels, Lenin and Stalin—established the materialist-dialectical world outlook and applied materialist dialectics with very great success to many aspects of the analysis of human history and of natural history, to many aspects of changes in society and in nature (as in the Soviet Union); but there are still many comrades, especially the doctrinaires, who are not clear about the problem of the particularity of contradiction. They do not understand that the universality of contradiction resides precisely in the particularity of contradiction. Nor do they understand how very significant it is for our further guidance in revolutionary practice to study the particularity of contradiction in the concrete things confronting us. Therefore, the problem of the particularity of contradiction should be studied with special attention and explained at sufficient length. For this reason, when we analyse the law of contradiction in things, we should first analyse the universality of contradiction, then analyse with special attention the particularity of contradiction, and finally return to the universality of contradiction.

The universality or absoluteness of contradiction has a two-fold meaning. One is that contradiction exists in the process of development of all things and the other is that in the process of development of each thing a movement of opposites exists from beginning to end.

Engels said: "Motion itself is a contradiction."[5] Lenin defined the law of the unity of opposites as "the recognition (discovery) of the contradictory, mutually exclusive, opposite tendencies in all phenomena and processes of nature (including mind and society)."[6] Are these views correct? Yes, they are. The interdependence of the contradictory aspects of a thing and the struggle between them determine the life and impel the development of that thing. There is nothing that does not contain contradiction; without contradiction there would be no world.

Contradiction is the basis of simple forms of motion (*e.g.,* mechanical motion) and still more the basis of complex forms of motion.

Engels explained the universality of contradiction in these terms:

> "If simple mechanical change of place contains a contradiction, this is even more true of the higher forms of motion of matter, and especially of organic life and its development. . . . Life consists just precisely in this—that a living thing is at each moment itself and yet something else. Life is therefore also a contradiction which is present in things and processes themselves, and which constantly originates and solves itself; and as soon as the contradiction ceases, life too comes to an end, and death steps in. We likewise saw that also in the sphere of thought we could not avoid contradictions, and that, for example, the contradiction between man's inherently unlimited faculty of knowledge and its actual realisation in men who are limited by their external conditions and limited also in their intellectual faculties finds its solution in what is, for us at least, a practically endless succession of generations, in infinite progress.
>
> ". . . One of the basic principles of higher mathematics is the contradiction. . . .
>
> "But even lower mathematics teems with contradictions."[7]

Lenin likewise explained the universality of contradiction as follows:

"In mathematics: + and −; differential and integral.
In mechanics: action and reaction.
In physics: positive and negative electricity.
In chemistry: the combination and dissociation of atoms.
In social science: the class struggle."[8]

In war, offence and defence, advance and retreat, victory and defeat are all, contradictory phenomena. Without the one, the other cannot exist. These two aspects struggle as well as unite with each other, constituting the totality of the war, impelling the war's development and solving the war's problems.

Every difference in man's concepts should be regarded as reflecting objective contradictions. Objective contradictions are reflected in subjective thought, constituting the movement in opposites of concepts, impelling the development of thought, and ceaselessly solving the problems that arise in man's thinking.

Within the Party, opposition and struggle between different ideas occur constantly; they reflect in the Party the class contradictions and the contradictions between the old and the new things in society. If in the Party there were neither contradictions nor ideological struggles to solve them, the Party's life would come to an end.

Thus the point is already clear: whether in simple or complex forms of motion, whether in objective or ideological phenomena, contradiction exists universally and in all processes. But does contradiction also exist at the initial stage of every process? In the process of development of everything, is there a movement of opposites from beginning to end?

Judging from the discussions in Soviet philosophical circles, the Deborin school holds the view that contradiction does not appear at the very beginning of a process, but only at a certain stage of its development. Consequently, up to that moment, the development of the process is not due to internal causes but to external ones. Thus, Deborin returns to the metaphysical theory of external causes and of mechanism. Applying such a view in the analysis of concrete problems, his school holds that under existing conditions in the Soviet Union, there are only differences but no contradictions between the kulaks and the peasants in general, thus agreeing entirely with Bukharin's view. In analysing the French Revolution, it holds that before the Revolution there were only differences but no contradictions in the Third Estate composed of the workers, the peasants and the bourgeoisie. These views are anti-Marxist. The Deborin school does not understand that every difference in the world already contains a contradiction, that difference implies precisely contradiction. Labour and capital have been in contradiction ever since they came into being, though at first the contradiction was not yet intensified. Even under the social conditions of the Soviet Union a difference exists between the workers and the peasants; this difference is a contradiction, though, unlike that between labour and capital, it will not become intensified into antagonism or assume the form of class struggle: in the course of socialist construction the workers and the peasants have formed a firm alliance and will gradually solve this contradiction in the process of development from socialism to communism. This is a question of distinction in the character of contradictions, not a matter of the presence or absence of them. Contradiction is universal, absolute, existing in all processes of the development of things and running through all processes from beginning to end.

What is the emergence of a new process? It is this: when the old unity and its constituent opposites yield place to a new unity and its constituent opposites, a new process emerges in place of the old. The old process is completed and the new one emerges. As the new process in its turn contains a new contradiction, the history of the development of its own contradiction begins.

Lenin pointed out that Marx in his *Capital* had given a model analysis of the movement of opposites which runs through the process of development of things from beginning to end. This is a method that must be applied in studying the process of development of all things. Lenin himself also correctly applied it and adhered to it in all his writings.

> "In his *Capital* Marx first analyses the simplest, most ordinary, funda-mental, most common and everyday *relation* of bourgeois (commodity) society, a relation that is encountered billions of times, viz., the ex-change of commodities. In this very simple phenomenon (in this 'cell' of bourgeois society) analysis reveals *all* the contradictions (or the germs of *all* the contradiction) of modern society. The subsequent exposition shows us the development (*both* growth *and* movement) of these con-tradictions and of this society in the sum of its individual parts, from its beginning to its end."

Having said this, Lenin continued: "Such must also be the method of exposi-tion (or study) of dialectics in general."[9]

Chinese Communists must master this method before they can correctly analyse the history and the present condition of the Chinese revolution as well as define its perspectives.

3. THE PARTICULARITY OF CONTRADICTION

Contradiction exists in the process of development of all things, and contra-diction runs through the process of development of each thing from beginning to end; this is the universality and absoluteness of contradiction which we have discussed above. Now we shall speak of the particularity and relativity of contradiction.

This problem should be approached from several angles. First, the contradic-tion in each form of motion of matter has its particularity. Man's knowledge of matter is knowledge of the forms of motion of matter, because there is nothing in the world except matter in motion and the motion of matter must assume certain forms. In considering each form of motion of matter, we must take into account the points which each has in common with other forms of motion. But what is especially important and constitutes the basis of our knowledge of things is that we must take into account the particular points of the motion of matter, namely, the qualitative difference between one form of motion and other forms. Only when we have taken this into account can we distinguish between things. Any form of motion contains within itself its own particular contradiction. This particular contradiction constitutes the particular quality which distinguishes one thing from all others. This is the internal cause or, as it may be called, the basis of one thousand and one ways in which things are different from one another. In nature many forms of motion exist: mechanical motion, sound, light, heat, electricity, decomposition, combination, and so on. All these forms depend upon one another as well as differ from one another qualitatively. The particular quality possessed by each form is determined by its own particular contradiction. This holds good not only of nature but also of society, and of thought. Every form of society, every mode of thought has its particular contradiction and particular quality.

The classification of scientific studies is based precisely upon the particular contradictions inherent in their objects. Thus a certain kind of contradiction peculiar to a certain field of phenomena constitutes the subject matter of a certain branch of science. For example, positive numbers and negative numbers in mathematics; action and reaction in mechanics; positive and negative electricity in physics; decomposition and combination in chemistry; productive forces and relations of production, classes and the struggle between the classes in social science; offence and defence in military science; idealism and materialism; the metaphysical outlook and the dialectical outlook in philosophy, and so on—it is because they each possess a particular contradiction and a particular quality that they are studied in different sciences. Of course, without recognising the universality of contradiction, we can in no way discover the universal cause or universal basis of the development of the motion of things; however, without studying the particularity of contradiction, we can in no way determine the particular quality of a thing that differs from those of other things, discover the particular cause or particular basis of the development of the motion of things, distinguish one thing from another, or mark out fields of scientific study.

According to the sequence in man's process of knowing, there is always a gradual extension from a knowledge of the individual thing to a knowledge of things in general. Man can proceed to generalisations and know the qualities common to things only after he has known the qualities peculiar to each of a great number of things. When man already knows such common qualities, he uses this knowledge as a guide and goes on to study various concrete things which have not yet been studied or have not yet been thoroughly studied, so as to find out their peculiar qualities; only thus can he supplement, enrich and develop his knowledge of the common qualities, and prevent such knowledge from becoming something withered and petrified. These are the two processes of knowing: one is from the particular to the general, and the other is from the general to the particular. Man's knowledge always proceeds in this cyclical, recurrent manner, and with each cycle (if it strictly conforms to scientific method) man's knowledge can be advanced and become more and more profound. Our doctrinaires make their mistakes because, on the one hand, they do not understand that we must study the particularity of contradiction and know the peculiar qualities of individual things before we can know adequately the universality of contradiction and the common qualities of various things; and, on the other hand, they do not understand that after we have known the common qualities of certain things, we must go on to study those concrete things that have not yet been thoroughly studied or have newly emerged. Our doctrinaires are lazybones; refusing to make any painstaking study of concrete things, they regard general truths as something emerging out of the void, and turn them into purely abstract formulae which people cannot grasp, thereby completely denying, as well as reversing, the normal order in which man comes to know truth. Nor do they understand the interconnection of the two processes in man's knowing, from the particular to the general and from the general to the particular; they do not understand at all the Marxist theory of knowledge.

It is not only necessary to study the particular contradiction and the quality determined thereby in every great system of forms of motion of matter, but also to study the particular contradiction and the quality of every form of motion of matter at each stage of its long course of development. In all forms of motion, each process of development that is real and not imaginary is qualitatively different. In our study we must emphasize and start from this point.

Qualitatively different contradictions can only be solved by qualitatively different methods. For example: the contradiction between the proletariat and the bourgeoisie is solved by the method of socialist revolution; the contradiction between the great masses of the people and the feudal system is solved by the method of democratic revolution; the contradiction between colonies and imperialism is solved by the method of national revolutionary war; the contradiction between the working class and the peasantry in socialist society is solved by the method of collectivisation and mechanisation of agriculture; the contradiction within the Communist Party is solved by the method of criticism and self-criticism; the contradiction between society and nature is solved by the method of developing the productive forces. Processes change, old processes and old contradictions disappear, new processes and new contradictions emerge, and the methods of solving contradictions differ accordingly. There is a basic difference between the contradictions solved by the February Revolution and the October Revolution in Russia, as well as between the methods used to solve them. The use of different methods to solve different contradictions is a principle which Marxist-Leninists must strictly observe. The doctrinaires do not observe this principle: they do not understand the differences between the various revolutionary situations, and consequently do not understand that different methods should be used to solve different contradictions; on the contrary, they uniformly adopt a formula which they fancy to be unalterable and inflexibly apply it everywhere, a procedure which can only bring setbacks to the revolution or make a great mess of what could have been done well.

In order to reveal the particularity of contradictions in their totality as well as their interconnection in the process of development of things, that is, to reveal the quality of the process of development of things, we must reveal the particularity of each aspect of the contradiction in the process, otherwise it is impossible to reveal the quality of the process: this is also a matter to which we must pay the utmost attention in our study.

A great thing or event contains many contradictions in the process of its development. For instance, in the process of China's bourgeois-democratic revolution there are the contradiction between the various oppressed classes in Chinese society and imperialism, the contradiction between the great masses of people and feudalism, the contradiction between the proletariat and the bourgeoisie, the contradiction between the peasantry together with the urban petty bourgeoisie on the one hand, and the bourgeoisie on the other, the contradiction between various reactionary ruling blocs, etc.; the situation is exceedingly complex. Not only do all these contradictions each have their own particularity and cannot be treated uniformly, but the two aspects of every contradiction also have each their own characteristics and cannot be treated uniformly. Not only should we who work for the Chinese revolution understand the particularity of each of the contradictions in the light of their totality, that is, from the interconnection of those contradictions, but we can understand the totality of the contradictions only by a study of each of their aspects. To understand each of the aspects of a contradiction is to understand the definite position each aspects occupies, the concrete form in which it comes into interdependence as well as conflict with its opposite, and the concrete means by which it struggles with its opposite when the two are interdependent and yet contradictory, as well as when the interdependence breaks up. The study of these problems is a matter of the utmost importance. Lenin was expressing this very idea when he said that the most essential thing in Marxism, the living soul of Marxism, is the concrete analysis of concrete conditions.[10] Contrary to Lenin's teaching, our doctrinaires never use their brains to analyse anything correctly; in their writings and speeches they always strike the keynote of the "eight-legged essay,"[11] which is void of any content, and have thus brought in our Party a very bad style in work.

In studying a problem, we must guard against subjectivism, one-sidedness and superficiality. Subjectivism, which I have discussed in my essay *On Practice,* consists in not looking at a problem objectively, that is, not looking at it from the materialist viewpoint. One-sidedness consists in not looking at a problem as a whole. For example: understanding only China but not Japan; understanding only the Communist Party but not the Kuomintang; understanding only the proletariat but not the bourgeoisie; understanding only the peasants but not the landlords; understanding only the favourable conditions but not the adverse conditions; understanding only the past but not the future; understanding only the unit but not the totality; understanding only the defects but not the achievements; understanding only the plaintiff but not the defendant; understanding only revolutionary work underground but not revolutionary work in the open; and so on. In a word, not understanding the characteristics of each aspect of a contradiction. This is called looking at a problem one-sidedly. Or it may be called seeing only the part but not the whole, seeing only the trees but not the wood. Consequently it is impossible to find the methods for solving contradictions, to accomplish the tasks of the revolution, to carry out the assignments well, or to develop correctly the ideological struggle in the Party. Discussing military science, Sun Tzu said: "Know the enemy and know yourself, and you can fight a hundred battles without disaster"; he was referring to two sides in a battle. Wei Cheng of the T'ang dynasty said: "To hear both sides makes you enlightened, and to hear only one side makes you benighted";[12] he also understood that one-sidedness is wrong. Yet our comrades often tend to look at problems one-sidedly; such people will often run up against snags. In *Water Margin*,[13] Sung Chiang launched three attacks on Chu village and was twice defeated because he had no clear knowledge of the conditions and applied the wrong methods. Later he changed his methods by first conducting an investigation into the situation and as a result he learnt about the intertwining roads; succeeded in disrupting the alliance between the Li, Hu and Chu villages; and won final victory in the third battle after secretly infiltrating his own soldiers in disguise into the enemy's camp, a strategem similar to that of the Trojan Horse in foreign legends. There are numerous examples of materialist dialectics in *Water Margin*, and the episode of the three attacks on Chu village can be considered the best. Lenin said:

> "In order really to know an object, we must embrace, study all its sides, all connections and 'mediation'. We shall never achieve this completely, but the demand for all-sidedness is a safeguard against mistakes and rigidity."[14]

We should remember his words. Superficiality is evinced when a person considers neither the characteristics of a contradiction as a whole nor the characteristics of each of its aspects, denies the necessity of penetrating into the thing and studying minutely the characteristics of the contradiction, but takes a glance at a distance and, having roughly noticed some features of the contradiction, would proceed to solve it (to answer a question, to settle a dispute, to execute a task, or to direct a military operation). Such a way of doing things never leads to anything but trouble. The reason why our comrades suffering from doctrinairism and empiricism have committed mistakes is precisely that their way of looking at things is subjective, one-sided and superficial. One-sidedness and superficiality are also subjectivism and entail a subjective method because, while all objective things are in reality interrelated and have each an inner necessity, some people do not mirror such conditions as they are but only look at things one-sidedly or superficially, knowing neither their interrelationship nor their inner necessity.

In the movement of opposites in the whole process of development of a thing, we must notice not only the special features of the interconnections and conditions of its various aspects but also the special features of every stage in the process of development.

The basic contradiction in the process of development of a thing, and the quality of the process determined by this basic contradiction, will not disappear until the process is completed; but the conditions of each stage in the long process of development of a thing often differ from those of another stage. This is because, although the nature of the basic contradiction in the development of a thing or in the quality of the process·has not changed, yet at the various stages in the long process of development the basic contradiction assumes an increasingly intensified form. Besides, among the numerous big and small contradictions determined or influenced by the basic contradiction, some become intensified, some are temporarily or partially solved or mitigated, and some emerge anew; consequently the process reveals itself as consisting of different stages. If people do not pay attention to the stages in the process of development of a thing, they cannot properly deal with its contradictions.

For example: when capitalism of the era of free competition developed into imperialism, there was no change in the character of the two classes in fundamental contradiction, the proletariat and the bourgeoisie, or in the capitalist nature of such a society; however, the contradiction between these two classes became intensified, the contradiction between monopoly capital and non-monopoly capital emerged, the contradiction between metropolitan countries and colonies became intensified, and the contradiction between the capitalist countries, that is, the contradiction caused by their uneven development, manifested itself in a particularly acute way, thus bringing about the special stage of capitalism, the stage of imperialism. The reason why Leninism is Marxism of the era of imperialism and of the proletarian revolution is that Lenin and Stalin have correctly explained these contradictions and correctly formulated the theory and tactics of the proletarian revolution for solving them.

An examination of the process of the bourgeois-democratic revolution in China, which began with the Revolution of 1911, also reveals several special stages. In particular, the revolution in the period of its bourgeois leadership and the revolution in the period of its proletarian leadership are marked off from each other as vastly different historical stages. That is, the leadership of the proletariat has basically changed the physiognomy of the revolution, and brought about a readjustment in class relations, a tremendous stirring of the peasant revolution, a thoroughgoing revolution against imperialism and feudalism, a possible transition from democratic revolution to socialist revolution, and so on. All these could not possibly happen when the revolution was under bourgeois leadership. Although there was no change in the nature of the basic contradiction of the whole process, in the antiimperialist, antifeudal, democratic-revolutionary nature of the process (with the semicolonial, semifeudal nature as its opposite), yet the process has gone through several stages of development in the course of some twenty years, during which many great events took place, such as the failure of the Revolution of 1911 and the establishment of the régime of the Northern clique of warlords, the establishment of the first national united front and the Revolution of 1924-7, the break up of the united front and the passing of the bourgeoisie into the counter-revolutionary camp, the wars between the new warlords, the Agrarian Revolutionary War, the establishment of the second national united front and the Anti-Japanese War. These stages contain such specific conditions as: the intensification of some contradictions (for example, the Agrarian Revolutionary War and the Japanese invasion of the four North-eastern provinces); the partial or temporary solution of other contradictions (for example, the liquidation of the Northern clique of warlords and our confiscation of the land of the landlords); and the fresh emergence of yet other contradictions (for example, the struggle between the new warlords, the landlords' recovery of their land after our loss of the revolutionary bases in the South).

To study the particularities of the contradictions at every stage in the process of development of a thing, we must not only observe them in their interconnection and their totality, but must consider each aspect of the contradictions at each stage of its development.

Take the Kuomintang and the Communist Party for instance. In the period of the first united front the Kuomintang carried out Sun Yat-sen's three cardinal policies of alliance with Russia, cooperation with the Communists and assistance to the workers and peasants, and therefore it was revolutionary and vigorous and represented an alliance of various classes in the democratic revolution. After 1927, however, the Kuomintang turned in the opposite direction and became the reactionary bloc of the landlords and the big bourgeoisie. After the Sian Incident in December 1936, it made another turn and began to move in the direction of cessation of the civil war and alliance with the Communist Party jointly to oppose Japanese imperialism. Such are the characteristics of the Kuomintang in its three stages. The formation of these characteristics is of course due to various causes. As to the Chinese Communist Party in the period of the first united front, it was party in its childhood and courageously led the Revolution of 1924-7; but it revealed itself as immature so far as concerns its understanding of the nature, tasks and methods of the revolution, and consequently Ch'en Tu-hsiu-ism, which appeared in the last period of this revolution, was able to have its affect and caused the defeat of this revolution. After 1927 the Communist Party again courageously led the Agrarian Revolutionary War and created the revolutionary army and revolutionary bases; however, it also committed mistakes of adventurism which brought serious losses to both the army and the bases. Since 1935 it has rectified these mistakes and led the new anti-Japanese united front; this great struggle is now developing. At the present stage the Communist Party is a party that has gone through the test of two revolutions and has acquired a rich store of experience. Such are the characteristics of the Chinese Communist Party in its three stages. The formation of these characteristics is also due to various causes. Without studying these characteristics we cannot understand the specific interrelations of the two parties at the various stages of their development; the establishment of the united front, the breaking up of the united front, and the establishment of another united front. But in order to study the various characteristics of the two parties we must—this is even more fundamental—study the class bases of the two parties, and the resultant contradictions between the Kuomintang and the Communist Party and other forces during different periods. For example: in the period of its first alliance with the Communist Party, the Kuomintang stood on the one hand in contradiction to foreign imperialism and was therefore opposed to it; while on the other it stood in contradiction to the great masses of the people at home, and, though it verbally promised to give many benefits to the toiling people, in reality it gave them very few or even none at all. In the period when it carried on the anti-Communist war, it collaborated with imperialism and feudalism to oppose the great masses of the people, writing off all the benefits which the great masses of the people had won in the revolution and thus intensifying its own contradiction with them. In the present period of the anti-Japanese War, the Kuomintang, standing in contradiction to Japanese imperialism, wants on the one hand to ally itself with the Communist Party, while on the other it does not slacken its struggle against, and its oppression of, the Communist Party and the Chinese people. As to the Communist Party, it always, no matter in which period, sides with the great masses of the people to oppose imperialism and feudalism; in the present period of the anti-Japanese War, because the Kuomintang shows itself in favour of resisting Japan, the Communist Party has adopted a mild policy towards it and the domestic feudal forces. These conditions have brought about, at one time, an alliance of the two parties, and at another time, a struggle; and even during the period of alliance, there also exists a complicated state of affairs in which alliance and struggle take place at the same time. If we do not study the characteristics of these aspects of the contradictions, we shall not only fail to understand the relation between each of the two parties and other forces, but also fail to understand the interrelation of the two parties.

From this it can be seen that in studying the specific nature of any contradiction—contradiction in various forms of motion of matter, contradiction in various forms of motion in every process of development, each aspect of the contradiction in every process of development, contradiction at various stages of every process of development and each aspect of the contradiction at the various stages of development—in studying the specific nature of all these contradictions, we should be free from any taint of subjective arbitrariness and must make a concrete analysis of them. Apart from a concrete analysis there can be no knowledge of the specific nature of any contradiction. We must all the time bear in mind Lenin's words: the concrete analysis of concrete conditions.

Marx and Engels were the first to supply us with an excellent model of such concrete analysis.

When Marx and Engels applied the law of contradiction in things to the study of the process of social history, they saw the contradiction between the productive forces and the relations of production; they saw the contradiction between the exploiting class and the exploited class, as well as the contradiction produced thereby between the economic foundation and its superstructures, such as politics and ideology; and they saw how these contradictions inevitably lead to different social revolutions in different class societies.

When Marx applied this law to the study of the economic structure of capitalist society, he saw that the basic contradiction of this society is the contradiction between the social character of production and the private character of ownership. It is manifested in the contradiction between the organised character of production in individual enterprises and the unorganised character of production in society as a whole. The class manifestation of this contradiction is the contradiction between the bourgeoisie and the proletariat.

Because of the vastness of the scope of things and the limitlessness of their development, what in one case is universality is in another changed into particularity. On the other hand, what in one case is particularity is in another changed into universality. The contradiction contained in the capitalist system between the socialisation of production and the private ownership of the means of production is something common to all countries where capitalism exists and develops; for capitalism, this constitutes the universality of contradiction. However, this contradiction in capitalism is something pertaining to a certain historical stage in the development of the class society in general; as far as the contradiction between the productive forces and the relations of production in class society in general is concerned, this constitutes the particularity of contradiction. But while revealing by analysis the particularity of every contradiction in capitalist society, Marx expounded even more profoundly, more adequately and more completely the universality of the contradiction between the productive forces and the relations of production in class society in general.

As the particular is connected with the universal, as not only the particularity of contradiction but also the universality of contradiction is inherent in everything, and as universality resides in particularity, so when we study a certain object, we ought to try to discover both of these aspects and their interconnection, to discover both particularity and universality within the object as well as their interconnection, and to discover the interconnection of this object and the many objects outside it. When Stalin explained the historical roots of Leninism in his famous work, *The Foundations of Leninism,* he analysed the international situation in which Leninism was born, together with various contradictions in capitalism which had reached their extreme under the conditions of imperialism, and analysed how these contradictions made the proletarian revolution a question of immediate action and how they created favourable conditions for a direct onslaught upon capitalism. Besides all these, he analysed the reasons why Russia became the home of Leninism, how Tsarist Russia represented the focus of all the contradictions of imperialism, and why the Russian proletariat could become the vanguard of the international revolutionary proletariat. In this way, Stalin analysed the universality of the contradiction in imperialism, showing how Leninism is Marxism of the era of imperialism and the proletarian revolution, and analysed the particularity of the imperialism of Tsarist Russia in the contradiction of imperialism in general, showing how Russia became the birthplace of the theory and tactics of the proletarian revolution and how in such a particularity is contained the universality of contradiction. This kind of analysis made by Stalin serves us as a model in understanding the particularity and the universality of contradiction and their interconnection.

On the question of applying dialectics to the study of objective phenomena, Marx and Engels, and likewise Lenin and Stalin, have always instructed people that they should not be tainted with any subjective arbitrariness and must discover, from the concrete conditions inherent in the actual objective movements, the concrete contradictions in those phenomena, the concrete role of each of the aspects of the contradictions, and the concrete interrelation of the contradictions. Our doctrinaires can never be in the right, because they have not taken such an attitude in study. We must take warning from the failure of doctrinarism and learn to acquire such an attitude in study—there is no other method of study.

The relation between the universality of contradiction and the particularity of contradiction is the relation between the common character and the individual character of contradictions. By the former we mean that contradiction exists in and runs through all processes from beginning to end: contradictions are movements, are things, are processes, are thoughts. To deny the contradiction in things is to deny everything. This is a universal principle for all times and all countries, which admits of no exceptions. Hence the common character or absoluteness. But this common character is contained in all individual characters; without individual character there can be no common character. If all individual characters were removed, what common character would remain? Individual characters are formed because each contradiction is a particular one. All individual characters exist conditionally and temporarily, hence they are relative.

This principle of common character and individual character, of absoluteness and relativity, is the quintessence of the problem of the contradiction in things; not to understand it is tantamount to abandoning dialectics.

4. THE PRINCIPAL CONTRADICTION AND THE PRINCIPAL ASPECT OF A CONTRADICTION

As regards the problem of the particularity of contradiction, there are still two sides which must be specially singled out for analysis, that is, the principal contradiction and the principal aspect of a contradiction.

In the process of development of a complex thing, many contradictions exist; among these, one is necessarily the principal contradiction whose existence and development determine or influence the existence and development of other contradictions.

For example, in capitalist society, the two opposing forces in contradiction, the proletariat and the bourgeoisie, form the principal contradiction. The other contradictions—for example the contradiction between the remnant feudal class and the bourgeoisie, the contradiction between the rural petty bourgeoisie and the bourgeoisie, the contradiction between the proletariat and the rural petty bourgeoisie, the contradiction between the liberal bourgeoisie and the monopolistic bourgeoisie, the contradiction between bourgeois democracy and bourgeois fascism, the contradiction between the capitalist countries themselves, the contradiction between imperialism and the colonies, etc.—are determined and influenced by this principal contradiction.

In semicolonial countries like China, the relationship between the principal contradiction and nonprincipal contradictions presents a complicated situation.

When imperialism wages a war of agression on such a country, the various classes in that country, apart from a small bunch of traitors, can temporarily unite to wage a national war against imperialism. At such a time, the contradiction between imperialism and that country becomes the principal contradiction, while all the contradictions among the various classes within that country (including the principal contradiction between the feudal system and the great masses of the people) are relegated temporarily to a secondary or subordinate position. Such was the case in China in the Opium War of 1840, the Sino-Japanese War of 1894, the Boxer War of 1900, and it is the case in the present Sino-Japanese War.

But in another situation, the relative positions of contradictions undergo a change. When imperialism does not apply the pressure of war, but adopts comparatively mild forms, political, economic, cultural, etc., to carry on its oppression, the ruling classes in the semicolonial countries will capitulate to imperialsim; the two will form an alliance for the joint oppression of the great masses of the people. At such a time, the great masses of the people often adopt the form of civil war to oppose the alliance of imperialism and the feudal class, while imperialism often adopts indirect methods in helping the reactionaries in the semicolonial countries to oppress the people without taking direct action: and the internal contradiction thereby becomes especially sharp. Such has been the case in China in the Revolutionary War of 1911, the Revolutionary War of 1924-7, and the ten years' Agrarian Revolutionary War since 1927. An analogous situation can also be found in the civil wars between the various reactionary ruling blocks in the semicolonial countries, *e.g.*, the wars between the warlords in China.

When a revolutionary civil war reaches the point of fundamentally threatening the existence of imperialism and its jackals—the domestic reactionaries— imperialism will, in an endeavor to maintain its rule, often adopt methods other than those mentioned above. It either tries to split up the revolutionary front from within or sends armed forces to help directly the domestic reactionaries. At such times, foreign imperialists and domestic reactionaries stand completely in the open at one pole while the great masses of the people stand at another, thus forming the principal contradiction which determines or influences the development of other contradictions. The aid given by various capitalist countries to the Russian reactionaries after the October Revolution is a case of armed intervention. Chiang Kai-shek's betrayal in 1927 is a case of disintegrating the revolutionary front.

But whatever happens, there is no doubt at all that at every stage in the process of development, there is only one principal contradiction which plays the leading role.

Thus if in any process a number of contradictions exist, only one of them is the principal contradiction playing the leading and decisive role while the rest occupy a secondary or subordinate position. So in studying any process—if it is a complicated process in which more than two contradictions exist—we must do our utmost to discover its principal contradiction. Once the principal contradiction is grasped, any problem can be readily solved. This is the method Marx taught us when he studied capitalist society. When Lenin and Stalin studied imperialism and the general crisis of capitalism, and when they studied Soviet economy, they also taught us this method. Thousands of scholars and practical workers do not understand this method, and the result is that, bewildered as if lost in a sea of mist, they cannot find the crux of a problem and naturally cannot find the method of solving contradictions.

As said above, we cannot treat all the contradictions in a process as being equal, but must distinguish between the principal and the secondary contradictions, and pay particular attention to grasping the principal one. But, in any contradiction, whether principal or secondary, can we treat the two contradictory aspects as being equal? No, we cannot. In any contradiction, the development of the contradictory aspects is uneven. Sometimes there seems to be a balance of forces, but that is only a temporary and relative state; the basic state is unevenness. Of the two contradictroy aspects, one must be the principal and the other the secondary. The principal aspect is that which plays the leading role in the contradiction. The quality of a thing is mainly determined by the principal aspect of the contradiction that has taken the dominant position.

But this state is not a fixed one; the principal and the nonprincipal aspects of a contradiction transform themselves into each other and the quality of a thing changes accordingly. In a certain process or at a certain stage in the development of a contradiction, the principal aspect is A and the nonprincipal is B; at another stage of development or in another process of development, the roles are reversed — a change determined by the extent of the increase or decrease in the strength with which each of the two aspects struggles against the other in the development of a thing.

We often speak of "the supersession of the old by the new". The supersession of the old by the new is the universal, for ever inviolable law of the world. A thing transforms itself into something else according to its nature and the conditions under which it finds itself and through different forms of leap; that is the process of the supersession of the old by the new. Everything contains a contradiction between its new aspect and its old aspect, which constitutes a series of intricate struggles. As a result of these struggles, the new aspect grows and rises and becomes dominant while the old aspect dwindles and gradually approaches extinction. And the moment the new aspect has won the dominant position over the old aspect, the quality of the old thing is mainly determined by the principal aspect of the contradiction that has won the dominant position. When the principal aspect of the contradiction which has won the dominant position undergoes a change, the quality of a thing changes accordingly.

In capitalist society, capitalism has changed its position from a subordinate one in the old era of feudal society into the dominant one, and the nature of society has also changed from feudal into capitalist. In the new era of capitalist society, feudal forces, originally dominant, have become subordinate, and then gradually approach extinction; such is the case, for example, in Britain and France. With the development of the productive forces, the bourgeoisie, from being a new class playing a progressive role, becomes an old class playing a reactionary role until it is finally overthrown by the proletariat and becomes a class which, deprived of privately owned means of production and of power, also gradually approaches extinction. The proletariat, which is much more numerous than the bourgeoisie and which grows up simultaneously with the bourgeoisie, but is under its rule, is a new force; from its initial position of subordination to the bourgeoisie, it gradually grows stronger and becomes a class which is indepedent and plays a leading role in history, until finally it seizes political power and becomes the ruling class. At such a time, the nature of society changes from that of the old capitalist society into that of the new socialist society. This is the path that the Soviet Union has already traversed and all other countries will inevitably traverse.

Take China, for instance. In the contradiction which makes China a semi-colony imperialism occupies the principal position and oppresses the Chinese people, while China has changed from an independent country into a semi-colony. But this state of affairs will inevitably change; in the struggle between the two sides, the strength of the Chinese people which grows under the leadership of the proletariat will inevitably change China from a semicolony into an independent country, whereas imperialism will be overthrown and the old China will be inevitably changed into a new China.

The change of the old China into a new China also involves a change in the situation between China's old forces of feudalism and her new forces of the people. The old feudal landlord class will be overthrown, and from being the ruler it will become the ruled and gradually approach extinction. The people under the leadership of the proletariat will, from being the ruled, become the rulers. At the same time, the nature of Chinese society will undergo a change, that is, the old, semicolonial and semifeudal society will change into a new, democratic society.

Instances of such mutual transformations are found in our past experience. The Manchu dynasty which ruled China for nearly three hundred years was overthrown during the Revolution of 1911, while the Revolutionary League under Sun Yat-sen's leadership won victory for a time. In the Revolutionary War of 1924-7, the revolutionary forces in the south representing the Communist-Kuomintang alliance, originally weak, grew strong and won victory in the Northern Expedition, while the northern clique of warlords, once all-powerful, was overthrown. In 1927, the people's forces led by the Communist Party became very weak under the attacks of the Kuomintang reactionary forces, but having eliminated opportunism within their ranks, they gradually became stronger once more. In the revolutionary bases under Communist leadership, the peasants, originally the ruled, have become rulers, while the landlords have undergone a reverse process. It is always in such a manner that the new displaces the old in the world, that the old is superseded by the new, that the old is eliminated and the new is brought forth, or that the old is thrown off and the new ushered in.

At certain times in the revolutionary struggle, difficulties outbalance advantages; then, difficulties constitute the principal aspect of the contradiction and advantages the secondary aspect. But through the efforts of revolutionaries, difficulties are gradually overcome, an advantageous new situation is created, and the difficult situation yields place to the advantageous one. Such was the case after the failure of the revolution in China in 1927 and during the Long March of the Chinese Red Army. In the present Sino-Japanese War China is again in a difficult position; but we can change this state of affairs and bring about a fundamental change in the situation of both China and Japan. Conversely, advantages can also be transformed in difficulties, if the revolutionaries commit mistakes. The victory of the revolution of 1924-7 turned into a defeat. The revolutionary bases that had grown in the souther provinces after 1927 all suffered defeat in 1934.

Such also is the contradiction in our studies when we pass from ignorance to knowledge. At the very beginning of our study of Marxism, our ignorance or scanty knowledge of Marxism stands in contradiction to knowledge of Marxism. But as a result of industrious study, ignorance can be transformed into knowledge, scanty knowledge into considerable knowledge, and blindness in the use of Marxism into the masterly application of it.

Some people think that this is not the case with certain contradictions. For example: in the contradiction between the productive forces and the relations of production, the productive forces are the principal aspect; in the contradiction between theory and practice, practice is the principal aspect; in the contradiction between the economic foundation and its superstructure, the economic foundation is the principal aspect: and there is no change in their respective positions. This is the view of mechanistic materialism, and not of dialectical maternialism. True, the productive forces, practice, and the economic foundation generally manifest themselves in the principal and decisive role; whoever denies this is not a materialist. But under certain conditions, such aspects as the relations of production, theory and the superstructure in turn manifest themselves in the principal and decisive role; this must also be admitted. When the productive forces cannot be developed unless the relations of production are changed, the change in the relations of productions plays the principal and decisive role. When, as Lenin put it, "Without a revolutionary theory, there can be no revolutionary movement,"[15] the creation and advocacy of the revolutionary theory plays the principal and decisive role. When a certain job (this applies to any job) is to be done but there is as yet no directive, method, plan or policy defining how to do it, the directive, method, plan or policy is the principal and decisive factor. When the superstructure (politics, culture and so on), hinders the development of the economic foundation, political and cultural reforms become the principal and decisive factors. In saying this, are we running counter to materialism? No. The reason is that while we recognise that in the development of history as a whole it is material things that determine spiritual things and social existence that determines social consciousness, at the same time we also recognise and must recognise the reaction of spiritual things and social consciousness on social existence, and the reaction of the superstructure on the economic foundation. This is not running counter to materialism; this is precisely avoiding mechanistic materialism and firmly upholding dialectical materialism.

If, in studying the problem of the particularity of contradiction, we do not study these two conditions—the principal contradiction and the nonprincipal contradictions in a process, as well as the principal aspect and the nonprincipal aspect of a contradiction—that is, if we do not study the distinctive character of these two conditions of contradiction, we shall then get bogged down in abstract studies and shall be unable to understand concretely the conditions of a contradiction, and consequently unable to find the correct method to solve it. The distinctive character of particularity of these two conditions of contradiction represents the unevenness of the contradictory forces. Nothing in the world develops with an absolutely all-around evenness, and we must oppose the theory of even development or the theory of equilibrium. At the same time, the concrete conditions of a contradiction and the change in the principal and nonprincipal aspects of a contradiction in its process of development, show precisely the force of new things in superseding the old. The study of various conditions of unevenness in the contradiction, the study of the principal contradiction and the nonprincipal contradictions, of the principal aspect and the nonprincipal aspect of a contradiction constitutes one of the important methods by which a revolutionary political party determines correctly its political and military, strategic and tactical drives. All Communists should note this.

5. THE IDENTITY AND STRUGGLE OF THE ASPECTS OF A CONTRADICTION

Having understood the problem of the universality and particularity of contradiction, we must proceed to study the problem of the identity and struggle of the aspects of contradiction.

Identity, unity, coincidence, interpermeation, interpenetration, interdependence (or interdependence for existence), interconnection of cooperation—all these different terms mean the same thing and refer to the following two conditions: first, each of the two aspects of every contradiction in the process of development of a thing finds the presupposition of its existence in the other aspect and both aspects coexist in an entity; second, each of the two contradictory aspects, according to given conditions, tends to transform itself into the other. This is what is meant by identity.
Lenin said:

> "Dialectics is such a theory: it studies how the opposites can be identical and how they become identical (how they change and become identical)—under what conditions they transform themselves into each other and become identical—why the human mind should not regard these opposites as dead, rigid things, but as living, conditional, changeable things which transform themselves into each other."[16]

What is the meaning of this passage of Lenin's?

The contradictory aspects in every process exclude each other, struggle with each other and are opposed to each other. Such contradictory aspects are contained without exception in the processes of all things in the world and in human thought. A simple process has only one pair of opposites, while a complex process has more than one pair. Various pairs of opposites are in turn opposed to one another. In this way all things in the objective world and human thought are formed and impelled to move.

But if this is so, there is an utter lack of identity, or unity. How then can we speak of identity or unity?

The reason is that a contradictory aspect cannot exist in isolation. Without the other aspect which is opposed to it, each aspect loses the condition of its existence. Just imagine, can any of the aspects of contradictory things or of contradictory concepts in the human mind exist independently? Without life, there would be no death; without death, there would be no life. Without "above", there would be no "below"; without "below", there would also be no "above". Without misfortune, there would be no good fortune; without good fortune, there would also be no misfortune. Without facility, there would be no difficulty; without difficulty, there would also be no facility. Without landlords, there would be no tenant-peasants; without tenant-peasants, there would also be no landlords. Without the bourgeoisie, there would be no proletariat; without a proletariat, there would also be no bourgeoisie. Without imperialist oppression of the nations, there would be no colonies and semicolonies; without colonies and semicolonies, there would also be no imperialist oppression of the nations. All opposite elements are like this: because of certain conditions, they are on the one hand opposed to each other and on the other hand they are interconnected, interpenetrating, interpermeating and interdependent; this character is called identity. All contradictory aspects, because of certain conditions, are characterized by nonidentity, hence they are spoken of as contradictory. But they are also characterized by identity, hence they are interconnected. When Lenin says that dialectic studies "how the opposites can be and how they become identical", he is referring to such a state of affairs. How can they be identical? Because of the condition of mutual sustenance of each other's existence. This is the first meaning of identity.

But is it enough to say merely that the contradictory aspects mutually sustain each other's existence, that is, there is identity between them and consequently they can coexist in an entity? No, it is not enough. The matter does not end with the interdependence of the two contradictory aspects for their existence; what is more important is the transformation of the contradictory things into each other. That is to say, each of the two contradictory aspects within a thing, because of certain conditions, tends to transform itself into the other, to transfer itself to the opposite position. This is the second meaning of the identity of contradiction.

Why is there also identity? You see, by means of revolution, the proletariat, once the ruled, becomes the ruler, while the bourgeoisie, originally the ruler, becomes the ruled, and is transferred to the position originally occupied by its opposite. This has already taken place in the Soviet Union and will take place throughout the world. I should like to ask: if there were no interconnection and identity of opposites under certain conditions, how could such a change take place?

The Kuomintang, which played a certain positive role at a certain stage in modern Chinese history, has, because of its inherent class nature and the temptations of imperialism (these being the conditions) become since 1927 a counterrevolutionary party; but, because of the intensification of the contradiction between China and Japan and the policy of the united front of the Communist Party (these being the conditions), it has been compelled to agree to resist Japan. Contradictory things change into one another, hence a certain identity is implied.

The agrarian revolution we have carried out is already and will be such a process in which the land-owning landlord class becomes a class deprived of its land, while the peasants, once deprived of their land, become small holders of land. The haves and the have-nots, gain and loss, are interconnected because of certain conditions; there is identity of the two sides. Under socialism, the system of the peasants' private ownership will in turn become the public ownership of socialist agriculture; this has already taken place in the Soviet Union and will take place throughout the world. Between private property and public property there is a bridge leading from one to the other, which in philosophy is called identity, or transformation into each other, or interpermeation.

To consolidate the dictatorship of the proletariat or the People's dictatorship is precisely to prepare the conditions for liquidating such a dictatorship and advancing to the higher stage of abolishing all state systems. To establish and develop the Communist Party is precisely to prepare the condition for abolishing the Communist Party and all party systems. To establish the revolutionary army under the leadership of the Communist Party and to carry on the revolutionary war is precisely to prepare the condition for abolishing war for ever. These contradictory things are at the same time complementary.

As everybody knows, war and peace transform themselves into each other. War is transformed into peace; for example, the First World War was transformed into the post-war peace; the civil war in China has now also ceased and internal peace has come about. Peace is transformed into war; for example, the Kuomintang-Communist co-operation of 1927 was transformed into war, and the peaceful world situation today may also be transformed into a Second World War. Why? Because in a class society such contradictory things as war and peace are characterised by identity under certain conditions.

All contradictory things are interconnected, and they not only coexist in an entity under certain conditions, but also transform themselves into each other under certain conditions—this is the whole meaning of the identity of contradictions. This is exactly what Lenin meant when he discussed, ". . . how they become identical (how they change and become identical)—under what conditions they transform themselves into each other and become identical. . . ."

Why should the human mind "not regard such opposites as dead, rigid things but as living, conditional, changeable things which transform themselves into each other?" Because that is just what objective things are. The unity or identity of the contradictory aspects in objective things is never a dead, rigid, but a living, conditional, changeable, temporary, relative matter; all contradictory aspects transform themselves, under certain conditions, into their opposites. Such a state of affairs, reflected in human thought, becomes the materialist-dialectical world outlook of Marxism. Only the reactionary ruling classes, past as well as present, and metaphysicians who are in their service, do not regard opposites as living, conditional, changeable things that transform themselves into each other, but as dead, rigid things, and propagate this erroneous view everywhere to delude the masses of the people, and thereby attain the aim of perpetuating their rule. The task of the Communists is precisely to expose such erroneous reactionary and metaphysical thought, to propagate the dialectics inherent in things, to hasten the transformation of things, and to attain the aim of the revolution.

In saying that contradictions become identical only under certain conditions we are referring to real and concrete contradictions, and also to real and concrete transformations of the contradictory aspects into each other. The innumerable transformations in mythology, for example, K'uafu's racing with the sun in the *Book of Mountains and Seas,* [17] Yi's shooting down of nine suns in *Huai Nan Tzu,* [18] Monkey's seventy-two metamorphoses in the *Pilgrimage to the West,* [19] the numerous episodes in the *Strange Tales From the Carefree Studio* [20] of ghosts and foxes metamorphosed into human beings, etc. — the transformations of opposites into each other as told in these legends are a sort of childish, imaginary, subjectively fancied transformations that are called forth among men by the innumerable transformations of complicated, real contradictions into each other, and are not concrete transformations as manifested in concrete contradictions. Marx said: "All mythology masters and dominates and shapes the forces of nature in and through the imagination, hence it disappears as soon as man gains mastery over the forces of nature." [21] Although stories of endless metamorphoses in such mythology (and also in nursery tales) can delight people because in them man's conquest of the forces of nature, etc., is imaginatively embodied and, moreover, the best mythology possesses, as Marx put it, "eternal charm", yet mythology is not based on concrete contradictions and therefore does not scientifically reflect reality. This is to say, in mythology or nursery tales the aspects that constitute contradiction have only a fancied identity, not a concrete one. Marxist dialectics is that which scientifically reflects the identity in changes of reality.

Why can only an egg be transformed into a chicken but not a stone? Why is there identity between war and peace and none between war and a stone? Why can human beings give birth only to human beings but not to anything else? The reason is simply that identity of contradiction exists only under certain necessary conditions. Without certain necessary conditions there can be no identity whatever.

Why is it that in Russia the bourgeois-democratic revolution of February 1917 was directly linked with the proletarian-socialist revolution of October of the same year, while in France the bourgeois revolution was not directly linked with a socialist revolution, and the Paris Commune of 1871 finally ended in failure? Why is it, on the other hand, that the nomadic system in Mongolia and Central Asia has been directly linked with socialism? Why is it that the Chinese revolution can avoid a capitalist future and can be directly linked with socialism without traversing the old historical path of the western countries, without passing through a period of bourgeois dictatorship? The reason is none other than the concrete conditions of the time. When certain necessary conditions are present, certain contradictions arise in the process of development of things and, what is more, these contradictions and all contradictions of this kind depend upon each other for existence and transform themselves into each other; otherwise nothing is possible.

Such is the problem of identity. When then is struggle? What is the relation between identity and struggle?

Lenin said:

> "The unity (coincidence, identity, resultant) of opposites is conditional, temporary, transitory, relative. The struggle of mutually exclusive opposites is absolute, just as development and motion are absolute."[22]

What does this passage from Lenin mean?

All processes have a beginning and an end; all processes transform themselves into their opposites. The stability of all processes is relative, but the mutability manifested in the transformation of one process into another is absolute.

The movement of all things assumes two forms: the form of relative rest and the form of conspicuous change. Both forms of movement are caused by the struggle of two contradictory factors contained in a thing itself. When the movement of a thing assumes the first form, it only undergoes a quantitative but not a qualitative change and consequently appears in a state of seeming rest. When the movement of a thing assumes the second form it has already reached a certain culminating point of the quantitative change of the first form, caused the dissolution of the entity, produced a qualitative change, and consequently appears as conspicuous change. Such unity, solidarity, amalgamation, harmony, balance, stalemate, deadlock, rest, stability, equilibrium, coagulation, attraction, as we see in daily life, are all the appearances of things in the state of quantitative change. On the other hand, the dissolution of the entity, the breakdown of such solidarity, amalgamation, harmony, balance, stalemate, deadlock, rest, stability, equilibrium, coagulation and attraction, and the change into their opposite states, are all the appearances of things in the state of qualitative change during the transformation of one process into another. Things are always transforming themselves from the first into the second form, while the struggle within the contradictions exist in both forms and reaches its solution through the second form. We say therefore that the unity of opposites is conditional, temporary and relative, while the struggle of mutually exclusive opposites is absolute.

When we said above that because there is identity between two opposite things, the two can coexist in an entity and can also be transformed into each other, we were referring to conditionality, that is to say, under certain conditions contradictory things can be united and can also be transformed into each other, but without such conditions, they cannot become contradictory, cannot coexist, and cannot transform themselves into one another. It is because the identity of contradiction obtains only under certain conditions that we say identity is conditional, relative. Here we add: the struggle within a contradiction runs throughout a process from beginning to end and causes one process to transform itself into another, and as the struggle within the contradiction is present everywhere, we say the struggle within the contradiction is unconditional, absolute.

Conditional, relative identity, combined with unconditional absolute struggle, constitutes the movement of opposites in all things.

We Chinese often say, "Things opposed to each other complement each other."[23] That is to say, there is identity of opposites. This remark is dialectical, and runs counter to metaphysics. To be "opposed to each other" means the mutual exclusion or struggle of the two contradictory aspects. To "complement each other" means that under certain conditions the two contradictory aspects become united and achieve identity. Struggle resides precisely in identity; without struggle there can be no identity.

In identity there is struggle, in particularity there is universality, in individual character there is common character. To quote Lenin, "there is an absolute even *within* the relative."[24]

6. THE ROLE OF ANTAGONISM IN CONTRADICTION

"What is antagonism?" is one of the questions concerning the struggle within a contradiction. Our answer is: antagonism is a form of struggle within a contradiction, but not the universal form.

In human history, antagonism between classes exists as a particular manifestation of the struggle within a contradiction. The contradiction between the exploiting class and the exploited class: the two contradictory classes coexist for a long time in one society, be it slave society, or a feudal or a capitalist society, and struggle with each other; but it is not until the contradiction between the two classes has developed to a certain stage that the two sides adopt the form of open antagonism which develops into a revolution. In a class society, the transformation of peace into war is also like that.

A bomb, before the explosion, is an entity in which contradictory things coexist because of certain conditions. The explosion takes place only when a new condition (ignition) is present. An analogous situation exists in all natural phenomena when they finally assume the form of open antagonism to solve old contradictions and to produce new things.

It is very important to know the situation. It enables us to understand that in a class society revolutions and revolutionary wars are inevitable, that apart from them the leap in social development cannot be made, the reactionary ruling classes cannot be overthrown, and the people cannot win political power. Communists must expose the deceitful propaganda of the reactionaires that social revolution is unnecessary and impossible, etc., and firmly uphold the Marxist-Leninist theory of social revolution so as to help the people to understand that social revolution is not only entirely necessary but also entirely possible, and that the whole history of mankind and the triumph of the Soviet Union confirms this scientific truth.

However, we must study concretely the conditions of various kinds of struggle within a contradiction and should not inappropriately impose the above-mentioned formula on everything. Contradiction and struggle are universal, absolute, but the methods for solving contradictions, that is, the forms of struggle, differ according to the differences in the nature of the contradictions. Some contradictions are characterised by open antagonism, some are not. Based on the concrete development of things, some contradictions, originally nonantagonistic, develop and become antagonistic, while some contradictions, originally antagonistic, develop and become nonantagonistic.

As we have pointed out above, the contradiction between correct ideology and erroneous ideologies within the Communist Party reflects in the Party the class contradictions when classes exist. In the beginning, or with regard to certain matters, such a contradiction need not immediately manifest itself as antagonistic. But with the development of the class struggle, it can also develop and become antagonistic. The history of the Communist Party of the Soviet Union shows us that the contradiction between the correct ideology of Lenin and Stalin and the erroneous ideologies of Trotsky, Bukharin and others, was in the beginning not yet manifested in an antagonistic form, but subsequently developed into antagonism. A similar case occurred in the history of the Chinese Communist Party. The contradiction between the correct ideology of many of our comrades in the Party and the erroneous ideologies of Ch'en Tu-hsiu, Chang Kuo-t'ao and others was also in the beginning not manifested in an antagonistic form, but subsequently developed into antagonism. At present the contradiction between the correct ideology and the erroneous ideologies in our Party is not manifested in an antagonistic form and, if comrades who have committed mistakes can correct them, it will not develop into antagonism. Therefore the Party on the one hand must carry on a serious struggle against erroneous ideologies, and on the other hand, must give the comrades who have committed mistakes sufficient opportunity to become aware of them. Under such conditions, struggles pushed to excess are obviously not appropriate. But if those people who have committed mistakes persist in them and increase the gravity of their mistakes, then it is possible that such contradictions will develop into antagonism.

Economically, in capitalist society (where the town under bourgeois rule ruthlessly exploits the countryside) and in the Kuomintang-controlled areas in China (where the town under the rule of foreign imperialism and the native big comprador bourgeoisie most savagely exploits the countryside), the contradiction between the town and the countryside is one of extreme antagonism. But in a socialist country and in our revolutionary bases, such an antagonistic contradiction becomes a non-antagonistic contradiction; and it will disappear when a Communist society is realised.

Lenin said: "Antagonism and contradiction are utterly different. Under Socialism, antagonism disappears, but contradiction exists".[25] That is to day, antagonism is only a form of struggle within a contradiction but not its universal form; we cannot impose the formula everywhere.

7. CONCLUSION

Now we can make a few remarks to sum up. The law of the contradiction in things, that is, the law of the unity of opposites, is the basic law of nature and society and therefore also the basic law of thought. It is the opposite of the metaphysical world outlook. It means a great revolution in the history of human knowledge. According to the viewpoint of dialectical materialism, contradiction exists in all processes of objective things and subjective thought and runs through all processes from beginning to end—this is the universality and absoluteness of contradiction. Contradictory things and each of their aspects have respectively their specific features—this is the particularity and relativity of contradiction. Contradictory things, according to certain conditions, are characterised by identity, and consequently can coexist in an entity and transform themselves each into its opposite—this again is the particularity and relativity of contradiction. But the struggle within the contradiction is ceaseless; it exists both when the opposites coexist and when they are transforming themselves into each other, and the struggle is especially manifest in the latter case—this again is the universality and absoluteness of contradiction. In studying the particularity and relativity of contradiction, we must note the distinction between what is principal and what is nonprincipal in contradictions as well as in contradictory aspects; in studying the universality of, and the struggle within, a contradiction, we must note the distinction between various forms of struggle within it; otherwise we shall commit mistakes. If, after study, we have really understood the essential points mentioned above, we shall be able to smash those doctrinaire ideas which run counter to the basic principles of Marxism-Leninism and are detrimental to our revolutionary cause, and also enable our experienced comrades to systematise their experiences so as to impart to them the character of principle and avoid repeating the mistakes of empiricism. These are a few simple conclusions we have reached in the study of the law of contradiction.

SPEECH AT THE LUSHAN CONFERENCE
(July 23, 1959)

This speech contains Mao's defense against attacks levelled at the Lushan conference following the failure of the Great Leap Forward. It is a somewhat rambling and disjointed speech, fierce and defiant, containing threats against the army and the party if they deserted him, and threats to organize his own personal military forces to challenge the present leadership. The speech is discussed in Chapter VI, pages 136 and 137. [Omissions by author.]

You have spoken so much; permit me to talk some now, won't you? I have taken sleeping pills thrice. Can't sleep.

Let me talk about this kind of opinion. After seeing the minutes, speeches, and documents of our comrades, and after listening to the speeches of certain comrades, I feel there are two tendencies and wish to speak about them here. One is untouchable, there being the tendency that one would "jump if touched at all." Wu Ch'ih-hui [the late Kuomintang official] said that Sun Fo would jump whenever he was touched. Thus, some people feel there is pressure, that is, they are unwilling to hear others say bad things and want others to say only good words, not willing to listen to bad words. I advise these comrades to listen. There are three kinds of words; and the mouth has two functions. A man has only one mouth, which is used, first, to eat, and second, to discharge the obligation of speaking. With ears one must listen. He wants to talk, and what can you do about it? There are some comrades who just don't want to listen to bad words. Good or bad, they are all words and we must listen to them. There are three kinds of words: one is correct, the second is basically correct or not too correct, and the third is basically incorrect or incorrect. Both ends are opposites; correct and incorrect are also opposites.

Now we are under attack both from within and without the party. The rightists said: Why did Ch'in Shih Huang-ti collapse? Because he built the Great Wall. Now that we have constructed the T'ien-an-men, we would also collapse; that's what the rightists alleged. I have not yet finished reading a segment of opinions within the party. The reflection of what has been manifested in a concentrated form in the Kiangsi Party School can now be found all over, and the views of all rightists have been published. The Kiangsi Party School is an intraparty representative. Some of them are rightists, wavering elements. They could not see the situation clearly, but they could change after some work had been done on them. Some people have historically had problems. They have undergone

Reprinted by permission of *Chinese Law and Government,* published by International Arts and Sciences Press, Inc., White Plains, New York 10603. From Winter 1968/69.

criticisms, and they also felt that everything was in a mess, such as the materials of the Kwangtung Military Region. All this has been said outside of the conference. What we do now is to combine the conference from both inside and outside. It is a pity that Lushan is too small and we can't invite all of them to come over, such as the Kiangsi Party School, Lo Lung-chi, Ch'en Ming-shu, etc. This is the responsibility of the Kiangsinese. The house is so small!

No matter what they say, it is muddled. This is also good; the more muddled they talked, the more one wanted to hear it. During the rectification we concocted the phrase of "stiffen the scalp to stand it." I have told some comrades that we must stand it, stand it by stiffening our scalp, but for how long? One month, three months, half a year, one year, three years, five years, eight or ten years? Some comrades would say "protracted war." I agreed with them, and such comrades were the majority.

Gentlemen of the audience, all of you have ears, and so please listen! It is nothing but muddled talk. Just because it is unpleasant, we want to listen. Welcome! If you would think in this way, it would not be so unpleasant to listen to. Why should we let others talk about it? The reason is that the Shen-chou [allusion to ancient China] will not sink, and heaven will not collapse. This is because we have done some good deeds and our loins are strong. The majority of our comrades have stiffened their loins, but why would they not do it? It was because for a period of time vegetables were scarce, there were not enough hairpins, no soap; there was an imbalance of proportions, the market was tense, everybody was tense, and the mental state became tense. I did not see any reason for tension. I was also tense; it would be untrue if I were to say there was no tension. You might be tense during the first half of the night, but upon taking sleeping pills after midnight, tension would disappear.

You say that we have deviated from the masses, but they still support us. I envision this as only temporary, maybe two or three months, about the time of the spring festival. I see that there is very good cooperation between the masses and ourselves. . . . In regard to this kind of extensive mass movement one cannot pour cold water to dampen enthusiasm, but one should only use persuasion. Comrades, your hearts are good. It is in fact difficult to accomplish as a matter of face; one can't be rash; there must be a step-by-step process. In eating meat, one can only consume one piece at a time, but never hope to be a fatso at one stroke. X X consumed one catty of meat daily, but did not even become fat in ten years. That the commander-in-chief [Chu Teh] and I are fat is not due to a single day. These cadres have led several hundred millions of people, among whom at least some 30 per cent are active elements, 30 per cent are passive elements, as well as landlords, rich peasants, reactionaries, undesirable elements, bureaucrats, middle peasants, and some poor peasants, and 40 per cent follow the mainstream. How many people are there to make up the 30 per cent? About 150 million people who must develop communes, establish mess halls, and undertake mammoth cooperation. They are extremely active and are willing to do it. You say that this is petty-bourgeois fervor? This is no petty bourgeoisie; they are poor peasants, lower middle peasants, proletariat, and semiproletariat. Those who follow the mainstream might also be disposed to form communes, and there are some 30 per cent who were unwilling. In short, adding 30 to 40 per cent makes a total of 70 per cent, or 350 million people, who, during a period of time, worked frantically. They wanted to do it. For two months around the time of spring festival, they became dismayed and changed. When cadres went to the countryside, they would no longer talk. They invited the cadres to eat potato congee, and their faces were bland, without any smiles. This was called blowing "communist wind." There must also be some analysis. Who were those who had some petty-bourgeois fervor? "Communist wind" consisted mainly of the cadres at the hsien and commune levels, especially some commune cadres who squeezed production brigades and teams. This was bad and the masses proved to be unreceptive. It became necessary to rectify and persuade them firmly. One month was spent for this, and by March or April this wind was repressed. What should be withdrawn has been withdrawn, and the accounts between communes and teams were cleared. This one month or more of accounting education has had its benefits, because in this short time it has enabled them to understand that equalization was impracticable, since this would cause them to "withdraw" or "transfer" their funds. We now hear that the majority have come over, but there were a few who still lacked "communism." Where can we find a school for short-term training classes? How can we enable the several hundred million population and the millions of cadres to receive education, to realize that the things must be returned and that they could not say that what is yours is mine and take them away at will. Even from ancient times there had never been such a rule, and even 10,000 years from now, it would not be possible to take what one wants. If there were ever such a case, it was that of Green and Red gangs in which the Green band stole and the Red band robbed, exploiting other people's labor without compensation and sabotaging equal value exchange. The government of Sung Chiang [hero of the novel *The Water Margin*, translated by Pearl Buck as *All Men Are Brothers*] was called the Hall of Loyalty and Righteousness. He looted the rich to help the poor, and because the loot belonged to local despots and vicious gentry, he could do it with impunity. Such a rule seemed to be permissible. What Sung Chiang robbed was the "Sheng-chen-wang"—tantamount to our beating the local despots—and what he looted was some ill-gotten property, and "any ill-gotten property could be robbed without encumbrance." Such property was squeezed from peasants and should therefore be returned to them. For a long time we have not resorted to striking at local despots. When we do this, it is all right to divide the land and confiscate it. This is because this is also ill-gotten wealth. However, it is a mistake to blow "communist wind" by seizing the properties of production brigades and teams, and by taking away their fat pigs and big cabbages. Even when we were dealing with the assets of imperialist countries, we still resorted to these three measures: requisition, procurement, and squeezing them out. How could we then exploit the wealth of the laboring people? How did we succeed in suppressing this wind within one month or so? This proved that our party was great, wise, and correct. If you won't believe it, there were historical data to prove it. During March, April, as well as May, several million cadres and several hundred millions of peasants were educated. They began to see the situation more clearly. It was primarily the cadres who did not understand before that this wealth was ill-gotten wealth. They could not draw a boundary line; they did not study political economy; they were ignorant of the law of value, equal value exchange, and distribution according to labor. In a few months they were convinced. There was probably no one who had understood everything perfectly, but many did understand about 70 or 80 per cent. They did not understand the textbooks, and were told to read them because cadres at the commune level must know something about political economy. It would be all right if one were illiterate; if one could understand something, there would be no need to read books. One could be educated by facts. Emperor Wu of the Liang dynasty had a prime minister by the name of Ch'en Fa-chih who was illiterate. The emperor asked him to compose a poem. Ch'en Fa-chih recited the poem, but asked someone else to write it down, saying that these scholars were not as good as he, who used his ears to learn. Of course, this does not mean that I oppose the elimination of illiteracy. . . . There was also the Ode of Imperial Decree by Hu-lü-chin, of the Northern dynasty, which reads: "The imperial decree is promulgated for the river under Yin-shan [mountain]; the heaven is like a canopy enveloping the fields all around; the sky is blue, and the wilderness is hazy; when wind sweeps over grass, cattle and lambs appear." This was also written by an illiterate. If an illiterate could become a prime minister, why can our commune cadres and peasants not hear political economy? It is my view that one can attend college, and that when it comes to economics, even the illiterate can also do it. After discussing it, he is bound to understand it. He can comprehend more easily than even the intellectuals. I have not read the textbooks myself. One should read some before one has the right to speak. It is necessary to squeeze out some time for the entire party and nation to launch a study movement.

Nobody knows how many inspections they have already conducted. Since the Chengchow Conference last year, inspections have been made repeatedly. They even carried out inspections when a 6th grade meeting affected a 5th grade meeting. People who came from Peking talked and talked, but they would not listen. We made a great many inspections, but you did not hear of them. Thus, I would advise these comrades to listen to other people, because they also have their own mouths as well as their own views. I notice that there are some problems which this conference cannot resolve. There are some who wouldn't give up their views. What they would like to do is to procrastinate — one year, two years, three years, or even five years. It won't do if you are not accustomed to listen to funny talks. What I say is that we must stiffen our scalps to stand it. All they can do is scold the three generations of our ancestors. When I was young and in the prime of my life, I would also be irritated whenever I heard some bad remarks. My attitude was that if others do not provoke me, I won't provoke them; whoever provokes me first, I will provoke him later. I have not abandoned this principle even now, though I have learned to listen. Let us stiffen our scalps to stand it and listen to them for a couple of weeks, and then counterattack. I would advise our comrades to listen. Whether you agree or not is your own business. If you won't agree, and if I am wrong, I will engage in self-criticism.

Second, I advise another segment of comrades that they must not waver during this crucial moment. As I see it, some comrades are wavering. They also say that the great leap forward, the general line, and the people's commune are all correct, but one must look for the direction of their ideology when they speak and the direction in which they speak. This segment of people belongs to the second category who are "basically correct, but only partly incorrect." They waver somewhat. There are some who would waver at the crucial moment and become irresolute during the great storms of history. There are four historical lines: the Li Li-san line, the Wang Ming line, the Kao-Jao [Kao Kang and Jao Shu-shih] line, and now the general line. If one cannot stand firm, one dances the rice-sprout song dance (the Kuomintang says that we are the rice-sprout song dynasty). They are worried and want to do their best for the country, and that is good. What kind of class should we call it? Bourgeoisie or petty bourgeoisie? I won't talk about this now. I have spoken at the Nanning Conference, at the Chengtu Conference, and at the party congress about the waverings of 1956 and 1957; instead of giving out dunce caps, they were interpreted as a problem of ideological methodology. If one should talk about the mad fervor of the petty bourgeoisie, one could also say, on the contrary, that the antiadventurism of that time was caused by sad and dismal pessimism and by the low-key attitude of the bourgeoisie. We don't want to give out dunce caps because these comrades were different from the rightists; they were also engaged in socialism, though they lacked experience, and whenever there were straws in the wind they would waver and oppose adventurism. Those who opposed adventurism then have now stood firm. . . . For instance, they say: "Where there is loss, there is also gain," and by putting "gain" behind, it would seem that they have mulled it over carefully. For instance, in the case of giving out dunce caps, this is the wavering character of the bouegeoisie or of the petty bourgeoisie. This is because the rightist factor has often been influenced by the bourgeoisie; under the pressure of imperialist bourgeoisie, one became a rightist.

When each production brigade made a single mistake, multiplied by some 700,000 production brigades, there would be some 700,000 items in all. Would it be possible to publish them fully? Moreover, the length of articles may vary, and I see that it may take at least a year to publish them. What will be the result? Our nation will collapse, and if by that time the imperialists did not come, our own people would also rise up to overthrow us. If the newspaper you are publishing will print only bad news, and if you have no heart to work, then it won't take a year, but it will perish within a week's time. When 700,000 items are published, and they are all bad things, then it is no longer a proletariat. This would be a bourgeois nation and it would become the bourgeois Chang Po-chün's Political Planning Institute. I am merely exaggerating. Suppose we do ten things, and nine of them are bad and are published in the newspapers. Then we are bound to perish, and should perish. In that event, I would go to the countryside to lead the peasants to overthrow the government. If the Liberation Army won't follow me, I will then find the Red Army. I think the Liberation Army will follow me.

I advise that some of the comrades pay attention to the problem of direction when they talk; the content of talk may be basically correct, but partly improper.

In order to ask others to be firm, one must be firm himself; in order to ask others not to waver, one must not waver himself. This is another lesson. As I see it, these comrades are not rightists, but middle-of-the-roaders. They are not leftists (leftists without quotation marks). I mention the word "direction" because some people have been frustrated and were worried. They could not stand firm; they wavered and went to stand in the middle. Whether they are left of the middle or right of the middle must still be analyzed. They have repeated the course of the comrades who erred during the latter half of 1956 and the first half of 1957. They are not rightists, though they have thrown themselves into the periphery of the rightists. They are still some 30 kilometers away from the rightists. This is because the rightists welcome such a view. It would indeed be a wonder if the rightists don't welcome the thesis held by these comrades. Such a peripheral policy is quite dangerous, and just wait and see if you don't believe it. I may offend some comrades when I say this publicly. If I don't say it now, it may be detrimental to these comrades.

Among the themes I raise may be added the problem of solidarity, to which I will now devote a passage. Raise the banner of solidarity, people's solidarity, national solidarity, party solidarity. I won't say whether this is useful or harmful to these comrades. Even if it is harmful, I must still talk about it. Our party is a Marxist political party. It is incumbent not only upon those of the first side to listen to others, but also upon those of the second side. People on both sides must listen to others. Did I not say that I want to speak? The first thing is that I want to speak; the second thing is that I want to listen to other people's talk. I was not in a hurry to speak, and have endured it by stiffening my scalp. Why can't I do it now? For twenty days I have shown my forbearance, and now the conference will soon be adjourned. We may just as well hold the conference until the end of the month. [George C.] Marshall went up to Lushan eight times; Chou En-lai went up to Lushan three times. Then why can't we go up Lushan once? We have the right to do so.

Now about the problem of mess halls. A mess hall is a good thing that cannot be unduly denounced. I am in favor of developing them successfully. It should be on the basis of voluntary participation; the grain should be delivered to the member-families, and any savings should be retained by the public. I would be satisfied if one-third of the mess halls could be maintained throughout the country. As soon as I mentioned this, Wu X X became very tense. Don't be afraid. There are still 90 per cent of the mess halls in Honan province that are under experiment and must not be dissolved. What I have said here is from a nationwide angle. Are there not four stages in dancing? "Stand on one side, try and try, then dance right on, until you die." Is there such an adage? Being an unpolished man, I am not too cultured. It would be all right if one-third of the peasants, about 150 million, persevered. My second hope is that there will be about one-half of the peasants, about 250 million in all. We can do this if there are more provinces and cities like Honan, Szechwan, Hunan, Yunan, and Shanghai. Some of the disbanded mess halls should be restored. The mess hall is not our invention; it has been created by the masses. In Honan, mess halls were established in 1956 before communization. In 1958, mess halls were developed rapidly. According to X X X, mess halls can liberate the labor force. I think there is another advantage, that is, it can economize resources. Without the latter, it cannot last. Can this be done? I am sure it can. I would suggest that the comrades of Honan try to undertake mechanization. For instance, by using running water, there is no need to carry it. In this way, labor can be saved, and it is also possible to economize resources. I am a middle-of-the-roader, and such provinces as Honan, Szechwan and Hupei belong to the left. Nonetheless, there came the rightists. The Ch'ang-li investigation group of the Chinese Academy of Sciences alleged that the mess hall had no merit at all, thereby attacking one point, without mentioning the rest. They emulated the method of the "Ode of Teng-t'u-tzu's Lust for Beautiful Women." Teng-t'u-tzu took Sung Yu to task on three charges: handsome and fond of women, adept in speech, unwilling to go into the harem; therefore Sung Yu was very dangerous. Sung Yu retorted: My handsomeness was endowed by my parents, and my teachers taught me to speak with eloquence. As for my fondness for women, this is not true. No other place has such exquisite women as the State of Ch'u; among the beautiful women of the State of Ch'u, the best are to be found in my town. In my town the daughter of the family on my east is peerless, of the proper height that cannot be increased or decreased by even one-tenth of an inch. . . . Teng-t'u-tzu was then a *tai-fu,* which is equivalent to today's minister of a ministry, and it would be a large ministry, such as a minister of the metallurgical industry, a minister of the coal industry, or a minister of what you call agriculture. The investigation group of the Academy of Sciences attacked only one point, without mentioning the rest. This attack was undoubtedly centered on such things as pork, hairpins, etc. Nobody can be without shortcomings; even Confucious had his mistakes. I have seen Lenin's own drafts that had been corrected pell-mell. If there were no errors why should he correct them? We may set up more mess halls. Let us experiment with them for one or two years, and I figure that they can be completed. The people's communes won't collapse; not a single one has collapsed yet. We are prepared for the collapse of one-half of them, and after 70 per cent have collapsed, we would still have 30 per cent left. If they must collapse, let them collapse. They are bound to collapse if not managed properly. The Communist Party must manage well—manage communes, manage all enterprises well, including agriculture, industry, commerce, communications and transportation, and culture and education. It is basically impossible to anticipate some things. Hasn't it been said that the party does not control the party? Now planning organs do not concern themselves with planning, and for a time they did not deal with planning. Planning organs are not limited to the [State] Planning Commission; there are also the other ministries, as well as local governments. It might be possible for the local governments to excuse them when, for a time, they failed to concern themselves with the general balance. Though the Planning Commission and the Central ministries have been established for a decade, they suddenly (decided) at Peitaiho that they would no longer handle the planning. This was called planned directive, which was tantamount to doing away with planning. The so-called noncontrol of planning meant the dispensing of a general balance, thus basically failing to calculate how much coal, steel, and communications would be needed. Coal and iron could not walk by themselves, and had to be transported by rolling stock. I did not anticipate this point. I and X X, and the premier, did not at all get involved in it. It was possible that I did not know about it, and this is indeed to exonerate myself even if I don't want to do so. This is because I was not the director of the Planning Commission. Before August of last year, I devoted my main energy to revolution. Being basically not versed in construction, I knew nothing about industrial planning. I said at the West Tower [at Chung-nan-hai, Peking]; Don't write about the wise leadership; I did not even exercise any control, and so what wisdom is there? However, comrades, in 1958 and 1959 the main responsibility has fallen on me and you should take me to task. In the past the responsibility could be laid to others—En-lai and X X—but now you should blame me because I really have not dealt with a great pile of things. Would the person who invented the human statue for burial not be deprived of his posterity [a reference to *Analects*]? Shall I be deprived of my posterity (one son killed in battle and another son insane)? Was it K'o Ch'ing-shih or I who invented the massive smelting of iron and steel? I say it was I. I had a talk with K'o Ch'ing-shih and said it would bring about 6 million tons. Later when I talked with others, there was an X X X who also felt it could be done. In June I set the target at 10,700,000 tons. It was published in the communique at Peitaiho. X X suggested it and I thought it would be all-right. This created a great disaster when 90 million people went ahead to smelt steel. The so-called inventor of the burial statue should be deprived of his children and grandchildren. Small native complexes [for iron smelting] were launched. . . . Many discussions were held, and they said it could be done, although it would be necessary to raise the quality, reduce cost, reduce the sulphur content, and produce really good iron. There would be some possibility if we would grasp it. The Communist Party has a method called grasping. Both the Communist Party and Chiang Kai-shek have each had two hands, but the hands of the former belonged to Communists, and they took it up when they grasped. It is necessary to grasp iron and steel, as well as grain, cotton, oil, ramie, silk, tea, sugar, and vegetables, plus tobacco and miscellaneous items. There are 12 items in agriculture, forestry, animal husbandry, subsidiary industry, and fishery that must be grasped, and there must be a general balance. Conditions vary in different localities, and so there cannot be a model for each hsien. There is a place called Chiu-kung-shan in Hupei, where bamboo and wood grow in its many mountains. Because they wanted to develop grain, bamboo and wood were neglected. There are places where tea and sugar cane do not grow. It is therefore necessary to make adjustments in accordance with local conditions. Hasn't the Soviet Union gone to procure pigs from areas inhabited by Moslems? How absurd this was!

There is an article on industrial planning that is quite good. As to the failure of the party to control party affairs, of planning organs to control planning and maintain a general balance, what have they been doing? Basically he was not worried; the premier worried, but he did not. When one does not worry and does not have zest, nothing can be achieved. Someone has criticized Comrade Li Fu-ch'un of the Planning Commission for "lingering when the feet want to move forward and stammering when the mouth wants to speak." Nonetheless, one must not be too impetuous, like Li K'uei [a character in *The Water Margin*], which also won't do. Lenin was full of enthusiasm and so he was welcomed by the masses. When one stammers in talking, it is usually because he has misgivings. During the first half-month, there were misgivings, but now the situation has been publicized. You have said what you wanted to say, and the minutes attest to that. If you have caught me in the wrong, you can punish me. Don't be afraid of wearing tight shoes. I have said at the Chengtu Conference that one should not be afraid of execution or of dismissal from the party. When a Communist and a senior cadre had so many misgivings, it must have been because he was apprehensive lest he speak improperly and be rectified. This is what you call "self-preservation by those who are astute"! As the adage says, disease comes into the mouth, but troubles come from the mouth. If I should do something disastrous today, two kinds of people would be disappointed with me; one kind would be those who are untouchable; the other kind, people whose direction is problematical. If you don't agree, you can refute it. I don't think it right to say that one cannot refute the Chairman. The fact is that you have all refuted me, though not by name perhaps. The views of the Kiangsi Party School and the party schools of the middle level were all refutations. They charged that the one who was the first to invent burial statues should be deprived of posterity. It was I who suggested and made the resolve for the smelting of 10,700,000 tons of steel, and the result was that 90 million people went ahead with it, X X [may mean "squandered"] People's Currency [*Jen-min pi*], and "the gains could not compensate for the losses." Next was the people's commune. I did not claim the right of inventing people's communes, but I had the right to suggest. In Shantung, a reporter asked me: "Is the commune good?" I said, "Good," and he immediately published it in the newspaper. This might be due to some petty-bourgeois fervor. Hereafter, newspaper reporters should leave [me alone].

I have committed two crimes, one of which involved calling for 10,700,000 tons of steel, or for massive steel smelting. If you supported it, you might just as well share some of it with me, but I was the first to make the burial statues and so cannot exonerate myself from the responsibility. As for the people's commune, the entire world has opposed it, including the Soviet Union. There is also the general line, for which, be it true or false, you also shared some responsibility. The general line has been implemented in industry and agriculture. As for the other big cannons, it is incumbent on the others to share some responsibility. Boss T'an [presumably T'an Chen-lin], you have had many big cannons, but they were not shot carefully and the communization was too fast. He began to talk when he was in Honan, and the records of Kiangsi and Chekiang spread rapidly. He did not speak carefully, and since he was not too sure, it would be better to be more careful. It is to his credit that he was full of zest and was willing to assume responsibility. This was better than those who seemed to be so sad and dismal. Nevertheless, in shooting cannons, one must be careful whenever vital problems are concerned. I have also shot three big cannons: the commune, steel smelting, and the general line. X X said that he was so rough that he could never be meticulous. I am like Chang Fei [a general of the Three Kingdoms] who, although crude, was careful at times. I said that the commune is a system of collective ownership. I said that the process of transition from a collective ownership system to a communist all-people's ownership system may take more than two five-year plans, and that it may take a twenty-five-year plan!

In regard to speed, Marx also committed many errors. He hoped every day for the advent of European revolution, but it did not come. There were devious repetitions and reverses, and there was no revolution before the time of his death. It was only by the time of Lenin that it came finally. Wasn't this impetuousness? Wasn't this bourgeois fanaticism? (X X interrupted: Lenin also said that the trend of world revolution had arrived, but it did not come later.) Marx also opposed the Paris Commune at the beginning, while Zinoviev was against the October Revolution. Zinoviev was executed later, but was Marx also executed? When the Paris Commune was established, he supported it. He thought that it would fail, but seeing that this was the first dictatorship of the proletariat, it would be good even though it lasted only three months. It seems to be impossible to judge the result if economic accounting is applied. We also had our Canton Commune, but the great revolution was a debacle. Will our present work be such a failure as in 1927? Will it be like the 26,000-mile long march, when most of the bastions were lost and the Soviet area was reduced to one-tenth of its original size? No, we cannot put it this way. Haven't we failed now? All comrades who have come to this conference have gained something; we have not failed completely. Isn't this a failure by and large? No, it is only a partial failure. We have paid a price, blown some "communist wind," and enabled the people of the entire nation to learn a lesson.

I have spoken twice on the problem of Stalin's socialist economics. It must now be studied more intensively. Otherwise, it won't be possible to develop and consolidate our enterprise.

As for the responsibility, X X X and X X X have had some responsibility, and X X X of the Ministry of Agriculture has had some responsibility. I was the first to be responsible. Old K'o, did you have some responsibility for your invention? (Old K'o: I have.) Was it smaller than mine? What you have done is merely a question of ideology. What I did was the smelting of 10,700,000 tons of steel and the participation of 90 million people in it, and this was a great disaster for which I must be responsible myself. Comrades, you should analyze your own responsibility and you will feel much better after you have made a clean slate of it. [Literally: "and your stomach will feel much more comfortable if you move your bowels and break wind."]

TALK ON PROBLEMS OF PHILOSOPHY

(August 18, 1964)

In an informal manner Mao discussed his view of Marxist philosophy with some comrades, including K'ang Sheng, the head of Mao's intelligence organization. Mao links his philosophy to the policy of sending cadres and students down to the countryside, and reminisces about his own experiences. He ridicules the concept of synthesis in Hegel and Marxism, and speculates on future evolutionary developments in line with his belief in Darwinism. See Chapter IX, pages 221 through 223. [Omissions by the author.]

It is only with class struggle that there is philosophy (it being useless to discuss the theory of knowledge apart from practice). It behooves comrades who study philosophy to go to the countryside. They should go this winter or next spring to take part in the class struggle. One should go even though one's health is poor. People won't die by going down to the countryside. There may be some flu, but it will be all right when they put on more clothes.

The way the liberal arts are presently being handled in colleges is no good. They go from book to book, and from concept to concept. How can philosophy emerge from books? The three components of Marxism are scientific socialism, philosophy, and political economics. They are based on sociology and class struggle: the struggle between the proletariat and the bourgeoisie. The Marxists found out that it would be futile for wishful thinking socialists to persuade the bourgeoisie to change their heart, and that they must depend on the class struggle of the proletariat. There had already been many strikes by that time. According to investigations of the English Parliament, it was found that a 12-hour work system was not as profitable to capitalists as an 8-hour work system. It was on this premise that Marxism evolved. It is only with class struggle as a basis that one can study philosophy. Whose philosophy? Marxist philosophy. There is also the economics of the proletariat which transformed classical economics. Those who study philosophy feel that philosophy comes first. This is wrong, for the first thing is class struggle. It is only when the oppressed begin to resist and search for a way out that they manage to find philosophy. Only by proceeding from this premise have we come to have Marxism-Leninism and to find philosophy. We have all come this way. It is because others wanted my head and Chiang Kai-shek wanted to kill me that I began to engage in class struggle and philosophy.

College students, those in the liberal arts, should begin to go down to the

Reprinted through the courtesy of U.S. Joint Publications Research Service JPRS 61269-2. From February, 1974.

countryside this winter. Those who are studying the sciences need not move now, though they may move once or twice. But all liberal arts students, students of history, political economics, literature, and law, must go. Everybody should go: Professors, instructors, administrative workers, and students, for a period of five months at a time. They should spend five months in the rural areas and five months in factories to acquire some perceptual knowledge. They should take a look at horses, cows, sheep, chickens, dogs and pigs, as well as rice, kaoliang, legumes, wheat and millet. In winter, one may not see crops, but at least one can see land, and people. Wherever they engage in class struggle can be considered to be a university where they can learn many things. What is Peking University and what is a university of the people? Which is better! I myself studied in the school of hard knocks [trans: "Green Forest Univ," school of the brigands where the law of the jungle prevails], where I managed to learn something. I read Confucius, the Four Books, and the Five Classics, and, after reading them for six years, I could recite them even though I couldn't understand them. I believed then in Confucius and even wrote some articles. Later I attended bourgeois schools for seven years. Six years plus seven years make a total of 13 years. I studied the whole bag of bourgeois natural sciences and social sciences. I also studied education. I spent five years in normal school and two years in middle school, including my time in the library. At that time I believed in Kant's dualism, especially idealism. I was originally a feudalist and a bourgeois democrat. Society made me turn to revolution. For several years I served as teacher and principal of a 4-year grammar school. I also taught history and Chinese literature in a 6-year school. Then I taught for a short while in a middle school, though I knew almost nothing. I joined the Communist party, joined the revolution, and I knew only that I wanted to make revolution. But revolt against what and how? Of course, it was to revolt against imperialism and against the old society. What is imperialism? I did not understand it too well. I understood even less about how to make revolution. What I learned in 13 years was useless for making revolution. I could use only the tool—language. Writing articles is a tool. As for the reasons they are basically useless.

Confucius said that "the benevolent person is humane and loves people." But which people did he love? All the people? Not on your life! Did he love the exploiters? Not completely, since he loved only some of them. Otherwise, why was it that Confucius failed to attain high office? [Trans.: i.e., Confucius was neither a full-fledged supporter of the exploiting class nor a man of the people. He was an ambivalent opportunist.] They did not want him, even though he loved them and sought to unify them. However, he almost starved, and was moved to declare that "the true gentleman remains firm in misfortune"...

As for the business of going down, it will begin this winter and next spring. You should go down by stages and in batches, to take part in class struggle. It is only thus that you can learn something and learn how to make revolution. You intellectuals live every day in your offices; you eat well, dress well, you never walk, and so you get sick. Clothing, food, housing and transportation are the four great essentials of life. By changing your living conditions from good to bad, by going down to take part in class struggle, and by steeling yourselves through the "four clean-ups" and "five antis," you intellectuals will change your appearance.

What kind of philosophy would you learn if you didn't engage in class struggle!

Go down and give it a try. You can come back if you become really sick, since it wouldn't do for you to die. If you become so sick as to approach death, then come back. Once you go down, you will be enthusiastic. (Comrade K'ang Sheng remarked: The Institute of Philosophy and Social Sciences of the Chinese Academy of Sciences should also go down, since it is fast becoming an institute of antiquities, a sort of fairyland where they no longer eat the food of human beings. Those in the Institute of Philosophy won't even read the *Kuang-ming Jih-pao.*). I read only the *Kuang-ming Jih-pao* and *Wen Hui Pao,* but not the *Jen-min Jih-pao* because it won't publish any articles of a theoretical nature. After my suggestion, they began to publish them. The *Chieh-fang-chun Pao* is very lively and readable. (Comade K'ang Sheng: The Institute of Literature shows no concern for the problems of Chou Ku-ch'eng [0719 6253 1007], while Sun Yeh-fang of the Economic Institute has been fooling around with Liberman's works and with capitalism.)

It is all right to engage in some capitalism. Society being so complex, wouldn't it be too monotonous to engage only in socialism to the exclusion of capitalism? Wouldn't that be too one-sided an approach, without any unity of opposites? Let them engage in it. It would support them, whether it was a frantic attack, demonstrations in the streets, or an armed revolt with rifles. Society is so complex that there is not a single commune, a single country, or a single Central Committee that doesn't have the need to implement the policy of one dividing into two. Look, hasn't the rural work department been abolished? It was engaged exclusively in contracting production to the peasant family, the "four great freedoms," credit loans, trade, labor hiring, and land transactions. It issued notices in the past. Teng Tzu-hui used to argue with me, and at the Central Committee meeting, he suggested that we launch the four great freedoms. To permanently consolidate the New Democracy would be tantamount to engaging in capitalism. The New Democracy is a bourgeois democratic revolution under the leadership of the proletariat. It should affect only the landlords and the compradore bourgeoisie, but not the national bourgeoisie. To distribute land to the peasants is to transform feudal landlord ownership into the ownership of individual peasants, which is still under the domain of the bourgeois revolution. It is by no means strange to distribute land, since MacArthur has distributed land in Japan and Napoleon also distributed land. Land reform cannot eliminate capitalism, and thus will never enable us to reach socialism.

In our nation now, about one-third of the power is controlled by the enemy or by those who sympathize with the enemy. We have been here for 15 years and have two-thirds of the domain. Today a party branch secretary can be bribed with a few packs of cigarettes and there's no telling what one could achieve by marrying his daughter off to such a person. In some areas land reform has been peaceful, and the land reform teams are rather weak. From the looks of things, there are more than a few problems at the present time.

I have received the materials on philosophical problems. (This refers to materials on the problem of contradictions—note of the recorder.) I have seen the outlines (referring to outlines of articles on criticizing the theory of combining two into one—recorder's note). I haven't found time to read the others yet. I saw also the materials on analysis and synthesis.

In gathering materials in this way, it seems that those on the laws of the unity of opposites, on the interpretations of the bourgeoisie, of Marx, Engels, Lenin and Stalin, and of revisionism are all good. The views of the bourgeoisie, Yang Hsien-chen, and the late Hegel have been around a long time, but they are even more nefarious today. There are also the teachings of [A.A.] Bogdanov [1873-1928] and [Anatolity] Lunachariskiy [1875-1933]. I have read Bogdanov's economics, Lenin also read it, and I seem to recall that he praised his section on original accumulation. (K'ang Sheng: Bogdanov's economics are quite possibly superior to anything coming out of modern revisionism. Kautsky's is superior to Khrushchev's, and Yugoslavia's is superior to that of the Soviet Union. [M.] Djilas [former aid to Tito, now out of favor there] had a few complimentary things to say about Lenin, namely that he engaged in some self-criticism on the China problem).

Stalin realized that he had made some mistakes on the China problem, and they were by no means small mistakes. We are a great nation of several hundred million people. He opposed our revolution and our seizure of political power. In order to seize political power throughout the entire nation, we had prepared for many years, and the entire war of resistance was preparation. If you read the documents of the Central Committee in that period including *On New Democracy,* you would have understood this. This is to say that it was impossible for us to set up a bourgeois dictatorship, and we could only establish a new democracy under proletarian leadership wherein we had a people's democratic dictatorship under the leadership of the proletariat. For some 80 years in China, all democratic revolutions under bourgeois leadership have failed. The democratic revolution which we led was bound to triumph. This was the only road, there was no other. This was the first step, and the second step was socialism. *On New Democracy* was the only comprehensive program. It dealt with politics, economics and culture, but not with military affairs. (K'ang Sheng: *On New Democracy* has had great significance on the world communist movement. I asked some Spanish comrades who said that their problem was that they undertook only bourgeois democracy, but not new democracy. They did not undertake these three things: the army, rural villages, and political power. They subjected their work entirely to the needs of the Soviet Union's foreign policy, with the result that nothing was accomplished.)

That is precisely what Ch'en Tu-hsiu did.

(Comrade K'ang Sheng: They [the Spanish] wanted the Communist party to organize the army and hand it over to others. This would have been useless.)

(Comrade K'ang Sheng: They did not want political power and did not mobilize the peasants. The Soviet Union told them that if they set up a dictatorship of the proletariat, England and France might oppose them and this would be bad for the Soviet Union.)

How about Cuba? Cuba sought both political power and an army, and she also mobilized her peasants. For this reason she succeeded.

(Comrade K'ang Sheng: When they fought, they also fought conventional battles, just like the bourgeoisie, and they made a last ditch stand in Madrid. They did everything they could to comply with the foreign policy of the Soviet Union.)

The Third International had not yet been dissolved, and we did not go along with it. The Tsun-i Conference did not go along with it. It was only after a decade of rectifications, at the time of the "Seventh [Party] Congress," that a decision was made ("The Decision on Certain Historical Problems") and the "leftists" were rectified. Those who were dogmatic basically failed to study China's special characteristics. Although they had spent more than ten years in the rural area, they did not study the agrarian land [issue], the productive relations or the class relations. One cannot gain an understanding of the rural villages by simply going there. One must study the relations between various classes and strata in the rural villages. It took more than ten years before I was able to understand them. I went to tea houses and gambling joints to meet everyone and investigate them. In 1925 I set up the Institute of the Peasant Movement to conduct rural investigations. I sought out poor peasants in my native village for investigation. They had no rice to eat, and their lives were dismal. There was a peasant whom I invited to play Chinese dominos (the cards consisting of T'ien, Ti, Jen, Ho, Mei ch'ien, Ch'ang-san, and Pan-teng). Afterward I invited him to dinner. Before, after and during the dinner, I talked with him, and learned how violent class struggle was in the rural villages. He was willing to talk to me because, first, I treated him like a person; secondly I invited him to eat, and thirdly he could win some money from me. I would lose to him, losing one or two silver dollars, and he was quite satisfied. There was a time when he was so desperate that he came to me to borrow one dollar. I gave him three dollars without expecting any repayment. It was impossible in those days to get any assistance which did not require repayment. My father used to feel that if a man did not look after himself, he would be damned by heaven and earth. My mother disagreed with him. When my father died, very few people came to his funeral, though many came to my mother's funeral. One time, some members of the Kolao Society [a secret brotherhood] buglarized our home. I thought it was a good thing because they stole things which they did not have, but my mother could not accept my view.

There occurred in Changsha a riot of rice looting and they even beat up the provincial governor. There were some peddlers, all natives of Hsiang-hsiang, who sold toasted beans in Changsha and were returning to their native villages. I stopped them to ask them what had happened. The green and Red Brotherhood in the countryside also held rallies and went out to raid the homes of some rich families. This was reported in the *Shun Pao* of Shanghai and troops were sent from Changsha to suppress them. Their discipline was poor; they robbed some middle peasants, thereby isolating themselves. One of the leaders went into hiding in the mountains, but he was captured and executed. Later, the village gentry held a meeting and killed several poor peasants. There was then no Communist party, and it was a sort of spontaneous class struggle.

Society pushed men like us onto the political stage. Who would have thought of promoting Marxism? We had never heard of it. What we have heard and read about were Confucius, Napoleon, Washington, Peter the Great, and Meiji Reformation, the three heroes of Italy, all of whom were part and parcel of capitalism. We read also about Franklin. He was born into a poor family, but later became a writer, and experimented with electricity. (Ch'en Po-ta: Franklin was the first to advance the thesis that man is the animal that makes tools.)

He did mention that man is the animal that makes tools. Before it was said that man is the thinking animal, and that "The function of the mind is to think," [trans. "Mencius"] thus saying that man is superior to all things. Who elected him to this post? He was self-appointed. All these theses evolved during the feudal age. Later, Marx suggested that because man can make tools, he is a social animal. Actually, it took mankind at least a million years to develop his brain and hands. Animals will develop further. I don't believe that it is only man that can have two hands, and that horses, cows and sheep won't advance anymore. Can it be that only apes can progress? Moreover, it is only one kind of ape that can progress, while others are all incapable of evolution? Will the horses, cows and sheep of a million or ten million years from now remain the same as they are now? I think they will change. All horses, cows and sheep and insects will change. Animals have evolved from plants, such as seaweed. Even Chang T'ai-yen knew about it. In his book about K'ang Yu-wei's views on revolution, [entitled: "Po K'ang Yu-wei Lun Ke-ming Shu," ("A Criticism of K'ang Yu wei's Views on Revolution")], he reasoned as follows. The earth was originally a dead earth, without plants, without water, and without air. it took tens of millions of years to produce water, and this water was not formed randomly from hydrogen and oxygen. Water also has its own history. Long ago, even the two gases, hydrogen and oxygen, did not exist. It was only with the emergence of hydrogen and oxygen that it became possible for these two elements to combine to form water.

We must study the history of natural sciences. We should read books. To read for the needs of struggle is greatly different from reading aimlessly. Fu Ying [a physical chemist] said that it takes millions of combinations before hydrogen and oxygen can form into water, and it is not simply a process of combining two into one. His words seem to be reasonable, and I want to talk with him about it. You must not reject everything about Fu Ying (speaking to XX).

In the past we did not deal very clearly with analysis and synthesis. We understand analysis a little better, but not much has been said about synthesis. I have asked Ai Ssu-ch'i about it, and he said that now we speak only about conceptual analysis and synthesis, not objective and practical synthesis and analysis. How should we have analyzed and synthesized the Communist party and the Kuomintang? The proletariat and the bourgeoisie? Landlords and peasants? The Chinese people and imperialism? In the case of the Communist party and the Kuomintang, how should we have analyzed and synthesized them? Our analysis involved nothing more than how much strength, how much land, how many people, how many party members, how many troops, and how many base areas, such as Yenan, we had. What were our weaknesses? We had no large cities, our army had only 1.2 million troops, and we had no outside help while the Kuomintang had enormous foreign aid. Comparing Yenan with

Shanghai, Yenan had only a population of 7,000. Adding the [party] organs and the [military] units, there were some 20,000 people, and it had only handicraft industry and agriculture. So how could it be compared with any large city? Our advantage was that we had the support of the people, while the Kuomintang had alienated them. Although they had more land, more armed forces and more arms, nevertheless, their soldiers had been conscripted forcibly, and these officers and soldiers were antagonistic. Of course, they also had some troops of considerable combat strength, and weren't easily routed. Their weakness lay in that they had been separated from the people. Whereas we aligned ourselves with the masses, they alienated them.

They spread the word that the Communist party shares property and wives, and they spread it even into the primary schools. They issued a song: "There are Chu Teh and Mao Tse-tung, who engage in slaughter and arson, and what would you do?" They taught school children to sing it. Having sung the song, they would question their parents and brothers, and this resulted in their making propaganda for us. There was a child who heard the song and went to ask his father about it and the latter replied: You need not ask me; you will see for yourself once you have grown up. This was a middle-of-the-roader. He then went to ask his uncle who scolded him saying: "What do you mean, killing and arson? I'd beat you if you insist on asking me again." It so happened that his uncle had been a member of the Communist Youth League. All the newspapers and radio stations scolded us. There were many newspapers, with a score or more in each city. Each party or faction had a paper, and they were all anti-Communist. Did the common people listen to them? Not on your life! All that has happened in China, we have experienced. China is a "sparrow." Even in foreign countries, there are bound to be rich people and poor people, counter-revolutionary and revolutionary and Marxist-Leninsts and revisionists. Don't you dare believe that everybody will believe the counter-revolutionary propaganda and rise up against us. We read the newspapers, do we not, and yet we haven't been influenced by them.

. . . .

How does one synthesize? The Kuomintang and the Communist party being two opposites, you have seen how they have been synthesized on the mainland, and it went like this: When their troops came, we swallowed them up, piece by piece. This is not Yang Hsien-chen's theory of combining two into one; nor is it a synthesis of peaceful coexistence. They do not want peaceful coexistence, they want to eat us up. Otherwise, why would they have attacked Yenan? Their troops ran all over Northern Shensi, except for three counties on the three borders. You have your freedom and we have ours. You had 250,000 men and we had 25,000 just a few brigades, and some 20,000 soldiers. Let's analyse how it was synthesized. Wherever you wanted to go, you went, and we ate up your army one bite at a time. If we could win, we fought; if not, we ran. There was a whole army which was completely wiped out between March 1947 and March 1948, after we eliminated tens of thousands of their troops. I-ch'uan was surrounded by us, and when Liu K'an an army commander, came to reinforce their troops, he was killed. Two of his division commanders were killed, the third was captured, and his entire army was routed. This was a case of synthesis. All his rifles, artillery and troops were synthesized i.e., absorbed by our side. Those who wanted to stay with us did so, while those who were unwilling to stay were given traveling expenses. After eliminating Liu K'an, a brigade in the city of I-ch'uan surrendered without fighting. What was the synthesis in the three great battles of Liao-Shen, P'ing-chin and Huai-Hai? Fu Tso-i had thus been synthesized, and all of his 400,000 troops surrendered their arms without firing a shot.

One eats one and the big fish devours the smaller; this is synthesis. This has never been written in the books; it is not written in my books. Yang Hsin-chen came out with his combining two into one, saying that synthesis is the linking together of two inseparable things. What kind of link is there in the world that cannot be separated? There are links, but they can always be separated. There is nothing that is inseparable. We have worked for more than two decades, and many of us have been swallowed by the enemy. When the 300,000 troops of the Red Army reached the Shensi-Kansu-Ninghsia border region, only 25,000 remained, all others had been eaten, routed, killed or wounded.

It is necessary to discuss unity of oposites on the basis of life. (Comrade K'ang Sheng: It won't do to merely discuss concepts.)

There should be synthesis when one analyzes; there should be analysis when one synthesizes.

When man eats animals and vegetables he first makes some analysis. Why doesn't he eat sand? If there is sand in rice, then it is not good to eat. Why won't man eat the grass which horses, cows and sheep consume, and eats only such vegetables as cabbages, etc. Such decisions are based on analysis. Shen Nung [legendary founder of Chinese agriculture and medicine]; tasted a hundred kinds of herbs, thereby making medicinal prescriptions. After many thousands of years, we have analyzed what can be eaten, and what cannot. Grasshoppers, snakes and turtles are edible; so are crabs, dogs and eels. Some foreigners won't eat them. People of North Shensi won't eat eels or fish; nor do they eat cats. There was a big flood along the Yellow River one year, and tens of thousands catties of fish were flushed onto the river banks, all of which were eventually made into fertilizer.

Mine is a native philosophy, and yours is foreign philosophy.

(Comrade K'ang Sheng: Chairman would you please talk about the problem of the three categories?)

Engels spoke about the three categories, but I don't believe two of them (unity of opposites is the most basic law; transmutation between quality and quantity, but there is basically no negation of negation.) To take the laws of transmutation betwen quality and quantity, negation of negation, and unity of opposites together is the trinominal, not the monistic theory [of origin]. What is most basic is the unity of opposites. Transmutation between quality and quantity is unity of opposites between quality and quantity. There is no such thing as the negation of negation. Affirmation, negation, affirmation, negation . . . in the development of things, there is in each phase both affirmation and negation. When slave society negated primitive society, it was affirmation in regard to feudal society.

Feudal society was a negation of slave society, and affirmation of capitalist society. Capitalist society was a negation of feudal society, and also an affirmation of socialist society.

How does one synthesize? Could it have been that primitive society and slave society coexisted? There was coexistence, but only to a limited degree. In the last analysis, primitive society had to be eliminated. There were also stages of social development, primitive society being divided into several stages. There were then still no sacrifices of women at burials, but they had to obey the men. At first, it was the men who obeyed the women, but it was then reversed and women obeyed men. There were a million or more years during which this stage of history was confused. Class society has been in existence less than 5,000 years. There were the so-called Lung-shan and Yang-shao cultures, the last stage of primitive society which featured pottery. In short, one ate another, one over-eliminated, and another society arose. Of course, the process of development was not completely pure. The slave system was still maintained in feudal society, but it was primarily a feudal system. There were some serfs, as well as industrial slaves, such as those engaged in handicrafts. Even capitalist society is not so pure and no matter how advanced capitalist society may be, there are also some backward portions, like the slavery in the southern part of the United States, Although Lincoln eliminated slavery, there are still Negro slaves and the struggle is rather violent. Some 20 million people are taking part in it, by no means a small number.

One eliminates another, growing, developing, and eliminating, this is true for all things. If one does not eliminate others, one will be eliminated himself. Why must man die? Even the nobility must also die. This is a natural law. The life of a forest is longer than human life, but it does not exceed a few thousand years. It won't do for there to be no death. If we could still see Confucius today, the earth would not be able to contain all mankind. I go along with Chuang-tzu's way of beating a basin and singing when his wife passed away. When someone dies, a celebration rally should be held to celebrate the victory of dialectics and the elimination of old things. Even socialism must die, for if it does not, there will be no communism. Communism will also last many millions of years. I don't believe that there won't be qualitative change in communism and that it won't pass through stages of quality changes to quantity. I can not believe that a specific characteristic can go on for millions of years without undergoing some change. According to dialectics, this is inconceivable. Take one principle for example: "From each according to his ability and to each according to his needs." After one million years, this would become a kind of economics. Do you believe this and have you thought about it? When that day comes, you won't need economists, since a textbook would do, and even dialectics would then be dead.

The life of dialectics is that it continues to head toward its opposite. Mankind will eventually reach its doomsday. When theologians talk about doomsday, it is pessimism used to scare people. When we speak about the destruction of mankind, we are saying that something more advanced then mankind will be produced. Man as we know him is very unsophisticated. Engels says that one must proceed from the kingdom of inevitability to the kingdom of freedom,

freedom being understood in comparison with inevitability. This sentence is not complete in that he has only mentioned half of it, without telling what comes next. Can one be free by merely understanding what is meant by freedom? Freedom is the understanding as well as the transformation of inevitability. One has to work at it. It won't do to merely understand what is meant by freedom. After one has found the rules, one must be able to apply them, by doing pioneer work, by breaking the earth, building houses, opening mines, and developing industries. When the population grows in the future and food becomes insufficient, it will be necessary to extract food from materials, and this is the sort of transformation which will bring freedom. Will it be so free in the future? Lenin has said that in the future there will be as many airplanes in the sky as flies, and what will happen if they become so rampant that they crash into each other? How will they be regulated and will there be that much freedom if they are so regulated. There are now about 10,000 buses in Peking, while in Tokyo there are some 100,000 (or is it 800,000?), and so they have plenty of automobile accidents. We have fewer vehicles, and moreover we educate our drivers and the people, and so we have fewer accidents. What will Peking be like 10,000 years from now? Will there be only 10,000 buses? New things will be invented. These tools of communication won't be needed, and men will be able to fly about by means of some sort of simple apparatus. One would be able to fly anywhere and land anywhere. Thus, it is not enough to simply understand inevitability, but one must be able to transform it.

I don't believe that there will be no division of stages in a communist society, and that there will be no qualitative changes. Lenin said that everything can be divided. Citing the atom as an example, he said that not only atoms are divisible, but electrons can also be divided. Nonetheless, it was deemed as indivisible before. The science of the fission of the nucleus is still relatively young, being only 20 or 30 years old. In the last few decades, scientists have analyzed the nucleus of atoms in which were found neutrons, antineutrons, mesotrons and antimesotrons. These are heavy, and there are also lighter ones. They were discovered primarily during and after World War II. The fissionability of electrons and atomic nuclei, was known long ago. In electric wire, copper and aluminum are used to separate external electrons. In the air at about 300 miles above the earth, the ionosphere has been discovered where electrons and atomic nuclei are separated. There is as yet no fission of electrons, but the day will certainly come when there will be. Chuang Tzu said: "If one takes away half of a foot-long hammer every day, there will be no end to it even after ten thousand generations." (*Chuang Tzu:* T'ien-hsia Pien, quoting Kung-sun and Lung-tzu.) This is true. If you don't believe it, you can try, and if it is exhaustible, then it is not science. Things are always developing, and this process goes on endlessly. Time and space are infinite. In space, both macrocosms and microcosms are infinite and indivisible. This is why scientists will always have work to do, even after one million years. I really enjoyed Sakata Soichi's [1911-0000, Japanese physicist] article on basic particles in the *Natural Sciences Research Bulletin*. I have never before seen such an article. He is a dialectical materialist and has quoted from Lenin: "The shortcoming of philosophers is that they do not engage in practical philosophy, and what they do is bookish philosophy."

We must bring out new things; otherwise, what would we do? And what would those that follow us do? New things exist in practical things, and so it is necessary to grasp practical things. . . .

Notes

Chapter I / Communism in China:
The Man, the Strategy and the Organization

1. For Mao's family background, see his interview with Edgar Snow, *Red Star Over China*, pp. 123-24.

2. Agnes Smedley, *Battle Hymn of China*, (New York: Da Capo Press, 1975), pp. 168-69.

3. Edgar Snow, p. 127. The chief dramatis personae of the *Romance of the Three Kingdoms* were Liu Pei, a member of the imperial house of Han and the Confucian model of virtue, and Ts'ao Ts'ao, a ruthless intriguer in the eyes of the traditional interpretation. Mao was claimed to have taken the unorthodox position of siding in his feelings with Ts'ao Ts'ao. See Schram, *The Political Thought of Mao Tse-tung*, p. 162. In his article, "A Reappraisal of the Case of Ts'ao Ts'ao," in *Wen Shih Lun chi* (Peking, 1961), Kuo Mo-jo, perhaps to please Mao, gives a revisionist assessment of Ts'ao Ts'ao's role in the historical novel. Regarding *Water Margin*, see Pearl Buck's translation under the title *All Men Are Brothers*. Of special interest is Mao's reinterpretation of the hero of this novel during political struggles in 1975.

4. Ibid., p. 133.

5. In retrospect, Mao has given to his main biographer Edgar Snow a rather excited description of the events of this time which in his recollection included revolutionary battles. In reality, the seizure of power included very little fighting, although the infighting between the original leaders of the local secret societies who came to power during the revoluton and the military commanders who took over led to some bloodshed after the Manchu government had fallen.

6. Edgar Snow, pp. 136-140.

7. For the text of Mao's essay see Stuart Schram, *The Political Thought of Mao Tse-tung*, pp. 94-102.

8. See Stuart Schram, *Mao Tse-tung*, p. 45.

9. During the fighting in World War I, Japan had taken over the German rights in Shantung province and then had gained additional privileges from China under the threat of military action — the infamous Twenty-one Demands of 1915.

10. These treaties, concluded by Great Britain, the U.S., France, Russia, Germany and later Japan and others, beginning with the Treaty of Nanking in 1842 at the end of

the opium war, had established numerous foreign rights and privileges in China.

11.   This article demonstrated the influence of Ch'en Tu-hsiu's concepts of science and democracy combined with a general admiration for the Russian Revolution and the military heroism of the Red Army. Mao expressed only a vague concept of the peasants, workers and others as part of the "great union of the popular masses," a concept which he never clearly defined. See Schram, *The Political Thought of Mao Tse-tung*, pp. 170-171, with reference to Hsiang-chiang P'ing-lun, Nos. 2, 3, and 4.

12.   Schram, p. 48.

13.   The term *masses* was a general Communist term, and it was in this meaning that Mao later used it. It had been applied by Lenin, when the Communist revolution was shifted from the industrial countries of the West to the essentially agrarian countries of Asia. In most of these Asian countries, including China, there was little, if any, class of industrial workers, the Marxian *proletariat*. In order to justify Communist leadership in these essentially nonproletarian societies, the term *toiling masses* signified a broader group of working people who then, as *oppressed popular masses* would take the place of the *proletariat* in the Communist doctrinal justification of their history. The term *toiling masses,* in German *werktätige Massen* appears to have first been used by the German socialist Karl Kautsky in extending the socialist revolution beyond the *proletariat*. Mao Tse-tung was to feel very much at home with this term which he used to characterize the large majority of the population whose support he claimed. Indeed, Mao's use of the term *proletariat* did not refer to the skilled workers but rather to these *masses* whom he claimed to lead.

14.   Yang Ch'ang-chi had died in January, 1920.

15.   The First and Second Communist International were organized in the 19th century by Marx and other socialists, but collapsed during World War I.

16.   The strategy of *national liberation movements* thus expanded the Communist doctrinal interpretation of history and was a second way towards communism as described in detail, for instance, in the main standard Soviet doctrinal textbook, *Fundamentals of Marxism-Leninism*, p. 394ff.

17.   Demetrio Boersner, *The Bolsheviks and the National and Colonial Question: 1917-1920*. Boersner provides a detailed history of the argument between two Marxist schools of thought about the role of the colonial world in relation to the proletarian revolution. Though the lines were not always that sharply drawn, Boersner distinguished between a *Western school* that thought emancipation of colonial people would come through the victory of the proletariat of the West, and an *Eastern school* which held that anticolonialism and nationalism in colonial countries would not only free these countries from rule by *imperial powers* but would also be a major instrument for bringing down *monopoly capitalism* in the West. Lenin and especially Stalin represent this school.

18.   This is not the place to treat in detail the problems of this untenable Communist interpretation which ignores among many other things the fact that in most periods of Chinese and other Asian histories the majority of peasants were small peasant

owners, that the landlords where they existed had no primogeniture as in some European peasant traditions, that land, therefore, was continuously divided and not a base of power nor even the major source of income for the upper social classes. All these and many other objections did not prevent the Communists from providing a doctrinal interpretation, applying to the non-Western world this unilateral interpretation of history on which their whole faith was founded. For an analysis of imperial Chinese society, see Chang Chung-li, *The Chinese Gentry* and *The Income of the Chinese Gentry,* both volumes with an analytical introduction by Franz Michael.

19. The agreement stated "Dr. Sun Yat-sen holds that the Communist order or even the Soviet system cannot actually be introduced into China, because there do not exist here the conditions for the successful establishment of either communism or sovietism. This view is entirely shared by Mr. Joffee, who is furthermore of the opinion that China's paramount and most pressing problem is to achieve national unification and attain full national independence, and regarding this great task, he has assured Dr. Sun that China has the warmest sympathy of the Russian people, and can count on the support of Russia . . ." See a.o., Milton J. T. Hsieh, *The Kuomintang: Selected Historical Documents, 1894-1969,* p. 71.

20. The contact began on December 23, 1921, when the Comintern agent, Maring, called on Sun, who, impressed by Maring's explanation of the Bolshevik Revolution, accepted the idea of Soviet support for his own revolution. In August, 1922, the original understanding was broadened by Sun's discussion with the Comintern agent, Joffee, who later continued the talks with Sun's representative, Liao Chung-k'ai in Japan, where the foundation was laid for the Sun-Joffee agreement. See Mao Ssu-ch'eng, *Min-kuo shih-wu-nien i-ch'ien chih Chiang Chieh-shih hsien-sheng,* p. 166.

21. The failure of Sun Yat-sen's revolution of 1911 can be attributed in part to Sun's lack of reliable military backing. Sun's main support had come from Ch'en Chiung-ming in Kwangtung who eventually turned against Sun. It was Ch'en's betrayal which led Sun to seek Soviet help. The main opposition to Sun's party came from the warlords of the North. In his vain attempts to overcome this resistance Sun tried in 1925 to gain the backing of northern provincial warlords without much success. Neither politically nor militarily had Sun been able to overcome the regional disintegration of the country.

22. J. V. Stalin, *Works,* Vol. 8 (January-November 1926), p. 379.

23. Mao Tse-tung, *Selected Works,* vol. 2, p. 268.

24. The Karakhan Manifesto drawn up by the Soviet Commissar of the People's Council in July of 1919 had promised the return to China of all Russian rights and privileges established by the treaties of the Tsarist government, including the Russian control of the Chinese Eastern Railroad in Manchuria—and without compensation. See Robert North, *Moscow and the Chinese Communists,* and Cheng, Tien-fong [Ch'eng T'ien-fang], *A History of the Sino-Soviet Relations,* pp. 108-9. When the Manifesto was published in the Soviet press a month later, the promise about the return of the Eastern Railroad was omitted and it has since been denied by the Soviet government

that this promise was ever made. There is, however, no reason to doubt the original version of the Karakhan Manifesto, which circulated in China in early 1920.

25. Benjamin I. Schwartz, *Chinese Communism and the Rise of Mao,* pp. 71-72.

26. See especially Ch'en Kung-po, *The Communist Movement in China,* edited and with an introduction by Martin Wilbur.

27. The Comintern representatives were said to have later tried to have this resolution revoked. See C. Martin Wilbur and Julie Lien-ying How, *Documents on Communism, Nationalism, and Soviet Advisers in China, 1918-1927.*

28. Ch'en himself had many personal meetings with Comintern agents, but did not share much of the information received with his party comrades. See Chang Kuo-t'ao, *The Rise of the Chinese Communist Party,* vol. I.

29. Schram, *Mao Tse-tung,* p. 59, and Ch'en Kung-po, p. 106.

30. For accounts of Mao's movements, see Schram, p. 61.

31. The record indicates that it was not easy for the Comintern representative to bring the Chinese Communists to understand the necessity of this form of cooperation with the Kuomintang. Having just grasped the doctrine of the class struggle as played out through the political parties representing their respective classes, it was hard for them to accept the order that the *vanguard* party of the proletariat had to join forces with the bourgeois enemy. But Moscow's authority prevailed and, as throughout, the Chinese Communist party followed Moscow's directives. This difficulty led later to a rather forced doctrinal explanation by Stalin of the Kuomintang as a party of not one but several classes. For Maring's problems in convincing the Chinese comrades and the necessity of claiming Comintern authority to have this policy accepted, see Jane Degras, ed., *The Communist International, 1919-1943: Documents,* vol. 2, p. 5.

32. As acting minister of the propaganda department of the Central Committee of the Kuomintang.

33. The term *cadre,* first used by Stalin, refers to a Communist functionary. *The Institute for the Peasant Movement* was first established in 1924 by P'eng P'ai, who was then secretary of the Kuomintang Agricultural Department, under which the Institute was placed. P'eng P'ai, who had organized the Hai-lu-feng peasant uprising was regarded as the Chinese Communist leader most familiar with peasant problems. For the Hai-lu-feng uprising, see Shinkichi Eto, "Hai-lu-feng, the First Chinese Soviet Government," *China Quarterly,* nos. 8 and 9 (October-December 1961 and January-March 1962).

34. Wang Chien-ming, *Chung-kuo Kung-chan-tang Shih-kao* (History of the Chinese Communist Party) (Taipei, 1965), vol. I, p. 187. At the same time, a political institute was set up in Canton. At this institute Mao gave a lecture, "The Peasant Problems." Graduates from this institute served as political cadres in the National Revolutionary Army in the northern expedition.

35. Ibid., p. 16.

36. Among the members were Shen Ting-i, Chang T'ai-lei (A Communist) and Wang Teng-yün. See Mao Ssu-ch'eng, ed., *Ming Kuo shih wu nien i-ch'ien chih Chiang Chieh-shih hsien-sheng* (Mr. Chiang Kai-shek before 1926) (Hong Kong: Lung Meng Publishing House, 1965), p. 201. An account of the journey is given in ibid., pp. 201-16.

37. Chiang did not see Lenin, who was too sick to receive him.

38. Ibid., pp. 217ff.

39. Tien-fong Cheng, *A History of Sino-Russian Relations,* pp. 133-34. According to another school of thought this assumption could not be proven and the incident was exaggerated.

40. For Mao's four resolutions which were discussed at the Kuomintang Central Committee meeting in February, 1924, after Mao's departure, Schram, *Mao Tse-tung,* pp. 68-69, with a reference to information by Roy Hofheinz, and *Chung-kuo Kuo-min-tang Chou K'an,* no. 9 (February 24, 1924).

41. Li Li-san had sarcastically referred to Mao as "Hu Han-min's secretary." See Edgar Snow, *Red Star Over China,* p. 145.

Chapter II / Mao and the Agrarian Revolution

1. In a speech at the Chinese Commission of the Executive Committee of the Comintern, Stalin stressed the importance for the Chinese Communists to establish their own military force; and in May, 1927, in a telegram to the Comintern agent, M. N. Roy, Stalin gave directions for a shift to a new radical line in the hope of possibly forcing the Kuomintang leaders still cooperating with the Communists to accept the Communist policy of agrarian revolution. The text of the telegram contained the order for preparations towards an independent military force: "This dependence on unreliable generals must be put to an end. Mobilize about 20,000 Communists, add about 50,000 revolutionary workers and peasants from Hunan, Hupeh, form several new army corps, utilize the students of the school for commanders and organize your own reliable army before it is too late. Otherwise there can be no guarantee against failures. It is a difficult matter but there is no other course." See J. V. Stalin, *Marxism and the National Colonial Question,* p. 249.

2. Jane Degras, ed., *The Communist International, 1919-1943: Documents,* vol. 2, p. 439.

3. Robert North and Zenoa Eudin, *M. N. Roy's Mission to China,* p. 111.

4. C. Martin Wilbur, "The Ashes of Defeat," *China Quarterly,* no. 18, pp. 3-54.

5. Ibid.

6.   At the final moment, the leadership in Moscow became dubious about the success of the plan for the Nanchang uprising and attempted to countermand the orders for the uprising, but the representative of the Chinese Central Committee, Chang Kuo-t'ao, who was sent to the city of Kiukang where several Communist leaders were preparing for the uprising, found that all preparations had been made and that the leaders were unwilling to cancel the action. See Chang Kuo-t'ao's letter to the Enlarged Conference, translated in ibid., pp. 44-52. While the Nationalist commander Chang Fa-k'uei would not join the rebellion, a number of his generals had been Communist party members. Among them were Yeh T'ing and Yeh Chien-ying, who were to have a distinguished career in the Red Army later. Still, only one of the Nationalist commanders, Ho Lung, a former bandit leader, came over to the Communist side, ibid.

7.   After the destruction of the main Communist force, Chu Teh was ordered by the Party Central to join up with a Nationalist troop commander, Fan Shih-sheng, who was a friend of Chu Teh, and become regimental commander under Fan. When Fan was ordered by the National Government to disarm Chu's force, he informed his friend Chu who departed with his unit in January, 1928 for Southern Hunan. See Kung Ch'u, *The Red Army and I* (Hong Kong: South Wind Publishing Company, 1965), pp. 96-100.

8.   The first phase of this *agrarian revolution* was still to be carried out under the Kuomintang flag and it took some time before the Chinese Communists were given the directive from Moscow that their newly established rural governments could raise the Communist flag and use the prestigious title of *Soviets* after the Russian Soviet model.

9.   Hsiao Tso-liang, *Chinese Communism in 1927, City vs. Countryside*, pp. 39-46.

10. The German term *Lumpen* means vagabond.

11. Mao Tse-tung, *Selected Works*, vol. 1, pp. 22-59.

12. Ibid., p. 22.

13. K. A. Wittfogel, "The Legend of Maoism," *China Quarterly*, no. 1 (January-March, 1969), p. 72f.

14. For these and other data, see the study by Hsiao Tso-liang, *Chinese Communism in 1927, City vs. Countryside*, pp. 43ff.

15. As Chang Kuo-t'ao stated: "although politically our comrades made active propaganda for land revolution, few realized how to make a land revolution." See Chang Kuo-t'ao, "Report, October 9, 1927," *Central Correspondence*, no. 7 (October 30, 1927), par. 2, quoted in Hsiao Tso-liang, *Chinese Communism in 1927, City vs. Countryside*, p. 47.

16. Hsiao Tso-liang, *Chinese Communism in 1927, City vs. Countryside*, p. 48, quoting Mao Tse-tung, "Investigations of the Rural Districts," p. 88.

17. Ibid.

18. Edgar Snow, p. 167.

19. In the argument between Mao and the Party Central, it must be understood that district centers in China were not as a rule cities in the Western sense. These centers were agricultural markets, but did not contain industrial development and no workers. The capture of such towns was therefore not necessarily a shift from rural peasant to proletarian urban revolution. Changsha, however, was more than such a rural district center, and Mao's plan indeed misinterpreted the purpose of Comintern policy. The intention of the party leadership was therefore clearly based on the strategy of fighting from the countryside to the city. Once the insurrection in the countryside had taken hold, the attack on urban centers meant in practice an attack on the county seats or smaller towns. Larger cities, such as Changsha, were not mentioned in the original insurrection plan and there is no evidence that special plans for uprisings in this and other major cities were actually formulated.

20. For the whole account of the Autumn Harvest uprisings, see the detailed description in Hsiao Tso-liang, *Chinese Communism in 1927, City vs. Countryside,* pp. 67-77.

21. Edgar Snow, *Red Star Over China,* pp. 167-68.

22. Ibid., p. 168.

23. The respective section of the "Resolution on Political Discipline" stated: "P'eng Kung-ta, Mao Tse-tung, I Li-yung, and Hsia Ming-han, members of the Hunan Provincial Committee, shall be removed from their present membership on the Provincial Committee . . . Comrade Mao Tse-tung was dispatched by the Central after the August 7 Emergency Conference to Hunan as special representative to reorganize the Hunan Provincial Committee and carry out the Central's autumn harvest insurrection policy. In fact, he was the center in the Hunan Provincial Committee. Comrade Mao should bear serious responsibility for the mistakes made by the Hunan Provincial Committee. He shall be dismissed as an alternate member of the Provisional Central Politburo." See the "Resolution on Political Discipline" adopted at the enlarged meeting of the CCP Central Provincial Political Bureau held on November 9-10, 1927. The full text of the resolution was published in *The Central Correspondence,* no. 13 (September 1927). Warren Kuo, *Analytical History of the Chinese Communist Party,* vol. 1, pp. 472-79.

24. Mao's disapproval of such raids was not to last long and appears more to have been a question of asserting his authority over Chu than a disregard for the policy of killing landlords and living on the land that became a standard part of the Communist guerilla warfare. At that time, however, Mao appears to have had a concept of broader political action and spoke of taking over the whole of Kiangsi province, making use of the conflict among Nationalist leaders. These projects of Mao were regarded in turn as unrealistic and fantastic by Chu and some of the commanders. See Otto Braun, "Von Schanghai Bis Yänan," *Horizont,* nos. 22, 23, 26-34, 35-38.

25.   See Mao Tse-tung, *Selected Works,* vol. I, pp. 105-115.

26.   Rule 1 — This refers to the traditional use of wooden doors as beds by quartered soldiers. Rule 8 — This version can be found in Agnes Smedley, *The Great Road,* p. 229; for a slightly different version, see Snow, p. 159.

27.   This use of the term *Red Guard* has to be distinguished from its later application during the Great Proletarian Cultural Revolution when *Red Guards* became the name for the high school and college students used by Mao as the vanguard of that movement.

28.   See Hsiao Tso-liang, *Power Relations Within the Chinese Communist Movement, 1930-1934,* pp. 14-38.

29.   Ibid., pp. 98-113.

30.   Schram, *Mao Tse-tung,* p. 152.

31.   For this and much of the following account, see Otto Braun's memoirs, "Von Schanghai Bis Yänan," which form an important documentary account of that period, interpreting it according to the Moscow line. Mao divided the regular forces into five military corps. The First, Third and Fifth corps were the main force, located in the Kiangsi Soviet and directly under Chu-Mao control. The Second Corps was the designation given to the force in western Hunan, south of the Yangtze under Ho Lung, and the Fourth Corps, north of the Yangtze River, was the unit of the O-yü-wan Soviet under the political control of Chang Kuo-t'ao, which was commanded by Hsü Hsiang-ch'ien. Many other local units, guerilla organizations and peasant self-defense forces under the Communist influence continued to exist and were as far as possible, at least nominally, incorporated into the central organization.

32.   Degras, vol. 2, p. 43.

33.   Mao, *Selected Works,* vol. 1, p. 124. For other versions, see also Edgar Snow, pp. 158-9, and Agnes Smedley, p. 229.

34.   Snow, p. 159. The main principles were ascribed to Chu Teh by Agnes Smedley, as well as by a former Red Army commander, Kung Ch'u in his memoirs, *The Red Army and I.* See Agnes Smedley, p. 229; Kung Ch'u, p. 133.

35.   See Li Tien-min, *Chou En-lai,* pp. 150-55; see also Edward E. Rice, *Mao's Way,* pp. 71, 527n.

36.   Braun.

37.   Mao had followed "a very hard, left course which not only consisted of the liquidation of great landowners and village usurers, but also hit heavily the middle stratum." He had often bypassed the families of Red soldiers in the land distribution, putting them off to the time of final victory, and had committed excesses during the establishment of cooperatives. Later, when Mao was reduced in authority

by the new arrivals from Shanghai, he shifted, according to Otto Braun, to the other extreme of too great a leniency to great landowners, usurers and commercial interests under the slogan "all for the peasants," hoping to broaden the social base of his Soviet government.

38. Mao, in line with his opposition to forward defense, appears to have claimed that the Fukien rebellion was a ruse to "trick" the Chinese Communist forces into a dangerous position.

39. See Kung Ch'u, pp. 395-400.

40. Only the rear guard, consisting mainly of local units, was decimated and it was soon decided to abandon the equipment and disband the large group of porters that had been assembled for transporting the machinery and supplies.

41. For an account of the Tsunyi Conference see Warren Kuo, *Analytical History of the Chinese Communist Party,* vol. 3, pp. 16ff. For documentation, see "Resolutions of the Tsunyi Conference," translated with a commentary by Jerome Ch'en, in *China Quarterly,* no. 40 (October-December 1969), pp. 1-38.

42. Po Ku lost his position of secretary general of the Central Committee and was replaced by Lo Fu, who had never been a strong independent figure and was willing to accept Mao's leadership. See especially Otto Braun's account of this move. See also Dieter Heinzig, "Otto Braun and the Tsunyi Conference" *China Quarterly,* no. 42 (April-June 1970), pp. 131-34. For an analysis see Richard Thornton, *China, The Struggle for Power, 1917-1972,* pp. 78-81.

Chapter III / Yenan

1. Another Communist commander, Hsü Hai-tung, had arrived in Shensi before Mao and joined forces with Liu and Kao.

2. Kao Kang and Liu Chih-tan had been arrested earlier by party representatives from Shanghai, but then were released by Mao Tse-tung and became Mao's loyal supporters. Liu Chih-tan was soon killed in battle. Kao Kang was to be purged by Mao in 1953. See Ch'en, Jerome, *Mao and the Chinese Revolution,* pp. 201-02. See also Chang Kuo-t'ao, vol. 2, p. 465.

3. During this whole period the author was professor in a Chinese State University in Hangchow and later in the interior, and had ample opportunity to observe the fast-changing Chinese domestic scene. He was struck by the abrupt change in the language with which the Chinese Communists treated the Western powers, echoing the Soviet line, once it had become known to the Shensi leadership.

4. For Mao Tse-tung's statement of the time, see *Selected Works,* vol. I, pp. 157, 164-65.

5. The author vividly remembers a strident protest in the fall of 1936 at the State University in Hangchow where he was teaching. To propagate the United Front

and a declaration of war against Japan, the students took over the University. Chiang Kai-shek arrived and met, first with the faculty and administration for a blistering lecture on their neglect of discipline; next with the student body, to explain his policy as a preparation for the inevitable stand against the very serious Japanese aggressor; and finally with two students, Communist party members, who had organized the protest and whom he strongly adivsed to leave the University forthwith, which they did. This ended the protest.

6. Warren Kuo, "The Zigzag Flight of the Red Army Troops," *Issues and Studies,* vol. 4, no. 10, p. 48.

7. In his Memoirs, Chang describes the humiliation of this trial. See Chang Kuo t'ao, vol. 2, pp. 512-17.

8. Sung Che-yüan had been appointed by the National Government with Japanese approval to the crucial position in Peking as a result of the Ho-Umetsu agreement in 1935. In this agreement, Chiang Kai-shek had accepted the Japanese demand that no appointment north of the Yellow River would be made without Japanese approval. Secretly, however, Sung Che-yüan had remained loyal to the Chinese national cause and was eventually to resist the Japanese attack at the Marco Polo Bridge incident, July 7, 1937, that led to the Sino-Japanese War.

9. This pledge, designed to cover Sung Che-yüan's clemency to the Communists in the eyes of the National Government, was obviously not meant seriously, and most of the Communists in question continued their work for their Party. Much later at the time of the Cultural Revolution this action was held against Liu Shao-ch'i, who was accused of having worked for the rehabilitation of traitors who had surrendered to the Nationalist cause even though, at the time, Liu had cleared his action with Mao.

10. Chang Hsüeh-liang was in regular communication with the Communist, had visited Paoan, and had a Communist representative at his headquarters. See Boorman, *Biographical Dictionary of Republican China,* vol. 1, pp. 61-68, and Chen, *Mao and the Chinese Revolution,* pp. 202-03.

11. Among others, see Chang Kuo-t'ao, vol. 2, pp. 480-90. See also Warren Kuo, vol. 3, pp. 228-29.

12. *Snow,* pp. 461-62; Rice, *Mao's Way,* pp. 91, 23n. See also Chang Kuo-t'ao, vol. 2, p. 484.

13. The Soviets had taken credit for saving Chiang Kai-shek's life. See statement by Molotov as quoted in Herbert Feis, *The China Tangle,* p. 180.

14. See Boorman, vol. 1, pp. 61-68. According to information given the author in 1947 by Ch'en Li-fu, there had been secret contact between the National Government and the Communists through Chou En-lai prior to the Sian kidnapping.

15. For a description of the Communist role in the Sian incident, see Chang Kuo-t'ao, pp. 480-90.

16. Chang Kuo-t'ao, vol. 2, p. 489.

17. Ibid.

18. Franz Michael, "University on the March," *Asia,* New York, 1939, pp. 18-19.

19. See Mao's intraparty directive of March 6, 1940, where he stressed that they had to "make sure that the Communists play the leading role in the organization of political power, and therefore the party members who occupy one-third of the places must be of high caliber. This will be enough to insure the party's leadership without a larger representation." See Mao, *Selected Works,* vol. 2, p. 418.

20. This was the same system later to be applied by the National Government in the land reform on Taiwan.

21. Rice, p. 94.

22. The first time was in September 1937 when troops of the 115th Communist Division of the Eighth Route Army staged a surprise attack against a large column of Japanese troops moving into Shensi province through P'inghsing Pass. This battle ended in a Communist victory, but since it had been the result of a Communist ambush it could not easily be repeated. The second battle between the Communists and the Japanese occurred in the summer of 1940 when Moscow pressed the Chinese Communists for renewed military effort to counter the danger of a Japanese attack against the Soviet Union at a time when the Soviet troops were under strong pressure by Hitler on the eastern front. As a result, the Eighth Route Army under the command of P'eng Teh-huai (P'eng Teh-huai had taken over from Lin Piao, who had been severely wounded in battle and was recovering from his wound in the Soviet Union where he remained until the end of the war) engaged the Japanese troops in a large offensive consisting of numerous actions by smaller units which proved to be very costly for the Communists. This series of battles in which about 400,000 men drawn from all division of the Eighth Route Army were involved became known as the Battle of the Hundred Regiments and was later propagandized by the Communists as a heroic feat. For the battle, see William Whitson, "The Field Army in Chinese Communist Military Politics," *China Quarterly,* no. 37 (January-March, 1969), pp. 5-6. The lesson of the costliness of the attempt to face the Japanese in an open offensive was one more reason that for the rest of the war the Communists never tried such an effort again and limited themselves to small-scale warfare behind the Japanese lines, moving in when the Japanese had penetrated an area to organize the people of the countryside behind the Japanese back under their own Communist administration. Mao later claimed that General P'eng Teh-huai had prepared this battle without consulting Mao.

23. Chi Wu, *Yi Ko Ke-Ming Ken-Chü-Ti Te Ch'eng Chang* (The Growth of a Revolutionary Zone Area), pp. 84-86 as cited in Richard Thornton's, *China, The Struggle for Power, 1917-1972,* p. 118 and n. 18.

24. This was the time when Otto Braun, the military representative of the Comintern who had remained with the Chinese Communists throughout the Long March

and in the first phase at Yenan, was recalled to Moscow. Otto Braun had lost his influence at the Tsunyi Conference and had from that time on functioned more as an observer than as a person of actual influence. See Braun's report.

25. Warren Kuo, "The Conflict Between Ch'en Shao-yü and Mao Tse-tung," part 1, *Issues and Studies*, vol. 5, no. 2 (November 1968), p. 35. See also Richard Thornton, *China, The Struggle for Power, 1917-1972*, pp. 105f.

26. Otto Braun.

27. It was this directive which was responsible for the leniency of Mao's action against Chang Kuo-t'ao who was only reprimanded but not purged in the Central Committee meeting of January 1938; however, Chang did not regain any authority. Later, when Stalin's protection was withdrawn, Chang had to fear for his life and defected from Yenan.

28. During the Cultural Revolution in 1967, in disapproval of violent factional infighting, Mao stated that it had not been important to him at Tsunyi to hold the leading position of party secretary as long as he could control the man in that position. In Mao's words: "They are fighting for the position of being 'the core.' That is not worth fighting for. The core is formed in the midst of struggle. At the Tsunyi Conference some people would have had me as the core, but I would have nothing of the kind. I thought I had better let Chang Wen-t'ien do the job." See *Survey of the China Mainland Press*, no. 4088 (December 28, 1967), p. 9 (hereafter cited as *SCMP*), as quoted in Edward E. Rice, *Mao's Way*, p. 86.

29. Yeh T'ing who had fled to Germany in 1927 after the collapse of the Nanch'ang uprising, had returned to command this army. The second in command was Hsiang Ying, who had been left behind in the Kiangsi Soviet at the time of the breakthrough and had been able to maintain a Communist unit and organization in that area. About Hsiang Ying's critical attitude toward Mao, see Otto Braun for an account of his night talk with Hsiang Ying before Braun left for the Long March. There Hsiang Ying, according to Braun, expressed his distrust and worry about Mao Tse-tung's ambitions and policies.

30. See Mao's speech "On the New Stage" *(Lun hsin chieh tuan),* published first in the journal, *Liberation* (November 1938) and translated in the *New China Daily* (January 1939), republished in Hong Kong by the new Democratic Publishing Company in 1948.

31. This speech was eliminated from Mao's *Selected Works*. A different version can be found in Mao's *Selected Works*, vol. 2, pp. 244ff, under the heading of "The Role of the Chinese Communist Party in the National Civil War."

32. Privately, however, claiming that the Kuomintang itself had prevented the institutionalization of the United Front, Mao maintained that the Communist party had to retain its own initiative and act independently without destroying the United Front. See Mao, *Selected Works*, vol. 2, pp. 215-16. "The question of independence and initiative within the United Front."

33. It may be possible to explain Mao's unusually cooperative position as his way of requiting Stalin's support for Mao's leadership of the Chinese Communist party. But Stalin's support went further. If Mao was to play the leading role in the Chinese Communist party, he needed the ideological equipment for this position and for this he appears to have received Soviet assistance at that time, as indeed he did later after the establishment of the People's Republic.

34. Kuo, "Disbandment of the New Fourth Army," *Issues and Studies,* vol. 6, no. 7 (April 1970), pp. 66-73.

35. Rice, pp. 97-98, and Warren Kuo, *Analytical History of the Chinese Communist Party,* vol. 4, pp. 252-312.

36. See Mineo Nakajima, *Gendai Chugoku-ron (China Today)* (Tokyo: Aoki Shoten, 1964), pp. 44-53.

37. Braun.

38. Meaning hostile contradictions to be resolved by violence. Other contradictions are "nonantagonistic" and can be resolved peacefully by persuasion.

39. To attack these "doctrinaires" Mao compared them with the scholars of late imperial times who had passed the examinations of the so-called "eight-legged essay,"—a rigid formalistic eight-point treatise far removed from reality—and who were incapable of dealing with real problems.

40. Mao lost the essential meaning of the dialectical concept as devised by Hegel. In the Hegelian concept of dialectics, the interplay of two opposed forces of thesis and antithesis in the realm of ideas lead to the emergence of a new synthesis. This synthesis again is a thesis that can be challenged by an antithesis and a new synthesis will emerge. The constant interplay of opposites thus leads to a progressive advance both in Hegelian and Marxist philosophy. This process is called the negation of the negation. Mao's description of dialectics omits the third element in the examples he gives and the conclusions he draws. Dialectics is, for Mao, simply a back and forth between two opposing forces in which one changes into the other—war changes to peace and peace to war; night changes to day and day to night; an egg will be transformed into a chicken, and Mao only wonders why it has to be an egg that under certain conditions will produce a chicken but not a stone; why human beings give birth to human beings, and not to anything else; and comes to the conclusion that the contradictions which he assumes exist only under certain necessary conditions.

    In conversations and in talks on "Question of Philosophy" in August 1964, Mao formally denied the tripod of this dialectical concept: "Engels talked about three categories, but as for me, I do not believe in two of those categories. The most basic thing is the unity of opposites and . . . there is no such thing as the negation of the negation." See *Chairman Mao Talks to the People; Talks and Letters,* ed. Stuart Schram, p. 226.

41. Mao quoted Stalin: "The question of colonies and semi-colonies is in essence a peasant question," and following Stalin, Mao gave the peasants the main role in

the Chinese revolution. See Mao Tse-tung, *Selected Works,* vol. 3, pp. 106-56.

42. Ibid., p. 156.

43. *Cheng-feng* is short for *Cheng-tun san feng,* literally translated as rectification of three styles. The rectification was to be carried out in the vocabulary of Maoist communism in order to correct "the approach in our study, the style in our party work, and in the tendency of our literary work." See Mao, "Rectify the Party's Style in Work," *Selected Works,* vol. 4, p. 28.

44. Braun.

45. For a documentation and general description of the *Chengfeng* movement, see Boyd Compton, *Mao's China: Party Reform Documents 1942-44.*

46. Kuo, vol. 4, pp. 603-06.

47. See, among others, Edgar Snow, p. 79ff.

48. For a short biographical description of Madame Mao, see the detailed account in Edward E. Rice, pp. 102-08, with reference to Chung Hua-min and Arthur C. Miller, *Madame Mao, a Profile of Chiang Ch'ing,* and Hao Jan-chu, "Mao's Wife: Chiang Ch'ing" in *China Quarterly,* no. 31 (July-September 1967) and Ting Wang, "Profile of Chiang Ch'ing, Mrs. Mao Tse-tung," *Far Eastern Economic Review,* no. 57 (August 1967).

49. Ibid.

50. See *SCMP,* no. 4089 (December 29, 1967), p. 1 and *Who's Who in Communist China,* vol. 1, p. 132, as cited in Edward E. Rice, p. 105.

51. *Chiang* means *river* and *Ch'ing* is *green* but also *pure or chaste.*

52. Mao is said to have threatened that if he would not be permitted to keep Chiang Ch'ing he would "go back to my native village and become a farmer." Though hardly seriously meant, this typical Mao statement may have convinced his colleagues that he was determined to have his will.

Chapter IV / Communist Victory

1. For this and the whole phase of American-Chinese negotiations during that time see the account in Richard C. Thornton, *China, The Struggle for Power 1917-1972,* pp. 146ff.

2. See Chiang Kai-shek, *Soviet Russia in China,* pp. 81-82: "He was my chief of staff in the China Theater of War, and I had great confidence in his recommendations. It may be recalled that the American Communists and their fellow-travelers were just then building up the Chinese Communists' reputation as 'agrarian reformers'

and as elements of a 'patriotic democratic party'; and were defaming me as a 'die-hard, reactionary Fascist.' Unfortunately, Stilwell was one of those taken in by these propaganda tactics. In the mistaken belief that the Chinese Communist forces, if placed under his command, would obey his orders and wholeheartedly fight the Japanese, he assured me that the Government could safely reequip them on the same basis as the Government forces and set them free for combat against the Japanese from where they were being held down by the Government's blockade. Moreover, the Government, he pointed out, could thus also release its forces immobilized on blockade duty for redeployment against the common enemy. Stilwell had no comprehension whatsoever of Communist intrigues . . . When Stilwell first came to China, I could have briefed him, regardless of his reactions one way or another, on Soviet Russia's intrigues and her designs on China. He might then have acquired a better understanding of the situation and been on his guard. In retrospect, I regret very much that I did not do this."

3. See statement by General Marshall after the failure of his mission when he complained that: "I have never been in a position to be certain of the development of attitudes in the innermost Chinese Communist circles. Most certainly, the course which the Chinese Communist Party has pursued in recent months indicated an unwillingness to make a fair compromise." Dun J. Li, *The Road to Communism: China Since 1912,* p. 276.

4. On Hurley's stopover in Moscow on the way to Chungking, V. M. Molotov repeated to him the statement made the year before by Stalin to Averill Harriman that the Soviet Union had no great interest in the Chinese Communists who were in their opinion not real Communists.

5. Upon leaving the airplane in Yenan, Hurley greeted a surprised Mao and Chou, who were waiting for him, with a loud Indian war whoop, according to Col. David D. Barrett, who was in charge of the American Military Mission in Yenan at the time. Rice, p. 110ff.

6. For an English translation of the Five Point Proposal see Dun J. Li, pp. 263-64.
    How strongly Mao seems to have resisted any agreement with Chiang Kai-shek, whom he apparently regarded as a personal opponent as well as the head of the National Government's opposition to Communist aspirations, can be inferred from an account of a meeting with Hurley in which Mao was said to have belabored Chiang Kai-shek to such a degree that Hurley felt compelled to ask: "Mr. Mao, are you Chinese or Japanese? Because what you said is exactly what the Japanese often said. As an intelligent Chinese I do not think that you should use the Japanese language to talk with me as a mediator. I hope, Mr. Mao, that you should think it over and change your attitude and then we can talk about negotiations." To this comment, Chou En-lai, who was present, reacted in conciliatory fashion: "Mr. Mao is a communist; and we communists always pay great attention to self-criticism. Therefore, Mr. Mao's criticism of the National Government and Mr. Chiang Kai-shek in front of you may astonish you as an American but is not strange for us communists. I hope, Mr. Hurley, you will understand this. From now on I will be the representative, and I am willing to follow you to Chungking to represent the Chinese Communist Party and open talks with the National Government." See Wang Chien-ming, *Chung-kuo Kung-chan-tang Shih-kao (History of the*

Chinese Communist Party), vol. 3, p. 46. See also Tso Shun-sheng, *Chin san-shih nien chien-wen tsa-chi (Random Notes and Reminiscences of the Last Thirty Years)* (Hong Kong: Liberty Publishing House, 1952), pp. 90-91. As a member of the delegation of minority party groups to Yenan, Tso had a long talk with Mao on July 4, 1945. He reported that Mao told him: "Mr. Chiang Kai-shek always believes that there is only one sun in the heaven and one king on earth. I don't believe that nonsense. Let him see, I will raise two suns."

7. Wang Ming remained a member of the Central Committee but not of the Polit-buro. He was appointed by Mao as principal of a girls' school, and finally left for Moscow. In his memoirs, *Half a Century of the CPC and Mao Tse-tung's Betrayal,* published in Moscow in 1975, Wang Ming accuses Mao of having attempted to poison him in Yenan. A Russian doctor presumably saved Wang Ming's life.

8. Mao Tse-tung, *Selected Works,* vol. 4, pp. 244-315.

9. Only once does Mao refer to the "illegal 'National Government.'"

10. See Stuart Schram, *Mao Tse-tung,* pp. 178-79. Composed earlier in Yenan, Mao first issued the poem in Chungking obviously to dramatize his arrival at his opponent's camp and to provoke answers in support or criticism of Mao's piece. The description of the majesty of the landscape of China, the prize to be won by valour, and the glorification combined with disparagement of the heroes of the past, were to serve as the proper introduction for the coming revolutionary hero of the day. See Appendix for poem.

11. A three-man group consisting of General Marshall, Chang Ch'ün for the Nationalists and Chou En-lai for the Communists, reached an agreement on January 5 on a military truce. During the PCC sessions they continued their meetings on military reorganization and the realization of the truce agreement.

12. In those provinces where actual control was divided between Nationalist and Communist forces, authority was shared. Depending on which side retained a larger part of the province, a Nationalist or a Communist were appointed as governor and vice-governor respectively. The Nationalists strenuously opposed the Communist attempt to establish their control in Kiangsu province in the lower Yangtze region, the very heart of Nationalist political, military and economic interests. The argument over local authority in Kiangsu was never settled and the dispute eventually contributed to the breakdown of the totality of the PCC settlements.

13. Nor had it been anticipated by some of the Chinese intelligentsia who had set hopes on avoidance of civil war. Their growing disenchantment was well expressed in an editorial in the *Ta Kung Pao* of December 1, 1945 (translated by Dun Li, *The Road to Communism: China Since 1912,* pp. 272f, under the title: "We would like to ask the CCP some questions."). The Communist duplicity emerges clearly from this editorial of the most influential independent Chinese daily of the time.

14. See *Foreign Relations of the United States,* vol. 6, pp. 541-42.

15. See Karroll Wetzel, "Out of the Jaws of Victory" (Ph.D. diss., The George Washington University, 1973).

16. Stalin extended this invitation through Chiang Kai-shek's son, Chiang Ching-kuo, who had been invited to Moscow.

17. Chiang Kai-shek's reaction is expressed in *Soviet Russia in China,* p. 102; "After very careful consideration, I realized that the future success or failure of our diplomacy would depend on how this particular situation was handled. I felt that if I should accept the invitation, we might have to endorse the Russian Communists' persistent strategem toward China, i.e., "cooperation" between the Kuomintang and the Chinese Communist Party, the establishment of a coalition government, and the inevitable complete dependence of China on Russia. All these formed integral parts in Moscow's scheme for China's "peaceful transformation." Once we succumbed to the scheme, it would seriously jeopardize our status as an independent country.

"On the other hand, if I should decline the invitation, it would of course disappoint Stalin, and, despairing of ever winning me over, he might become even more overt in his support of his Chinese puppets' subversive activities against the Government, and close the door to any possibility of a rapprochment. World opinion had already been confused by the Communists' international propaganda. Most of the democratic nations had chosen to appease Russia in the Sino-Soviet dispute. Their attitude toward my Government was coldly aloof to the point of pessimism. They thought they could preserve their own economic interests in China even if the Chinese Communists should seize power.

"Finally, after a thorough discussion with senior members of the Government and the Kuomintang, it was unanimously decided that we should base our decision on China's permanent national interests rather than on the shifting world condition. Since even such great sacrifices as China had been forced to make under the Sino-Soviet Treaty of Friendship and Alliance had failed to satisfy Soviet Russia, we realized that there was no point in my meeting Stalin."

18. See Wetzel's dissertation. Also see Thornton, pp. 196-207.

19. Mao's *Selected Works,* vol. 5, pp. 81-84.

20. Ibid., p. 415.

21. Ibid.

22. Schram, *Chairman Mao Talks to the People,* p. 191.

23. The equivalent of $300 million in credits was granted by the Soviet Union in this first agreement.

24. For the text of the marriage law, see *The Marriage Law of the People's Republic of China,* pp. 1-10; for an excellent account of the subject, see Marinus Johan Meijer, *Marriage Law and Policy in the Chinese People's Republic.*

25. For the text of the Agrarian Reform Act and other relevant regulations, see *The*

Agrarian Reform Law of the People's Republic of China.

26. Richard L. Walker, *China Under Communism: The First Five Years,* pp. 218-19. Professor Walker's data are based on estimates provided by the Free Trade Union Committee of the American Federation of Labor and other estimates including figures given by the Chinese Communist officials. See also Richard L. Walker, *The Human Cost of Communism in China.*

27. For this campaign, see Robert T. Lifton, *Thought Reform and the Psychology of Totalism: A Study of "Brainwashing" in China.*

28. As an example, an administrative specialist in agriculture would be checked by a similar specialist in the party structure. What made the control even more complete was the fact that the officials of both hierarchies were party members and, thus, under party discipline. The interlocking of these two hierarchies was especially noticeable in the frequent practice of Communist appointments under which the first secretary of the Provincial Party Committee held frequently concurrently the post of vice governor in the provincial administration while the governor of the province often concurrently held the position of Second Secretary of the provincial party organization.

Chapter V / Handling the Soviet Connection

1. See, among others, O. Vladimirov and V. Ryanzantsev, *Stranitsy politicheskoi biografii Mao Tse-duna (Pages from Mao's Political Biography)* (Moscow: Izdotelstro Politichesko; Literatury, 1969). See also Otto Braun, "Von Schanghai bis Jaenan," (From Shanghai to Yenan) *Horizont,* nos. 32, 23, 26-34, 35-38 (1969).

2. The fact that Stalin admitted to Yugoslav Communists that he had at the end of World War II encouraged the Chinese Communists to compromise with Chiang Kai-shek because he did not believe in their imminent victory does not disprove in any way the general tenor of Soviet policy towards support. It can be held that at the time Mao Tse-tung himself did not expect that the final victory was so close at hand. See also Mao's comment about Stalin's misjudgment of the Chinese Communist chances of victory in 1945 and his worry of Mao's political Titoism, dispelled only at the time of the Korean war referred to in Chapter IV, n. 24.

3. Robert K. Bowie and John K. Fairbank, *Communist China 1955-1959, Political Documents with Analysis,* p. 3.

4. Among those who tried to replace Mao were men like T'an Chen-lin, who in 1953 "took the lead in sending a joint letter asking our great leader, Chairman Mao, to 'take a rest' " and Chu Teh, who was later accused of having ambitions to become himself Mao's successor. See *SCMP,* no. 3962 (April 10, 1967), p. 9.

5. The Kao-Jao "clique" was later accused of having, at this meeting, "madly assailed Chairman Mao." See *SCMP,* no. 4179 (May 16, 1968), pp. 5-6.

6. For a very useful account of the Kao Kang affair, see Edward E. Rice, *Mao's Way*, pp. 129-232, with references to documentary information.

7. "The Chairman of the People's Republic of China commands the armed forces of the country and is Chairman of the Council of National Defense." Article 42. For the text, see Peter S. H. Tang, *Communist China Today*, vol. 2, p. 99.

8. See Mao's speech, *People's Daily*, October 17, 1955, which was originally delivered at the Conference of Provincial and Local Party Secretaries on July 31, 1955.

9. An interesting account of the method of Communist propaganda can be found in the book by Robert Loh, *Escape from Red China*. Mr. Loh was one of the model liberated capitalists used by the Communists for interviews with foreign visitors. This account of his interviews was made public by him after his escape.

10. The shift in Chinese population to this area was later extended and affected the population composition in Sinkiang and Tibet. Turkish and Tibetan ethnic groups began to be outnumbered by Chinese immigrants resulting in destruction of the ethnic and cultural identity which these former Chinese dependencies had retained under imperial rule of traditional China.

11. For this literary housecleaning, see Merle Goldman, "The Hu Feng Campaign of 1955," in *Literary Dissent in Communist China*, pp. 127-157.

12. For the text of the constitution of 1954, see Peter S. H. Tang, *Communist China Today*, vol. 2, pp. 90-110.

13. The railroad rights were returned in 1952 to Chinese management, but the naval base of Port Arthur was retained temporarily "on the invitation" of Peking, evidently because the Korean War had not yet been concluded.

14. See Stuart Schram, ed., *Chairman Mao Talks to the People. Talks and Letters, 1956-1971*, p. 99. At the same time, Mao expressed his criticism of "Khrushchev's complete demolition of Stalin at one blow."

15. *SCMP*, no. 527 (March 10, 1953), pp. 1-3.

16. For the remarks by Chu Teh (representing Mao) at the opening of the Congress, see *SCMP*, no. 1231 (February 20, 1956), p. 36.

17. Donald Zagoria, *The Sino-Soviet Conflict, 1956-1961*, pp. 42-45. Gives an account of the reaction in China.

18. For the text of Party Statutes of 1956, see Tang, *Communist China Today*, vol. 2, pp. 112-133.

19. See, among others, Robert K. Bowie and John K. Fairbank, (foreword) *Communist China 1955-1959, Political Documents with Analysis*, pp. 234ff.

20. See *People's Daily,* (June 13, 1956).

21. Ibid.

22. The term *contradictions* refers to the opposing principles of dialectics in Marxist doctrine. In his earlier speech on contradictions in 1938, Mao had dealt with this concept. The distinction between the two types of contradications was not new in Communist theory, but its emphasis by Mao introduced a new political principle that was to become crucial in Mao's struggle with the Party.

23. For the text of Mao's speech see, *Let a Hundred Flowers Bloom; The Complete Text of 'The Correct Handling of Contradictions Among the People' By Mao Tse-tung Chairman, Communist Party of China,* with notes and introduction by G. F. Hudson (New York: Tamiment Institute).

24. By 1975 the Communists claimed that twelve million young people had been "sent down to the countryside," since 1957.

25. In addition to reform labor camps to which millions were sent for undetermined periods of time, other forced labor camps existed from which there was no return. The system, so well known from Soviet history had its parallel in China. See Bao Kuo-wang [Jean Pasqualini] and Rudolph Chelminski, *Prisoner of Mao.* A personal account of an inmate of one of these camps who was able to return only because he happened to be a French citizen and De Gaulle intervened for him at the time of the establishment of French-Chinese relations. In his account, Pasqualini estimates that at any given time about six million Chinese were working in these camps where work goals were maintained by means of food allocation and obedience became a matter of sheer survival.

26. After the Comintern had been abolished by Stalin in 1943 and the Cominform by Khrushchev in 1956, the intraparty conferences became the only formal framework for discussion and resolutions of general Communist policies.

27. For Mao's speech see *Peking Review,* vol. 2, no. 36 (September 6, 1963), p. 10. For Mao's proposed harder line policy, see *Peking Review* vol. 2, no. 37 (September 13, 1963), pp. 10-12, and Appendix.

Chapter VI / The Sino-Soviet Conflict

1. See *Policy Review,* vol. 15 (June 10, 1958).

2. Schram, *Mao Tse-tung,* p. 292.

3. See Franz Shurmann, *Ideology and Organization in Communist China,* p. 493 and references given there.

4. Li Cho-ming, *The Statistical System of Communist China.*

5. Chou En-lai admitted, for instance, that the grain production figures of 375 million tons had been "a little high" and that, in fact, instead of 375 million, only 250 million tons had been produced, a figure for which there was, however, as little reliable statistical evidence as there had been for the first exorbitant one. Steel production was now claimed to have been eight million tons instead of close to 11 million tons and the prospect for 1959 was substantially lowered.

6. See Valentine Chu, "The Famine Makers," *New Leader,* June 11, 1962.

7. Mao himself later declared in a well-known statement to Japanese visitors that he was made to feel like a "father at his own funeral," and was shunted aside. That this demotion was not accepted without struggle is also evident from Mao's attempt to maintain the right to call decisive meetings of the leadership of party and government. The chairman of the Republic was in charge of the Supreme State Conferences in which major political matters were discussed. When such a Supreme State Conference was called in September 1960 by Mao's successor as chairman of the Republic, Liu Shao-chi, Mao on his own called a similar meeting a month later to discuss an almost identical program to that taken up previously by his successor.

8. The Soviets on the other hand resented Mao's recklessness in starting a confrontation with the U.S. in disregard of specific Soviet opposition. For a more detailed account, see Edward F. Rice, *Mao's Way,* pp. 154-156.

9. Unable to accommodate this sudden influx the British authorities attempted to return most of the refugees to the People's Republic and tried to induce the Communist authorities to stem the tide. But at least 140,000 remained in British territory.

10. For the text of the Moscow statement, see *China Quarterly,* no. 5 (January-March 1961).

11. Zagoria, *The Soviet-Sino Conflict, 1956-61,* p. 99.

12. According to all accounts, the Lushan meeting was a dramatic confrontation between Mao and P'eng Teh-huai who had the support of other military leaders and many of the non-military members of the Central Committee. See David A. Charles, "The Dismissal of Marshal P'eng Teh-huai," *China Quarterly,* October-December, 1961; Union Research Institute, *The Case of P'eng Teh-huai 1959-1968;* J. D. Simmonds, "P'eng Teh-huai, A Chronological Reexamination," *China Quarterly,* no. 37 (January-March 1969).

13. For the text of Mao's violent and gross speech, see Appendix.

14. In his speech Khrushchev also strongly warned against military adventures that might lead to war. See Rice, pp. 157, 158.

15. Ibid., pp. 154-156.

16. Richard Lowenthal, "Diplomacy and Revolution: The Dialectics of a Dispute,"

China Quarterly, no. 5 (January-March 1961), p. 18.

17. For the texts of the letter of the Central Committee of the Chinese Communist party in answer to the letter of the Central Committee of the Soviet Union, as well as for the nine detailed comments on the specific issues of the ideological conflict, see *The Polemic on the General Line of the International Communist Movement* (Peking: Foreign Language Press, 1965).

18. They were actually drafted by Teng Hsiao-p'ing who thus, at this time, was at least in the matter of the Sino-Soviet relations, fully supporting Mao Tse-tung by actually serving as his very skillful doctrinal interpreter.

19. Lo Jui-ch'ing, however, was to turn against Mao at the outset of the Cultural Revolution in 1965.

20. See *Peking Review* (September 28, 1962).

21. See Richard Baum and Frederick C. Teiwes, *Ssuch'ing: The Socialist Education Movement of 1962 to 1966* (Berkeley: University of California Press, 1968.)

22. See *SCMP,* no. 138, pp. 5-17.

Chapter VII / The Great Proletarian Cultural Revolution

1. Liu Shao-ch'i, *How To Be A Good Communist,* p. 14.

2. Ibid., pp. 89-91

3. Between 1962 and 1966, 15 million copies of Liu's book were said to have been sold in comparison to about a million and a half sets of Mao's *Selected Works.* For this and a more detailed description of the Party's attack against Mao Tse-tung's claim of infallibility, see Rice, *Mao's Way,* pp. 184-88.

4. Ibid.

5. See James R. Pusey, *Wu Han: Attacking the Present through the Past* (Cambridge: Harvard University Press, 1969).

6. *Current Background,* no. 842 (December 8, 1967), p. 7

7. "In the Theatre; Chiang Ch'ing's Model Plays," *China News Analysis,* no. 1038 (April 13, 1976).

8. P'eng Chen had compared the new operas rather drastically with the Chinese practice of dressing young children with slit pants that permitted them to relieve themselves without parental aid. To P'eng these plays were "still in the stage of wearing trousers with a slit in the seat." See *Current Background,* no. 842, pp. 12-14, quoted in Rice, p. 206.

9. With the exception of K'ang Sheng who claimed that his signature under P'eng's circular letter had been added without permission.

10. *Current Background,* no. 852 (May 6, 1968,) pp. 2-6.

11. *SCMP,* no. 3866 (January 24, 1967), pp. 1-3.

12. Of special interest was the takeover of *People's Daily.* This organ of the Central Committee was seized on June 1, 1966. From that date on the appearance of the newspaper changed. Each day it carried a quotation from Mao Tse-tung beside its name. Editorial space to propagate the Thought of Mao Tse-tung was also greatly increased.

13. Published in *People's Daily* on June 19 and in all other Peking papers, the letter was reprinted June 24 in English in the *Peking Review.*

14. The victory of the Thought of Mao Tse-tung was apparent in a *People's Daily* editorial of July 1, 1966, reprinted in a red color issue No. 27 of the *Peking Review* on the same day. The article, "Long Live Mao Tse-tung's Thought," ascribed all Communist success in China to the Thought of Mao Tse-tung. All the Party's victories in the forty-five years since its founding were called "The Great Victories of Mao Tse-tung's Thought."

15. *Peking Review* (September 3, 1965).

16. The strategem used by Mao to seize Lo Jui-ch'ing, who was not only the chief of staff but also head of military intelligence, is not known; one story reported to the author has it that Lo was taken prisoner by a ruse when he visited Mao Tse-tung in Hangchow and joined Mao in a boat ride on the West Lake.

17. One of the miracles reported by the papers, for instance, had it that one of the many swimmers who had jumped into the water of the Yangtze River to follow Mao's example had carried a sign with the inscription, "Long live Chairman Mao." Not used to this handicap while swimming, the enthusiastic follower had gone under and swallowed a good deal of Yangtze water before being pulled out. When brought to, he claimed that as a result of Mao's feat the water had tasted incredibly sweet—indeed an extraordinary transformation of the Yangtze water. For an account of these and many other episodes of the swim, see "Did he try to walk on it?" *The Economist* vol. 220, no. 6414 (London, July 30, 1966), p. 439.

18. Arthur Waley, trans. *Wu Ch'en-en, (Monkey).*

19. *Joint Publications Research Service,* August 25, 1967, p. 9, as referred to in Rice, pp. 249-50.

20. For example, children from the Eighth Route Army families and veterans of the Korean War were admitted to schools and a group of them were sent to Wuhan in 1958 to study philosophy. All they had in preparation was a strong political ambition but little real education. *China News Analysis,* no. 634 (October 28, 1966), pp. 4ff, gives many examples and general comment.

21. See statement of June 3 about the "glorious responsibility of the leftist students" who were "the heart of the movement" of revolution and whose slogan was "students give lessons to teachers." Ibid., p. 5.

22. *China News Analysis,* no. 642 (January 6, 1967), p. 3.

23. *Current Background,* no. 852 (May 6, 1968), p. 8. For the attacks by these Maoist organizations against their more fortunate school mates of better social background and education, see also *China News Analysis,* no. 634 (October 28, 1966), p. 4, with examples of Red Guard posters, threatening the schoolmates of better background; and *China News Analysis,* no. 636 (November 11, 1966), article "Five Red Guard Letters," for examples of the crude language used by the radicals in the defamation of their opponents.

24. *People's Daily,* August 9, 1966, as quoted in *China News Analysis,* no. 634, p. 6.

25. The term *Red Guards* was first used by a Tsinghua University middle school group on June 24, 1966 and was then adopted as the most suitable slogan for the whole movement.

26. "The revolutionary students in many schools, when they heard the broadcast [of the resolution] immediately organized, lifted high the picture of Chairman Mao and the sayings of Mao, beat drums and sang revolutionary songs." *People's Daily,* August 9, 1966, as quoted in *China News Analysis,* no. 634, p. 6.

27. In Lin Piao's speech at the first T'ien-an-men meeting in August 1966, the Red Guards were instructed to destroy the Four Olds and establish the Four News. *People's Daily,* August 18, 1966.

28. *People's Daily,* August 29, 1966, as quoted in *SCMP,* no. 3773 (September 2, 1966), p. 9-10.

29. M. A. Gibson, "Terror at the Hands of the Red Guards," *Life,* vol. 62, no. 22 (June 2, 1967), pp. 22-29; 63-66.

30. Ibid., p. 29.

31. Rice, pp. 257-58, for Mao's statements as derived from Red Guard and other sources.

32. As Chou En-lai said, "Now students come to Peking to exchange experiences from over the country, and Peking students go to other places to carry out revolutionary travel. This is a good thing, we support you." See Chou En-lai's speech at the rally in Peking on August 31 as reported in *People's Daily* that date. These exchanges could, and later did, serve another purpose, that of political alliances. They became dangerous as a strategem of the Red Guards to strengthen their power nationwide and were later suppressed.

33. According to this remarkable document, Liu admitted among his many mistakes

during the Cultural Revolution that he and the party's Central Committee had permitted the Peking City Committee to send work teams to the schools; these teams had attempted to suppress the mass movement, did not permit street demonstrations and wall posters, and created fights between students which spread all over the country resulting in counterrevolutionary peril within the schools. Liu had not understood the Thought of Mao Tse-tung and had not learned from the masses.

34. *People's Daily* and *Red Flag* (September 7 and 15, 1966), and Chou's statements, *China News Analysis,* no. 629 (September 16, 1967).

35. *SCMP,* no. 3852 (July 4, 1967), p. 3.

36. *China News Analysis,* no. 644 (January 13, 1967), p. 3.

37. *China News Analysis,* no. 642 (January 6, 1967), p. 6, reporting accounts by Japanese journalists.

38. *China News Analysis,* no. 644, p. 3.

39. An example was the general headquarters of the Shanghai Revolutionary Upheaval Workers, which consisted of thirty-two units including "the Second Military camp of Shanghai workers who went to the north and returned"; "the Revolutionary Committee of Red Guards in Shanghai University and specialized colleges and schools"; the "Red Guard Army Directory of the combined committee of Shanghai Revolutionary Upheaval"; the "revolutionary upheaval liaison station in the Shanghai party and government offices"; and many others. *People's Daily* (February 5, 1967). How typical and acceptable this proliferation of revolutionary organizations was can be deduced from the fact that when shortly thereafter the call to "seize power" came, Shanghai and the revolutionary rebels there were cited as the best model.

40. This and other directives of the time were issued under the name of the Central Committee of the party, the State Council, the Military Affairs Committee, and the Cultural Revolution group. *Current Background,* no. 852 (May 6, 1968).

41. For Mao's fear that the enemy was penetrating the revolutionary ranks, see *China News Analysis,* no. 649 (Feb. 24, 1967).

42. Hereafter referred to as the PLA.

43. *Current Background,* no. 852 (May 6, 1968).

44. The strategic reserves were stationed at Wuhan.

45. *Current Background,* no. 852 (May 6, 1968), pp. 54-55.

46. *Peking Review,* nos. 14, 15 and 16 (April, 1966) and *SCMP,* no. 521 (April 25, 1966).

47. The respective paragraphs read: "It is necessary to institute a system of general elections, like that of the Paris Commune, for electing members to the cultural revolutionary groups and committees and delgates to the cultural revolutionary

congresses. The lists of candidates should be put forward by the revolutionary masses after full discussion and the elections should be held after the masses have discussed the lists over and over again. The masses are entitled at any time to criticize members of the cultural revolutionary groups and committees and delegates elected to the cultural revolutionary congresses. If these members or delegates prove incompetent, they can be replaced through election or recalled by the masses after discussion."

48. "Shanghai Commune," *China News Analysis,* no. 714.

49. *SCMP,* no. 4147 (March 27, 1968).

50. Ibid.

51. Parris H. Chang, "China's Revolutionary Committees; Two Cases Studies Heilung-chiang and Honan," *Current Scene,* no. 1 (June, 1968).

52. *Peking Review,* no. 935 (August 26, 1966).

53. *Current Background,* no. 852 (May 6, 1968), p. 115.

54. Ibid., pp. 63, 68-69, 78, 84, 91.

55. Ibid., p. 119.

56. A detailed account of this incident can be found in *Union Research Institute* (Hong Kong [Kowloon]), vol. 48, nos. 10, 23, and vol. 49, no. 13.

57. *China News Analysis,* no. 193 (October 26, 1967).

58. The British holdings consisted of the island of Hong Kong acquired at the Treaty of Nanking in 1842 and expanded to include the peninsula of Kowloon, acquired in 1860 to which the "New Territories" were added in 1898 as a "99-year lease" to expire in July 1997, when the New Territories are supposed to return to China.

59. The influx of Chinese refugees is continuing at a rate of about 30,000 people a year. This number is an estimated one-third of those who attempt to escape but fail in the majority by being captured by the Chinese border guards or perish by drowning.

60. It was Khrushchev's derision which enraged Mao and caused him to point to the "imperialist" Czarist predecessors of the Soviet Union who had taken a large chunk of Chinese territory on the northwestern border by "unequal treaties" concluded at a time of Imperial China's greatest weakness.

61. Both men and women were sexually molested in the most vulgar manner by female and male Red Guards, respectively. For an account of this incident, see Rice, pp. 377-378.

62. For the field armies traditions, see William W. Whitson, *The Chinese Communist High Command, 1928-1969: A Study of Military Politics.*

63. "Revolutionary Committee Leadership—China's Current Provincial Authorities," *Current Scene,* vol. 2, no. 18 (October 18, 1968).

64. For the cruelty of these vicious fights in which victims had eyes gouged out and ears and noses cut off, see *Union Research Institute,* 48 (August 8, 1967), pp. 152-53.

65. Huang Yung-sheng, a member of Lin Piao's former Fourth Field Army group, was military commander.

66. John Gittings, *Far Eastern Economic Review,* no. 26 (June 23-29, 1968), pp. 648-50.

67. Rice, pp. 437-40.

68. This elevation of Mao's Thought to a quasireligious authority was then transferred from the schools to all administrative offices and even to the people's homes.

69. A Pakistani mission had brought the gift of mangoes used by Mao for this demonstration of support of the new teams. The mango gift was widely celebrated in the press and became the symbol of the Mao Thought Propaganda teams who were to take over the Cultural Revolution.

70. *China News Analysis,* no. 728 (October 11, 1968), p. 5.

71. *China News Analysis,* no. 728 (October 11 and 14, 1968), pp. 6-7.

Chapter VIII / Mao and the Succession

1. *Peking Review,* no. 14 (April 4, 1969), pp. 7-9; no. 16 (April 18, 1969), pp. 7-9; no. 18 (April 30, 1969), pp. 16-35.

2. *Peking Review,* no. 18 (April 30, 1969), pp. 36-39.

3. *Peking Review,* no. 15 (April 10, 1970), pp. 3-10; and special issue, (May 8, 1970), pp. 3-6.

4. Text and reference in Chinese Information Service, *Background on China,* B 72-76.

5. *Issues and Studies,* no. 10, pp. 95-97.

6. Ibid.

7. Ibid.

8. *Issues and Studies,* no. 12, p. 68, and *New York Times,* December 12, 1972.

9. Cheng Wei-shan and Li Hsüeh-feng, officers of the former Fourth Field Army.

10. See Chung-fa nos. 4, 20, in *Issues and Studies,* vol. 8 (May 1972), pp. 77-83 and vol. 9 (December 1972), pp. 92-96.

11. Documents of the CCP Central Committee, Chung-fa (1972) no. 4, in *Issues and Studies*, no. 8 (May 1972), pp. 77-83.

12. *Issues and Studies*, no. 12 (September 1972), p. 69.

13. Chien Tieh, "A Study of a Document Concerning the Lin Piao Incident," *Issues and Studies*, no. 12 (September 1972), pp. 41ff.

14. Ibid.

15. Yang Yung-kuo (also spelled Yang Jung-Kuo), "Confucius—A Thinker Who Stubbornly Upheld the Slave System," *Peking Review*, no. 41 (October 12, 1973), pp. 5-9.

16. *Peking Review*, nos. 35 and 36 (combined issue) (Sept. 7, 1973), pp. 17-25.

17. Ibid., pp. 26-29.

18. Ibid., pp. 29-33.

19. See "Outline of Education of Situation for Companies," *Issues and Studies*, vol. 10, no. 9 (June 1974), pp. 90-100 and no. 10 (July 1974), pp. 94-105.

20. "CCP Central Committee Documents on The Criticism of Lin Piao and Confucius." *Issues and Studies*, vol. 10, no. 11 (August 1974), pp. 109-113.

21. See *Red Flag*, no. 11 (November 1973), pp. 30-40.

22. For text of report see *Background on China*, 75-05 (January 23, 1975). Chou En-lai's Report to the National People's Congress on "Government Work."

23. See *Peking Review*, (January 23, 1976).

24. See *The New York Times*, (April 8, 1976), p. 16. Text of Peking changes and account of disturbance.

25. *Peking Review*, no. 15 (April 12, 1974), pp. 6-11.

26. For an English translation, see Pearl Buck's *All Men Are Brothers*.

27. *Background on China*, B75-015 (June 12, 1975). Text of Chiang Ch'ing's secret talk to Chinese Communist diplomats.

28. *Background on China*, B75-08 (March 12, 1975). Wang Hung-wen's secret report at the CCP.CC "Reading Class."

29. *Background on China*, B75-11 (April 23, 1975). Text of Chang Ch'un-ch'iao's article intensifying campaign.

30. "Two Revealing Speeches by Hua Kuo-feng in 1975," *China News Analysis*, no. 1038 (April 13, 1976).

31. *Tibetan Review*, vol. 10, nos. 9 and 10 (September-October 1975).

Chapter IX / The Verdict of History?

1. Benjamin I. Schwartz, *Chinese Communism and the Rise of Mao.* Schwartz held that the rural-based communism was an isolated development in the hinterland of China, cut off from any influence by directions from either Moscow or the Chinese Communist leadership in Shanghai. This interpretation was challenged by a number of scholars, especially Karl August Wittfogel. *China Quarterly,* nos. 1 and 2 (1960), "Debate of Chinese Communist History," with essays by Wittfogel on "The Legend of Maoism" and the retort by Schwartz on the "Legend of the Legend of Maoism" followed by a final retort by Wittfogel.

2. Hsiao Tso-liang, *Power Relations Within the Chinese Communist Movement, 1930-1934; The Land Revolution in China 1930-1934: A Study of Documents,* and *The Chinese Communism in 1927, City vs. Countryside.* Richard Thornton, "The Emergence of a Comintern Policy Towards China," *The Comintern Historical Highlights,* ed. Drachkovitch and Lazitch, and *The Comintern and the Chinese Communists 1928-1931.*

3. Stuart Schram, *The Political Thought of Mao Tse-tung* and *Mao Tse-tung.* The opposite view has been expressed by Arthur Cohen, *The Communism of Mao Tse-tung.*

4. Franz Michael, "Ideology and the Cult of Mao," *Communist China, 1949-69, A Twenty-year Appraisal,* ed. Frank N. Trager and William Henderson.

5. Chang Kuo-t'ao, *The Rise of the Chinese Communist Party, 1928-1938,* vol. 2, p.511.

6. According to *Khrushchev Remembers,* pp. 464-5, Mao wrote a letter to Stalin asking him to recommend a Marxist philosopher who might come to China to edit Mao's works. Mao wanted an educated man to put his works into proper shape and catch mistakes in Marxist philosophy before Mao's writings were published. Yudin was chosen and sent to Peking. Yudin became very close to Mao who went to see Yudin more often than Yudin called on Mao. Indeed, Stalin became worried lest Yudin would not show proper respect for Mao. But the relationship ended when Mao turned anti-Soviet.

7. Statement made by Mao at the plenary session of the Eighth Central Committee, September 1962. *Current Background,* no. 842, p. 7.

8. See Chapter V.

9. *Chairman Mao Talks to the People,* see Appendix.

10. Ibid., pp. 212-230.

Appendix: Documents
On Contradiction

[1] V. I. Lenin, "Conspectus of Hegel's *Lectures on the History of Philosophy*", *Collected Works,* Russ. ed., Moscow, 1958, Vol. XXXVIII, p. 249.

[2]In his essay "On the Question of Dialectics", Lenin said, "The splitting in two of a single whole and the cognition of its contradictory parts (see the quotation from Philo on Heraclitus at the beginning of Section 3 'On Cognition' in Lassalle's book on Heraclitus) is the *essence* (one of the 'essentials', one of the principal, if not the principal, characteristics or features) of dialectics." (*Collected Works*, Russ. ed., Moscow, 1958, Vol. XXXVIII, p. 357.) In his "Conspectus of Hegel's *The Science of Logic*", he said, "In brief, dialectics can be defined as the doctrine of the unity of opposites. This grasps the kernel of dialectics, but it requires explanations and development." (*Ibid.*, p. 215).

[3]V. I. Lenin, "On the Question of Dialectics", *Collected Works*, Russ. ed., Moscow, 1958, Vol. XXXVIII, p. 358.

[4]A saying of Tung Chung-shu (179-104 B.C.), a well-known exponent of Confucianism in the Han Dynasty.

[5]Frederick Engels, "Dialectics. Quantity and Quality", *Anti-Dühring*, Eng. ed., FLPH, Moscow, 1959, p. 166.

[6]V. I. Lenin, "On the Question of Dialectics", *Collected Works*, Russ. ed., Moscow, 1958, Vol. XXXVIII, pp. 357-58.

[7]Frederick Engels, *op. cit.*, pp. 166-67.

[8]V. I. Lenin, "On the Question of Dialectics", *Collected Works*, Russ. ed., Moscow, 1958, Vol. XXXVIII, p. 357.

[9]*Ibid.*, pp. 358-59.

[10]See "Problems of Strategy in China's Revolutionary War", Note 10, p. 251 of this volume.

[11]See *ibid.*, Note 2, p. 249 of this volume.

[12]Wei Cheng (A.D. 580-643) was a statesman and historian of the Tang Dynasty.

[13]*Shui Hu Chuan (Heroes of the Marshes)*, a famous 14th century Chinese novel, describes a peasant war towards the end of the Northern Sung Dynasty. Chu Village was in the vicinity of Liangshanpo, where Sung Chiang, leader of the peasant uprising and hero of the novel, established his base. Chu Chao-feng, the head of this village, was a despotic landlord.

[14]V. I. Lenin, "Once Again on the Trade Unions, the Present Situation and the Mistakes of Trotsky and Bukharin", *Selected Works*, Eng. ed., International Publishers, New York, 1943, Vol. IX, p. 66.

[15]V. I. Lenin, "What Is to Be Done?", *Collected Works*, Eng. ed., FLPH, Moscow, 1961, Vol. V, p. 369.

[16]V. I. Lenin, "Conspectus of Hegel's *The Science of Logic*", *Collected Works*, Russ. ed., Moscow, 1958, Vol. XXXVIII, pp. 97-98.

[17]*Shan Hai Ching (Book of Mountains and Seas)* was written in the era of the Warring States (403-221 B.C.). In one of its fables Kua Fu, a superman, pursued and overtook the sun. But he died of thirst, whereupon his staff was transformed into the forest of Teng.

[18]Yi is one of the legendary heroes of ancient China, famous for his archery. According to a legend in *Huai Nan Tzu*, compiled in the 2nd century B.C., there were ten suns in the sky in the days of Emperor Yao. To put an end to the damage to vegetation caused by these scorching suns, Emperor Yao ordered Yi to shoot them down. In another legend recorded by Wang Yi (2nd century A.D.), the archer is said to have shot down nine of the ten suns.

[19]*Hsi Yu Chi (Pilgrimage to the West)* is a 16th century novel, the hero of which is the monkey god Sun Wu-kung. He could miraculously change at will into seventy-two different shapes, such as a bird, a tree and a stone.

[20]The *Strange Tales of Liao Chai*, written by Pu Sung-ling in the 17th century, is a well-known collection of 431 tales, mostly about ghosts and fox spirits.

[21]Karl Marx, "Introduction to the Critique of Political Economy", *A Contribution to the Critique of Political Economy*, Eng. ed., Chicago, 1904, pp. 310-11.

[22]V. I. Lenin, "On the Question of Dialectics", *Collected Works*, Russ. ed., Moscow, 1958, Vol. XXXVIII, p. 358.

[23]The saying "Things that oppose each other also complement each other" first appeared in the *History of the Earlier Han Dynasty* by Pan Ku, a celebrated historian in the 1st century A.D. It has long been a popular saying.

[24]V. I. Lenin, "On the Question of Dialectics", *Collected Works*, Russ, ed., Moscow, 1958, Vol. XXXVIII, p. 358.

[25]V. I. Lenin, "Remarks on N. I. Bukharin's *Economics of the Transitional Period*", *Selected Works*, Russ. ed., Moscow-Leningrad, 1931, Vol. XI, p. 357.

Bibliography

Selected Books and Articles

Agrarian Reform Law of the People's Republic of China, The. Peking: Foreign Languages Press, 1953.

Bao, Kuo-wang [Jean Pasqualini] and Chelminski, Rudolph. *Prisoner of Mao.* New York: Cowark, McCann & Geoghegan, 1973.

Boersner, Demetrio. *The Bolsheviks and the National and Colonial Question: 1917-1920.* Geneva: Librairie E. Drog, 1957.

Boorman, Howard L. *Biographical Dictionary of Republican China.* 4 vol. New York: Columbia University Press, 1967-1971.

Bowie, Robert K. and Fairbank, John K. (foreword). *Communist China 1955-1959, Political Documents with Analysis.* Cambridge: Harvard University Press, 1962.

Buck, Pearl. *All Men Are Brothers.* New York: Grove Press, 1937.

Case of P'eng Teh-huai, 1959-1963, The. Hong Kong: Union Research Institute, 1968.

Chang Chung-li. *The Chinese Gentry.* Seattle: University of Washington Press, 1955.

_____. *The Income of the Chinese Gentry.* Seattle: University of Washington Press, 1962.

Chang Kuo-t'ao. *The Rise of the Chinese Communist Party, 1921-1938.* Vol. 1, 2. Lawrence, Kansas: University Press of Kansas, 1971.

Cheng, Tien-fong. *A History of Sino-Soviet Relations.* Washington, D.C.: Public Affairs Press, 1957.

Ch'en, Jerome. *Mao and the Chinese Revolution.* London: Oxford University Press, 1965.

Ch'en Kung-po. *The Communist Movement in China.* Edited by Martin Wilbur. New York: Octagon Books, 1966.

Chiang Kai-shek. *Soviet Russia in China.* Revised abridged edition. New York: Farrar, Strauss & Giroux, 1965.

Chu, Valentine. "The Famine Makers." *New Leader* (June 11, 1962).

Chung Hua-min and Miller, Arthur C. *Madame Mao, A Profile of Chiang Ch'ing.* Hong Kong: Union Research Institute, 1968.

Cohen, Arthur. *The Communism of Mao Tse-tung.* Chicago: University of Chicago Press, 1964.

Compton, Boyd. *Mao's China: Party Reform Documents, 1942-44.* Seattle: University of Washington Press, 1952.

Degras, Jane, ed. *The Communist International, 1919-1943: Documents.* 3 vols. New York: Praeger, 1964.

Feis, Herbert. *The China Tangle: The American Effort in China from Pearl Harbour to the Marshall Mission.* Princeton, N.J.: Princeton University Press, 1953.

Foreign Relations of the United States. Diplomatic Papers, China 1942-49, vol. 6. Washington, D.C.: Government Printing Office, 1956.

Fundamentals of Marxism-Leninism. Moscow: Foreign Languages Publishing House, 1963.

Gibson, M. A. "Terror at the Hands of the Red Guards." *Life,* vol. 62, no. 22 (June 2, 1967).

Goldman, Merle. *Literary Dissent in Communist China.* Cambridge, Ma.: Harvard University Press, 1967.

Hsiao Tso-liang. *Chinese Communism in 1927, City vs. Countryside.* Hong Kong: Chinese University of Hong Kong, 1970.

_____. *Power Relations Within the Chinese Communist Movement, 1930-1934: A Study of Documents.* Seattle: University of Washington Press, 1961.

Hsieh, Milton J.T. *The Kuomintang: Selected Historical Documents, 1894-1969.* New York: St. Johns University Press, 1970.

Hudson, G. F. Notes and introduction to *Let a Hundred Flowers Bloom: The Complete Text of 'The Correct Handling of Contradictions Among the Peoples',* by Mao Tse-tung. New York: Tamiment Institute, n.d.

Khrushchev, Nikita Sergeevich. *Khrushchev Remembers.* Translated and edited by Strobe Talbott. Boston: Little, Brown, and Company, 1974.

Kuo, Warren. *Analytical History of the Chinese Communist Party,* vols. 1-4. Taipei: Institute of International Relations, 1966, 1968, 1970, 1971.

Li Cho-min. *The Statistical System of Communist China.* Berkeley: University of California Press, 1962.

Li, Dun J. *The Road to Communism: China Since 1912.* New York: Van Nostrand Reinhold Company, 1969.

Li Tien-min. *Chou En-lai.* Taipei: Institute of International Relations, 1970.

Lifton, Robert T. *Thought Reform and the Psychology of Totalism: A Study of "Brainwashing" in China.* New York: Random House, 1968.

Liu Shao-ch'i. *How to be a Good Communist.* Peking: Foreign Languages Press, 1964.

Loh, Robert. *Escape from Red China.* New York: Coward, McCann, 1962.

Marriage Law of the People's Republic of China, The. Peking: Foreign Languages Press, 1959.

Mao Tse-tung. *Selected Works.* 5 vols. New York: International Publishers, 1954-1962.

Meijer, Marinus Johan. *Marriage Law and Policy in the Chinese People's Republic.* Hong Kong: Hong Kong Military Press, 1971.

Michael, Franz. "Ideology and the Cult of Mao." In *Communist China, 1949-1969, A Twenty-year Appraisal,* edited by Frank N. Trager and William Henderson. New York: New York University Press, 1970.

North, Robert. *Moscow and the Chinese Communists.* 2nd ed. Stanford, California: Stanford University Press, 1963.

_____ and Eudin, Zenoa, *M. N. Roy's Mission to China.* Berkeley: Berkeley University Press, 1963.

Polemic on the General Line of the International Communist Movement, The. Peking: Foreign Language Press, 1965.

Rice, Edward E. *Mao's Way.* Berkeley: University of California Press, 1963.

Schram, Stuart R. *The Political Thought of Mao Tse-tung.* New York: Praeger, 1963.

_____. *Mao Tse-tung.* New York: Simon and Schuster, 1966.

_____, ed. *Chairman Mao Talks to the People: Talks and Letters, 1956-1971.* New York: Pantheon Books, 1974.

Schurmann, Franz. *Ideology and Organization in Communist China.* Berkeley: University of California Press, 1968.

Schwartz, Benjamin I. *Chinese Communism and the Rise of Mao.* Cambridge: University of Harvard Press, 1957.

Smedley, Agnes, *The Great Road: The Life and Times of Chu Teh.* New York: Monthly Review Press, 1956.

Snow, Edgar. *Red Star Over China.* New York: Grove Press, 1961.

Stalin, J. V. *Marxism and the National and Colonial Question.* vol. 8 (January-November 1926). Moscow: Foreign Languages Publishing House, 1953.

_____. *Marxism and the National Question.* Moscow: Foreign Languages Publishing House, 1950.

Tang, Peter S. H. *Communist China Today.* 2 vols. Washington, D.C.: Research Institute on the Sino-Soviet Bloc, 1957, 1958.

Thornton, Richard C. *China, The Struggle for Power, 1917-1972.* Bloomington: Indiana University Press, 1973.

_____. "The Emergence of a New Comintern Strategy for China, 1928." In *The Comintern: Historical Highlights,* edited by Milorad M. Drachkovitch. New York: Praeger, 1966.

_____. *The Comintern and the Chinese Communists: 1928-1931.* Seattle: University of Washington Press, 1969.

Ting Wang. "Profile of Chiang Ch'ing, Mrs. Mao Tse-tung." *Far Eastern Economic Review,* no. 57 (August 1967).

Waley, Arthur, trans. *Wu Ch'en-en (Monkey).* New York: Penguin Books, 1971.

Walker, Richard L. *China Under Communism: The First Five Years.* New Haven: Yale University Press, 1955.

_____. *The Human Cost of Communism in China.* Washington, D.C.: Senate Committee on the Judiciary, n.d.

Wetzel, Karroll. "Out of the Jaws of Victory." Ph.D. dissertation, The George Washington University, 1973.

Whiting, Allen S. and General Sheng Shih-tsai. *Sinkiang: Pawn or Pivot.* East Lansing, Michigan: State University Press, 1958.

Whitson, William W. *The Chinese High Command: A History of Communist Military Politics, 1927-1971.* New York: Praeger, 1973.

Who's Who in Communist China. Hong Kong: Union Research Institute, 1969.

Wilbur, C. Martin and Lien-ying-How, Julie. *Documents on Communism, Nationalism, and Soviet Advisers in China, 1918-1927.* New York: Columbia University Press, 1956.

Zagoria, Donald. *The Sino-Soviet Conflict, 1956-1961.* New York: Atheneum, 1964.

Journals

Background on China. New York: Chinese Information Service.

Current Scene. Hong Kong: Green Pagoda Press, Ltd.

China Quarterly. London: Contemporary China Institute of the New School of Oriental and African Studies, London University.

Issues and Studies. Taipei: Institute of International Relations.

China News Analysis. Hong Kong: G.P.O. Box 3225.

Peking Review. Peking: Foreign Languages Press.

Survey of the China Mainland Press. Hong Kong: American Consulate General. Cited as *SCMP* throughout this work.

Index